THE CHILLIWACKS AND THEIR NEIGHBORS

Oliver N. Wells

edited by
Ralph Maud
Brent Galloway
Marie Weeden

Talonbooks • Vancouver • 1987

published with assistance from the Canada Council

Talonbooks
104-3100 Production Way
Bunaby, British Columbia
V5A 4R4 Canada

Typeset in Times by Pièce de Résistance; printed and bound in Canada by Hignell Printing Ltd.

Second Printing: August 1997

On the cover: Centre—John Wallace carving mythical creature on a canoe. Clockwise from top left—Billy Sepass and Rose Sepass; Edwin Wells (standing at left), Hamilton Lainge and Billy Sepass (seated, left to right) with hunting companions not now identifiable; Mrs Matilda Thomas with basket work; Mrs Amy Cooper (standing) and Mrs Mary Peters working on a tapestry; Mrs Harriet Johnny weaving; John Wallace hollowing out a canoe.

The editors and publisher wish to acknowledge the valuable help of Randy Bouchard and Dorothy Kennedy of the B. C. Indian Language Project at all stages in the preparation of this volume.

Canadian Cataloguing in Publication Data

Wells, Oliver, 1907-1970.
The Chilliwacks and their neighbors

Includes bibliographical references.
ISBN 0-88922-255-X

1. Chilliwack Indians. 2. Indians of North America - British Columbia - Chilliwack. I. Maud, Ralph, 1928- II. Title.
E99.C5523W44 1987 971.1'00497 C87-091478-2

Contents

Preface

This publication is the culmination of the many pleasurable hours that my father, Oliver N. Wells, spent researching Chilliwack Native history as he visited and interviewed his Native friends. I can still picture him on many a winter night sitting at the dining room table in our old home, Edenbank, searching through books and articles for which he had sent from as far away as London and New York, in order to find out all that he could about the history of the Chilliwacks. Often his old reel-to-reel tape recorder would be there beside him, and we would see him listening intently to his tapes, transcribing sections from his latest interviews, or composing questions for his next. I can still see his face lighting up with enthusiasm as he told me that, during his visit with Mrs August Jim, she had told him that she had been born in an underground skummel. That was one of the moments that symbolized what his project was all about—a desire to touch the past.

It was over a decade later, while listening to these tapes with Ralph Maud and Brent Galloway, as we slowly and meticulously transcribed each word, that I not only experienced again my father's unique and infectious enthusiasm for his project, but that I also came to know his rewards. The three of us spent many afternoons and evenings working in the old dining room at Edenbank, as he had. But by then Oliver Wells was gone.

Marie Weeden and Oliver Wells on a bench below Elk Mountain, overlooking Gordon Wells's ranch on Chilliwack River.

I had often heard my father remark what a great privilege it was to have been able to experience these visits with his Native friends. Together they enjoyed renewing memories and stories of the past. I know he found the interviews a fascinating and rewarding task. Oliver's brother, Casey, had agreed to assist by studying the Halkomelem words and developing a practical method of writing the language. Casey was fascinated with the project and spent hours working out details.

On his first visit with Dan Milo, Oliver took Dan for a drive around the valley and brought him to Edenbank for a cup of "Sara's good tea." Dan felt comfortable at the farm, having been there so many times in his 97 years. Often he had come with his father, who had worked for the Wells family in the late 1800s. I remember that Dad was amazed at Dan's memory, and I remember how everyone marvelled at his magnificent talent of presentation. He spoke with the authority of a master storyteller.

My father's death after a motor vehicle accident in Scotland left a great hollowness in our lives. It was impossible to believe that this vibrant and loving man was gone. His death left unpublished his book-length manuscript of the history of his beloved Edenbank, as well as the final draft of his anthology, "The Chilliwacks and Their Neighbors."

It was my wish that both of these projects could be completed and I therefore consulted with Wilson Duff, Peter Macnair at the Provincial Museum, and Dr More at UBC. Each of these men, after reading over the manuscript, expressed the desire to see Oliver's interview tapes completely transcribed before any publication took place. Eventually Dr Ralph Maud of SFU and Dr Brent Galloway, who was working at Coqualeetza, agreed to get this project under way. Through the co-operation of Andrea Laforet and Peter Macnair, the tapes were copied at the Provincial Museum, and I was sent these copies. There were approximately fifty cassettes in all. Thanks to the enthusiasm and generosity of Ralph Maud, who volunteered to do the initial transcribing, we were soon deeply involved with our project. Brent added the Halkomelem words, sometimes consulting with Edna Bob and Amelia Douglas at Coqualeetza. I shared the task of rechecking the transcripts with Ralph and Brent in weekly listening sessions when our schedules permitted. We were involved with this project for several years. On completion we had approximately 1000 pages of transcriptions. It had been a time-consuming but extremely rewarding task.

I believe that my father was first enticed to research local Indian history in 1962 when he was invited to write an introduction to Eloise Street's *Sepass Poems*. Chief Billy Sepass had related these legends to Mrs Street, and when the time came to publish she turned to Oliver because Sepass had been a good friend of Oliver and his father, Edwin Wells. Oliver talked to old-timers who vividly remembered "Old Billy," and searched his own memories for times spent in his company. Oliver always spoke of Billy Sepass with great respect and warmth.

No one could carve a canoe like Billy Sepass. When I was young, Chief Sepass's last canoe rested beside the creek at Edenbank, turned over to slough off the heavy rains. I loved the days when my father and I quietly guided that canoe under the small bridges and on through the bird sanctuary, which he had created along the banks of streams. Later I remember Dad oiling it and hanging it up between the rafters in the barn, preserving it for the museum that he hoped we would someday have in Chilliwack. When Oliver was young, Chief Sepass had carved a huge freighting canoe which he used on Chilliwack Lake. He had often accompanied Edwin and his family as they hunted and scouted trails into the local mountain ranges. Old Billy had felled huge timbers neatly into line on many dangerously narrow stretches along the ridges of Liumchen. Bridge Bailey, who was a frequent hunting companion of Billy Sepass, has told me that the highlight of their evening campfires was listening to Old Billy share his wonderful stories.

After writing his sketch of Chief Sepass, Oliver expanded his interest in Native history, and everyone with whom he discussed his new project readily responded to his infectious enthusiasm. His Native friends welcomed him into their homes, where together they reminisced and recounted the old days, the old ways, and the old Halkomelem language. He and Casey eventually completed and published a booklet on Halkomelem in 1965. This booklet was used in the first classes in which the Native language was taught at Tzeachten. At the same time Oliver searched out Native artists and craftsmen and arranged for them to display their work both provincially and nationally. He regretted that no one was carving canoes any more. With the discovery that John Wallace of Soowahlie had been an experienced carver, Oliver scouted out a satisfactory log and persuaded him to come to Edenbank and carve a canoe.

Oliver Wells and his daughter, Marie, at Edenbank, c. 1952.

My father never ceased to marvel at the dexterity with which John Wallace carved out his huge Salish canoes, taking a step or two back, then carefully "eyeing" it, until with a deft movement of the axe against firm cedar the perfect stroke was made. He wrote later that John "carved out an old style shovel-nosed canoe . . . with the skill of an accomplished artist." After John had spent many hours and days of contouring the sides, hollowing the center, and stretching the ribs of each canoe, its graceful form would take shape. I remember watching as Oliver would help John when the canoe needed lifting, heating, stretching or staining. Together they would launch the canoes in the Luckakuck Creek in front of our old home.

There was a quiet contentment that existed between John and Oliver as they worked on the canoes in the horse barn. I remember the satisfaction showing in Oliver's eyes as he watched John at work. Because John had lost a leg in a logging accident he would rest periodically and the two men would "visit" for a while. Curled shavings from John's axe and plane lay deep on the stable floor and in the air there was the aroma of cedar. Old "Queenie," our border collie, lay patiently nearby.

Over the years John carved nine canoes in the horse barn at Edenbank. After Oliver died, John came walking up the driveway to see me. He had come to say how badly he felt that his good friend was gone. I understood so well. I thanked him and encouraged him to come back and finish the almost completed canoe in the horse barn. He did not come back. Six months later John was gone too. I always wondered if it was because "Ollie" wasn't there to make sure there was oil in the tank for his stove at home or groceries in his cupboard. John died of pneumonia.

During the years that Oliver was doing his tape recording and editing he produced not only the Halkomelem language booklet but also *Indian Territory 1858*—a detailed, illustrated map of the Chilliwack and neighboring tribes as they were in 1858. In addition he published *Squamish Legends*, based on his visits to August Jack Khahtsahlano and Dominic Charlie, and *Myths & Legends of the Staw-loh Indians*, from local interviews. At the same time he was involved in many community activities and farmed over eighty acres, raising Aberdeen Angus beef cattle and a large flock of sheep. Almost single-handedly, he took off about fifty acres of hay twice a year, bringing it in on a sweep specially designed for the front of his tractor, with just one or two neighborhood boys for help. He told Mr Jeffcott during this first interview (tape No. 13) that he'd "be down again after he brought in next week's hay." His days were long and full. Much of his research was done in the evening after the day's chores were completed.

Upon discovering that the Native women of the Stalo had been expert blanket weavers and that examples of their art were exhibited in the finest museums in the world, Oliver became extremely interested in trying to help revive the art. One day over dinner at Edenbank, I remember him saying, "Wouldn't it be wonderful if once again this area could become famous for its weaving!" That statement was the beginning of another major Oliver Wells project.

Mrs Amy Cooper, who had been a friend of the family for many years, encouraged Dad in all his research and introduced him to Mary Peters of Seabird Island. I recall his great joy when he found that Mary was still using the weaving techniques of her ancestors and was willing to experiment using naturally-dyed wool from his sheep at the farm. I remember his enthusiasm as he told of her talents; each time she completed a beautiful rug, he brought it home to show us all.

The ceremonial rug that she eventually completed was a work of art. Through his encouragement many other talented women gradually began again the task of threading the loom to recreate a special part of their artistic heritage. I remember his working in our old basement, constructing sturdy looms for each weaver. For the largest looms he used straight strong trees and rounded them smoothly with the axe for the crossbars. I still have one of these looms at home.

Josephine Kelly, who lived at Soowahlie, agreed to spin his North Country Cheviot wool for him, and Dad began experimenting with natural dyes. He read all he could concerning the traditional uses that the Native people had made of plants, lichens, fruits and nutshells, and soon was producing warm earthy colours that were gorgeous. Weaving classes came from SFU, UBC, and handicraft clubs and shops in Vancouver, to see his work and to discuss his methods of dyeing. He showed the visitors the superbly crafted hangings that Mary Peters and soon Adeline Lorenzetto, Martha James, Irene James, and Annabel Stewart were producing from Josephine's spinning. Soon others were spinning and weaving as well. The dyeing project grew in dimension and nearly monopolized the shed that Sara used for drying walnuts. Two oil stoves were set up and brightly dyed wool hung everywhere.

Listening to my father's voice on tape, as we did almost weekly for so many months, has been a poignant experience for me. As the seasons changed at Edenbank, I often looked out, as I listened, to where I had so often seen him at work on the land, in the sanctuary, or coming up from the barn. Memories flooded my heart. What a privilege it was for me to know the spirit of such a man.

As Ralph Maud, Brent Galloway and I neared the completion of this project, we realized that we wanted to present the transcriptions in such a way that they would capture the essence of not only the historical information but also the experience of those moments of communication that took place between Oliver and his Native friends. Ralph took on the task of editing, and I am impressed with the way he has put the interviews together and the sections he has chosen. To me he has indeed captured what Oliver Wells and his informants wished to convey and preserve.

Just before his recent death, I had a short visit with Chief Ritchie Malloway, Bob Joe's brother and a very good friend of my father. I mentioned to Ritchie that I was preparing a preface for this publication and that I found it difficult to explain the feeling that Dad had for this work and what sort of a man he was. I asked Ritchie how he would describe him. His sincere and dignified reply says it all so well: "We grew up together, we were neighbors and friends. He was one of us." What can I possibly add?

Marie Weeden

I wish to express my thanks to everyone who has contributed to the completion of this volume. I am especially grateful to the following:

Peter Macnair, the late Willard Ireland, the late Wilson Duff, Andrea Laforet, Barbara Efrat, Edwin J. Allen, Jr, Art More, Randy Bouchard, Dorothy Kennedy, Jay Powell, Vickie Jensen, Reuben Ware, Larry & Terry Thompson, Wayne Suttles, the late Chief Richard Malloway, Mrs Malloway, Donna Cook, Chilliwack Museum Staff, Ray Wells, Mr & Mrs Bridge Bailey, Frank Malloway and the Staff at Coqualeetza, Edna Bob, Amelia Douglas, the late Sadie Thompson, Imbert Orchard, Don Baird, SFU Instructional Media Centre, Norman & Pat Todd, Social Sciences & Humanities Research Council of Canada, Mabel Walter, David Allen, Josephine & Mike Kelly, Del & Ed Kelly, Mary O'Connol, Alice Wells, Betty & Bob Purkiss, Murdock Maclaughin, Neil Smith, *Chilliwack Progress*, Crisca Bierwert Russell, Wendy Galloway, Dick Weeden.

Traditional feast honors great leader Oliver Wells

The late Richard Malloway, with his son Frank Malloway.

"Oliver Wells was a different kind of man; he had a great heart, a great heart for our people and some day I hope we will get another friend like him."

Chief Richard Malloway paid those words of deep tribute to Oliver Wells on Friday, when the native people of the district held a traditional "feast" to mark the passing of a "great leader."

Nearly 150 Indians and non-Indians, including the brothers of Mr. Wells, crowded into Tzeachten Hall for a noon meal served by the Indian Homemakers.

Chief Malloway, who grew up with Mr. Wells, explained the deep sense of shock felt by the native people when they learned that Mr. Wells died last week following a car crash in Scotland.

"It was something that we did not want to believe—that our great friend was gone. He was someone that we will never forget. He was a true friend," Chief Malloway said.

To indicate the respect which the native people held for Mr. Wells, Chief Malloway pointed out that he (Mr. Wells) was the only white man invited to the spiritual dances held at certain times throughout the year. "We are very careful who we invite to spiritual dances, but we invited Mr. Wells because we could trust him as a true friend."

Referring to an Indian belief, Chief Malloway said, "when we leave this cruel country we don't go, we just change life and in that way I hope he (Mr. Wells) is with us this afternoon and time to come." [*Extract.*]

(*from* The Chilliwack Progress, *10 November 1970*)

Tribute to Oliver Wells

This tribute to Oliver Wells was written by former Sardis resident Allan Fotheringham, who is now a widely read columnist.

One always regrets the things one did not get around to doing. In Canada's Centennial year with all the elaborate talk of monuments and historical dates and politicians, I longed to tell someone that this is not what a country's centenary is all about. I meant to write an article stating one thing: Oliver Wells is what Canada's birthday party is all about. A man who loved the land and lived on it and nourished it in the tradition of his father and his father's father who founded Edenbank Farm in 1867—the year the country was born; a man who worked quietly and raised a fine family and served his community and whose influence spread in ripples far beyond the confines of that handsome green estate of his on the banks of the little Luck-a-kuck stream in a tiny British Columbia town that few Canadians have ever heard of or ever will. Ollie Wells and the 100 years of Edenbank was what centennial was all about.

I never did get around to writing this article and now Oliver N. Wells is no longer with us. His farm and his family and his example remain to remind us in this month of the national crisis of so much that is fine about Canada.

The first day I arrived in B.C. as a boy, I was taken to Edenbank and met Ollie Wells. To someone from a less favored area of Canada there was indeed something of Eden to the setting. It was a warm September day in 1942 and the lush fruit was dropping on the ground. The Canada geese were prancing over the lawn and occasionally buffeting silly newcomers who ventured too close. The fields were full of good cattle. There was a rich smell of horses and a sleek collie dog danced behind the feet of Ollie.

I've never forgotten that idyllic scene and yet it would be a mistake to think that Edenbank "just happened." Old photographs of that same scene taken in 1900 reveal for us the myth that the good old days were all serene and beautiful. It was a raw, crude setting in those early days of A.C. Wells and later Ollie's father E.A. Wells. It took years of care and a loving eye to transform that early raw scene of gravel bars into the showpiece that became Edenbank. The farm was built just as were the bloodlines of the prize-winning Ayrshire herds and just as was the structure of Ollie's life.

He based his life on building. Through his own work and from his own base at Edenbank he became a respected naturalist, anthropologist, artist and writer. He did research on Indian art through the British Museum. Anthropologists from the University of Washington came to study his findings.

Decades before the word ecology became fashionable, Ollie Wells was devoting a prime section of his land to his famous sanctuary as a refuge for birds.

He knew instinctively what the editorial writers and politicians have only now finally grasped: that a land that cannot support animals will not long support man. He was a truly educated person who knew that man must—first of all—be at peace with his surroundings.

Long before the trends of society that brought forth the cries of "power" from frustrated racial and native minorities, he was quietly working to encourage native Indians to realize their potential and regain their pride through long-neglected crafts. Amidst all the glitter and dazzle and architectural gimmickry of Expo, a visitor suddenly had a flash of insight into the real Canada when he turned a corner and came upon a brilliant, colorful example of the Salish weaving in a tapestry revived and inspired by Ollie Wells.

Through it all there was a humanity that shone through. He had a rich sense of enjoyment. I remember the laugh. No one who heard Ollie Wells laugh could mistake it for any other. No gathering, however discreet, could resist the richocheting echo of his deep laughter once it gathered strength and billowed forth.

Through all the years of building, of developing his fine Edenbank herd, of doing his own research and documentation and correspondence by night, he never travelled abroad. Breeders and naturalists and admirers from Britain, New Zealand and afar made the pilgrimage to Edenbank, to confer with him and to accept his open hospitality. After all those years it is stunning irony that he received his fatal injuries only hours away from at last seeing some of those old friends and viewing some of those farms. Just outside Inverness he died in the land which produced the animals he loved; the Ayrshire, the Angus, the Cheviot. He was 63 and he had accomplished so much.

Ollie Wells was a good man. He was a gentle man. He was a Christian man. He was a kind man. He was in the finest sense, a man.

—from *The Chilliwack Progress*, 10 November 1970; reprinted in Allan Fotheringham, *Collected & Bound* (Vancouver: November House, 1972), pp. 162-164.

Memories of the Tape-recordings

As long as I remember, driving up the Canyon to rivers or coast areas, or in the Cariboo, Oliver would always get into conversation with any Native people he met. He would ask if they had known Chief Billy Sepass or Bob Joe or any Chilliwack Indians. I think he always planned to study the background of our local tribes.

Someone might tell him of a friend of a friend who carved model canoes, or a woman who made baskets. Then he would plan to visit these people. I know he would do chores early, and we would leave (with a thermos of tea and a lunch) for Hope or Yale or Laidlaw. Oliver would be so eager as he knocked at someone's door for the first time. I would be in the car nearby. The door would open a few inches, if a woman answered. He would talk awhile, then point me out, and I would smile and say something. Soon the door would open wide, and she might bring out a basket she had made. I could tell by Oliver's face if he felt he had made a good contact.

Adeline Lorenzetto showing Sara Wells her first experiments with Salish designs.

When he greeted the men he would use some Native word he knew, and the Indian would smile to hear it—usually not correctly pronounced. Always when we went again the door opened wide.

I remember a visit to Chehalis to see a basket maker, Ada Peters. Badly crippled, she was sitting on a couch with a large bowl of water surrounded with prepared cedar-roots. Making baskets was her life—beautiful papoose beds, etc. When she spoke it was in cultured English. Oliver asked her if she had gone to "All Hallows School" at Yale, and she had. (Edna Malloway went there too.) Oliver's theme, when he found someone so efficient in her craft, was: teach it to the younger women. The same with Mary Peters, the weaver; we took her to demonstrate her work, and when we would get her home and the loom and all unloaded, he would say, "Teach your grandchildren," and Mary would smile and nod her head to say yes. And how she did! Think of Monica and Elizabeth and others there.

Locally, Dan Milo was the oldest Native who was interested in what Oliver was doing to help preserve the Halkomelem language. Dan was very old and blind, but his memory and mind were clear. Oliver was impressed with the love and respect that surrounded him, his grandchildren and great-grandchildren—they would all come out to see him into the car. When he would arrive, Oliver would seat him in the big kitchen window, and we would have tea and cakes. After a little while I would clear the table and the tape recorder would be placed, and all explained. Oliver would have a list of questions that would bring out the history he hoped to gain. Dan, blind and with no audience, would begin: "My friends, who are listening to my stories . . ." They would talk in the kitchen for a long time. Then Oliver would play the tape back to him. This would be a rewarding day for Oliver.

Sara and Oliver Wells in the "Chinook" canoe made by John Wallace.

As John Wallace carved canoes in our horse barn, Oliver worked with him, always questioning him and gaining knowledge of what John remembered. We always had a big tea early. Oliver didn't know how well he ate. *And* John always thanked me!

Through Major Matthews, Oliver became interested in Chief August Jack Khahtsahlano and Dominic Charlie and the Squamish Indians. One day we took some model canoes made by a Chehalis Indian to North Vancouver to Mr Chamberlain, who owned the Tomahawk Cafe, a man keenly interested in Indian crafts. He had a marvellous collection in the cafe. But the model canoes Oliver took had no interest to him—too elaborate and *painted*. He wanted only the natural. He was a friend of August Jack's, told Oliver of him, and warned him that if Chief August thought Oliver's interest was merely personal he would not cooperate. So we drove to Squamish and visited August Jack. No trouble. August Jack took Oliver to his heart. He and Mary Ann, his wife, came out to meet me. Oliver took their pictures, and a date was made to return with the tape-recorder. That was a very happy recording day for Oliver.

Sara Wells

Introduction to "The Chilliwacks and Their Neighbors"

(September 1965)

About ten years ago I commenced making notes and seeking out information concerning the early history of our Native people. This effort continued to gain momentum, and during the past three years I have enjoyed the privilege of having many tape-recorded interviews with my older friends among the Native people. To supplement this material I have searched deeply into the records of the earliest explorers, fur-traders, surveyors, pioneer settlers and early missionaries. From the material assembled I trust I can present to you in the following pages something of an anthology,[1] which will bring to your mind a true picture of the Native in his native land.

Among the Chilliwacks and their neighbors there are still a few who were born before the time of the establishment of the reserves. When they have passed, it will be too late to record the Native's interpretation of life as it was in the homes of their people.

With the coming of settlers, the Natives lost the freedom of their native land: on reserves set aside for them, they became wards of the government, and were given some assistance in adapting themselves to a new way of life. It has been a century of trial for the Indian. Much that had been theirs that was fine was destroyed and lost. Much that they were proud of still remains, but goes unnoticed by those who have not the eyes to see nor the desire to comprehend.

A new day is already begun for the Native. Many no longer feel the need of the protection of the reserve. The youth are now for the most part an integrated part of the community. In schools and sports and in the social life of the community they are taking their rightful place among the people of Canada. Some will cling to their native heritage and retain those fine characteristics which belong to them as a people. Others will drift into and become part of the nation of Canadians in which little interest is taken in origin of their parent stock.

A hundred years from now, if the trend in population-increase continues at such a favourable rate for the Indians in relation to other segments of the population, the council chambers of the tribal chiefs may well be the country's parliament buildings. But this is a record of the life of those fine Native people—the Chilliwacks and their neighbors—who lived for the most part in peace and plenty, and in harmony with nature and their fellow man, more than 100 years ago.

---

[1]If Oliver had completed his project, *The Chilliwacks and their Neighbors* would have been an anthology including extracts pertinent to the area, from the work of Franz Boas, Charles Hill-Tout, Wilson Duff, Reverend Thomas Crosby, Roderick Haig-Brown, John Edgar Gibbard, P. R. Jeffcott, J. K. Lord, to name only a few. Modesty would have prevented him from including much of his own researches. The present volume takes *The Chilliwacks and their Neighbors* as an appropriate title under which to present a full, if not complete, picture of Oliver Wells's contribution to the ethnology of area.

"THE CHILLIWACKS AND THEIR NEIGHBORS"

Present-day landmarks mentioned most often
in the Wells interviews.
See also Oliver Wells's map
"Indian Territory, 1858."

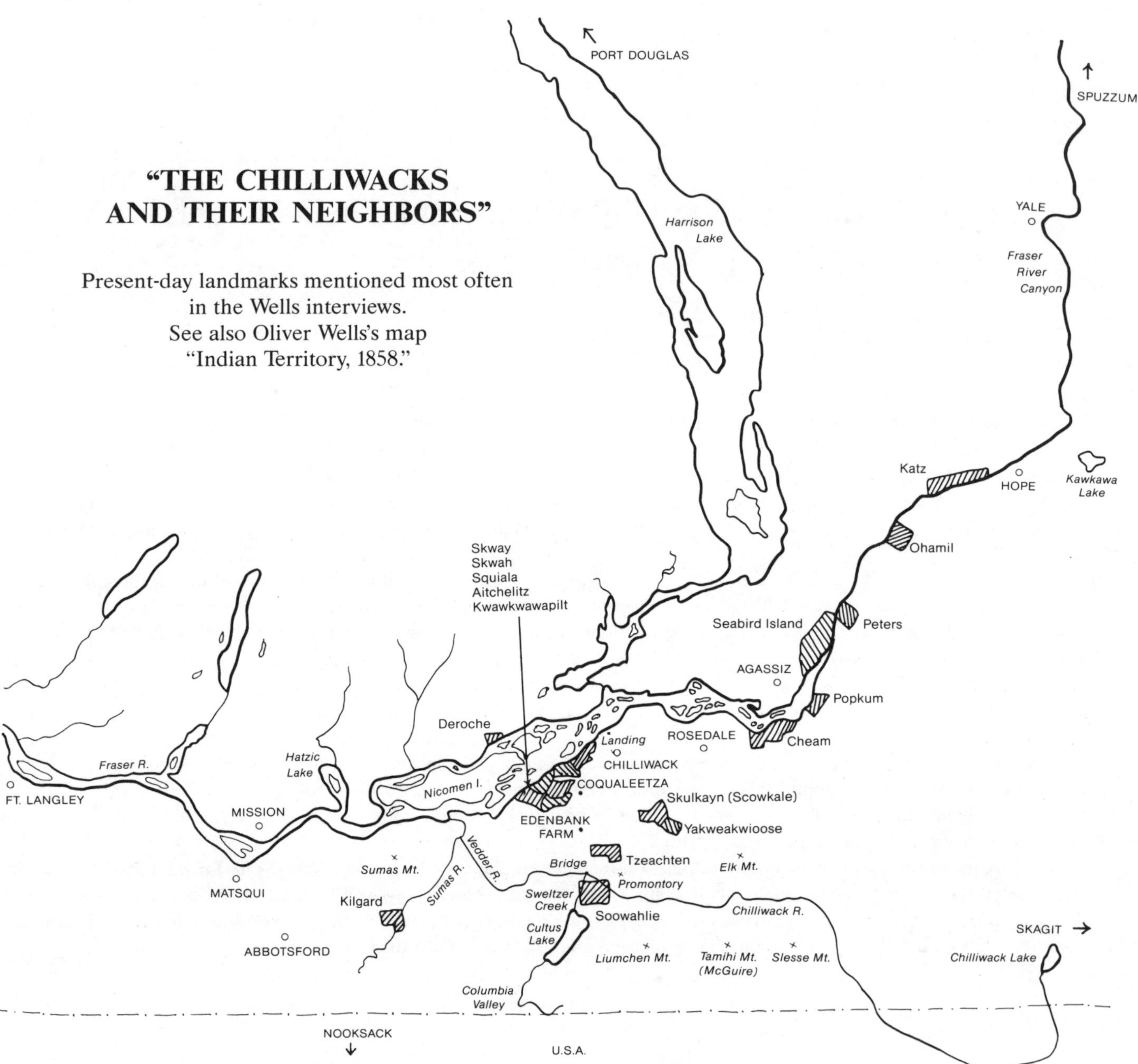

Note: Not to scale; boundaries very approximate.

Geological Background to Legendary History of the Tribes

It was early in the morning on a July day in 1964 that I sat on top of a vantage point on Elk Mt, high above the Chilliwack River Valley, which lay to the south of me, about 4500 feet below. As I sat watching the clouds rising out of the valley of the Chihlkwayuhk (as the river was known to the Natives), my mind went back to the words which I had read in Prof Hill-Tout's *Report to the British Association for the Advancement of Science* in 1902. He asked how long the Chilliwack had lived here on the river from which they had taken their name, and a chief replied: *''we have always lived here,* looking up at the sky and the mountains.'' In 1962, sixty years later, I recorded on tape the same question directed to Bob Joe, the last great historian of the tribe. His reply was: ''we have lived here since time immemorial, thousands of years.''

Oliver Wells looking out from Elk Mountain towards the Fraser River Valley, in the late 1960s. Photo by Robert Young.

My thoughts again turned to the scene before me. The clouds had lifted out of the deep valley, yet hung in mists in a shroud around the snow-covered peak of Mt Selesse (pronounced Seleesee by the Natives). At the foot of the peak, 8000 feet below its summit, its namesake, Selesse Creek, wound its course through a long deep valley leading to the south. About eleven miles up this valley, in 1858, the Boundary Line survey crew were cutting a trail to the International Boundary Line, which they were in the process of establishing. Capt. C.W. Wilson, who was in charge of supplies, recorded in well-chosen words the beauty of the landscape in that then-virgin country: ''Rewarded by the finest view ever seen in this country, we were right under the peaks of the Chekoimuck Mts, which formed a semi-circle basin in which lay four glaciers high above us. From the four glaciers about 30 cascades fell 150 to 200 ft in height, and, uniting above us, formed the Chikoyoum stream, while Selesse ran away to the left.'' His description, with Native names for the streams, seemed to support the legendary history of the tribe that Selesse was the original homeland.

For an hour the mist clung to the sharp peak, which I wished to photograph. I had time to study the valley below, where the Selesse joined the Chilliwack. I tried to visualize the valley as it was in 1920, when I rode a saddle horse for hours under the great forest of giant trees over the bench lands toward Chilliwack Lake. That age-old trail was cut a foot deep in the moss-covered floor of the forest. And now as I looked, I realized that there was evidence of bench lands all along the valley below, and that the river was slowly cutting down through table lands, even as the Thompson River has done in the great bench lands of the Interior. The level plateau areas could only have been formed by water, which could only have come from glaciers. There, then, could be part of the answer to the question of how long was the period of time which the Native referred to as *''we have always lived here.''*

A few weeks after returning from the mountain trip, I was visiting with Edmund Joe Peters of Seabird Island Reserve at Agassiz. I had been doing some tape-recording, and as I left I asked him if the Indians had any knowledge of the Fraser River having at one time run through the Chilliwack Valley south of Little Mountain. ''No, Oliver,'' he said, ''but the old people used to believe that one time there was a big slide came off of Cheam. That's what made all the rough country there near Cheam. And it pushed the Fraser over, so that it stopped running into those channels, and then the Cheam Lake came on top of the slide. When they cut the CNR right-of-way throught the slide they found logs 30 ft deep.'' Here, then, was another legend or myth which related to legendary history, which, if based on fact, might have some significance in the early history of the local tribes.

I determined to find proof, if possible, of the age or period in which these land formations were made. From the B.C. Department of Agriculture and the Federal Department of Mines and Technical Surveys I obtained maps of the Sumas-Chilliwack and Kent municipalities, which had been prepared under the direction of Dr Armstrong, and published in 1960. From these sources some interesting information was gleaned and noted. Briefly: the last Glacial Period of the area was known as the Sumas Ice Sheet, which advanced from the Cascades not more than 11,500 years ago. The ice, which had extended at great depths (700 ft) over the whole valley to a point a few miles west of Abbotsford, gradually withdrew, clearing out of the upper Chilliwack River valley before it left the Sumas-Chilliwack valley. During this period the Chilliwack River found its outlet to salt water by going through the Cultus Lake and Columbia Valley, and on out to Puget Sound throught what is now Washington State. This would mean that the water was lifted to a considerable depth above Vedder Crossing, where an ice mass blocked off what was later the river's outlet from the mountains. At various up-river points there was a build-up of the plateau areas, as lakes formed behind the glaciers, from which the lacustrine deposits flowed to settle on the lake bottoms. After the final withdrawl of ice, the river gradually cut down through the plateau areas, frequently causing great landslides, which continue even to this day. Dr Borden has estimated that Indians were living at Yale 9000 years ago. It is possible that the early ancestors of the Chilliwacks may well have been living on the upper benches of the Chilliwack River at that time—"before the river sprang from the mountains," as Prof Hill-Tout was told. This may well have been witnessed as the Chilliwack finally breaking through at what is now Vedder Crossing. So it would seem that the Chihlkwayuhks have likely lived in this, their ancestral homeland, for thousands of years, even as their legendary history claims they have.

Stone Sculpture

Very fine specimens of stone sculpture have been found in the Chilliwack area, two of them at least on comparatively high land, both east and west of Mt Shannon (or Little Mountain), north-east of Chilliwack city centre. The area in which they were found may well have been some of the earliest formed land, built up by deposits of the Fraser River, whose course at one time straddled this rocky outcrop in the valley's floor. Timber growing on the area at the time of White settlement might indicate this land had risen above flood water from 600 to 1000 years ago.

One of the finest specimens of this culture is now in the Chilliwack Museum, part of the Allan Watson Collection of artifacts.

Ceremonial bowl found near Camp Slough, Rosedale area.

Bowl in the shape of a bird, from the Watson Collection.

Soapstone pygmy owl, found at Unsworth's Farm.

It is a beautiful example of craftsmanship in dark grey soapstone. It might be described as representing a human figure, with uplifted face, seated and holding a bowl in its lap. The head is covered from behind with a well-carved likeness of an animal's head. From the back at the shoulders protrudes a short neck, on which has been carved another head with an uplifted face.

Another fine specimen of stone sculpture in the Allan Watson Collection, possibly of the same period, is a bird, slightly crouched on sturdy legs, with closely held wings, which are lifted to hold a bowl between them on the back. Another bowl of this type was recently illustrated in *The Beaver* magazine of the Hudson's Bay Company, in an article written by Thomas H. Ainsworth, former curator of the Vancouver City Museum. This bowl was also found in the Chilliwack area.

These objects of a distinct cultural type were located in Pilalt territory when White contact was first made with the tribes. The Pilalt have no knowledge of these objects or the culture they represent. Published literature at this time does not give us any enlightenment on the relationship between these sculptures and the arts of existing tribes. If connection could be made, it would reinforce the claim that these lands have been occupied continuously for thousands of years.

These soapstone figures should not be confused with the many small Salish bowls which have been found in the Chilliwack area. One of these of special interest is an owl carved out of volcanic rock. It is without doubt a good likeness of the Pigmy owl, looked upon as an ill omen by the Chilliwacks. This little owl figure with a bowl on its back was found at an old village site on the upper Atchelitz Creek, where many other items of interest were plowed up.

Their Native Land

The Chilliwacks and their neighbors were hunters as well as fishermen; among them were those who prided themselves on their ability as runners and mountaineers. The principal hunting ranges of the Chilliwacks were Liumchen and Elk Mountain, which were a truly Native paradise. Prior to White settlement and for some time thereafter, they hunted and trapped far back into the Cascades, in Skagit country to the east and Nooksack country to the south. In all, it was a recognized tribal hunting ground of approximately 400 square miles. Heavy stands of timber on the lower slopes gave way to open country at about 4000 ft, above which was Alpine park land, a great resource for native food plants and berries.

The Pilalt tribe had access to hunting grounds in the eastern end of Chilliwack valley and the mountains further east, the feeding grounds of large elk herds. The Pilalt occupied and controlled an area of approximately 50 square miles, back from the Fraser River. The river itself, however, was a right-of-way for all Salish tribes through Pilalt territory.

Sumas Lake's 10,000 acres expanded to cover 30,000 acres when the Fraser was in flood. Surrounded by sloughs and grassy prairie, it was a natural wild fowl reserve. Sumas Mountain and the forest areas to the south where the Sumas met the Nooksack carried a plentiful supply of venison. In all, the Sumas tribe controlled about 30 square miles.

The Tait lived close to the Fraser River north of Cheam in numerous villages, over which towered the high mountains where they went for game, berries, and roots, to supplement their fish diet. Mountain goats were plentiful, which they hunted for the wool-like hair with which women wove blankets. The Tait had about 30 miles of the Fraser as their homeland, but each year in the fishing season they allowed peaceful passage upriver to all the Coast Salish. Within the memory of older members of the tribe, the Tait Indians made regular hunting trips in the fall into the watersheds of the Chilliwack and Nooksack rivers, returning by way of the Fraser, sometimes after it was frozen over, with their canoes laden with dried venison and bear fat.

Mountains Which Lived in the Native Legends

Cheam peak, rising high above the lands of the Tait and Pilalt tribes, is the most distinguished feature of the landscape of this locality. The Pilalt, with one of their principal villages known as Cheam, have come to believe that the mountain took its name from the same meaning as the village, i.e. "wild strawberry place," since these berries are plentiful on the mountain. However, the Tait people, in whose territory the peak stands, consider it to be like one of them; for, according to legends which still come to light from the minds of the old people, the mountain knows when any member of the tribe dies—even in distant places—and the mountain is heard to moan in sorrow. It is known to them as Theethuhlkay, "the mother mountain." The word literally means "joined together," and refers to three "sons," the three peaks attached to her to the east. The mother mountain also had three daughters, the youngest of which she is said to hold in her arms. It is the little peak near the summit, visible as you come down Jones Hill. There are legends also concerning the ancestors of the people of Popkum, who came down from Theethuhlkay. The Native name of the peak was recorded by the Boundary Line Survey Commission in 1857-60 (*U.S. Geological Survey Bulletin* No. 174).

The Native name of Sumas Mt, Tuhk'kayuhq, means "gap left when large chunk broke off." This meaning is given by Dan Milo, and is also recorded by Wilson Duff in his *Upper Stalo Indians*. In the legend of the flood, Tuhk'kayuhq was above water, and many canoes were moored to its top. When the large chunk broke off, these canoes, full of people, drifted to various places, including Lummi Island and Bella Coola, which accounts for these tribes of long ago using the same Salish language.

To those who would retain the Native names which our mountains acquired from the local tribes, it is regrettable that the name of Tamihi Mt was changed to McGuire Mt. McGuire was a pioneer settler in the Chilliwack River area. The Native name goes far back into the history of the Chilliwacks. In ancient times, according to legend, it was to this mountain that the deformed or misfits in communal life were taken by their guardians. Here on Tamihi they were left to fend for themselves, and there was little chance of survival. T'ehmeehiy in the Chilliwack language means "the place of the deformed." There is a splendid view of it up river from Vedder Bridge.

Tamihi Mountain.

Rivers and Streams

It has been firmly established that Chilliwack refers to the action of "going back upstream"—to the head at Chilliwack Lake, according to Bob Joe. This explanation was also that of Chief Sepass. Albert Louie, another old historian of the tribe, said that when a canoe has reached the point where it can be paddled no further between two banks it has reached what he terms "chihlahlqw'." Harry Edwards stressed that it was the action of "following back up the stream." Mrs Albert Cooper is of the opinion that the name refers to the action of a backwater in "going back upstream." If a canoe was launched at the "chihluhk," the backwater carried it upstream. I asked Dan Milo to say in Halkomelem the following sentence: "I am going upstream." His reply was: "As spoken by 'up-river people'—lah chihlteeihl; as spoken by the Chilliwacks—lah chihlkwayhaywihl." Without doubt the original Native word "chihlkwayuhk" meant "going back upstream."

According to the older Natives of the Chilliwack tribe, the Coqualeetza prior to White settlement was a small stream which flowed from springs located within a mile of Steetahs, what is now Vedder Crossing; and Indians had homes along this stream south of the present Sardis. "The place of cleansing" or "the place of washing of blankets" is the meaning now attributed to the name "Kohkwahleet'tha." However, the true meaning is "the beating of blankets," which act, as Dan Milo clearly stated, is part of the washing process. Albert Louie says that the name came originally from the story in which the men, who were being pursued by their wives, knew they were very close at hand because they could hear them beating their blankets in anger. His explanation is very similar to that given by Hill-Tout in the "Blanket Beating" legend.

In pre-White days, the Atchelitz was a spring water stream rising within a mile of the Crossing, Steetaws. It flowed northerly across the valley just above the lowlands of Sumas to join the Chilliwack at a point near Squiala. A'tselihts means "the place where you come to a point and can go no further." Chief Sepass indicated on his map that at one time, possible 400 years ago, the Atchelitz was known as Yookuhkahmihn, and that it was then the water course of the Chilliwack River.

Another spring water stream, the Kateseslie had its source south-east of the present town of Sardis. At the time of White settlement it was navigable by canoe to where the Sardis post office is now located. The highway cloverleaf on Vedder Road covers part of the old Kateseslie stream bed. Along this stream the Natives collected slough grass for use in basket making.

An early photograph of Edenbank Farm. Luckakuck Stream is in the foreground.

According to Dan Milo, the name Luckakuck means "to straddle." The stream derived its name from the fact that the Natives often slipped and straddled a foot-log which they walked to cross it. Albert Louie explained that originally it was a slough connecting the Kateseslie to the Coqualeetza in times of high water. Old maps indicate it was likely an extension of the old Lakuhway Channel, which at one time carried the full stream of the Chilliwack River to the Fraser.

The Semmihault was the only tributary coming into the old Chilliwack River from the east. The meaning of the name is not known; Bob Joe said it was the same word as the name of the old Chilliwack language. Catholic Tommy spoke of his father having travelled via canoe from the Fraser to the foothills on this stream. It is the home of the legendary seelkee, described by John Wallace.

Thoowehlmen, meaning "the river that changed its course," was the route of the Chilliwack River from Vedder Crossing to Sumas Lake about 400 years ago, according to Chief Sepass and Bob Joe. When White settlement came, there was no sign of what is now Vedder River.

The Chilliwack-Vedder-Sumas

Over a long period of years, the Chilliwack River has been an important factor in the lives of the people of the Chilliwack Valley. Always admired for its beauty spots and its steelhead runs, it is becoming increasingly recognized as a tourist attraction of great importance.

Occasionally, during the winter months when our mountains are loaded with deep snow, a Chinook wind comes, bringing high temperatures and rain. Then the river becomes a torrent overnight, often rising at the rate of one foot an hour. In flood, it carries all before it. In earlier years, before the valley was logged, great trees were carried downstream to form jam piles, which overnight would swing the river, and a new channel would be cut. During the flood years of 1918 and 1935, from within sight of the present Vedder Crossing bridge, some 20 acres of the old Teskey Farm was swept away; the old bridge went out, along with 10 acres of old cherry orchard below it. The channel in this area is now cut deep and straight, and it is not likely that we will ever again see the river run so high that the roots of floating trees will drag on the bridge as they pass underneath.

The first record I have of the White man on the river is one taken from the Hudson's Bay Company's Journal: "In Dec. 1828 a party from the Fort (Langley) went up the Fraser, explored Sumas Lake, then continued up the Fraser and entered the Chilwhoo-yook—but they could not mount the current beyond the distance of 10 miles.''

The Indians then living along the Chilliwack were located above what is now known as Vedder Crossing, and according to Indian history they traversed the river by canoe from the Fraser to Chilliwack Lake. It is the belief of the Indians that long ago the Chilliwack flowed West from Vedder Crossing into Sumas Lake. Later, it swung East from Vedder Crossing, and then North-East across the valley to join the Fraser east of Little Mountain, through the Elk Creek channel. It mattered little to the Indians whether the river flowed east or west; it carried their canoes and their food, the great runs of salmon.

Chilliwack River from the foothills of Elk Mountain. A deer traverses the logged slope.

When the White settlers arrived, the river flowed north from Vedder Crossing, following the channel (now almost dry) which is now bordered by the Chilliwack River Road, entering the Fraser just above Chilliwack Mountain. At this time, the east end of the valley was mostly a bog area, recorded on the early survey maps of Chilliwack as late as 1886 as ''an area of Beaver dams and swamps.'' Settlement of the valley, which had begun in 1859, extended along the banks of the Chilliwack, from the Fraser upstream. By 1870 when the Indian villages along the River became established as Reserves, most of the land along the river was settled on, either by Indians or Whites.

The Vedder Hotel, on the south end of the bridge at Vedder Crossing, before the massive erosion of the land. This photograph was owned by Mrs Amy Cooper.

In a heavy freshet in 1872, log jams formed in the old Chilliwack and blocked the river; its waters overflowed to break through and form new channels—to the west through the Atchelitz and the Luckakuck. One of the valley's earliest settlers was Volkert Vedder, who with his sons took up large tracts of land at the north-east corner of Sumas Lake, near where the town of Yarrow is now located. In the diary of A.S. Vedder, there is a note recorded in March 1874 which reads ''first muddy water in Vedder Creek.'' This muddy water was the vanguard of water bearing down from the Chilliwack, which, within living memory, had had no connection with Vedder Creek. In the big freshet of the spring of 1882 when the Fraser rose to a height of 23 feet, the Chilliwack River again carried in its run-off great quantities of trees and debris, which formed jam piles in its established channels, and turned the river, which then roared down the valley toward Sumas Lake. In the spring of 1894, when the valley residents saw the Fraser rise to a height of 25 feet, the Chilliwack established itself in what was to become known as Vedder River, and flowed west into Sumas Lake.

Almost every pioneer district has a bit of its history which is described as a ''feud.'' If Chilliwack had one, it was because no one wanted the Chilliwack River! During the years of heavy freshets between 1872 and 1894, the settlers in the Sardis, Atchelitz and Sumas strove to hold the river in check with only horses and cable, fallen timber, and dynamite to work with. When the river swung down the Luckakuck, falling 60 feet in 2 1/2 miles, it tore out acres of rich farmlands, and when it swung through the Atchelitz and Sumas areas, it flooded much good land. Neighbors banded together to protect their land; both dynamite and legal charges were laid and exploded.

Only the Indians remained unperturbed. The river that was named after them no longer flowed by their homes; but, as is characteristic of the people, they adjusted themselves to the changes without a fuss. They took their canoes in the wagons they had gotten from the White man over the White man's roads to fish where the fish were running.

Mr F.N. Sinclair of Chilliwack was the engineer who submitted the plan for the dyking and draining of Sumas Lake. In a brief, which he prepared for publication afterwards, Mr Sinclair makes reference to the fact that some 33,000 acres, which was river-built from deposits made by the Fraser and Chilliwack Rivers, was reclaimed. The Vedder River was confined to the Vedder Canal, to carry it across the prairie east of what had been Sumas Lake, to the Sumas River, just before the Sumas reaches the Fraser. Thus the Chilliwack River, source of sustenance for the Native people, both destroyer and builder of the lands of Chilliwack, was finally brought under control. Originally know by the Natives as the Ch.ihl-KWAY-uhk meaning, "to go back upstream," it stretches from the Cascades to the Fraser. It is now known as THE CHILLIWACK, THE VEDDER, VEDDER CANAL, then THE SUMAS, before it joins THE FRASER.

The Subjugation of the Native

While the title to this section may seem to strike up a feeling of resentment in many people, it is nevertheless the most appropriate term to cover the actions of the White man during the period of twelve years, between 1858 and 1870, when he literally "took over" the tribal lands of the Ch.ihl-KWAY-uhk and neighboring tribes.

Before 1858, these Native tribes knew no boundaries; with the exception of those natural boundaries established between themselves by mutual consent. After 1870 they had no alternative other than to recognize survey lines around small areas, which were *reserved* for them.

Before 1858, they lived in comparative harmony, with each tribal unit recognizing its own leaders as counsellor, and authority. After 1870, all *natural* authority was lost; and small family tribal units were grouped together, and became subject to the laws of the intruder in their land.

Before 1858, the religious beliefs of the Native people were founded on ancient beliefs—plus an infiltration of Christian code, which had come to them through their own "Prophets" and religious leaders. After 1870, the Native people for the most part, accepted the teachings of the various Christian beliefs. But, in the grasping of the new faith, the strength with which their *old* religious beliefs had governed their lives, was lost; and only a few attained the old stability in the new faith.

Before 1858, the tribes moved their home-sites at will, in harmony with the seasons and their way of life. After 1870, this "way of life" was no longer one of freedom of movement.

Before 1858, their established trade values were based on beaver skins, blankets or salmon. After 1870, the White man's gold and silver were the "symbol of exchange."

So, in all these things, the Native became subject to, or under the domination of "The White Man," the intruder in their lands. And it was the "White Man" who inflicted his egotistic ideals on the People.

The onrush of miners was one of the main causes of the abrupt change in the way of life of the STAW-loh tribes along the Fraser. Roderick Haig-Brown, in *The Living Land,* wrote that little of what was valuable in Native culture

> was apparent to the gold miners and white settlers who moved in, in such great numbers, in 1858. Where the Indian could help, he was used; but the earlier shortages of labour and local knowledge soon ceased to be a factor, and the Indians became an inconvenience rather than anything else. By 1862 the smallpox epidemic was raging northward and inland, from Victoria. Tuberculosis and other white diseases began their steady inroads, and liquor was doing its damage amongst a people completely unused to it, and unprepared for it. By 1885 a total population of 70,000 had declined to 28,000 or less. Whole villages, and in some cases entire language groups had been wiped out.

During the period in which the reserves of land were being set aside for the home-sites of the Natives, they came under the influence of Christianity. This was not a gentle force. The strength of character possessed by the missionaries who came among the Native people was powerful. To them there was but one faith, their own; and each faith in its rivalry to possess the souls of the Native people wrought condemnation on beliefs of their White brothers if of contrary faith. In one field of thought only were they in accord, namely that the religious beliefs and customs of the Native people were such that they must be set aside or destroyed. The gateway to salvation was not open to the Native until he put on White man's clothes, took a White man's name and accepted the White man's God. Strangely enough, until he had done this and totally renounced all those fine things which belonged to his Native culture, he was, in the eyes of the Christian, a pagan.

However desirable it may be that a people be known as Christian, however fine the lives of the Native people have been who accepted Christianity and became true Christians, the destruction of the faith of the Native in himself and in the religious ceremonies (which had for generations led them to be thankful and respectful) was a blow by which the Native people were struck down and from which they have been slow to recover.

Oliver Wells

A Note on the Text of the Interviews

We have tried to edit the interviews in such a way that the participants might have enjoyed reading the selections without embarrassment. Fidelity to the actual words and dialects used seemed to be the best policy, on the assumption that speakers would rather be recognizably themselves than given a false "standard" English. The selection is representative of all the different subjects discussed by Oliver Wells with his informants. We have naturally chosen the more interesting moments rather than the parts where the questions and answers were less rewarding. None of the livelier exchanges has been excluded; there were, given the extremely good feeling that pervaded all the interviews, no unpleasant moments to hide. All the myths and legends told in English on the tapes have been included verbatim. Otherwise, normal concern to avoid repetition has governed editorial choices.

To make a readable, publishable book out of approximately fifty hours of tapes meant that a great deal had to be omitted—just how much can be surmised from the complete list of interviews given at the end of this note, where it can be seen that only about two-thirds of the recorded interviews have been included (and then only a percentage of the material in those). Scholars and other interested persons may contact the editors to consult the full transcriptions, which will perhaps eventually be stored in some electronically retrievable form.

Omissions are not indicated in this edition; dots are used for incomplete or interrupted sentences. Titles (in square brackets) have been supplied for the stories.

Most of the photographs used were taken by Oliver Wells or members of the Wells family, and are in the possession of Marie Weeden. Some photographs were obtained by Oliver Wells from sources unknown at this time; we regret being unable to provide proper credit.

Oliver Wells's pronunciation of Indian words is given in his own Practical Phonetic System. The Halkomelem words of the Native informants have been transcribed by Brent Galloway in the orthography described by him in the following note.

We are indebted to Randy Bouchard and Dorothy Kennedy of the B.C. Indian Language Project, and to Dr Louis Miranda of the Squamish Indian band, for making the initial transcription of the interviews with August Jack and Dominic Charlie, and for supplying the spelling of Squamish words and answers to specific questions. They should not be held responsible for any errors that may exist in the present edition.

Ralph Maud

Oliver Wells Interviews and Publications (those interviews used in the present volume are numbered):

	14 March 1954	Mrs Amy Cooper (not recorded)
	7 February 1962	Introduction to Eloise Street's *Sepass Poems*
(1)	8 January 1962	Dan Milo, with Jack Stevenson
(2)	8 February 1962	Mrs Amy Cooper
(3)	8 February 1962	Bob Joe

	21 October 1962	Dan Milo, speech at Soowahlie Hall opening (not recorded)
	1962	Dan Milo (not recorded)
	23 October 1962	Mrs August Jim (not recorded)
(4)	30 October 1962	Mrs August Jim & Mrs Amy Cooper
	15 February 1963	Tzeatchen spirit dance; newspaper report by Oliver Wells
	1 October 1963	Mrs Amy Cooper (not recorded)
	12 December 1963	Mrs Amy Cooper (not recorded)
(5)	16 January 1964	Bob Joe
(6)	31 January 1964	Dan Milo (tape not extant)
	10 May 1964	Bob Joe
(6)	July 1964	Dan Milo
	August 1964	Edmund Joe Peters & Mary Peters
(7)	16 September 1964	Edmund Joe Peters & Mary Peters
(8)	8 October 1964	Harry Edwards
	6 November 1964	Edmund Joe Peters & Mary Peters
(9)	24 November 1964	Mrs Amy Cooper
	4 December 1964	Dan Milo
(10)	5 December 1964	Bob Joe
	17 December 1964	Mrs Amy Cooper (not recorded)
	5 January 1964	*A Vocabulary of Native Words in the Halkomelem Language*
	24 February 1965	Mrs August Jim & Mrs Amy Cooper
	26 February 1965	John Wallace
(11)	3 July 1965	Mrs Amy Cooper
(12)	9 July 1965	August Jack Khahtsahlano
(13)	12 July 1965	P.R. Jeffcott
(14)	28 July 1965	Albert Louie
(15)	4 August 1965	Dominic Charlie
(14)	5 August 1965	Albert Louie
	13 September 1965	August Jack Khahtsahlano
	2 October 1965	John Wallace
	November 1965	Mrs Amy Cooper
(16)	2 November 1965	August Jack Khahtsahlano
(17)	15 November 1965	Dominic Charlie
	3 December 1965	Bridge Bailey
	17 January 1966	John Wallace (not recorded)
	June 1966	*Squamish Legends*
(18)	11 September 1966	J.W. Kelleher and family
(18)	6 October 1966	J.W. Kelleher and family
	1966	*Indian Territory 1858*
(19)	28 September 1967	Mrs Lena Hope
(20)	3 October 1967	John Wallace
	4 October 1967	Mrs Mary Charles
	31 March 1968	Mrs Amy Cooper
	26 September 1968	John Wallace (not recorded)
	Spring 1969	*Salish Weaving, Primitive and Modern*
	1969	*A Vocabulary of Native Words in the Halkomelem Language* (2nd edn)
	1970	*Myths and Legends of the STAW-loh Indians*

The Significance of the Halkomelem Language Material

As described elsewhere in this volume, both Oliver and Casey Wells were interested in preserving as much information as they could on the culture, the language, and the history of the local Indian people in recording these tapes. I met Oliver only once, in my first summer of linguistic fieldwork with Mrs Amy Cooper, in 1970. He was returning an artifact he had borrowed for a talk or display on Stalo history. I was impressed by all that he had done. In 1973 I met his brother, Casey, and for a month we had many interesting conversations on their work with the Indian people. Oliver had passed away in 1970 but Casey let me listen to and copy many of the tapes they had made. By this time I realized the significance of their work on many levels. On just one level, some of the words and explanations they obtained have never been gotten from anyone else.

Oliver and Casey, a founder of radio station CHWK in Chilliwack, had both studied the work of Franz Boas, Charles Hill-Tout, Wilson Duff, and others, and Casey (perhaps from his radio work) had learned about the International Phonetic Alphabet in some detail. From this Casey developed a writing system, the PPS (Practical Phonetic System), capable of fully transcribing the local Indian language, upriver dialects of Halkomelem.

In 1962 and 1963 a graduate student in linguistics, Jimmy Harris, from the University of Washington, had been working with Dan Milo, and showed Oliver and Casey the advantages of taping interviews. He brought up some blank reel-to-reel tapes for Oliver to begin taping his own interviews. Casey went along on some of the interviews and transcribed the Halkomelem words at home afterward. Later Oliver also learned to transcribe in PPS and also prepared fuller transcripts of the English conversations of some of the tapes. The words were copied onto file slips, and re-elicited and compared just as is done by professional linguists.

The goal of the Halkomelem work was not only to preserve but also to transcribe the language in a system that could be typed on a normal typewriter, printed in newspapers, and read easily enough to give an approximation to the Indian place names and words. Casey wrote up two explanations of his PPS, one for casual readers, and one for announcers and more serious readers (to get closer to being able to produce the actual sounds and words). At his request I prepared a third explanation, PPS, Part 3 (1974), to give explanations and equivalences to the International Phonetic Alphabet for Indian people, linguists, and others wanting to pronounce each sound exactly.

The publications of Oliver Wells (see bibliography) and of Casey Wells (*Anthology of Valley History*, etc.) had all Halkomelem words written in the PPS system. The second edition of *A Vocabulary of Native Words in the Halkomelem Language as used by the Native People of the Lower Fraser Valley, B.C.* (1969) had approximately 1336 words listed in it plus 60 place names with literal meanings and nice biographies of the main speakers Oliver worked with. His other publications on place names, legends, Salish weaving, etc. are equally rich in information. In transcribing the tapes which Oliver (and sometimes Casey) made, Ralph and Marie and I were impressed by the expertise Oliver had in working with Indian elders, and the informed and knowledgeable questions he asked. He often brought lists of questions, excerpts from books, transcriptions from previous interviews, etc. to the interviews, and he always brought his knowledge as a descendant of pioneering families in the area. More importantly he found Native elders who were very knowledgeable in many areas, and he fully explored and preserved much of this valuable and interesting information for all of us.

When I began my work towards a linguistic grammar of Halkomelem in 1970, many of the elders he had worked with were already gone, some being the last to know the old ways in certain fields (Albert Louie on the Pilalt dialect, Bob Joe and Dan

Milo in many areas, and John Wallace on canoe-making in the traditional ways). In 1975 I joined the staff at Coqualeetza Education Training Centre in Sardis to set up the Halkomelem Language Program. Some of the elders there (and in the Nooksack tribe in Washington) had been trained in a practical writing system different from the PPS, the Stó:lō writing system. Rather than waste that training and cause confusion with competing systems it was decided to stick with the Stó:lō writing system in our language program. Others had used the PPS at the classes in Sardis in the early 1970s. But the Stó:lō writing system was officially adopted by Coqualeetza and is now in wide use throughout classes in the Fraser Valley. For that reason, Ralph, Marie and I decided that I should transcribe the Halkomelem words in the Oliver Wells tapes in the Stó:lō writing system, so that the Indian people could make instant use of all the material. It is a phonemic writing system except for the symbols ts and ch (allophones) and ts’ and ch’ (allophones) which are difficult to predict.

The words Stalo and Halkomelem are spellings which have been used for a number of years and are still used by linguists and anthropologists. In the Stó:lō writing system, the two words would be spelled Stó:lō and Halq’eméylem, to show their pronunciation in all the upriver dialects of Halkomelem. The upriver dialects include Tait, Pilalt, Chehalis, Chilliwack, Sumas (and perhaps Scowlitz). Perhaps fifty fluent elder speakers remain of all these dialects together, some in Washington. But some younger people are studying the language through classes at Chehalis, Seabird Island, and Chilliwack.

What follows here is a key relating the Stó:lō writing system to the Americanist International Phonetic Alphabet and to the PPS (so that readers of earlier works by Oliver Wells or Casey Wells can interpret their Halkomelem transcriptions). This section concludes with a description for the layman or the language student (as in PPS, Part 3) of how these sounds are made. We hope this will make this volume of use to a wide range of people, both Indian and non-Indian, researcher and interested casual reader alike, as Oliver and Casey Wells intended.

Stó:lō Writing System	Americanist IPA	PPS
a	= [a] before length (:) or under stress (´ or `)	ah
a	= [ɛ] when not under stress (´ or `)	eh
ch	= [č] (allophone of /c/)	ch
ch’	= [č’] (allophone of /c’/)	ch’
e	= [i] between palatal sounds (l, lh, x, y, s, ts, ts’)	ih
e	= [ʊ] between labialized sounds (m, w, kw, kw’, qw, qw’, xw, x̲w)	u
e	= [ə] (or carot) (elsewhere)	uh, e
h	= [h]	h
i	= [i]	ee
k	= [k^h] or [k^y] (aspirated except after s)	k
k’	= [k’] or [k'^y] (free variation)	k’
kw	= [k^{wh}] (aspirated except after s)	kw
kw’	= [k'^w]	kw’
l	= [l]	l
lh	= [ł]	ł
m	= [m]	m
o	= [a]	a
o	= [ɔ] between labialized sounds in free variation with [a], esp. found in speech of Bob Joe	aw
ō	= [o]	oh
p	= [p^h] (aspirated except after s)	p
p’	= [p’]	p’
q	= [q^h] (aspirated except after s)	q
q’	= [q’]	q’
qw	= [q^{wh}] (aspirated except after s)	qw
qw’	= [q'^w]	qw’
s	= [s]	s
sh	= [š] (only found before xw, allophone of /s/)	sh

t	= [t^{h}] (aspirated except after s)	t
t'	= [t']	t'
th	= [θ]	th
th'	= [tθ'] (affricate, glottalized)	th'
tl'	= [ƛ']	tl'
ts	= [c] (allophone of /c/)	ts
ts'	= [c'] (allophone of /c'/)	ts'
u	= [u]	oo
w	= [w]	w
x	= [x^{y}]	~~k~~
xw	= [x^{w}]	~~kw~~, ~~w~~
x̲	= [x̣]	~~q~~
x̲w	= [x̣^{w}]	~~qw~~
y	= [y]	y
'	= [ʔ] (glottal stop, not written at word-beginning before vowel, rare [hyphenated] after obstruents, common elsewhere)	'
´	= [´] (high pitch stress) (written over the vowel)	syllable in CAPS
`	= [`] (mid pitch stress) (written over the vowel) low pitch (no stress) is not written	in CAPS
:	= [·] (length, usually of vowel, one mora; sometimes of consonants such as sonorants)	:

The vowels can be compared with English sounds:

a	as in English ''fat'', ''bat'' (when under ´ or ` or before w or y) or as in English ''sell'', ''bet'' (elsewhere)
e	as in English ''sill'', ''bill''(when between palatal sounds l, lh, x, y, s, ts, ts', k, k') or as in English ''pull'', ''bull'' (when between labialized sounds m, w, kw, kw', qw, qw', xw, x̲w) or as in English ''mutt'', ''what'' (elsewhere)
i	as in English ''antique'', ''beet'', ''eel''
o	as in English ''pot'', ''mop'', ''father'', ''bother'' or as in English ''law'' for Bob Joe between labialized sounds
ō	as in English ''no'',, ''go'', ''crow''
u	as in English ''Sue'', ''soon'', ''moon'', ''flu''

Most vowels can be followed by [y] or [w] in the same syllable:

Stó:lō	Americanist IPA	PPS
aw	= [æw] (as in English ''cow'')	ahw
ay	= [æy] (rare in English, some have it in ''sang'')	ahy
ew	= [əw] (as in Canadian English ''about'')	uhw
ey	= [ey] (as in English ''bait'')	ay
iw	= [iw] (as in English ''peewee'' minus the last ''ee'')	eew
iy	= [iy] (as in English ''beet'')	eey
ow	= [aw] (as in English ''ah well'' minus the last ''ell'')	aw
oy	= [ay] (as in English ''bite'')	iy
ōw	= [ow] (as in English ''bowl'')	ohw

The only consonants which are pronounced like those in English are: p as in English ''pill'' and ''spin'', t as in English ''tick'' and ''stand'', ch as in English ''church'', ts as in English ''rats'', k as in English ''king'' and ''skill'', kw as in English ''inkwell'' and ''queen'', th as in English ''thin'' (but not voiced as in ''this'' or ''the''), sh as in English ''shine'', s as in English ''sill'', h as in English ''hat'', m as in English ''man'' and ''bottom'', l as in English ''land'' and ''camels'', y as in English ''yes'' and ''say'', and w as in English ''wood'' and ''how''.

This leaves eighteen (18) sounds, most of which do not ever occur in English. The best way to learn them is by practicing with a speaker of Halq'eméylem.

The sound written with q in Halq'eméylem is not pronounced like a ''qu'' in English (that sound is written kw in Halq'eméylem). Instead the Halq'eméylem q is more like a plain k but further back in the throat. While a plain k is made by raising the middle of the tongue to touch the hard palate, Halq'eméylem q is made by raising the very back of the tongue to touch the soft palate. This requires careful listening and careful practice. A helpful hint is to keep the middle of the tongue either very flat or cupped at the bottom of the mouth; if the middle arches up and touches the hard palate at any place you will get a k not a q. The sound written with a qw is made just like the q but with rounded lips. Neither the q nor the qw sound is heard in English.

There are ten (10) consonants written with an apostrophe: ch', k', kw', p', q', qw', t', th', ts', and tl'. These are popped or glottalized consonants. None of these sounds occur in English. They are all begun by putting the lips or tongue in the same place you would to make the plain consonant (ch, k, kw, p, q, qw, t, th, ts, and t (for tl')). But you press the tongue harder against whatever it is touching at the top of the mouth, and let the air pressure build up behind it quite strongly. After a lot of pressure has built up behind the point of stoppage, you drop the tongue suddenly to let the air out with a hard pop. Your vocal cords also close off the windpipe and tighten to help build up the air pressure, and they are snapped open suddenly to help make the pop. For p' it is the lips that are pressed together tighter and opened suddenly with a pop. For tl' the tongue stops the air as it would for the ''t'', but after the pressure is built up one or both sides of the tongue are dropped suddenly while the tongue tip stays touching the ridge behind the upper teeth. This produces a ''t'' popped with the side of the tongue. Right after the pop the tip of the tongue is dropped and this lets out the ''l'' sound. The tl' requires more explaining than the other popped sounds because there is no plain tl. Th' occurs in English ''width'' and ''breadth''.

The sound written with a plain apostrophe ' occurs mainly after vowels in Halq'eméylem but also is found after s, xw, x̲w, m, l, y, and w. It is called a glottal stop by linguists. It is found in a few words in English, like ''mutton'' or ''button'' or Cockney English ''bottle'' (spelled with ''tt'') or beginning each ''uh'' in ''uh-uh'' (the sound meaning 'no') or the sound beginning ''earns'' in ''Mary earns'' when pronounced differently from ''Mary yearns''. The glottal stop is a marginal sound in English, but it is a regular consonant in Halq'eméylem. One more point is important to remember: glottal stop rarely (if ever) occurs after a consonant such as p, th, t, ch, ts, k, kw, q, or qw. When and if it does it is pronounced as a separate consonant and is written with a dash to separate it from the p, ts, or whatever. One of the only examples I have found so far in 10,000 words is 'éts-'ets ''to stutter''; the ts-' is pronounced as two sounds, not as a single popped ts'. (Whenever you see p', th', t', tl', ch', ts', k', kw', q', or qw', these are popped consonants, each pronounced as a single sound).

The lh sound is made by putting your tongue in position to say an ''l'' but then blowing air (like an ''h'') around the sides of the tongue. The friction sound of the air against the sides of the tongue produces the sound. This sound does not occur as a regular consonant in English, but may be heard after ''k'' sound in a few words like ''clean'' (klhin) or ''clear'' or ''climb''.

Finally there are four blown x sounds: x, xw, x̲ and x̲w. These and all the blown sounds are produced by raising the tongue to narrow the passage of air till you hear the friction of the air. It works much like squeezing a hose which has a flow of air or water; when it is squeezed at one point it increases the pressure and makes a louder sound. The plain x is made with the middle of the tongue raised roughly in the same place as it is put to make a y as in ''yawn''. But instead of using your voice you just blow air and it produces a friction sound between the middle of the tongue and the front of the hard palate. English has this sound first in ''Hugh'' or ''hew''. Xw is made with the tongue raised a little further back, by the middle of the hard palate (roof of the mouth), but it also requires rounded lips. It sounds a lot like ''wh'' in some words in English but with more friction on the roof of the mouth. x̲ is made still further back, in fact with the back of the tongue raised close to the soft palate (where the q is made). German has this sound in ''ach'' for example, and Scottish has it in ''loch'' meaning ''lake''. The x̲w̲ is made in the same back place as x̲ but is also made with round lips. It is like a blown qw while x̲ is like a blown q.

Almost all Halq'eméylem words have at least one stressed vowel (like á or à or í for example). Some words have several stressed vowels (like pípehò:m or shxw'ílámá:lá). In some languages stress is predictable: always on the next to last vowel, etc. But in Halq'eméylem stress is not predictable and it must be learned with each word. Fluent speakers of Halq'eméylem can ignore the stress marks here if they know the word. But if the word or the reader is new the stress marks are needed to tell which part of the word is said louder and higher. Without this a speaker will have a foreign accent or will say the wrong word.

Stress (´ or `) does not change the pronunciation of a vowel (qwá:l 'mosquito' and qwà:l 'talk' both rhyme with English ''pal''). Stress means the vowel is pronounced fairly loud and with a higher melody than if the vowel was unstressed. High stress (shown by ´ over a vowel) has the highest pitch, about four (4) notes above a vowel without a stress mark. Mid stress (shown by ` over a vowel) has a medium pitch, about two (2) notes above a vowel without stress. Thus pípehò:m has a melody somewhat like 5-1-3 on a musical instrument. Stress is only written over a vowel, never over a consonant.

Length is shown as a colon (:); it means that the sound before the length is prolonged or dragged out twice as long as a sound without a following length mark. Vowels with a long mark always also have high stress or mid stress. Vowels with high stress and a long mark have a melody gliding from highest pitch to lowest all in the same vowel (qwá:l $^{5}—_{1}$). Vowels with mid stress and length have a prolonged middle pitch and no glide (qwà:l 3→).

Only about twenty (20) words have no stress anywhere on the word (they are said without raising one's voice pitch at all, for example, welh 'already' and xwel 'still'). And only a few words in the whole language have no vowels at all (kws, kw's, tl'). But more (difficult) consonants can occur right together in Halq'eméylem words than can in English words, for example, skw'xá:m 'number', slhq'á:tses 'Friday, 5:00', kw'qwém 'hatchet', ch'á:yxwttsel 'I dried it' (the first t and the ts are each pronounced), and ts'eheyelháwtxws 'his church building'. Some of the combinations can be difficult to pronounce, for example, ts'ekwx̱elhtsthóxchexw 'fry it for me!'

Finally, notice that there are systematic groups of sounds which are spelled in systematic ways: ten popped or glottalized sounds all shown with an apostrophe (p', th', t', tl', ch', ts', k', kw', q', qw'); six sounds made on the soft palate shown with a q or underlined x̱ (q, q', qw, qw', x̱, x̱w); six sounds made on the hard palate shown with a k or an x (k, k' kw, kw', x, xw); three sounds made on the side of the tongue and shown with an l (tl', lh, l); seven sounds made with lip rounding shown with a w (w, kw, kw', xw, qw, qw', x̱w), and nine sounds made by blowing shown with h, x or s as part of the symbol (th, lh, sh, h, x, xw, s, x̱, x̱w).

The Nooksack place names in the P. R. Jeffcott interview (#13 below) are not in PPS, but in Jeffcott's own spellings, found in his *Nooksack Tales and Trails*. For recent research, see Galloway and Richardson, ''Nooksack Place Names, An Ethnohistorical and Linguistic Approach,'' 1983 Salish Conference proceedings pp. 133-196.

Brent Galloway

PART I

BEGINNINGS

Eloise Street Harries (centre) and Oliver Wells (right) presenting a copy of Sepass Poems *to Gerald Sepass (left), grandson of Chief K'hhalserten Sepass. This photograph is part of the publicity material in* Sepass Poems *(1963) in the Smithsonian Institution; courtesy of Wayne Suttles.*

As a Prologue to the interviews we present two documents that indicate clearly the position from which Oliver Wells began his ethnographic work among the Native people of the Chilliwack area. The first piece is a typescript in the Chilliwack Museum, signed and dated 1 November 1959, and sketches very briefly the history of the Methodist church in its relations with local Indians, a story in which (it should be added) the Wells family played a prominent role.

Secondly, we reprint, with permission of the Sepass Trust, Oliver's Introduction to Eloise Street's *Sepass Poems* (1963; 2nd ed. *Sepass Tales* 1974). Eloise Street was an adventurous thinker on the subject of Indian history, and the editor of a magazine, *Indian Time*, dedicated to reforging the Native identity. Her correspondence with Oliver Wells is extensive. Her invitation to him to write the Introduction on Billy Sepass was a turning point in the direction of his life.

Early Work of the Church Among the Indians

A review of the early church work in the Valley would not be complete without special reference to the missionary work among the Indians, who at that time outnumbered the White population many times.

In January, 1868, Rev Crosby came up the Fraser in a canoe manned by Indians, in bitterly cold weather, to start his work, preaching to them in their own language.

His first service, after leaving the Fraser River at Sumas Landing, was at an Indian camp at the head of Sumas Lake known as Nah-nates. From there he went to Soowahlie (Cultus Lake Reserve), then to Skowkale (near Sardis), then to Squiala at the mouth of the Chilliwack River, and then back to Sumas. Thus the Indian by the hundreds learned of Christianity from one who spoke their own language, the native tongue used before the coming of the fur trade and the Chinook jargon.

In September of 1870 the first Camp meeting was held in Chilliwack—where that river joins the Fraser. Steamships chartered for the occasion brought large numbers of Whites from Victoria and New Westminster, while Indians came from the north and from Vancouver Island as well as a great many from this locality.

Frontispiece photograph from Rev Thomas Crosby, Among the An-ko-me-nums *(Toronto: William Briggs, 1907).*

Rev Crosby was an outstanding leader, and it was not long before there were a number of converts among the Native people who became disciples working with Rev Crosby, much as the disciples followed Christ in bible times.

The pamphlet The Coqualeetza Story 1886-1956, *owned by Oliver Wells, describes the history of the Coqualeetza Industrial Institute. The brick building was erected in 1894 at the cost of $35,000 including furnishings. At the time of opening there were 63 pupils on the roll, with a staff of five. It replaced a fire-damaged wooden Coqualeetza Home built in 1889 by Rev C. M. Tate, who had before that held a school for Indian children in his home on Knight Road, Chilliwack.*

The first gathering of Indian children for the purpose of christian teaching of the Methodist Church was held in a big rough-board house near the Atchelitz Church. Instruction was given every Sabbath.

Rev C.M. Tate followed Rev Crosby. In 1886 Rev and Mrs Tate began teaching and training the Indian children in their home near Coqualeetza. Through efforts of the Women's Missionary Society of the Church, the first Coqualeetza Indian Residential School and Home was built in 1888. Mrs Lizzie Uslick, still resident of Skowkale Reserve at Sardis, was one of the pupils who attended the first school.

This early building was destroyed by fire in 1891, and Rev Tate pressed for the building of a new school; the large red brick building which stood until 1923 was officially opened in 1894, with 100 students enrolled. The new Coqualeetza Residential School of the Methodist Church was opened in 1924 and housed 273 students. The late Rev Dr Raley, who spent his life in Indian work, was for over twenty years its Principal.

In 1941 Coqualeetza was converted from a Residential School to a hospital for the Indians, and Dr W.S. Barclay became Medical Superintendent.

Among the many contributions Coqualeetza has made to the work of the church, none was more outstanding than the development of Rev Peter Kelly, who came to Coqualeetza as a boy about 1894 and who in recent years after a lifetime of work among the Indians of the Province, was accorded the honor of becoming President of the B.C. Conference of the United Church of Canada.

Churches for the Indians were established at Skowkale and at Soowahlie Reserves. For many years they were active centres of church work. While the Skowkale church no longer stands, the little church at Soowahlie has recently been brought back into active use.

Among the Indians, Rev Crosby mentioned several in his book *Among the An-ko-me-nums*:

Tsit-see-mit-stom—the old warrior Chief of the Sumas whose camp was at Nah-nates was a convert of the first Camp Meeting of 1870. This old warrior chief was one who led the defence of the local tribes against the slave-seeking tribes who invaded their territory.

David Sallosalton—who as a boy came to the mission house and was later to be a leading preacher among the people of the Chilliwack reserves.

Captain John—Sua-lis of Cultus Lake, who for 35 years was a faithful Native assistant to Rev Crosby.

Chief William Sepass—of Skowkale, a devoted class leader and one of the great Indian chiefs who worked with the church for the good of the Native people.

We are fortunate today in having with us a number of our Indians who represent the tribes of our local Native people. Of the church they are ''Hi-sh Closk Tillicums'' (very good friends):

Mrs Francis Kelly
Mrs Cawley—a Coqualeetza student
Mrs R. Malloway
Mr and Mrs Ed Kelly—Coqualeetza students
Chief John Hall—a Coqualeetza student
Mr Oliver Uslick
Mrs Uslick Sr—of the first Coqualeetza school
Mrs David Sepass and daughter
Captain John's grandson—Andy Commodore, and his son and wife, Mr and Mrs Norman Commodore
Mr Albert Cooper.

Oliver N. Wells
Sardis, B.C.
November 1, 1959

Rev Peter Kelly, who had been a student at Coqualeetza 62 years before, returned to the district during 17-18 February 1962 to officiate at the opening of Soowahlie Hall. Oliver Wells tape-recorded the proceedings.

Khal-agh-il-til, Chief Sepass

Chief in the Making

The Indian stood motionless behind the trunk of the largest tree he could find on the ridge; he was waiting for the grizzly to come into sight.

The previous day he had made his way up the old trail which the Native people had used for generations in their frequent forays after berries and *mowich* (deer). It led up from the wooded foothills into the great open park lands of Elk Mountain. In the evening he had camped beside the little lake at the 4000-foot level in the high valley east of the ridge. Before sunrise he was making his way toward Cheam Peak, that high outpost of the Cascades which rises to 7000 feet above the valley of the Chilliwack, the land of his people. He was alone; his mission in this high, wild country was twofold. He had come that he might be alone to consider the plight of his people, and to gain strength and wisdom to become their *siem* (leader).

His mother was the daughter of a Thompson River chieftain, and through her, according to the custom of the Salish people, he had inherited a chief's station in the life of the tribe. As a boy, he had seen Fort Hope established by the Hudson's Bay Company. From his uncle, then Chief Khal-agh-thit-til, he had learned of the great gatherings of the tribes at Yale, ceremonial gatherings where the songs of the tribes were sung and where their legends were told so that succeeding generations would know and remember. Here, too, the tribal dances were held, and the medicine men strove ever to hold their dominant position in the lives of the people.

As a youth, he lived with his family in the valley of the Chilliwack. He had been carefully trained by his uncle, Chief Khal-agh-thit-til, in preparation for the day when he would take the old Chief's place as hereditary chief. He had learned much concerning the stars, their meaning and movements; he knew the history and the legends of his people, and was familiar with the sacred religious rites and customs of the Salish people. His name was Khal-agh-il-til, which carried a reference to the Deity.

Now, as he moved slowly through the draws and over the ridges, no movement or sound escaped his notice; yet his mind was with his people. For generations they had lived in contentment in small bands along the Chilliwack, in pit houses with their split cedar roofs and in the great long houses. Their homes were in a land of plenty: fish crowded each other in their annual runs up the river; game was plentiful and easily taken; life was easy. There was time for feastings, dancing, and the various religious rituals which were important events in their life.

But the White Man had come—first the fur trader, then the gold seeker—and had bought his furs and used his canoes. Trade goods and coins meant wealth and distinction to the Indians, and they had worked hard and prospered.

From his Thompson mother he had learned the precepts and teachings of the Salish people. He reviewed them in his mind: "It is bad to steal"; "It is bad to be unvirtuous"; "It is bad to lie"; "It is bad to be lazy"; "It is bad to commit adultery"; "It is bad to boast if you are not great"; "It is bad to be cowardly"; "It is bad to be inhospitable or stingy"; "It is bad to be quarrelsome." These precepts he vowed he would keep forever, but he knew they were disappearing from the homes of his people that had been invaded by the White Man's firewater.

After the gold seekers had come the White settlers, laying claim to the lands along the lower Chilliwack, the lands where his people had their homes. With them had come the missionaries. First came the Catholics, speaking of the Great Spirit and their Book of Prayer, which his people had heard about from the tribes to the south. Then had come Crosby, who spoke the

Halkomelem tongue, the language of the Tsilli-Way-ukhs; he told them of the Great Spirit and his Son Christ who had been on earth. Khal-agh-il-til had listened, and with his people was content to recognize this Spirit-Over-All-Spirits.

As he made his way along the ridge, he asked the Great Spirit to guide him that he might lead his people through much that they did not understand.

By midmorning he was climbing an open ridge leading up to the great rocky triangle of Cheam Peak itself. Here he hoped to find the answer to his troubled spirit, and here he hoped to prove his valor. He would search out a grizzly, and after killing him and eating the flesh of his head, he would climb to the peak of Cheam, and from this point he would look out over the valley of the Chilliwack and make peace with the Great Spirit.

Now the Indian was again the hunter; he waited, knowing full well the grizzly he had seen from the ridge would soon leave the great rock slides on which he was feeding and would climb up toward the rock bluffs above, coming out over the ridge where he now waited in silence. With a nerve of steel, the Indian waited without fear. He was alone; his weapon was a Hudson's Bay musket, a muzzle-loader. He would have but one shot; there would be no chance to reload. Should the grizzly see him at close range, he knew the bear would charge and the hunting knife in his belt would be his only defense. He knew his people would recognize his greatness if he could kill a grizzly with a musket. The great claws would adorn his ceremonial dress. He knew the wind was right; he must wait until the bear was close enough—until he knew he could place his shot in the vital organs. He knew the musket could not fell a grizzly with one shot, so great was his strength.

The bear came slowly up onto the ridge. The barrel of the musket drew down slowly, and the Indian's eye held steady through the sights as the bear drew closer. Closer he came, until at last the moment he had waited for arrived. As the great bear's head swung out of the way and through the sights the bare chest appeared, Khal-agh-il-til pressed the trigger. The ball struck home, and the bear recoiled under the shock; for a moment he swayed, and then with a roar he raised himself on his hind legs to his full height, searching for his enemy. Already the smoke that might have given the bear a clue had cleared; the gun barrel was as still as death. The Indian stood motionless: this was the fatal moment; his heartbeat quickened—would the bear see him and charge? The force of the shot was making the grizzly cringe, but he held his position a moment longer as he searched in vain for his adversary. Then, uncertainly, he lowered himself onto all fours, turned to go back whence he had come, and retreated into the rocky bluffs.

The Indian relaxed. He knew he had sent the bullet home and that he had but to wait for the bear to die; he had made his kill. In the afternoon, Khal-agh-il-til took up the trail of blood on the rocks and soon located his kill. The grizzly had retreated into a rocky crevice to die. Dressing the carcass, he skinned out the head, and feasted in preparation for the climb up the narrow rocky ridge to the Peak. Mindful of the customs of his ancestors, he placed the bear's skull on a rocky point as a mark of respect that would please the spirit of the bear. With renewed strength and courage, he mounted the Peak.

The Tribes of His People: The Halkomelem

Monarch of all he surveyed, Khal-agh-il-til stood on the crest of Cheam Peak. It was 1870. He was yet only halfway through the long life that he was to live, but the foundation of the character which was to develop in this man had already been laid.

Born in the early 1840s, his early training was that of the Salish people, as practiced for generations before the coming of the White Man's influence. His was, however, of a special significance which extended far beyond the normal training to hunt and to fish and to take his place in the daily life of the tribe. He had been chosen by his grandfather to transmit to succeeding generations those religious and legendary beliefs which his people had carried with them as they had moved from the lands to the south up into the Thompson River country, down the Fraser, and up the Chilliwack to join the tribes who for generations had lived in peace and plenty.

These tribes had formerly lived high up the river among its mountain fastnesses in order to avoid being raided by the dreaded Cowichans, who, until the establishment of Fort Langley by the Hudson's Bay Company, had periodically come up the Fraser in their great war canoes to plunder and take slaves. Settled now along the river from the Fraser to the mountains, the Tcilqeuk or Tsilli-Way-ukh (Chilliwacks) lived in family groups, each of which as an extended family looked to its own head man or leader for guidance in all things. They had not as yet come to know or recognize a chief among them as a man whose word was law.

As young Khal-agh-il-til watched from his vantage point on Cheam Peak, nearly 7000 feet above the valley floor, the sun sank behind the horizon; the sky caught up and reflected its glory along the mighty Fraser. From the sea to the foot of the Peak on which he stood, the great river became a river of gold. Covering much of the valley floor, it stretched out its many arms around and among the tribes of the Stalo, the River People—the Halkomelem, as they were known by the language they spoke.

To the north, seemingly almost beneath the Peak on which he stood, the river rushed by as it left behind the numerous canyon villages of the Tait tribe, whose pit houses had lined its banks in many places from Yale down to Popkum. Far to the north, beyond the river, stretched the land of the Chehalis, whose territory covered the watershed of that river and the south end of Harrison Lake. The Scowlitz tribe, however, held the mouth of the Harrison River; these tribes were friendly to the Pilalt and Chilliwack tribes.

Turning now to the west, the great river spread out in the wider valley, and the reflected light rising to the mountain tops etched in clearly defined lines the sloughs and islands and tributaries of the mighty river as its now placid current flowed westward to the sea. The Pilalt tribe, who spoke a slightly different language from that of the people of the Chilliwack, held sway on both sides of the Fraser from Popkum down to the mouth of the Chilliwack. Close under Cheam, Hope Slough broke away from the Fraser and often ran full to the tops of its high banks. Here a main village of the tribe had their homes at a village known as Ciam—("Wild Strawberry Place").

Midway along the Slough, another large village was located at Schelowat, and at the west end of the Slough where it again joined the Fraser was the village of Skwali. These were the neighbors of the Chilliwacks, living like them in pit houses during winter months and in temporary shelters during the summer.

And now, as his gaze swung farther west and south, the young Indian's blood stirred as he traced the waters of the Chilliwack from its confluence with the Fraser to the seclusion of its upper reaches, which lay hidden behind the mountains to the south.

Again the Indian lifted his gaze and looked far to the south, over the homes of the Chilliwacks, over Cultus Lake gleaming silver in the dying light as the sun set, to where Mount Baker rose, with the sun's last rays reflecting from its eternal snows. Beyond Mount Baker, far to the south, was the land of his ancestors. To them he owed much—his desire to rise to the heights of leadership with humility and yet with a proud bearing. He had been born with a chief's station in life; he had been trained and schooled in the wisdom and knowledge a leader must have; he would pray for strength and courage to lead his people in the days ahead. For he had the wisdom to see that their way of life was not going to be as it had been in the past.

He was mindful of the fact that Chief Hal-lal-ton of Shaulkel had not long to live, and that the Chief's daughter was eager for her husband, Short Charlie, to be the next chief. To him also had come word that the people of the Chilliwack would favour him.

In the morning he would pray to K'HHalls, the Sun God, as the sun rose over the great peaks to the east, over the Skagit country—whence the grizzly had come.

The Influence of the White Man

Soon after the coming of the settlers, old Chief Hal-lal-ton of Shaulkel died. At a great gathering of all the people of the Chilliwack, Khal-agh-il-til was to become known as Chief K'HHalserten Sepass, the central figure of leadership in the villages of the Chilliwacks and the tribes of the upper Stalo. He was the son of William Sepass of Shaulkel, who in turn was the son of Sepass, who had come from the Shuswaps. From his mother he had inherited recognition by the Thompson tribes, whose influence extended down into the Canyon. From the Thompsons he had chosen his first wife, and they had established a home among the Chilliwacks. His sister had married into the neighboring tribes to the west, the Sumas, and the influence of the family was felt over a large area of the valley.

William Sepass with his first wife, Rose, the daughter of Thompson Uslick. Oliver has a note: "she was the mother of eight of his children, most of whom died of TB before health services were available to counteract the disease."

The year 1867 was to see events take place which were to affect the life of Chief Sepass gravely. That year Reverend Edward White, grandfather of Eloise Street, was one of the first visitors to the home of A.C. Wells, who had established a farm in the same year on the Ketsesly and Coqualeetza Sloughs, where the village of Sardis how stands. Reverend White recommended to the Methodist Church that a missionary be sent to work among the Indians and the White settlers living along the Chilliwack. In 1869 Reverend Thomas Crosby, having spent two years among the Indians at Nanaimo and having learned to speak the Halkomelem language fluently, set out from Nanaimo in a dugout canoe, and a week later he arrived at the home of A.C. Wells, having crossed the Gulf and ascended the Fraser and Chilliwack Rivers alone. In his book *Among the An-ko-me-nums*, Reverend Crosby refers to the conversion of old Chief Hal-lal-ton at Skowale: "Chief Hal-lal-ton of Skowale [was] a Chief of the old school, and when he was converted he brought his whole tribe with him."

Sepass, already the recognized leader among his people, became a close friend of A.C. Wells and later of his son, Ed Wells; still later he became a friend of the writer, Oliver N. Wells, who from 1923 until the death of the old Chief in the early 1940s accompanied him on many trips into the mountains.

With the establishment of the reserves, Sepass, as chief of the Skowkale Reserve, took pride in the leadership he was able to give his people when their government expected them to change their way of life from their long-established custom of living off the products made available to them by nature. He established a fine residence surrounded by a stately evergreen hedge, a fruit orchard, a large barn, and well-tilled fields. As a young man, Sepass worked for A.C. Wells, pioneer Chilliwack farmer, and his ambition and good judgment soon created within him the ability to lead his people into agricultural pursuits, at which for some years they were quite successful.

The Wells farm, long known as Edenbank, carries to this day a monument in nature set firmly in place by young Sepass when he worked for A.C. Wells in 1882. Near the present residence it stands, a native blue spruce; now eighty years old, it measures twelve feet in circumference.

Chief Sepass became recognized not only by the numerous villages of the Chilliwacks as their leader but also by all the tribes of the Stalo as the spokesman for the Native peoples. He was a master of the language of the ancient Chilliwacks, of the Halkomelem language, and of the Chinook jargon, the trade language used by the Indians and early settlers as their common means of communication. In the highest sense he was to represent his people.

Sepass adopted the White Man's religion. While his Native spirit called him still to the Potlatch or the ceremonies of his people, he was one of the most gifted in expressing his prayers to the Great Spirit. In the White Man's church, to which he accompanied his friends, he spoke in great reverence and with gifted eloquence in his native tongue. It was the writer's privilege to hear him repeat in all reverence the "Lord's Prayer" in the language of the Chilliwacks.

Hunter, Trapper, and Canoe-Maker

As a hunter, the Chief had no equal. He killed at least two grizzly bears with a Hudson's Bay musket before he became the proud owner of a .303 Savage, with which he was a dead shot. Much of his game he killed by taking up a position on a game trail. In 1923 the writer, as a young lad, was a member of a group guided by Chief Sepass on the first trip made into the Liumchen Mountain country with the hope of establishing a permanent trail. Crossing the Chilliwack River in a small dugout canoe, the Chief ferried the party across the fast stream one or two at a time; he led them up the old Mount Baker trail past great beaver dams to Tamihi Creek. There they camped overnight, and the next morning they started a steep climb which took them up and out on top between the precipitous peaks of Church Mountain (or Twin Sisters) at 4500 feet. Here camp was made.

Edwin Wells and Billy Sepass at Elk Mountain, c. 1905. Left to right: Edwin Wells, Harry Uslick, Ray Wells, Billy Sepass.

The Chief announced in the evening that he would go after *mowich.* He had with him a deer-call of his own making. Moving down a long slope, he took up a position alone and began his wait, calling occasionally. He had not long to wait—an inquisitive deer came slowly up the hill. When it was close enough, Sepass pressed the trigger and dropped it; the bullet had gone through the chest and heart, making an instant kill.

A lifelong companion of Chief Sepass, Ed Wells ranked high on his long list of friends. He accompanied the Chief on many a hunting trip and frequently was taken to visit the trapline which the Chief maintained throughout his life. On one occasion he was granted the exciting if dubious pleasure of making the kill when evidence showed that a cougar had been caught in a trap. The Chief had fastened the trap chain to a strong, light anchor pole which allowed free movement but no chance to escape. When after careful stalking the cougar was finally located, it was too late for considered shooting. The cougar was waiting for them behind a log and was already coming through the air when the Chief stopped his spring in mid air with a quick and deadly shot.

His skill in canoe-making was unsurpassed. He made many during his lifetime—small shovel-nosed ones for use on the swift Chilliwack, larger ones for use on the Fraser. At the Chilliwack Arts Festival in 1961, a dugout cedar canoe twenty-two feet long, which had been made by Chief Sepass forty-five years earlier, was the feature attraction at the exhibit of Indian Crafts. The graceful lines of the craft are as perfect and symmetrical today as when it was purchased by Oliver N. Wells from the Sepass family soon after the Chief's death. The canoe had been made by the Chief on the banks of the Chilliwack River above Tamihi Creek; its maiden voyage took its maker down the river and out into the Fraser, where he used it daily to tend his nets.

Possibly the Chief's closest brush with death was when driftwood once caught his net, overturned the canoe, and threw him into the Fraser River. He was rescued by one of his people who saw the accident and put out into the current to save him.

Sepass himself had been the hero in a river accident years before. In 1887, when the Chilliwack River was a roaring torrent, Sepass was piloting a canoe load of settlers across the River. Running with the current at a high speed, the canoe struck a submerged rock with such force as it neared the shoreline that the bow was split and water came pouring in. Sepass immediately threw himself forward face down in the bow of the canoe and wrapped his arms around the split bow, holding it together until a landing was accomplished.

Oliver Wells's caption on the back of this old photograph: "Chief Billy Sepass at left, with 10 men in the big freighter canoe he made at Chilliwack Lake about 1924."

Man of Solitude

The valley of the Chilliwack River and the hills surrounding Cultus Lake became the Chief's hunting ground. The solitude of the deep, timber-covered valley was to him a congenial companion as he passed along familiar trails. The River knew the silent passing of his canoe, the quiver of his salmon nets; the river banks knew the tread of his untiring step as he visited his trapline. The beaver at work in their ponds paused to watch his passing and felt no fear, for he was one of them, a part of the world in which they lived. When the hunt was on, the deer and the bear tried in vain to elude his stealthy stalk.

Chief Billy Sepass, July 1926.

The Lake, known to his people as Cultus, was to him of absorbing interest. He knew the legends of the evil spirits that dwelt therein, whose wrath and violence were responsible for the violent storms which often swept over the Lake, and he knew of the Slollicum—the Mystery of the Lake.

The mountains surrounding the Lake held much that was dear to him—the deep, still forests were as a cathedral to him where he might meditate. To the east, the mountain towered above the Lake, and from its steep upper slopes he often watched the Lake below in all its various changing moods. As he sought out the deer in their midday lair, in the timber on the ledges overlooking the Lake, he would pause and listen in watchful waiting, with the patience known only to those of his race. Often, as he watched, the calm surface of the lake would be broken by a swiftly running ripple, streaking across the surface before a breeze; and in the quiet of the great timbers he would hear the whisper of the wind in the tree tops. Then suddenly from the valley to the southwest a wind would spring out over the lake and the waves would rise. Scarce moments later, the whitecaps would be curling over the breakers as they sped across the lake to crash upon the rocky shore. Overhead the great timbers would moan and bend with the wind. Far below him, the lake would once again have become Swailtza-tha-Way-lee—the Storm Lake.

Across the lake, the rocky bluffs of the shoreline rose up into the timber-covered mountain which extended to the west and south of the land of the Nooksacks. How well the Chief knew the ancient trail that ran along the northern slope, under the big timbers where no underbrush grew, to the lodge of Mesatchee Sam, a Nooksack who with his family guarded the long trail which led from the land of the Nooksacks through the lands of the Chilliwacks, their fellow tribesmen, to the great fisheries of the Fraser at Yale. The daughter of Mesatchee Sam had become his second wife, for the dread disease which took so many of his family had taken also the life of his first wife. Years of travel and hunting had made the Chief familiar with this mountain, which rose in irregular formation as a ridge between Cultus Lake and the Old Sumas Lake. He knew of its bold outcropping of rocky bluffs; he knew of its mineral licks, the haunts of the deer, its spring-water streams, and the network of deer trails which to him were the only requirement in cross-country travel.

Chief Sepass's Declining Years and Great Decision

For over half a century, Chief Sepass watched the passing of the old way of life among his people. The land which had been theirs for so long was quickly being occupied by White settlers. Reserves had been established on which tribes had to live, with the old custom of recognition of a head man of the family units being replaced by the election of chiefs. Growing agricultural crops and hiring out as labor had replaced much of their former independent life of hunting and fishing. The coming of the misssionaries and the White Man's laws had changed the beliefs and ceremonies of his people.

As a convert to Christianity, he was its staunch supporter, but he was loath to relinquish the old customs and ceremonies. He had attended and taken part in the last great Potlatch of the Chilliwacks which had been held at Tzeachten. At the turn of the century, the Potlatch had been outlawed, but there, under protective guards posted on all trails, old Bill Uslick had summoned the tribes from near and far, and the sound of drums and rattles which rose and fell in rhythmic chant was heard for days.

Sepass had often joined in the New Year ceremony of mourning for those who died during the past year, and he knew that these and other customs would soon be only of the past. He knew the ways of his people would never again provide for the keeping of those ancient customs. The legends and myths which had been passed on to him in song would soon be lost forever. As their guardian, he was expected to pass them on to succeeding generations.

The loss of his son Eddie, whose passing he mourned so deeply, seemed to have closed the door forever on the normal giving of his inheritance. Eddie had died before he was seven years old. His playmate for the few years of his life had been Jack Stevenson, who was born the same year. One day years after the boy's death, the old Chief stood silently waiting at the gate of a field which Jack was plowing. It was on the Skowkale Reserve, not far from the graveyard. Unnoticed he had come, and he stood quietly, waiting with the patience of his kind, until the team was unhitched and the day's work was done. Then he spoke to his son's playmate of years long past in the Chinook language familiar to them both. *''Mamook chako yahwa''*—''Come with me yonder.''

The grave was marked by a simple headpiece which the old Chief himself had carved from cedar, carefully making the letters and figures which had been outlined by Reverend Crosby. The inscription read simply, ''EDDIE. 1880-1886.'' The old Chief spoke simply of the bond of their friendship. *''Mika delate closhe tillikum''*—''You were his close friend.'' There was a moment's silence, and then he spoke again: *''Yaka klatawa hopa yaka tillikum''*—''He has gone to his people.''

Quietly they turned, leaving behind memories of the past, and slowly made their way back to the team—to life as they now knew it, so far removed from the life they both had known before the death of Eddie.

Among the early missionaries who befriended Sepass as a young man was Reverend Edward White, one of the first four missionaries sent out by the Wesleyan Methodist Church. These four had come before Reverend Crosby, who had converted Sepass to his faith. Now, in his search for a means to record for all time the songs of his people, Sepass went to the home of Reverend White's daughter, Mrs C.L. Street, who could speak fluently his own language—the dialect of the Chilliwack Indians. Through her translation, which was recorded by Eloise, her daughter, the songs were set down in rhythmic form as the Chief directed. Some four years of patient translation were spent before the work was completed. The Chief's only request was in fact a decree: that the poems should be published as he had given them so that his people would not forget their great past. Eloise Street agreed to this compact, and has herein kept faith with the old Chief.

Chief Sepass, renowned yet humble, respected by Indian and White Man alike, was a friend of everyone; all who knew him called him friend. His later life was spent for the most part out in the world of nature, which he loved and respected, hunting, fishing, and tending his trapline along the rivers and returning again and again to the mountains which had long been the hunting grounds of his people. His countenance was always serene and yet stern; his faith in the Great Spirit was steadfast.

In 1943 he passed into the Great Beyond, leaving behind a record of achievement unsurpassed by any Indian of his time.

Oliver N. Wells
7 February 1962

1. Dan Milo—I

Dan Milo and his grandchildren, 1964.

Oliver Wells in his *A Vocabulary of Native Words in the Halkomelem Language* (1965) wrote of Dan Milo as follows:

> Born at Scowkale on October 10, 1867, Dan Milo is the oldest of the Native people who have assisted with this publication. A much-loved great-grandfather, Dan lives at the old homesite with his family.
>
> His ancestors, according to the legend, flew into the valley, and for this reason, his father's name was Sloh-kwih-LAH-loh, meaning "flying away." The name "Milo" was given to his father by Mrs A.C. Wells, wife of the pioneer settler.
>
> Dan has a broad knowledge of history in general, and in particular, that of the language, legends,

and stories of the Natives. As a storyteller he has no peer.

In his younger days, Dan "got around." He worked in the logging camps, on the River Boats of the Fraser, and with the Boundary Line Survey crews that established the boundary line "markers" on the peaks of the Cascade Mountains.

As a young lad, Dan was among the first group of Native children who were gathered by Rev C.M. Tate (the founder of Coqualeetza Residential School) into his home that they might be given schooling. In the first little school, built by Mr Tate near his home, Dan acted as Interpreter, in which capacity it was necessary for him to use Halkomelem, Chinook and English, in order to transmit messages from the Native children to the teacher and return.

Dan has had considerable pleasure during his lifetime as a member of the Native Brass Bands, who established enviable reputations. For over 80 years it can be said that Dan has played his fiddle to entertain his friends, and translated the Halkomelem language into English for the benefit of linguists and professors. During recent years he spent two weeks as a "paid" guest at the home of Jim Harris, linguist of the University of Washington, who was most appreciative of Dan's stay with them. He is blind now, but his wit is sharp and his memory clear.

This first of the recorded interviews took place, according to the "tape log," on 8 January 1962. The location is Dan Milo's house in the Skulkayn Reserve, more commonly known as Scowkale.

Dan Milo at Scowkale
8 January 1962 (with visitor Jack Stevenson)

WELLS: First of all I should say that this is Oliver Wells interviewing Dan Milo, and Mr Milo is now going to give us one of the early stories of the Chilliwack Indians.

MILO: The same story that I said about that young girl who left the place there, where they all died?

WELLS: Yeah. Down at Yarrow?

MILO: Yarrow, yeah.

[ORIGIN LEGEND]

Well, there was a boy from Kilgard. In them days they used to call that place Semáth. That means Sumas. Well, that one boy was left by himself. All his people died. So he went home. And the next morning he made up his mind to come over there and see who was living at Yarrow, where he saw that smoke coming out of a big house where there was a lot of Indians living. When he come there, he went right into the house there. There was just that one girl left, after she had all the bodies put away. So that is the first time he ever saw this girl. So he got acquainted with her. So he got real acquainted, and they married right there. So they stayed together. And that's where the language that the Indians are using started from. They went over to Nicomen, where there was a lot of Indians there. That was the only people that used the language that the Indians are using now, today.

WELLS: Is that the language they call the Halkomelem?

MILO: Yeah. Because it's the name of the place, Leq'ámél. That's how they call it Hálq'éméylem.

WELLS: The name of that island was Nicomen Island? And how do you say Nicomen in...?

MILO: Leq'ámél. And that's how that word speaks that way, Hálq'éméylem, when they speak the language they used then. They come home. They raised childrens, and that's how the people began to speak that Hálq'éméylem language. All their children speak the same.

WELLS: All the Chilliwack Indians learned to speak...?

MILO: The real Ch'elxwíqw Indian, they have a different language altogether. That's what they call the Chilliwack today, the right way to pronounce the name of the people that used to live right here. They used to live up there at Th'ewálí [Soowahlie] Reserve. That's Ch'elxwíqw. They used to speak a way different language, something like they used over here at Skagit.

WELLS: In the early days the Chilliwack Indians lived high up the Chilliwack River at many places? Up Tamihi and Slesse, a long time ago?

MILO: No.

WELLS: Not in your time?

MILO: Only when they go hunt mowech [deer], you know. And mountain sheep.

WELLS: And do you have the Indian word for "sheep"? There are no sheep in this valley, no mountain sheep, eh? How about the word "salmon," for the big spring salmon?

MILO: The real Chilliwack salmon, they'd have called them—those that's running the Fraser River—sqwéx̱em. But those that runs in the Chilliwack River, swá:ychel. All the different rivers runs out from the Fraser River, the fish got their names. The fish that runs into Chehalis, they call them pó:qw', that's spring salmon.

WELLS: And the sockeye? The sockeye salmon?

MILO: Théqi.

WELLS: How about the streams here? Where does the Coqualeetza get its name?

MILO: The Coqualeetza? It was a spring. It run out from the schoolhouse across here. And that's where the Indians used to come and cleanse their washing. And that word, kw'eqwálíth'a—they used to clout it with a stick, you know, to dry them. They have their blanket or something hanging, and they start to hit it with a stick, you know, to dry, drain the water out of it, you know. That's why they call that creek Kw'oqwálíth'a.

WELLS: I see. That's good. Well, there used to be a small slough. It went through where Sardis is now. Kateseslie?

MILO: Katsesló:y, yeah. That was part of that Kw'oqwálíth'a that went through Sardis there, come out to the Cottonwood Corner.

WELLS: Well, then, this Luckakuck. What does Luckakuck mean?

MILO: Lexexéq—somebody straddle a log or something. I don't now how it become named that, you know.

WELLS: The Indian word means "straddling a log"?

MILO: Yeah. I'm going to tell you how Sepass is named here in Scowkale. The grandfather of Chief William Sepass, he walked all the ways from Shuswap, and landed here; and he married William Sepass' grandmother. After a while he went home to Shuswap, and he never come back again. And William Sepass' father, he growed up, and then he gotten married. And he got William Sepass, his son. So the latest William Sepass he named the name of his great-grandfather that came from Shuswap.

WELLS: I see. William Sepass' first wife, was she a Thompson River girl too?

MILO: That's old Thompson Uslick's daughter. Old Mrs Thompson Uslick was partly from Thompson. Merritt. And he was partly from Cultus Lake, Soowahlie Reserve, old Thompson Uslick. Because, way back in the early days here, the corner of the Soowahlie Reserve runs as far as Wells' place, just a little ways back here. Well, he was living there, the old Thompson Uslick was living there when the White people came and they couldn't find no place that is open for anybody. That's how the Indian reserves got so small, you know. They just leave it to them to pick out as much land they can use. So that's how the Chilliwack valley was opened for White people when they first come in this valley.

WELLS: I see. Well, this Thompson Uslick, where did you say his...?

MILO: Just a little ways up here. You know, there was an apple orchard back there, some years ago. His planting was there, you know. There was some apple trees growed there.

WELLS: Oh, yeah, up here at Tzeachten?

MILO: No, right here on your place.

WELLS: Oh, right on the farm here?

MILO: Yeah.

WELLS: Oh, is that right?

MILO: Yeah.

WELLS: Well!

MILO: Old Harry Uslick was a boy already. Robert, his older brother, and Jack, Jack Uslick, they were kids at that time. Yeah, that's the way it went.

WELLS: Yeah. They lived right at—above, on the corner of the Wells farm, like?

MILO: Yeah. Between this house and Stevenson's place.

WELLS: Oh yeah? Well!

Your family, Dan, where did your father come from?

MILO: Well, he was really from Ch'elxwíqw, Chilliwack here, that was on the Chilliwack River. And he lived right there where I lived. There's a cabin across the creek, you know, from the Fletcher's house. Well, that's where my father's house was, before the high water of the Chilliwack River came and eat up that place, that kind of bend there.

WELLS: The old Thompson Uslick, would he speak English, or would he still stay with the old Indian language?

MILO: Well, all the Indians in their time—my father's the same—they only speak Chinook. They learn that from the Hudson Bay.

WELLS: Yeah, but some of the Indians used it even before the Hudson Bay come? Trade language, eh?

MILO: Yeah. Myself, when I was a boy, I learned how to speak Chinook just listening to my father speaking to the

Mrs Tate and Rev Tate at the Mission house on Knight Road, with pupils.

pioneers in this valley here. There was A.C. Wells, one of them, and the Kipps. They all speak Chinook. And my father learn how to speak it, and when he speaks to the—

you know, he speaks Chinook. And when I was a kid, about twelve years of age, I learned how to speak Chinook myself. When I went to school at the Coqualeetza, C.M. Tate was the man that started the first school on the end of the Knight's Road at Sardis. And there was a bunch of us went to school there. And they had a young schoolteacher there, and she had a heck of a time with us, you know. We couldn't speak English. So Mrs Tate, she teaches us sometimes because, myself, I speak Chinook, so I interpret, speaking Chinook to Mrs Tate. I used to have a book from some of the missionaires in Kamloops, and they used to call it "Kamloops Wawa." Well, there used to be some kind of a shorthand writing there, you know.

WELLS: I have a few words here in English, and you tell me what they are in Chinook: "Hurry up and go away."

MILO: Hyas kloshe mika klatawa.

WELLS: "Where are you going?"

MILO: Kah mika klatawa?

WELLS: "Very good friend."

MILO: Delate kloshe tillikum.

WELLS: Very good. How old are you, Dan?

MILO: Ninety-seven.

WELLS: Ninety-seven! Oh, that's very good.

•

WELLS: This is an interview between Jack Stevenson[1] and Dan Milo, with Oliver Wells acting as moderator. You two

Jack Stevenson with Oliver Wells, at the confluence of the Atchelitz and the Fraser Rivers.

are old tillikums, and I really just wanted to get you on this record to have a conversation between you in Chinook.

STEVENSON: Nawitka [Yes].

WELLS: You were telling about the explosion on one of the river boats. Maybe we could get a bit on that first.

STEVENSON: The *Ramona*. Captain Seymour.

WELLS: Did you work on that, Dan?

MILO: Well, the time we got exploded, you know, I wasn't working on the boat. I was just travelling, I and my wife and my kids. Well, the night before leaving New Westminster they asked me if I can help them along till they come to Chilliwack. I said, "All right." Well, I wasn't working; I found myself a bib overalls, and I put that on top of my dress pants. Well, that's what saved me from being burnt real bad. It was just my face, and down my hand there. You could see the scars from where the jacket was buttoned tight. Captain Seymour, he was so excited he was going to throw the anchor down without having it tied. But someone seen him, you know, and told him the

"The Ramona." Photograph courtesy of the Chilliwack Museum and Historical Society.

anchor wasn't tied. So they tied it, and anchored right there at the head of the Langley Island there.

WELLS: Did it kill anybody in the explosion?

STEVENSON: Two women, Dan.

MILO: Two womens got drowned.

STEVENSON: Blew them right off the steamer.

MILO: One was getting off at West Landing, and the other one just come down from up the upper deck to bid goodbye to this lady that's going off. While they were there talking—you know the glass there where you can see the water when it's on the steam?—It was full all the time, but it went down all at once. It must have been plugged. That's what give so much heat on the boilier.

STEVENSON: Klatawa pe [Go then] Westminster, St Mary's Hospital.

---

[1]Jack Stevenson, described by Oliver in a typescript note as "a lifelong friend of the Chilliwack Indians," lived and farmed on Stevenson Road, named after his father, Robert Stevenson, a pioneer of Sardis from Northern Ireland. According to a typescript in the Chilliwack Museum, "the Indians named Robert 'the man afraid of nothing.'"

MILO: Nawitka [Yes].
STEVENSON: Konaway mimie yahka memaloose [All downstream she die].
MILO: Delate memaloose [Truly dead].
STEVENSON: Nawitka [Yes].
WOMAN'S VOICE: The kids want to hear you talk Chinook.
STEVENSON: Nem [Name] Luckakuck "slippery log." Konaway inati [All across] yahka keellapi pe chuck [he fall off then water]. Hiyu solleks [Plenty angry]; wawa [say] Luckakuck. Nika tumtum yahka [I think it] cuss-word.

•

WELLS: What were the families that lived on the Soowahlie Reserve? Up at Cultus Lake.
STEVENSON: Indian David; Thompson Tommy; Humpback Sampson; Commodore; Captain John; Harry Capit.
MILO: Nawitka [Yes]. Konaway memaloose [All dead], Jack. Okoke man mika kwunnum, konaway klaska memaloose [These men you count, all they dead].
WELLS: Well, the Coopers?
STEVENSON: George Cooper's mother was an Indian, and his father was a White man. Doctor George was a full-blooded Indian, a medicine man. And he was George Cooper's half-brother.
WELLS: I see. Well then, in the burial ground up at Soowahlie, there's King David, and a large family.
MILO: That's Indian David's son.
STEVENSON: His oldest boy.
MILO: Do you remember Bertrand that was over at Blaine, Jack?
STEVENSON: Yes. Charlie.
MILO: Well, that's old Captain John's sister, Mrs Bertrand. Well, he had a son by the name of Tommy.
STEVENSON: I know him. Bertrand.
MILO: Tommy Bertrand. You now, he went after a girl that was in Coqualeetza school, when he already had a young woman from Lytton. He had her at Harry Uslick's place here. Harry wasn't at home. I guess the Coqualeetza people heard about this, you know, that the girl was in the family way. So they were going to put him in jail.
STEVENSON: Yes. I saw the policemen, Jed Nichol and Nat Cary; I met them going out there to Harry Uslick's to arrest Bertrand. Bertrand went upstairs to change his clothes, and he jumped out of the upstairs window, and he run. And he got away.
MILO: He went upstairs. He told the policemen, "My coat is upstairs. I'll go up there and put it on; then I'll go with you."
WELLS: In the early days one time, didn't they lock up an Indian in Chilliwack jail, and the Indians were in such numbers that they forced them to let him go?
STEVENSON: I don't remember.
WELLS: I heard that once. Only one time that I heard there was ever any trouble, like.
STEVENSON: But the Indians had a very strong sense of justice.
MILO: Yeah.
WELLS: Now, you've listed the older Indians at the Soowahlie Reserve; who were the oldest Indians at Tzeachten?
STEVENSON: James Wealick, Fred Wealick, Jimmy Michell.
MILO: Bill Uslick.
STEVENSON: Bill Uslick, Harry Uslick, and Jack Uslick.
WELLS: Well, then, go down to Scowkale and Yakweakwioose.
STEVENSON: The Yakweakwioose and the Scowkale, they're practically all one. One side is Catholic, and other side Protestant. There was Malloway, Doctor Bob, and Louie.
WELLS: Is that Albert Louie's father?
STEVENSON: Albert Louie's father. And then Thompson Uslick, and Milo.
MILO: Old Jack.
STEVENSON: Little Jack, Long Charlie, Short Charlie... There's another one in there, and I can't think of his name.
WELLS: Who was the last one, opposite Albert Knight's house?
STEVENSON: Long Charlie. No, that was Little Jack.
MILO: Little Jack, yeah.
WELLS: That was Jack. We used his horses one of the first times when I went up Liumchen.
MILO: Scowkale Jack. He didn't belong to Scowkale though.
STEVENSON: He was Thompson River, wasn't he?
MILO: No, he was from—his father was from Ruby Creek.
WELLS: Chief Billy Sepass, he was the only Indian that had land on the west side of the Chilliwack River, eh?
MILO: I'll tell you. The Scowkale didn't have that place where Sepass was, there, on the side of the creek. But there was Sepass himself, he was just a young man—that's before he married Uslick's daughter—and then the old Chief X̲elálhten's son. He was quite young: and they didn't have no place to stay. So that's how the Indian agent give this place where Sepass was, there, on the side of the creek. There was X̲elálhten; that was the old chief before Sepass.
WELLS: Is that the same family? Sepass' uncle?
MILO: No, no. This Short Charlie that they called him, he was from Cultus Lake family. When he married X̲elálhten's daughter, he stayed right there at Scowkale. And they stayed there all together, you know, until X̲elálhten died. They didn't have no chief for some time; so this old lady, Short Charlie's wife, wanted her husband to become chief. So they got the whole Chilliwack to vote on that. But they liked Sepass better than they do Short Charlie. So Sepass he win, and become chief.

Scowkale Church. Photo: Archives of the United Church Conference, B.C.

WELLS: I see. Well, now, there was another reserve down the Chilliwack River.

STEVENSON: Squiala.

WELLS: Squiala. Who was in there?

STEVENSON: Willie Dick.

MILO: William Dick, the old man Dick, and his son, William. That's close to Al Evans's place there across the slough. But that S<u>x</u>woyehá:la [Squiala], that's way over, towards the Chilliwack Landing. You know why that place is called S<u>x</u>woyehá:la? That's where they used to have that thing they have when they're dancing.

WELLS: Oh, the mask?

MILO: Yeah, the mask. They call it s<u>x</u>wóy<u>x</u>wey. That's where they used to have it, there. They are the only people that had that mask. And there was another group of Indians right over here on the end of Higginson Road, on that side of the road—that's when that river was running, Chilliwack River—S<u>x</u>wóy<u>x</u>wey they called that place. There used to be a lot of Indians there a long long time ago, I guess. I didn't see it. S<u>x</u>wóy<u>x</u>weyle. That's where they used to have that mask, yeah.

WELLS: When my grandfather first came to the valley, hewas at a big Indian spirit dance or something that lasted for days, and he said they worked up into such a frenzy that they would grab up the dogs or anything that was around and dance right through the fire with them.

MILO: Well, I'll tell you a little story. I didn't see it, but that's what my mother used to tell me. Those Indians way back in the early days—my mother was just a little girl—the dance didn't start till after Christmas in them days, and they used to do a lot of things that a person wouldn't think anybody could do that, where there's a man that used to grab a red-hot stone. He used to have it in the fire the whole time the dance was going on. And the other man in that same place, at Scowkale, he used to grab hold of, just roll up a dry fish, and shove it, you know, and let it go, you know. Well, when the time comes that those guys going to dance, they hide all the babies. If he get hold of a baby, he eat it up. But if he gets hold of a dog, you know, he gets hold of a dog and tears it up, you know.

WELLS: My grandfather said he actually saw them pick up a dog and tear chunks out of it with their teeth.

STEVENSON: Eat it. Raw dog.

WELLS: That was as late as my grandfather's time.

MILO: Yeah. Well, my mother was watching that man when he start to dance, and there was a stone there in the fire, just red-hot, real red-hot. And he had his hands oiled, you know, got some grease on it. He grabbed hold of that stone, and when he get started dancing, my god, it's just like when you're frying something on a frying pan. His hands were making smoking. After he come round once around the hall, he throw that stone in the fire again. Well, that's a little bit of a devil, isn't it?

WELLS: Well, they worked up into quite a frenzy, like, didn't they? I attended a kind of mourning dance, or a mourning celebration in which they were mourning the people that died during the year before. And that was up at Tzeachten, and that would be about 1925 or somewhere there. I heard the drums going one night when I come home. And there was a big dance on, like, and I went up, and there was no other White man there except one man from the Vedder Crossing, and I just was stood at the door. But I was told afterwards that they were mourning the dead that had died the year before. And on the left side of the hall around the wall was a lot of the old women, and they were just weeping and wailing to beat the band. And then in the centre every once in a while there'd be one young fellow that would come out in a kind of a dance. And there were drums and rattles and stuff going over here.

MILO: That kind of dance, it started from way up, way up Thompson, Shuswap, and way back there, right down. And it would be about after Christmas that they'd get started here. Farther down, crossed over to Vancouver Island, they get on later, way late in the springtime.

WELLS: Would the same people move down through, or...?

MILO: That song seems like it travels down here.

STEVENSON: When they made potlatch unlawful, old Bill Uslick put on one. And he gave away all his stuff, his horses, his cattle, his wagon. He had it going for three or four days. And they grabbed him and they put him in jail for six months. Jim Mercer saw him coming home from jail, and he says: "Kah mika mitlite, Bill? Where have you been?" "Skookum [strong] house."

MILO: *(laughs)*

STEVENSON: "Mika Protestant, okook sun? You Protestant today?" "Halo [No]." "Catholic?" "Halo [No]. Just siwash."

MILO: *(laughing)* What's the meaning of that "siwash" anyway?

STEVENSON: It's a Mexican word that means "a mule."[2]

WELLS: It doesn't belong to the Indian language, eh?

MILO: No. I was working in a logging camp down here at Seabird. I was just going in. I used to be on the whistle punk, you know. I know there was a log coming, out where the donkey was, and those logs run against a stump and got stuck. And the hook-tender, he was just coming along: "Here," he says, "grab ahold of that line and siwash that stump over there." I said, "I'll siwash you," I says to him.

STEVENSON: *(laughing)* You know what that means, Ollie? It's just a wrap on the stump, and they call it a siwash.

WELLS: Oh, yeah. I see.

STEVENSON: Danny, he didn't understand us.

MILO: "Siwash the stump," he says. "I'll siwash you—!"

STEVENSON: Hiyu chahko [Plenty become] hiyu sollecks [plenty mad]! If you want to get into a fight with an Indian, call him a "siwash." He'll fight you.

MILO: Delate sollecks [Right angry].

STEVENSON: Nawitka [Yes].

MILO: Nawitka.

•

WELLS: Well, would you tell us—your mother would be one of the older type Indians, doing the things like the Indians used to do—can you tell us how she would have you make yourself hardy when you were a boy?

MILO: CHWK. I think I give it to them too.[3] But only hear it once through the radio. That's when I was still at Coqualeetza. And CHWK quit coming there and taking my stories. The doctors didn't like them to come there. The University used to come there and take some meanings of Indian words too. Well, are you going to take it now?

WELLS: Yeah, it's on now.

MILO: Yeah. When I was a boy about ten years of age, how my mother used to treat me, she used to treat me kind of rough. When I got up in the morning in the winter time, you know, when the east wind is blowing hard, as long as the creek is open: "Throw those pants down!" (I'd be dragging my pants on to go warm myself on the heater.)

[2]"Siwash," the Chinook Jargon word for a Native Indian, is usually said to be derived from the French "sauvage" (savage).

[3]Murdock Maclachlan of the local Chilliwack radio station interviewed Dan Milo and other Native people (including Mrs Augustine Joseph of Cheam, and John Hall). Wells made notes from these recordings.

"Throw that pants down and take your shirt off. Go down to the creek and jump in." I'd take my shirt off, and run down to the creek. And there was a plank there that goes way out to the water that's running, for their drinking water. And I'd jump right in that water. I come out of the water across the creek. And I swum back. My mother tells me before I went down: "You feel down there and find a stick that's well soaked, that's stayed down there. And rub yourself with it. That'll give you a long life. You'll live old that way."

WELLS: I think she must have been right, Dan, because you've lived for ninety-seven years, and that's about as good as anybody can do.

MILO: "If you don't do that," my grandfather said to me, "every time sickness comes, they'll be taking you up to the graveyard."

Coqualeetza Indian brass band. Rev Barraclough is the left of the three seated men. Oliver Wells wrote of Dan Milo, "Dan has had considerable pleasure during his lifetime as a member of the Native Brass Bands, who established enviable reputations."

2. Mrs Amy Cooper—I

Oliver Wells wrote of Mrs Amy Cooper in the *Vocabulary* pamphlet as follows:

> Mrs Cooper has very clear memories of her childhood, both at home and at Coqualeetza Residential School. She was one of the group of Native children who moved from Reverend C.M. Tate's school into Coqualeetza when it was opened.
>
> As with other students of the early church schools, the high standard of character and academic training of the teachers of that day had a lasting influence on Mrs Cooper. She became proficient in music and household arts. Her dignity and respect for elders, natural to the Native people, were here developed still further.
>
> Her one regret, when her period of formal education had come to a close, was that she had been deprived of the privilege of speaking her own native language while at Coqualeetza.
>
> Her marriage to William Commodore, a grandson of Captain John Sualis, of Soowahlie, gave her an opportunity to rebuild her knowledge of the Halkomelem language and learn much of the history of the Chilliwack tribe. After the death of Mr Commodore she married Albert Cooper, who is a grand-nephew of the late Captain John.
>
> Mrs Cooper's interest and assistance has been largely responsible for this project being undertaken and developed. She has a good command of English and a wide knowledge of Native Culture, in the preservation of which she takes a keen interest. Her home is the site of the old village of K̶AY-luhs, to which village the few remaining Natives moved from the upper Ch.ihl-K̶WAY-uhk when their old village site was destroyed by a slide.

Mrs Cooper's house, where the interview took place, is on the north side of Chilliwack Lake Road about half a mile from Vedder Crossing, i.e. on the other side of the river from the main Soowahlie Reserve land.

Mrs Amy Cooper at Soowahlie, 8 February 1962

WELLS: Well, it's good to be able to talk with you, Mrs Cooper; and I would be glad if you could tell us what you know about the Indians of the Chilliwack River, and maybe especially those that live up on the Soowahlie.

MRS COOPER: Well, Soowahlie was the motherland of Chilliwack. And all the people lived up there. There wasn't any other reserve, you see.

WELLS: The first of the Indians that were living at Soowahlie, it seems to me one time you referred to them as "sun-worshippers."

MRS COOPER: Yes.[1]

[1]The reference here is to an early interview of 14 March 1954. Oliver did not tape it, but made notes, which included the following:

> Indian families, living in homes near where the cemetery is now, were known as "early risers." They were supposed to have risen and eaten before sun up and not to have eaten again until after sunset. This was the custom and training common in the homes of the "nobles" or upper class of the tribe.

WELLS: Where were they, against the mountain, along the Sweltzer Creek?

MRS COOPER: Well, towards where the old church is, across the stream. They were all classed. There was the

Mrs Amy Cooper.

aristocrats, and the seconds, and then there was low class, and then there was the slaves.

WELLS: That would be about from the time the Whites came—earlier than that?

MRS COOPER: Oh, earlier, far earlier. And then they went out, you see, down to Atchelitz, Squiala, and all that. Well, those Indians from there claim that they come from Sch'el-xwíqw, Chilliwack. But Sts'elxwíqw means sts'élexw, and sts'élexw means "backwater," see?

WELLS: Well, that's interesting. Yeah, I'm glad to hear that explanation.

MRS COOPER: And the backwater was at the Vedder, and it went up towards here, and up in the creek there, see. That's what sts'élexw means, and sts'élexw is "backwater."

WELLS: One thing I wanted to inquire about was the different families. One of the older Indians, I understand, was Indian David. Was he of the Soowahlie?

MRS COOPER: Yes, his mother was.

WELLS: Of these various Indians, there might be something in particular which should be mentioned. This Indian David, he was the father of King David, wasn't he? I notice there's quite a large family.[2] Did they have any particular interest in life? Were they canoe-makers or...?

MRS COOPER: No, no. David was far younger than Thompson Uslick and Captain John. They were the older ones. David worked for your grandfather; as a young man, he worked there for—oh, until he was past middle-age.

WELLS: Then there was one Indian that I knew myself, Harry Capit. And one thing I wanted to inquire, and you may know. It was understood that Harry Capit was a great man for hunting deer. And that he used dogs, before it became illegal, I believe.

MRS COOPER: Well, they had hound dogs, real hound dogs, those black dogs with the great big long ears.

WELLS: Did they? And they would turn them loose?

MRS COOPER: Turn the dogs loose out on the mountain there, and they'd chase the deer right down into the lake; and soon as they got to the lake there, well, just a head would be showing, and Harry'd shoot it then. He'd wait with a canoe down at the lake, and he always brought home his deer.

WELLS: Did any of the other Indians hunt in that manner?

MRS COOPER: No, none of them would, because they didn't like the meat.

WELLS: After it had been run by the dogs it'd be too hot by the time it was killed.

MRS COOPER: Yes.

WELLS: I was going to ask about the Sweltzer Creek, or the creek that comes out of Cultus Lake. What was the first name?

MRS COOPER: Swílhcha. That's Cultus Lake. But the white man couldn't say Swílhcha. It used to get pretty rough, and the surveyors would go there and fish trout, and, well, they just couldn't get any trout, I don't know why. The Indians used to get the trout and all that. Then, there were certain places where the Indian went to be by himself for weeks and weeks to be an Indian doctor, and they said that it was "cultus" place, see. So the surveyors thought that "cultus" was an Indian word, and called it Cultus Lake.

WELLS: I see. The word "cultus," is it a true Indian word or...?

MRS COOPER: No, it's Chinook. It's "bad" in Chinook.

WELLS: The original name was Suhweelt'zuh?

MRS COOPER: Swílhcha.

[2]Wells noted in a manuscript workbook: "In the graveyard at Soowahlie is a grim reminder of the terrible mortality among the Native people when they became exposed to the White man's diseases. In the cemetery, there is a headstone which records the death of King David and five of his children."

WELLS: And does that mean "storm lake"?

MRS COOPER: Well, to tell you the truth, that's one word

Panoramic view of the "motherland of the Chilliwack," Cultus Lake, with Columbia Valley in the foreground, and Soowahlie Reserve in the middle distance. Aerial photograph by Casey Wells.

I couldn't pronounce when they would start pronouncing Indian words, and I couldn't get them to tell me. Maybe Dan Milo would know.

WELLS: Did the Indians live in the Columbia Valley?[3]

MRS COOPER: No, they hunted over there. And they just lived, you know, where the keekwilee houses were made, between the church and the graveyard. They were made there.

WELLS: They dug into the ground, and then put a cedar slab roof over it, yeah.

MRS COOPER: And they say it could hold thirty people in there. My mother lived in one of them.

Capt John of Soowahlie, and his wife, Sally Ann.

WELLS: In the early days, did any of the Indians live out on the flats where the Kellys are now?

MRS COOPER: Not until Captain John got to be chief. There was one chief before Captain John, an old, old man, Captain John's uncle, and he didn't last long there, and I can't even pronounce his name.

WELLS: Captain John, his name was John Swalihs, was it?

MRS COOPER: Swóles.

WELLS: And the Commodore family is descended from Captain John, is that right?

MRS COOPER: Yes. Captain John and his wife Sally Ann had only one child, and that was Commodore's wife, Sara.

WELLS: And what Commodore was that?

MRS COOPER: He came from Kilgard, and marrying the chief's daughter, well, he just stayed here.

WELLS: Would he be the father of Andy Commodore?

MRS COOPER: Grandfather.

WELLS: And the chieftainship, then, has been in that family?

MRS COOPER: The first chief, I don't know his name; that was Captain John's uncle. Then Captain John. Then George Cooper is Captain John's nephew; and when George

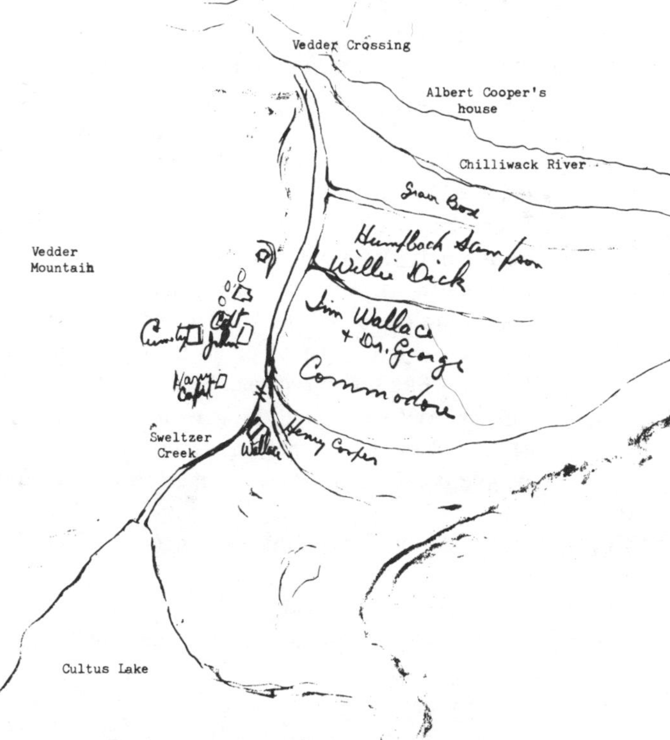

Sketch by Oliver Wells of the location of houses on the Soowahlie Reserve, made during a later interview with Mrs Cooper (probably March 1968). Further place names added by the editors.

Cooper died, then Albert got it. And then he sent in his resignation, and then he handed over to Norman, you see. So there's only been five generations there since the White man came. That's not very many, is it?

---

[3]This valley, a fertile area south of Cultus Lake, between the Lake and the Border, should not be confused with the great Columbia River system.

WELLS: Where did the Indians have their burial ground before they established that graveyard?

MRS COOPER: They had it where John Wallace is living. They didn't bury them. They had them in boxes. They made boxes, and they put them in. And they didn't lay them down. They put the knees right up here, and then when another one there died, they put that one in until that box is full. I got lost in the woods one time, and I come across one of them. And nobody would believe me. And, say, were they big people! They must have been, with great big heads, and all their teeth on. And their bones were so long that, when it got washed out, the Vedder was just strewed with all the skulls and the bones there. And doctors from Vancouver came up to pick them up. And they had their teeth, and they were all laying there facing the sun when I saw them, all grinning at me. And they had solid, good teeth.

WELLS: Is that right? Would that be out where the river is now?

MRS COOPER: That box was there, and nothing bothered it. And nobody'd believe me until they saw all the bones strewn down. Then old Willie Dick went and picked it up and brought it up to the graveyard and buried it.

WELLS: Well.

MRS COOPER: Years ago, when the old people used to tell the younger generation there that there was a famine once—did you ever hear of that?

WELLS: No.

MRS COOPER:

[ORIGIN LEGEND]

There was a famine that everything there—well, I suppose like in India and other places there—that they couldn't save anything. And they couldn't dig anything to put away, like these wild potatoes and other things there that they used to dig, roots and that. All that there was died off, and what didn't die off the bugs got it. They didn't say it was grasshoppers. And they said the worms ate it; and all the berries there, they were all worm-eaten. And the fish never came up. The creeks there was so dry there, that the fish never came up. And, according to the Soowahlies, everyone died but a woman; and she saw them all just doubling over, she says, when they were getting too weak. There was nothing to eat; so she went and got cedar bark, and made herself a pair of corsets, like, and bound that up, and she was able to stand and breathe. And then she went down to a little creek down at South Sumas. Now I don't know where that creek is; but I saw it once when we went out when I was a kid there to pick cranberries. I don't know if it's around Ling's or someplace there. And she went there. And what did she get? Minnows! So the only thing she could do to catch them was to weave a little net and make a little scoop-net out of grass there. And she got the minnows. And that's how she lived. Then, when she got stronger and the spring came and the roots came back and the other stuff there that they eat, you know, she went back home and gathered up all the bones, skin and bones, and cleaned out the big long-house that she lived in. She got that clean. But she didn't have a dog or she didn't have a man, woman, or child to talk to. And she was all by herself till one day a man showed up. And he came from Lake Whatcom. He was the only one that was survived over at Lake Whatcom. And they say that's where the Soowahlie people come from, from the man from Lake Whatcom and this woman from Soowahlie.

WELLS: Well, that's one reason that the language would be similar too.

MRS COOPER: Well, they had no line; there was no borderline there. My son-in-law was over last, oh, about nine months ago, and he says people are still fighting over that man's name. But he came to Soowahlie, and he died and he was buried in Soowahlie, and that's where the generation come from. But they say that there used to be a famine, and that was the worst, when they all died.

WELLS: Did the Indians live up the Chilliwack River in the earlier times?

MRS COOPER: Up this way? Yes. I've heard that from old Captain John and the old-timers talking about it when there was just a few survived that avalanche that came down and went right over the village they had there. There was a lot of them up there.

WELLS: Up where the mud-slide is?

MRS COOPER: I don't know where it is, but they say that you could see where part of it broke off, and that part came down and the other part is up, but this came right down on the village and killed them all.

WELLS: Was the Wealick family originally up in this area?

MRS COOPER: Fred and James Wealick's mother come from Kilgard, and old Wealick went over there and lived there until the Indian Department started taking over from the Indians and telling them they had to get back to their own reserves and settle down. So Tzeachten wasn't taken up, so they settled in Tzeachten. And Jack Uslick settled there because he had a Wealick woman. And Wealick's an Indian name.

WELLS: Well, now, I was wondering about that. Do you now what it means?
MRS COOPER: No, but I can pronounce it in the Indian. And Uslick's Indian.
WELLS: Malloway wouldn't be?
MRS COOPER: Malloway's Indian. I can't pronounce it, the Indian, but it's Malloway. Milo's Indian.[4] Sepass is Indian.

•

WELLS: You were going to tell me about the Indian legend concerning Mount Cheam and Mount Baker. What is that story?

Mt Cheam is "really and honestly a dog's head when the snow is just off, you can see it. You can see the ears and it looks like it's just above water. It's really a dog head but it wouldn't go back to the family, the man family" (Mrs Amy Cooper, February 8, 1962). Illustration by Oliver Wells, from Myths and Legends of the Stawloh Indians *(1970).*

[LEGEND OF MT CHEAM]

MRS. COOPER: Well, Mount Cheam is a lady, and Mount Baker is a man. (This is an old legend.) So Mount Baker, he comes over and he looks for a wife, and he finds a nice-looking girl. So he takes her over to the State of Washington. They live there and they have three boys, Mount Hood, Mount Rainier—I can't tell you what the other one is. And they have three girls, but the boys are the oldest ones. After the boys grew up and she had three little girls, she says, "I had better go back home," she says, "to my people, to the Fraser River." So she comes back, and she says: "I'll stand guard," she says, "I'll stand and guard the Fraser River, that no harm comes to my people, and no harm comes to the fish that comes up to feed them."
WELLS: Well, that's very interesting.
MRS COOPER: That's the legend. And then she takes her three children, and she stands up there. And coming down from up the road, there's three little points, and those three little points are her children. They say she holds the smallest one in her hand. And behind her, towards this way, is the dog head of the dog that followed her, and she told the dog to go back home, and it stood there, and stayed there. So I guess right now there, if the snow isn't all off, you could see that dog head plain. Did you ever see it?
WELLS: Yeah. Some people call that the creeping prospector.
MRS COOPER: No, it's really honestly a dog head there.

---

[4]Oliver writes in his workbook: "The name Milo was given to Dan Milo's father by Mrs A.C. Wells when Milo was working on the farm of the writer's grandfather, A.C. Wells." By the time of a later interview (November 1965) Mrs Cooper has asked Mrs David about the name Malloway, and says of Julius Malloway (Richard Malloway's father): "He was baptised Julius Manuel,and the Indians tried to say 'Manuel' and they couldn't do it, and went on trying until they got Malloway." Brent Galloway writes the following explanation:

> According to Chief Richard Malloway, his grandfather Th'eláchiyatel received the name Manuel after a riverboat on which he worked on the Fraser River. Upriver Halkomelem speakers would normally change all n's to l's, and thus Manuel became Málewal. The final "l" was changed to "y" on Chief Malloway's name by the paymaster at Coqualeetza Hospital, who wrote the name Malloway on analogy with the Scotch-Irish names like Galloway. This change happened during the time Chief Malloway (not then chief) worked at Coqualeetza Hospital. The connection is proven by the Stalo band lists for 1878. The one for "Ya.kwi.a.kwi.oos Village" shows "Sah.lait.se.ate.tun Manuel" among others. Th'eláchiyatel is now the Indian name of Chief Richard Malloway, so Manuel on the list is clearly his ancestor. Richard is the son of Julius Malloway (Siyémches) (born 1870, died Sept. 12, 1948) and wife Mary (1858-1967) who are buried in the Yakweakwioose Cemetery. Also buried there is "Thalaltchyatil Malloway" with no dates on his stone. But this must be the father of Julius Malloway, i.e., Th'eláchiyatel Manuel, who was shown on the 1878 band list with a wife, one son and two daughters.

WELLS: You told me one time about the mountain Tamihi, and that legend of how it got its name. And it means "barren mountain" or something like that, eh?

MRS COOPER: "Hermaphrodite."

WELLS: "Hermaphrodite"?

•

WELLS: I have this little Methodist hymnbook here. I think you may remember having used it, Mrs Cooper, when you were at Coqualeetza? Did you ever sing out of it in the Halkomelem?

MRS COOPER: We used to sing down at Scowkale Church.

WELLS: I wish we could...

MRS COOPER: We sang "Come Thou Fountain."

WELLS: Yes.

MRS COOPER: "Shall We gather at the River?"[5]

Chehál talhlímelh q'ép lí te stó:lō,
Stó:lōs kw'e Chí:chelh Siyá:m
la la la la la la la la
Lí kw'e chíchelh te éy téméxw
Chelál talhlímelh q'ép lí te stó:lō
la la la la la la la la
Chelál talhlímelh q'ép lí te stó:lō,
Te stó:lōs te Chíchelh Siyám.

It's a long time that I've ever heard or tried to sing it. I've forgotten the words.

WELLS: Well, you've done very well.

MRS COOPER: I'm the only one on the Soowahlie Reserve that could talk the Indian language. And I had to learn it. I guess that's why I never forgot.

WELLS: Well, one of these days there'll be some of the younger generation—and I heard of one or two already that have asked their parents what the Indian language was like—and if we could get a song recorded, just like you were singing now, why, then, we have the English for it, and we'd have the tune and we'd have the pronounciation on the tape, and it wouldn't be long before anyone could pick it up.

MRS COOPER: They don't understand, not any of them. Only just Dan Milo.

Albert and Amy Cooper outside their house on the Chilliwack River Road.

[5]Mrs Cooper is singing hymn #19 in the *Indian Methodist Hymnbook*, compiled by Crosby, Tate and Barraclough in 1898.

3. Bob Joe—I

Oliver Wells wrote the following in his workbook:

> Few have the privilege of sitting in on an interview with an Indian whose mind has retained the knowledge of tribal history to the extent that is evidenced by the following script.
>
> Having made an appointment with Bob Joe for a tape recorded interview, I went to his home at Tzeachten on February 8, 1962, and was greeted pleasantly by Bob, who was then 80 years old.
>
> Bob is the recognized historian of the Chilliwacks; his interview is an example of the care with which tribal history was passed down from one generation to the next. Though he has had very little education and no training in the art of delivery, Bob's discourse is concise and to the point. It is informative and has an air of finality which is convincing. The information given has been proven reliable by research undertaken since the recording was made.

Bob Joe at Tzeachten, 8 February 1962

WELLS: We'll record a few things which I wanted to ask you, Bob. And one thing: what was the name of your family, and can you tell me the Indian name?

JOE: There were four brothers; each one of those brothers had a name. Well, it appears at that time, time immemorial, thousands of years ago, the oldest brother was Wilíléq; the next brother, Th'eláchiyatel; the next brother, Yex̱wéylem; the last brother, the fourth brother, Siyámches.

WELLS: Those are good straight Indian names from way back.

JOE: At that time, Malloway is a White man's name, given, not from our heritage.

WELLS: But the Malloway family descended from these four?

JOE: Yeah, from these four, which is a large family today. Captain John, Captain John's son, daughter, great-grandchildren, they're descended from them four that I just named.

WELLS: Did these families, like the Wealick family that lives here now, did they come down from the Soowahlie Reserve area? Was the family originally higher up the river?

JOE: The main headquarters of the Chilliwack tribe was up at Chilliwack Lake, Sx̱óchaqel. Well, as time went on, they kept a-moving down, that is the headquarters of these four that governed that tribe of Indians. They used the Chilliwack River down as far as the stone house, Láx̱ewey. Qwemílíts, that's Chilliwack Mountain.

WELLS: Was that the house that was built by the Millers?

JOE: That was built where the first store was there.

WELLS: That's where the Sumas River joins the Fraser?

JOE: Yeah, I think so; around there. Well now, they have their tribal territories. So that the Chilliwack tribe, they joined the Pelólhxw [Pilalt], that's Chilliwack Landing today. And on this side they came in contact with the Skagit; further down, Nooksack; and come further down, Semáth [Sumas], today called Kilgard.

WELLS: Some of the earliest Indian homes in the valley were along the Sweltzer Creek, were they?

JOE: Yeah, Soowahlie there. They moved their headquarters down four times. The last headquarters was down here toward around Higginson. They call that Sx̱wó:yx̱weyle.

WELLS: I was talking with Dan Milo, I guess, and he

indicated that that was quite a large strong band of Indians, and at that gathering they used this mask.

JOE: Yeah, that sx̱wó:yx̱wey, that came in after that, oh, years after.

Bob Joe.

WELLS: The mask got the name from the people?

JOE: Yeah. When they disbanded from Sxwó:yx̱weyle, some of them went down to Láx̱ewey [Lackaway], Qwemílíts, Shxwá:y [Skway], Qweqwe'ópelhp [Kwawkwawapilt], Sx̱woyehále [Squiala], Áthelets [Aitchelitz]. And some of them come up this way. They made their homes down here at Kitabush [Kickbush]. There's another name for that.[1] That's where one of the largest bands were. And Sq'awqé:yl, Scowkale, then Yeqwyeqwíws [Yakweakwioose], then Ch'iyáqtel [Tzeachten] here. But at that time, you see, there was part of the Chilliwack tribe live toward Columbia Valley.

WELLS: I often wondered. Did they actually live up through the other end of the lake?

JOE: Yeah. Their tribal territory was from Láx̱ewey, Miller's stone house, right over to Maple Falls. The Chilliwack tribal territory was almost to that road going down Chilliwack Landing, Steamboat Landing, across the valley; up to Elk Creek Falls, straight back to Sx̱óchaquel [Chilliwack Lake], and the same around that way.

WELLS: To get back to ask you about some of these families: Albert Louie, did his family live there?

JOE: Louie's father comes from the same family as we do. Same family.

WELLS: Been there for generations and generations.

JOE: And the population of that tribe of Indians may be a thousand to one, comparing the population today. You'll see for yourself the history of Vancouver Island, where it's stated there were thirty thousand Indians and only fifteen hundred Whites. That's the time of Sir James Douglas. What happened to those thirty thousand Indians?

WELLS: I guess the small-pox plagues took a pretty bad toll.

JOE: For enough they did, yeah.

WELLS: Well, I should go and talk to Albert Louie some time, eh? Louie's pretty near a hundred years old now, is he? He would remember almost back to the time of the long-houses, eh?

JOE: He should remember.

WELLS: I read records of the long-houses down at Squiaala. When the first survey party come in in '65 they camped down there, the Government Survey party; and they described a big long-house with the mats for divisions.

JOE: The so-called long-houses—there was a house that they call Qoqóláx̱el, and it was about, oh, maybe a quarter of a mile above where the bridge is now, above Vedder Crossing.

WELLS: On the flats in there?

JOE: Qoqóláx̱el. This house just had one door. There was no back door, just a front door. And the front door was made out of one whole tree. A large person couldn't walk in straight, had to go in sideways. And the pillars, the posts, in there and outside was all carved. And for some reason or other—I guess it was my fault—I never asked the old man, that's James Michell, what they are. At the door, on top of the door, can you guess what that carving was? A maple leaf.

WELLS: Is that right?

JOE: A maple leaf. And below that, the beaver. Often today, they say, "The maple leaf forever." They took the beaver out. We come down with that history, with the beaver.

WELLS: Well, that's interesting, you know. There's not many records of carvings and house posts this far up from the coast, are there?

JOE: No. I only saw one. That was down Qweqwe'ópelhp [Kwawkwawapilt]. A man by the name—they give him the

[1]By the next interview (#5), Bob Joe remembered the name of the village as Sékw'sekw'emáy, meaning "birch grove." As an informant for Wilson Duff, he translated the name as "where birch trees grow" (see *The Upper Stalo Indians* p. 38).

name Alpős; must be Alphonse. And this post, the animal that they carved on that is not in existence today. They call that "sí:lhqey." When it comes out of the water, the pond or the lake, just a big round ball. And one head will come out one side of the ball, and the other head will come out the other. And on the back were round, not diamond shape, all round. The body was black, the main body, but this here was red and white, the centre dark.

WELLS: What did you call it again?

JOE: Sí:lhqey.

WELLS: There's no use my trying to pronounce these names, but if I ask you, why, then, I have them recorded.

JOE: Yeah.

A representation of the double-headed serpent described by Bob Joe in the interview of 8 February 1962. Oliver's drawing has been authenticated by the signature, "Robert Joe."

[LEGEND OF THE TWO-HEADED SERPENT]

When Isaac Kipp lived there where his house is still there yet, well, my grandfather George went down there, not only him, fifteen or twenty men more or less went down there to help Ike cut the hay. Well, one day Isaac Kipp there missed a cow that was just about due to calve, so he called my grandfather. "Why don't we go look for that cow, George." And they went back, and about where the fairground is now, there was ponds there; it wasn't a true lake; it didn't go deep, soft grass swamp. Even then they see a big duck come out of the water, and then the duck seems to go up in the air. And this big ball come up. And, according to grandfather, Isaac Kipp told him, he says, "Don't turn around. If you do you'll get sick." Well, at that time they knew what that sílhqey would do; so they stood there. And it was dry dry ground where they were on the edge of this pond, but by the time that big black ball disappeared in the air, the water was up here.

WELLS: Well!

JOE: Isaac Kipp told the old man, he says, "Wade back up," he says. So they back-tracked. They got to a higher bank, and they sat down. And Isaac Kipp told the old man, "I don't feel good," he said. "My bowels," he said "is all upset." *(Laughs.)* So he took two plugs of smoking tobacco, "T & B" I think it was. He give the old man a big chunk. He says, "You take and chew it up and swallow it." Well, they did, both of them. But it wouldn't work at all. *(Laughs.)* And it sort of came back, started to throw up. And what they threw up was little chunks of stick, what you find in the bottom of a pond. How'd that come in there?

WELLS: Isaac Kipp, he was my grandfather on my mother's side, you know. These first settlers that come in, like Kipp and Reece, they actually come in and sat right down on Indian land, didn't they? The Indians must have been quite friendly or they would have got in trouble, because they were only three or four of them to begin with.

JOE: On this part they were friendly. Yeah, old Thompson Uslick—that's when the Survey came along: "Thompson, this land don't belong to you. It belongs to the White man." Well, I forgot now what the name of your grandfather's—just below, the one who got drowned.

WELLS: Oh, yeah, Sickers?

JOE: Sickers. Well, somebody else lived there, you see. Well, when they were told that that land belong to the White man, they moved out.

WELLS: No uprising.

JOE: No. Well, before that is when the representative of the Crown made her tour through British Columbia. They met her at X̱woxwlá:lhp, that's Yale.

WELLS: That's Yale?

JOE: X̱woxwlá:lhp means "a willow tree." That's where the agreement was made, given by this young woman, young English woman, I suppose the daughter of Queen Victoria. And the leader or chief at that time—his name was Líqwtem there—was given a staff and a flag. And the other leader was here at Cheam. They called him Alaksís. I guess his name was Alec. He was given another staff and flag. There was three of those staff given to the lower tribes of Indians.

The other one was given down at Musqueam. Qsí:làlxw, that's the name of this other leader. And that staff, it's over on Vancouver Island; great-great-great-grand-daughter of Qsí:làlxw married over there. They still have it over there. What they had here, they had a fire, and ours went up.

WELLS: Before the reserves were set out, were there a number of Indian families living on the west side of the Chilliwack River, the part where Yakweakwioose is now?

JOE: Yes, there was.

WELLS: Was there an early graveyard in there? Chief Sepass, he made a map for my dad one time, and he showed an early graveyard about where the Lapum property is now.[2]

JOE: Yes. There was a graveyard in there. But these graveyards at the time, you see, they wasn't buried. They were in large boxes. They just lay on top of the ground. They were about four feet in depth; and then width, six or seven feet, maybe eight feet.

WELLS: When there was another death, they'd just keep packing them in? Some were buried in a sitting position?

JOE: You find them further up the river.

WELLS: Yes. Mrs Cooper mentioned there was a graveyard washed out by the river.

JOE: Yeah, that graveyard was there where that bridge crosses the Soowahlie creek now, just below. I saw the graveyard was there. And it wasn't very long, the freshet come along and wash everything away.

WELLS: And they just put the boxes on top of the ground?

JOE: Yeah. They were going to build a road from Bailey's over to South Sumas Road. So the Council came after us: "You got to move your graveyard down that way." And we did. That's in my time, you see. So they asked T'ixw-elátse: "You remember where this Wilíléq and his brothers were buried?" "I don't know. You go down to the old lady." Sally—the name of the old lady—"Yes," she says, "I remember. If you find the bone with six bracelets, that's Wilíléq and the sister, if you find the hair in two braid, about that large, with brass braided with the hair." We dug up this old grave, and sure enough there was—we found only five bracelets. Joe Swóles, when they first found that, took one, and instead of keeping it in a good safe place, he perched it on top of a stump. Somebody else got it lost. So it's over here on Tzeachten cemetery. And that brass or copper or whatever it was was as thin as paper. Wherever that came from we don't know. I believe up till now, if you go there and dig it up, you'll still find that. Each braid was about that long, about two feet. And they say when the young lady was standing her hair was down on the ground. This Wilíléq was born, and his mother wasn't feeling well after. And this happened to be in the summer time, and the people went out to the Fraser to get their wish for dried salmon. Wilíléq's mother—that was after one month—she took kind of a fit, or whatever it was. And they called someone over: "Does the woman feel bad?" "No, it's a child." And while she was in that stage of life, rain and wind, thunder, and then this child was born, thirty days, according to that "almanac," a long string tied in knots.

WELLS: That's the way they kept their calendar?

JOE: There was thirty knots; that's thirty days. That's Wilíléq's sister. Brother and sister. She didn't marry. She was single.

WELLS: I was going to ask you about when the young Indians wanted to get married, did the parents have anything to do with it?

JOE: Oh, yes, the parents had the full power to choose the man they wanted for their daughter. And at that time, none of the young ladies went here or there alone. It was either the aunt or the grandmother went with them to look after them. And not only them. Young men were hunters; they had to be looked after, otherwise their spirit or their energy would be lost, you see. Now, they had their old ceremonies at that time. They married, there was no ring. "Are you going to take that woman as you lawful wife?" "Yes." They ask the same question of this young lady as this young man.

WELLS: Who would be the official, the head man of the family?

JOE: Oh, yeah. It would be the head man of the tribe.

WELLS: In the old days they called them "seeahm" or something like that?

JOE: Yeah, siyám. Siyám means "a master," "the master," siyám. Well, there's another master: Chíchelh Siyám. Chíchelh Siyám means "the High Master"; that's the Great Almighty.

WELLS: That was the Great Spirit to the Indians, yeah?

JOE: Yes, long before the White race come to this country. And as far as that Bible was concerned, there's two or three in there, they worked pretty close to the Bible.

WELLS: Is that right?

JOE: They did. You daren't go over there and get you another man's wife. No, you daren't fool around. If you did, you're either going to be hurt or be killed. And if your hands got too crooked, take things, and awful punishment at that time. They take and strip you, turn you out. That's your punishment for stealing.

WELLS: My father would tell me that they would—the family and all the hired men at the farm—would get in the wagon and go for a picnic for the day. There might be twenty-five, fifty Indians around, but they'd just simply drive away and forget about the place. And there was never anything ever touched on the farm. Nobody ever worried about the

---

[2]Donna H. Cook's M.A. thesis *Early Settlements in the Chilliwack Valley* (UBC 1979) offers a number of maps indicating the lands owned by early settlers. Illustration #22 gives the Lapum house as 7195 Chilliwack River Road. Oliver and Bob Joe go through the Sepass Map place-names together in interview #5.

Indians stealing anything. And as long as I can remember I can never hear my parents or my grandparents ever refer to an Indian that he might steal. Sometimes a few of them would make mistakes, you might say; but if they were a friend of yours, why, you don't need to worry about them stealing.

JOE: About that time now, you're travelling, you come to a house on the row of houses: it was never locked. You go in and help yourself. If there's anything to cook to eat, help yourself. But never take anything with you. And that happened several times, and before this man here was half a day off, they caught him. They stripped him off; let him go. That's the punishment. The old-timers, they held their principles sacred. "Sx̲áx̲e." That's the nearest I can come: "something that is precious."

[STORY OF SIWASH ROCK]

This happened in the Squamish tribe. There was a family came up this way. It took them about three days, maybe a little more, from Capilano. Capilano is an Indian name: Qoyápelálexw. Qoyápelálexw, that's Chief Joe's name, handed down from way back. This young man came up, and in three days and a half he'd get up to Hope, maybe a little above. Now this young man got a woman from there. He married there, and went down. And one of the places where they lived there at that time was Qweqwe'ópelhp; that's on Stanley Park. And they had their rule: you go out there to hunt seal at a certain time, not any other time. Now, if you went out there, you had to get the permission of your leader, your siyám. Well, this young man wouldn't go by those rules. He went out there alone. Now, he was warned: "The next time you go out there," he says, "you'll stay right there; you'll never come ashore." He was warned. He was out there. They come out, and they come back; and he's still there today. Siwash Rock. That's Siwash Rock today, it's that young man that took that woman from up here. But his wife, she still lived, and her people are still up here, buried up at Trafalgar Bar.

WELLS: I can remember going into Uslick's place, Harry Uslick's, with my dad; and Uslick gave us a portion of a large sturgeon. This sturgeon was in a small wagon or a democrat; and it was about eight to ten feet long, about a foot square in the body, like. And he would have caught that out in the Fraser, I guess, eh?

JOE: Yeah, that's it. Now, that's another story. From Musqueam, that's there on Point Grey, the people can come from there up as far as Saddle Rock, Five Mile Creek, what they call Ts'okw'á:m. Twenty, twenty-five years back, I happened to be up there, and some of the old-timers, Dennis Peters and Isaac James and several others, they wanted to put up a monument for this large grave, like I was telling you, in the big boxes. Well, the little cemetery's there today; Í:yem it's called. That's the name of that place. So the fishing grounds can be used by all the tribes from Musqueam up, up to Saddle Rock. They were allowed it. That's the agreement. 'Cause they spoke almost the same dialect, some little heavier, some little quicker.

WELLS: The Nooksack people, they would come over too, would they? At times, to the Fraser?

JOE: No. Not much. About that time, part of the Nooksack River came through Sumas, emptied out on this Sumas River. Well, the salmon went up that way.

WELLS: Years ago I went to the west end of Chilliwack Mt with my father. I think he went to see an old Indian that lived there. I don't remember the name. But either that Indian told me the stories, or my dad told me, that sometimes the Thompson River Indians would come overland to hunt in these high Liumchen areas and the Skagit and in through here, and sometimes they would maybe dry their meat and bring it out down the Chilliwack River to the Fraser and go up the Fraser, is that right?

JOE: Yeah, that's right. But they had to get their permission.

WELLS: I've heard stories—I don't know whether Chief Sepass or my father or where, but I've heard stories of Indians going into a cave where they knew the bear was, before he come out in spring.

JOE: Yeah, that's right. There was an old man that lived down here just this side of Ritchie [Malloway]. They nicknamed him Little Jimmy. Jimmy Skówk his name was, a hunter, a small man. That's when they had the muzzle-loaders. So there's a bear in a cave. Well, he got one and drug it out. And he could hear more in there, and the air from there was, well, warm. "There must be more in there." He crawled right in there, no flashlight. (*Laughs.*) Something was blinking over there!

WELLS: Did the Indians use these bearskins in their dances and for ceremonial?

JOE: Some of them did. There was a man from Vancouver—I think he was a reporter for the *Sun*—he came here and started to ask me questions. So I told him. He asked me this 'ere question. He says: "When a woman is expecting to give birth to a child, do you have a doctor? What did they do? Did they have water? Hot water?" Some of them did. Some of them didn't have it. It was, at that time, after the woman got through with that, there's a creek over there, ice-cold water. She went and bathed. Even my mother went there, and gave birth to one of her children, and dropped him in the cold water. Never hurt a thing. There's a woman up here called Sarah Salt, and about twenty-five years ago, went up on the mountain back of Hope to pick mountain blueberries. She was expecting. These other women there they missed Sarah. Sarah Salt was her name. They hollered. No Sarah. And they walked back. And she says: "Where you folks going? You going back home?" "Yeah. We had to come down and look for you." "Oh, yeah. I'm here." "What have you got in your arms?" "That's my baby."[3]

---

[3]Oliver writes in his workbook a note headed "Conclusion":

> Bob Joe then tells of the rugged strength of the Indian Women, of their going into cold streams after childbirth without ill effects. His mother did. I met his mother at the door of her home in 1960. She was 103 years old. She is still living at the time of this writing.

4. Mrs August Jim

Oliver Wells dedicated his *Vocabulary of the Halkomelem Language* to Mrs August Jim, and described her as follows:

> Mrs Jim was born in 1871 and has spent her entire life at Ohamil. She resides with her daughter-in-law, Mrs Edmond Lorenzetto and her grandson Joe.
>
> Her Native name, Squh-WAHTH-uhl-wuht, comes from the myth concerning the origin of the SKWIY-kway mask.
>
> During her lifetime, Mrs Jim has been an accomplished basket-maker, doing the fine work of the Canyon people. She was a weaver of the Kah-SEEL-tuh (tump-line), which she and others used in order to carry the packs during their frequent trips into the high mountains. Her beautiful tump-lines won recognition for her work at the Canadian Handicraft exhibit in Montreal in 1964.
>
> Her contribution to the production of this booklet has been one of inspiration. Her voice will be one of the last to carry the Native language with clarity of accent and expression.

Of Joe Lorenzetto, Oliver wrote:

> Joe was born at Ohamil in 1911. He is one of the very few of the younger generation who has retained much of the old culture, the knowledge of which he has great ability to depict in hand-craft and in oral presentation.
>
> He is a son of the late Edmond Lorenzetto, who was described by Wilson Duff as the best source of information on the Tait tribe.
>
> Joe Lorenzetto has contributed much of interest concerning the various types of Native canoes which once frequented the Fraser River. Of these he has carved beautiful models, one of which is the old Stalo canoe, used by the Natives below Yale. This was the WHAL-kwih-LIH-chum, a model of which was purchased by the Canadian Handicraft Guild for exhibition purposes. To Joe should go the credit of re-establishing the design of this old type of canoe, the name of which means ''the canoe which is easily dragged over the sand-bars.''

Mrs August Jim and her husband, daughter and son-in-law were among Wilson's Duff's chief informants during his field work of 1949-50. He pays tribute to them on p. 9 of *The Upper Stalo Indians* (1952):

> Edmond Lorenzetto, about 55, has spent virtually all his life at Ohamil or at Katz, across the river. Both of his parents and all of his Indian grandparents were from the same immediate area. Edmond received his surname from a Spaniard who married his grandmother. He does not remember this man, but does remember admiringly his grandmother's second husband, ''an Indian doctor for good things.'' Although the youngest of my principal informants, Edmond has always taken a deep interest in the old culture,

and he proved to be my best source of information on the Tait. A gentle, patient, and reflective man, Edmond embodies many of the most attractive attitudes of the old culture: pacifism, generosity, respect for age.

Mrs Lorenzetto, a few years younger than Edmond, was also a good informant on some subjects, especially on the attitudes of people of high rank. Her father had come from what had for generations been regarded as the highest-ranking family of the Hope area. Her mother was from a high-ranking Langley family; her maternal grandmother had come from Lummi. Mrs E.L. is very conscious of her high rank. She is proud of her far-flung relations with well-respected families and is aware that despite her parents' teaching of an attitude of outward humility, she still receives from others the deference and respect due her high social position.

Mr and Mrs August Jim, both over 80, also live on the Ohamil Reserve about a hundred yards from E.L., who is Mrs Jim's son. August was born at Hope; his father was from the former village on Seabird Island; his mother was from Musqueam. He is a good informant, but seldom did his knowledge of a subject exceed that of his son-in-law. Mrs Jim speaks no English, but often added comments which August or Edmond translated. It was good to have Mr and Mrs Jim near by while staying with Edmond. The frequent visits to the "old people" presented welcome changes of pace and gave an opportunity to check on obscure points as they arose.

Mrs August Jim.

Mrs August Jim, with Joe Lorenzetto and Mrs Amy Cooper, at Ohamil, 30 October 1962 (with visitor Willie George)[1]

WELLS: Have you lived here all your life, Mrs Jim?

MRS COOPER: *(Laughs.)*

WELLS: Mrs Cooper, would you ask...?

MRS JIM: [I don't understand, so I don't talk. You are a White man, but we are Indian.][2]

LORENZETTO: [Since you were born have you always lived here?]

MRS JIM: [I have, yes.]

LORENZETTO: She stays here all the time. All the time.

WELLS: She's lived here all the time?

LORENZETTO: Yeah, lived here all her life.

WELLS: And she's always just talked the Halkomelem language—she hasn't talked English?

LORENZETTO: No. [You never talk English? You don't know it?]

MRS JIM: [No. Oh, the old people, my grandparent raised me.]

LORENZETTO: Just her grandparents that raised her when she was a small kid. She never went to school.

WELLS: I see, yeah, I see. Well, I wonder if I could get her to tell us some of the Indian legends of the district, stories which she has of the legends. When I was talking with Dan Milo, he told me one or two legends, and Mrs Cooper told me a legend about the Cheam peak, but maybe your

[1]Mrs Sara Wells's diary indicates that there was a preliminary visit on 23 October 1962, and on 30 October 1962 Oliver "used tape recorder." William George was the chief of the Ohamil reserve (Laidlaw) at the time of the interview, and dropped in unexpectedly.

[2]For this interview, square brackets have been used to enclose the English translation of Halkomelem spoken sentences. Brent Galloway has supplied a strictly literal rendering of the phrases. See Brent Galloway's "Halkomelem Speech Events," a paper read at the Salish Conference 1981.

grandmother had some legends of this area, which she would tell in her own language. And then you could tell me, so that we'd have it. Would you ask her, Mrs Cooper, about what legends she might tell us?

MRS COOPER: Joe can say that one better than me. [The legend of the woman.]

MRS JIM: [The legend of the Lhílheqi.]

LORENZETTO: [The legend of Lhílheqi. Yes.]

MRS JIM: [Yes.]

MRS COOPER: Go ahead.

WELLS: If you would ask her, and then occasionally you'd tell us in English what she has told us.

MRS COOPER: [The story of Lhílheqi. He wants to find out about it.]

MRS JIM: [In the Indians' own words?]

MRS COOPER: [Yes.]

MRS JIM:

Mt Cheam. Photograph by Casey Wells.

[LEGEND OF CHEAM PEAK]

[It's only that the Indians say that the Lhílheqi people were sisters close in age, but I don't remember how many. So the youngest sister cried and cried. She wants to be the one sitting right in front and looking at the water in the river. And so the youngest sister stayed right in front, facing upriver. At least, that used to be the talk of the Indians of long ago. Then something happened to start transforming them to become like that, to become a mountain.]

MRS COOPER: [A woman?]

MRS JIM: [Women.]

MRS COOPER: There are two sisters, and—.

MRS JIM: [There may have been three people, I think.]

MRS COOPER: There may have been three of them, and they were always arguing about who would be in the front to face the river there, so that they could see the river and watch the river.

MRS JIM: [It was the youngest that was the one who was put in front. She's watching everybody travelling by paddling along.]

MRS COOPER: Well, she says that the youngest one is in the front there, so she could watch them as they're paddling up the river. [Then what happened?]

MRS JIM: [The one transforming the people in the past started to keep on, and so they became mountains.]

MRS COOPER: Joe, what does that mean: x̲ex̲éyt?

MRS JIM: [He changed them.]

MRS COOPER: Changing the people.

MRS JIM: [So those became a mountain.]

MRS COOPER: And they turned into the mountain.[3]

---

[3]Dan Milo, in a recorded interview of 4 December 1964, summarizes the legend of Cheam peak in its traditional form, then adds a more recent bit of mythology:

> This great big mountain there, it was a woman at one time. And she had three boys that's living behind her. And the one that's in front of her, sitting in front of her, that was a little girl there. She wants to be out there near the river so she can see people travelling on the river. There's a lake behind that mountain Lhílheqey, a little on that side, a great big lake. And there was a woman that was picking berries up there, up at that big mountain. And they looked down at that lake there; by golly, there was a steamboat coming. That's before there ever was a steamboat around this valley. There was a steamboat coming towards them, with a whole lot of people in the boat. And the reason why they didn't go right down when they saw that steamboat was coming, there was a man there that was just hairy, taking the little clothes that's in there and throwing them outside of the tent. His body is just hair that's all. Well, the steamboat comes out of sight when it landed there. They come down; they wanted to see the people that's in it, a lot of people. That's the first time they ever saw a steamboat at that time. They got down there, and there's nothing down there at all. (*Laughs.*)

WELLS: That's a story somewhat similar to the legend in the Bible.

MRS COOPER: Yes, Lot's wife.

MRS JIM: [So she's still a child, the Indians past were talking together. I've forgotten lots.]

MRS COOPER: [You said that you were born when the earth shook itself.]

MRS JIM: [Yes. Later the ground was being shaken, and I was born in the pithouse, inside. The Indians were inside.]

MRS COOPER: Her parents were living in this keekwilee house there when she was born, and there must have been an earthquake that the house moved. And there was just a slight tremor the next day. And that's how old? How old is she, Joe?

LORENZETTO: Let's see, she'd be ninety-one, going on ninety-one now.

MRS COOPER: Ninety-one in December. There must've been an earthquake, then, ninety-one years ago.

WELLS: The word "keekwilee," that is...?

MRS COOPER: That's Chinook.

WELLS: That's Chinook, is it? What is the Indian name?

MRS JIM: Sqémél, sqémél.

MRS COOPER: Sqémél.

WELLS: And these homes, they were large enough for a large number of people?

MRS COOPER: [How many people were there inside the pithouse?]

MRS JIM: [I don't know. It was big. It must have been like this little house, the whole room was as big, when I started to become a little aware.]

MRS COOPER: Mother says about thirty used to go in, thirty people. She lived in a sqémél around here.[4]

WELLS: Some of them would be smaller, would they? Just one-family dwellings?

MRS COOPER: No, more than one.

WELLS: And they put the ladder up through the centre?

MRS COOPER: Well, she says it wasn't bigger than that.

WELLS: The stovepipe?

MRS COOPER: Hewed, yes.

MRS JIM: [And it's all really chopped just like this where you foot goes.]

MRS COOPER: Good toes to crawl up.

WELLS: And the steps were cut in the post?

MRS COOPER: Yeah. And that's where the ends went. I don't know how it was fixed there. But that was where the smoke went out too. Mother says they used to go up like cats.

MRS JIM: [I don't know when they must have started to take me outside. That's before I began to get big when it must have already started to be spring.]

MRS COOPER: That would be: She left the following spring after she was born, and then she left.

LORENZETTO: Yeah, that's right.

MRS COOPER: [Then where did they go?]

MRS JIM: [Then they went inside what they had made, many little houses, sort of planks, still the work of Indians long ago. They went inside when it was summer.]

MRS COOPER: Yeah, they moved out of the keekwilee houses in the spring there. They just went in there for the winter.

WELLS: I see. Were the keekwilee homes generally near the river, or sometimes back on the mountain?

MRS COOPER: [Is the pithouse near the river?]

MRS JIM: [No. But it's not too near the mountain, nor too far either.]

MRS COOPER: It's between the river and the mountain, she says.

WELLS: And when the men were fishing, before they had the White man's nets, did they do their fishing with nets, or did they do it with spears and hooks?

MRS COOPER: [What did they use, the ones who went drift-netting?]

MRS JIM: [They're making rope Indian style.]

MRS COOPER: [Indian hemp.]

MRS JIM: [Net, yes, the fibre like the grass that grows.]

Mrs August Jim and Mrs Amy Cooper.

MRS COOPER: [It's from the Similkameen that they...]

MRS JIM: [It was from there when it was being sold by the Indians here.]

MRS COOPER: Well, these people down here didn't have the grass that they have up in the Okanagan, and the grass is about so long, and they take that grass, and then they'd do this with it there, and get all the dirt off, because they were afraid of rattlesnakes, see? And they wouldn't let children play with it. They were very careful about the dust of it anyway. And then they used that when it got soft, and then they spun that on their knees there. Or some of them make a little horse there where they used to spin it.

WELLS: To weave these nets?

MRS COOPER: Yes. Different knot.

MRS JIM: [It's just like the sack-net, not like the long ones like the White man.]

MRS JIM: I've seen the sack-nets there, and it must be

[4]Mrs Cooper's mother, Mrs Amelia Lorenzetto, was also raised in a pit house.

a good ten to twelve feet wide. Those are really sack-nets.

LORENZETTO: Yeah.

MRS COOPER: There's two canoes goes out. And the one at the bow there has rocks, and they throw that in there. And the fish just comes down, gets in the sack-net, and, say, that's heavy! But this grass will hold it, hold it a lot better than the twine of today.

WELLS: Well, would the Indians here get the grass from the upper country, or did they use something else?

MRS COOPER: They used to come down and sell it. They were always welcome to get it, you see.

MRS JIM: [And it was their dried salmon that those Indians wanted, fish here.]

MRS COOPER: They got the dry salmon from down here to take up, take back to the Similkameen. And they used to bring down a lot of dried saskatoons too. And soapberries.

MRS JIM: Sx̱wő́sem.

MRS COOPER: You know what sx̱wő́sem is?

WELLS: No.

MRS COOPER: Indian ice-cream? Haven't you ever seen it? It's berries. There's a lot along the Allison Pass there. And they're red, like currants, but very tender. And you just take that, and whip it up, and it foams up like ice cream there. And you put sugar in it, and enjoy eating it.

WELLS: Is that this white berry that's on a bush?

MRS COOPER: No, no. This is up on the Allison Pass.

WELLS: It's a red berry. What do you call the saskatoon berries?

MRS COOPER: [Is it only what they dry that is called sk'ak'áxwe?]

MRS JIM: [Yes.]

MRS COOPER: [What is it named when it is still growing?]

MRS JIM: [The name of the berries still just on the tree is tseslát̓s.]

MRS COOPER: Tseslát̓s, while it's on the bush; and after they've dried it, they call it sk'ak'áxwe. Both hard to say!

WELLS: I won't try to say them. When I was looking up some information on the local Indians, it referred to the fact that the grizzly bear was very much respected in that they, when they were hunting, they would do certain things, and they would not do other things, because they did not want the spirit of the grizzly bear to think badly of them. Can Mrs Jim tell me anything on that, or maybe can you, Joe?

LORENZETTO: [No, no. The Indians chased the grizzly away, didn't they?]

MRS JIM: [Yes.]

LORENZETTO: [That's because it's not food of the Indians.]

MRS JIM: [Yes. It's not food for the Indians because they were acquainted with it long ago in the past.]

LORENZETTO: Of course, these grizzly bear, the old Indian long time ago, they don't bother with them, because it's their ancestor, and they don't eat it. They left them alone, unless they want a hide, you know, well, they'd kill it, and get just the hide.

Joe Lorenzetto and Mrs Amy Cooper.

MRS JIM: [It's only the one that was mauled by the grizzly. He understands that he'll be killed when people start to chase him.]

MRS COOPER: They never touched the people unless the people went after them, the grizzlies there, and knew that they were going to be killed, and that's when they fought back.

WELLS: Did the Indians here in the early days go into the caves and kill bear when they were in hibernation in the wintertime, when the bear was asleep?

MRS COOPER: [Did a person used to go inside the den of the bear to kill him while he was still sleeping?]

MRS JIM: [They used to, they must have. Yes. There will sometimes come to be a hole in the fallen snow. The breath is from the really deep hole. Then they really sneak up on it carefully. They dig it out. They kill it.]

MRS COOPER: [Then someone really did go into the hole?]

MRS JIM: [No. There's nobody like that here that went into the hole. There used to be an old man that we knew, that one that had his hand eaten, right over here. He must have felt inside the den, and was bitten on the hand from the inside.]

LORENZETTO: Well, you know, the bear is breathing way down in the hole, and then there's a lot of snow, and they see there's a steam out of it. That comes through, and then a small little hole right in the snow, and then they know the bear is way under there.

MRS COOPER: The man stuck his hand in.

LORENZETTO: Yeah, he stuck his hand way in there. He was going to grab the bear, and then the bear just bit him.

WELLS: He was already awake in the spring!

MRS COOPER: Well, didn't they get a rope and crawl in from the top, and then pull the bear up?

LORENZETTO: I don't know.

MRS COOPER: I used to hear Billy Sepass's sister tell that. Was pretty hard to believe.

WELLS: In talking with Bob Joe at Chilliwack, he said that there were instances where one fellow especially, he would go into the cave—sometimes there was more than one go into the cave—sometimes there was more than one bear—but the bears were dormant enough so they would kill them in the cave.

MRS COOPER: Well, this woman there, Billy Sepass's sister, I used to go and sit there and listen to her, and she says there that the little man went in through the hole the bear goes in. And then he'd get this rope, and the bear would be asleep, and he'd always look for the male bear, because the female had cubs. And the two outside there would pull on this rope there, and the bear wouldn't even wake up, she says, even when it was just choked to death. And they'd get it out through this hole. [That's Sláwá'iya's story. She told me the story herself. That was the one she called Hímél.]

MRS JIM: [Yes.]

MRS COOPER: [Did he have any younger siblings?]

MRS JIM: [None. There was only Hímél around that I knew. He was from upriver.]

•

MRS COOPER: This is Mr Wells. This is Willie George, the Chief here.

WELLS: Pleased to meet you, Willie. I come up today with a tape recorder to ask Mrs Jim about her language, to get as much as I can of the old language on the tape.

GEORGE: Oh?

WELLS: So that I was asking her questions, and Mrs Cooper helps me.

GEORGE: [Are you understanding?]

MRS COOPER: [I know how to be talking.]

GEORGE: [That's it.]

MRS COOPER: [I've really forgotten it. I haven't talked for a long time.]

GEORGE: [Oh, it's all right.]

MRS COOPER: [There's nobody that I converse with regularly. Everybody has already forgotten the words. There's only my elder sister, Agnes; only she still knows it.[5] When you see her, get her to talk.]

GEORGE: [O.K. What happened to you folks? What were you folks doing?]

MRS JIM: [He took a seat on the copper pot over there.]

WELLS: No, you sit down. I'm glad to have you talk because it comes on the microphone... I was asking Mrs Cooper about sign language, and she thought the Indians used sign language up here more than some other places. What do you say? Would your mother know? Did they talk a distance with just using their hands?

MRS COOPER: Mum used to use it there when she lived up in Yale and when they used to holler from across the river here, and she just made the sign languages with her arms and her hands when the river made such noise you couldn't holler and tell. They did a lot of that up in Yale.

GEORGE: Yeah, I know that sign, but I forget. My god, it takes a lot of....

WELLS: Ask her if they talked across the river with just using their hands, eh?

MRS JIM: [I wonder if it's X̲elhálh she is talking about.]

GEORGE: [Yes.]

MRS JIM: [X̲éylx̲elemòs was a taboo person; there's nothing...]

GEORGE: [Just that you are on the other side, talking...]

MRS JIM: [You don't know anything. You are a fresh child, beside me. I know much. It's that I've forgotten it. They got there, the changing people got there. They were called Transformers. That person, like a supernatural creature, was winning. His eye is fixed, one of his eyes is over his neck. So the people[6] started to look; they went inside his house, and then started to get bent over backward by him, and then started to become laid out. You just don't look in the inside of his house.]

GEORGE: [Is that X̲éylx̲elemòs?]

MRS JIM: [Yes. It got to the third time he was approached, and now he was beaten, and so became a rock.]

WELLS: What does she say?

MRS COOPER: What does she mean, X̲éylx̲elemòs?

GEORGE: Oh, this guy from....

MRS JIM: [The name of the one from X̲elhálh, who was changed; then he became a rock.]

The three-mile canyon above Yale, probably taken by Frederick Dally, 1867-70. Courtesy of the British Columbia Provincial Museum, Victoria, B.C.

---

[5] Mrs Cooper's half-sister was Mrs Agnes (Murphy) Smith, of Silver Creek, near Hope.

[6] The "people" are the Transformers, trying to out-stare the mythical Xéylxelemòs, who resisted successfully for a while, but was eventually changed into Lady Franklin Rock, in the Fraser River between Yale and the village, Xelhálh, across from Yale.

MRS COOPER: Where's X̲elhálh?

GEORGE: The other side of Yale, on this end of the tunnel. Yeah, there's a man there owned the place, and nobody go in there.

MRS JIM: [There's nobody that ordered him around, when only he lived there.]

WELLS: Does she think they used the sign language to talk without talking to them?

LORENZETTO: [They're telling someone news from the other side, that's just their hand they use.]

MRS JIM: [That's ''í:wtsesm'' they call it. It was just known what the hands were doing.]

WELLS: What do you say when you want someone to come across the river in a canoe?

MRS JIM: T'ákwel. [Come across.]

MRS COOPER: T'ákwel.

WELLS: And if you say the river is running very fast?

MRS COOPER: Le x̲wṓm. [It's going fast.]

MRS JIM: Q'éyéx̲. [Whirlpool.]

GEORGE: You're going to cross over it, go right straight over. [Don't be running away from the whirlpool.]

WELLS: Straight across.

MRS COOPER: Why? I'd try to get away from it, if it was me.

MRS JIM: [And so come to die with your canoe.]

GEORGE: Oh, yeah, you hit that q'oyéx̲ pretty good; you just fly. Away you go. Hit another one.

WELLS: Oh, you use the outside of the whirlpool to get you going, eh? It helps you go fast?

GEORGE: Yeah, yeah. I crossed with my aunt, you know. I was sixteen years old. My uncle says, ''You take them over.'' ''O.K.''

MRS COOPER: Did you get across?

GEORGE: No, we hit that whirlpool and come right back in! We came right back where we started from. (*Laughter.*)

WELLS: Two or three years ago, a young fellow, he was a friend of mine, he was crossing the river above Hope to log, you know, and just a small motor on the back of a small boat. And he got caught in a whirlpool, and the whirlpool took the back end down like this, and he went under. He went down and he never come up.[7]

GEORGE: That's Petéyn [Odlum, B.C.]. That's a strong whirlpool there.

WELLS: How do you say ''very strong''?

GEORGE: ''Eyém.'' [It is strong.]

WELLS: Good. If you say ''to come''?

GEORGE: Emí. Emí kw'e ahíw. ''Coming up the river.''

WELLS: Oh, I see, yeah.

GEORGE: ''Pótlem.'' When the wind starts to blow, you ''pótlem'' up to Yale.

WELLS: What's ''potlem,'' then? When the wind blows from the west?

GEORGE: ''Sail.'' You put your sail up.

WELLS: ''Potlem,'' eh? Did the Indians always use sails?

GEORGE: Oh, yeah.

WELLS: What would they make them out of, blankets? Before the White people's cloth come, what did they make them out of?

GEORGE: No, they never used sail before. They just paddled.

MRS COOPER: Sure they did, Willie. They used bulrushes. They used that bulrush, slháwél.

GEORGE: Yeah, that slháwél. It don't grow here.

MRS COOPER: There's a lot grows down our way.

WELLS: On the lower Fraser they'd use it more.

GEORGE: You never see that slháwél, uh?

WELLS: The rush blanket? Yes, Mrs David Charles from Seabird Island, she let me have one for exhibition in Chilliwack. Nobody makes them now, eh?

GEORGE: No.

MRS COOPER: Were the needles hers?

WELLS: Yeah.

MRS COOPER: I had a couple of them, but they got burnt in the old house.

MRS JIM: [And so you just have none. That happened to mine. The ones I used to have were stolen from me.]

WELLS: Ask Mrs Jim how many goats it takes to make a goat-hair blanket.

MRS JIM: [Is it six? Oh, I don't know. My grandmother and I used to help each other in making it, but I don't know how many it takes to finish one goat-wool blanket.]

Mrs Mary Charles exhibiting a rush mat she has made.

MRS COOPER: She used to help her grandmother make them. You know, tease it. But she doesn't know how many would make one blanket. [Is there anything else that goes in the blanket besides mountain goat?]

MRS JIM: [They dusted it with something like flour. They call it st'ewṓqw'. It's from the ground.]

MRS COOPER: St'ewṓqw'.

WELLS: What does that mean?

MRS JIM: [It must be that it's fast in spinning its wool.]

MRS COOPER: Sort of a clay. There's some up on the

---

[7]This was Tony Way, who with his brother David, came from England in the late 1940s, and settled in the Chilliwack River valley.

Vedder Mountain. And they take that and burn it, and it turns white like powder, like as fine as talcum powder. And they use that right on the wool, the goat wool, because it's so rough, and it makes it easier to spin.

GEORGE: It makes the wool stick together, you know, that st'ewṓqw'.

MRS COOPER: That's after they make it into powder they call it st'ewṓqw'.

WELLS: I never heard of that before.

MRS COOPER: Oh, I used to see Captain John make it. He always had that for his wife.

GEORGE: You know what they call this face powder? St'ewṓqw'esem.

MRS COOPER: You mean "powdering up" is st'ewṓqw'esem?

GEORGE: Yeah.

WELLS: That's really good.

MRS COOPER: So what about the paint?

MRS JIM: Temélh. [Red ochre paint.]

WELLS: Yeah. I should ask Mrs Jim what ceremonies the Indians used to have. Did you have a feast or something when the first salmon come up every year? Can you ask her what dances, what ceremonies they had?

MRS COOPER: [It's the person's dream when he's dancing.]

WELLS: In the fall of the year, from this time on.

MRS JIM: [There was only one old person that was here who I knew; he just had the dream vision of a mink. Mink are just little animals, so he went to dive fom the shore, and got out on the island just over there. Oh, there was lots of flaky ice, not quite solid. People got out in a canoe and followed him, but already he'd got inside the pit house. The Indian was in there dancing, the Mink was really dancing.]

WELLS: Can you tell me what she said, just in short?

GEORGE: Yeah. This guy, he dive in the river.

MRS COOPER: His power was the Mink.

GEORGE: Yeah, his power was the Mink. And these guys follow him, you know. He's going to swim across this river here to that island. When they got there this guy was dancing in the other keekwilee house over there.

MRS COOPER: And he went right under the ice to get across?

MRS JIM: [He dived, he went and reached the other side. The land right over here is with the female owner, my late step-parent. Anyway, that's a true story they sometimes told.]

MRS COOPER: [Is it his spirit power?]

MRS JIM: [It's his dream vision that came to him. He was made to play by the Mink. Then he went crazy, they say, began to get possessed, and then he did that, dove in the water.]

MRS COOPER: Well, Bob Joe explained to you how they start Indian dancing, didn't he?

WELLS: Well, no.

MRS COOPER: When they get this power there, and they, they—oh, I can't really explain it. They seem to forget, and get in another world where this Mink would be, and the Mink there would tease him and talk to him, and then pretty soon he's imitating it, and then he'll dance like it. So when he had that power, he had power enough to go in the river on this side and go right across and get into another keekwilee house under the ice.

GEORGE: Well, these guys followed him, you know, and get across, and there he was. He's over there dancing.

MRS JIM: [So he's sick; he's sick so he dances.]

WELLS: When my grandfather first came among the Indians at the Chilliwack there, he went to one or two of their spirit dances, like, you know. And he said they'd gradually get up into a frenzy, and then they'd dance right through the fire. And Bob Joe said they would pick up, they would grease their hands. They had a certain way of doing it. They'd grease their hands, and they'd pick up a hot rock, and just keep moving it, and their hands would be just steaming, but they'd keep it going.

MRS COOPER: Like Jimmy Poole.

GEORGE: Yeah. Jimmy Poole, he grabbed that red-hot pipe.

MRS COOPER: Stovepipe. And his hands would be just like that, no burns.

GEORGE: No. And he looked like a White man too.

MRS COOPER: Red beard, red hair.

WELLS: Did they have any special ceremony when the first salmon come every year, like now we have Thanksgiving service?

LORENZETTO: Oh yeah.

MRS COOPER: The first fish that was caught there, they called their friends and they all gathered up and ate the first fish that was caught. Isn't that right, Willie?

GEORGE: Yeah. Yeah. They learn how to set their net, you know; that's a dip net. Sack-net. That's the way they catch the fish. They go after the run and they tie them on a log, let it drift. There's a bunch down Siwash Creek; when it comes into the eddy, they catch that log full of fish there.

WELLS: They would use a log that was drifting, and put the net underneath, like?

GEORGE: Yeah, then

Joe Lorenzetto carving a model canoe.

down Siwash Creek there's some fellows there going to catch that log.

WELLS: Most of the fish were caught up on the canyon on the dip-nets, I guess, eh? What do you call a dip-net?

MRS COOPER: What do you call a dip-net in the Indian? Come on Joe.

LORENZETTO: [What is it called? Q'émes, isn't it?]

MRS JIM: Q'emóstel.

MRS COOPER: Q'emóstel. I knew it but I couldn't think of it.

MRS JIM: [I never used it, but I remembered its name.]

GEORGE: No, we never used that for, oh, about 30 years now.

WELLS: Oh, that type of net, eh?

GEORGE: That q'emóstel, yeah. The old chief here, old Pat from Katz, we go up Yale, you know, they know how to fix that.

LORENZETTO: It's only me that knows how to fix it around here, make that dip-net.

•

WELLS: I think we have this ready now. This is an interview with Mrs August Jim, who is going to sing for us in her own language.

MRS JIM: Mm?

MRS COOPER: [It doesn't matter if it's a hymn or if it's our late ancestor's song.]

WELLS: If you would like to sing with her for one hymn, Mrs Cooper, it would be good.

Mrs August Jim, wearing traditional tump-line.

MRS JIM: [I've gone and forgotten many of them. What was always heard was "The Sweet By and By."]

[*Song*]

WELLS: What is the name of the song which Mrs Jim just sang?

MRS COOPER: That's a very old song there, "On the Cross."

WELLS: It was sung in the early days by the....

MRS COOPER: Yes, by the United Church.

Song transcribed by Brent Galloway.

[Mrs Jim sings again, with Mrs Cooper joining in.]

WELLS: That's fine.
MRS JIM: [It's impossible, my dry throat.]
WELLS: And the name of that one, Mrs Cooper?
MRS COOPER: "Come Thou Fount of Every Blessing."[8]
MRS JIM: (*Singing*)
[Oh, where I used to walk.
Oh, where I used to walk.
I see where I used to walk and I cry.
The place where I used to walk was beautiful.
Oh, where I used to walk.
Oh where I used to walk.
The place where I used to walk was good, anyway.
Where I used to walk was beautiful and I cry.]
MRS COOPER: [That's called?]
MRS JIM: [The song?]
MRS COOPER: [What is its name?]
MRS JIM: [It has no name. It's only her song.]
MRS COOPER: [It's only her song then when she travels?]
MRS JIM: [She travels. She gets here travelling, and sees the land where she used to be. Then she sings that song.]
MRS COOPER: It's just a travelling song. As you went past the place before and you seen it again, then you sang the song.[9]
WELLS: I would like to ask Mrs Jim if the needle I made is all right for use in making mats.
MRS COOPER: [Is that all right?]
MRS JIM: [Yes. But it used to be a little more like this. It becomes a little more bent when it...]
MRS COOPER: She says that's got to be bent a little more.
MRS JIM: [And then that's this, here.]
MRS COOPER: Well, she's got one! (*Laughter*) [Is it his? Did he finish this?]
MRS JIM: [No. This one is real Indian style. The one they went and stole, which was like this one, was my late grandmother's, and I have only this one. It must have been a really lazy old person to steal.]
MRS COOPER: She says somebody there stole her grandmother's.
MRS JIM: [This is close to what I owned. I guess what he stole was four like this one.]
MRS COOPER: Gee whiz.
WELLS: Mrs Thomas, I think, will make a mat for me if I get the rushes for her. Will you ask Mrs Jim if she'll make one?

Mrs Matilda Thomas with Nancy Purkiss, Oliver Wells's granddaughter, who is watching Mrs Thomas make a rush mat.

MRS COOPER: [He wants one.]
WELLS: If I get the rushes?
MRS COOPER: [He's asking, if he gets the cattails, will you make it?]
MRS JIM: [I don't think I can make it. I guess maybe I can sort of manage to make it.]
MRS COOPER: [Oh, you never made them before?]
MRS JIM: [Little.]
MRS COOPER: Uh-huh. She'd make a small one.
WELLS: Yes, well, that would be fine. I'd like a small one.
MRS JIM: [Yes.]
WELLS: These are the oldest bulrushes I've got. At home I have some that are more dry, but they're younger, they're smaller.
MRS COOPER: [It's like twine. It's like twine.]
MRS JIM: [Oh, that's just what they spin, they say.]
WELLS: Are these too old or too young or all right?
MRS COOPER: [He wants to know if this is all right.]
MRS JIM: [Maybe, if only it's made longer, it's all right.]
MRS COOPER: She says that that one's a good one.
WELLS: Is this one too old?
MRS JIM: [That's too old.]
MRS COOPER: She says it's old.
WELLS: This is too old, is it?
MRS JIM: [Yes.]

---

[8]This is hymn #44 in the *Indian Methodist Hymnbook*, compiled by Crosby, Tate, and Barraclough in 1898. The Halkomelem words in the hymnbook are almost identical to those sung on this tape by Mrs Jim and Mrs Cooper.

[9]Mrs Jim's daughter, Mrs Kate Lorenzetto Karlsen, composed this personal lyric. Wilson Duff refers to it in *The Upper Stalo Indians* (1952) p. 127:

> E.L.'s [Edmond Lorenzetto's] sister, going back to her childhood home and seeing the path she had formerly walked along, made up this song:—
>
> Oh my tracks are still there, where I used to walk,
> Oh my trail is still nice,
> I nearly cried when I saw my tracks.

Cecilia Thomas's singing of this song has been recorded by Brent Galloway.

WELLS: I have some more in the car, which are younger, and they may be good for a small mat. I'll bring them in and you tell me if they're all right.

MRS COOPER: [It will be just you that picks out what you're going to want. Anyway you can't give him this. You will use it.]

MRS JIM: [We'll give it to him. Oh, I'm not sure I can manage to make the bulrush mat. I guess it's only if I look to Joe that I'll manage to make it.]

MRS COOPER: [But who else makes them? There's no one that makes them. He's going to go over to Seabird and ask if Daniel Thomas's wife...]

MRS JIM: [There's no woman.]

MRS COOPER: She tells me there that Mrs Daniel Thomas there doesn't make them.

WELLS: No? Is that right?

MRS JIM: [It's only her mother who was making it.]

MRS COOPER: Her mother used to make them.

WELLS: Oh, I see. Well. Mrs Thomas, I asked her if she would make one, and she said she had no one to get the bulrushes. Is this all right, or is this too young? I cut these about three weeks ago, and these I cut about a week ago.

MRS COOPER: Where'd you get this?

WELLS: At our place. Just a few. They've just started.

MRS COOPER: She says if there's anything wrong with the needles, Joe will fix it.

WELLS: Good.

MRS COOPER: Joe's awfully good with his hands. [Is it all right with just what is here?]

MRS JIM: [Oh, if it's this, it's just fine.]

MRS COOPER: [It's good that he's brought it, anyway.]

MRS JIM: [You saw Joe's work, didn't you?]

MRS COOPER: This is Joe's work.

WELLS: Joe's work, eh? That's an old type of spoon similar to what they used to make here. I should take it to the Museum. Would he let me have it for the Museum?

MRS COOPER: [Is this yours?]

MRS JIM: [It's my own. Joe made it for me.]

MRS COOPER: It's hers. [Is it O.K. if the White man takes it and then stores it wherever they are being stored?]

MRS JIM: [Yes, just possibly. Joe might get mad that it was too good to let go.]

MRS COOPER: Joe gave it to her, and she'll have to ask Joe if she let it go first.

WELLS: I read in one of the books where they use nettles for making string. Did you ever make twine from nettles, for making fish-nets?

MRS COOPER: [The stinging nettle]

MRS JIM: [I never tried it.]

MRS COOPER: She never tried it.

WELLS: You're not too old to try. The book said that near the bottom it's tough, and they take it—I don't know just how; but this fibre on the outside, apparently they thread that. You never make string out of that?

MRS JIM: [Maybe so. I don't know. Then maybe our ancestors were making tumplines. I didn't see it.]

MRS COOPER: She's heard there something about the nettles, but she never saw any of it. She says that's way back.

•

MRS JIM: [Our tree there used to be growing far up river.]

MRS COOPER: This one. What is it? Don't they get red when they get ripe? Or is that the color?

WELLS: I believe that's a wild juniper. It grows on the mountains?

MRS JIM: Á:'a. [Yes.]

MRS COOPER: [Are you going to grow it?]

MRS JIM: [I want to try it, yes.]

MRS COOPER: She's going to plant it. She's a great one for that, you know. This rhoda—what do you call them? Rhododendron.

MRS JIM: [It will be a tree again, and its branches are being pruned by Joe.]

MRS COOPER: Yeah. And you're going to plant it?

MRS JIM: [Yes.]

WELLS: It's very pretty.

MRS COOPER: Yéx̱chetlha te xwelítem. [Give it to the White man.] You know what's "xwelítem"?

WELLS: No.

MRS COOPER: "White man." (*Laughter.*) You better learn that. Everybody else knows what it is.

MRS JIM: [You give him it.]

MRS COOPER: (*Laughing.*) She says this is for you.

PART II

The Language, the Map, and the Loom

Behind Oliver's ethnographic work was a deep-seated affection for his Indian neighbors, which was reciprocated. As his work enters a stage of consolidation, it is given the impetus of a unique historic event, the Tzeachten spirit dance of 15 February 1963. Oliver was one of the few outsiders (perhaps the only one) invited. He was moved to write an account of the event, which we include here from a typescript version submitted to the *Chilliwack Progress* and printed in the issue of 20 February 1963.

The sense that there was a revival of Indian spirit and culture to which he could add his contribution spurred Oliver on toward making his researches public. He intensified his efforts to gather and anthologize all the previous writings on the Chilliwacks and their neighbors. As far as his interviewing was concerned, he started to concentrate on the Indian language and on a map of the territory. By the end of 1964 he was able to feel he could publish *A Vocabulary of Native Words in the Halkomelem Language*, and he had done most of the work on his *Indian Territory 1858*, though publication of the map was delayed. His visits to Mary Peters inaugurated the revival of Salish weaving.

Native Dancing Returns to Chilliwack

They came from Nooksack, Everson, LaConner, Musqueam, Chehalis, Seabird, and Lummi—seven tribes speaking seven different dialects. The ancient custom of the Season of Dancing, which prevailed among the Coast Salish, was reborn in a great gathering of some 400 Indians, who responded to invitations to gather at Tzeachten Hall. They gathered not to be entertained in the fashion of the White Man's dance, but to unite in a fellowship in which expression was given to their age-old desire to dance as their spirit moved them. There was no mirth, no jesting, no applause. From the oldest veteran of yesteryear, who unconsciously took up the beat of the drummer with the quiet clapping of her hands, to the youngest youth, whose hands fell naturally to the tapping of the rhythm with a pair of sticks, the tribes were as one with the beat of the drums.

Young men of the YPPA, headed by Frank Malloway, whose slogan was "this tribal custom shall not die," organized the event, which hosted some 400 guests in a hall 30 x 45 feet in size with a small adjoining kitchen. The entire event was orderly, and all proceedings were carried out with traditional dignity. It was at Tzeachten that the last great potlatch of the Chilliwacks had taken place, and because of it the Chief was punished by the White man's law. Here now, the youth of the tribes accepted the guidance of their older chiefs, and order was preserved in their own fashion. The cars were parked in orderly array. The food for the feast was taken to the kitchen, where it was made ready for the midnight sitting. As they entered the hall each tribe was assigned its location, where it remained as a group. And so around the hall a packed mass of Natives presented a spectacle which was most impressive. In the front row, the dancers, with faces painted and some in costume; beside them their drummers, with gaily painted raw-hide drums of various sizes and design. Behind them, their supporters, who would lead the chant, picking it up from each dancer. Behind them, the older men and women, and those with babes in arms. In the centre of the hall, where in ancient times the open fire would blaze, a large drum heater formed the hub for the dancing area, and round this each dancer moved as his dance required.

Chief Ritchie Malloway gave oversight to the proceedings, and Bob Joe, Tzeachten's oldest resident, moved about in quiet dignity, forever on the alert that nothing should interfere with the dancers. Things moved along in continuous order without any visible direction. Visiting tribes, by virtue of their being so, were among the first to dance, and from each tribe the dancers were drawn as the spirit moved them. As if by instinct, the movement of dancers onto the floor followed down along the hall, like a slowly moving river, which caught up in its current a dancer who felt the urge to perform before the people that they might know how his inner feelings expressed themselves.

In all some 20 or 25 drums were ready to take up the beat. Possibly a dozen rattles, each with clusters of deer hooves, and a dozen heavy dancing staffs, carved and painted, with great clusters of deer-hoof rattles, made up the picturesque assembly of instruments. As each dancer gave voice to the urge to dance, the drums and rattles would commence a gently vibrant acceptance of the coming dance, as they gathered around the dancer, their drums gradually building up the courage of the dancer to leave his seat and move out onto the floor. By then he would have established the rhythm and beat of his dance, which the head drummer would pick up and transfer, as if by magic, to every drum and rattle in the hall. Attendants would often move out with a dancer and slowly precede the dancer with a graceful lifting gesture of their hands, and around the hall dozens of voices would rise to join the chant in perfect rhythm.

Dances varied with the theme of the story which the dance was portraying. Often the drums would be muffled in their beat, and the rattles would take up a tremulous quiver. Then the mood would change, and the drums held high overhead would break out in violent strokes, the dancing staffs would rise and fall with resounding beat upon the floor, and the hall would ring and vibrate as the beat was taken up in unison by a hundred voices.

When the dance was coming to an end, the dancer would withdraw from the centre of attraction, and, as his voice and figure withdrew, another voice would draw the muffled drums to pick up his or her theme, and gradually draw that dancer out.

At 1 a.m. the dancers rested and the feast was served. Two long tables were quickly laid with the places neatly set, and food in great quantities with many delicacies spread in neat array. The more distant guests were seated first—120 thus were served, and then the tables cleared and 120 more sat down, and again the never-ending supply of food poured out, and again the tables were cleared. Then a hundred more sat down, the Chilliwacks and friends who had been doing all the necessary things to make the feast a grand success, and then, last but not least, at 3 a.m. those ladies whose hands had toiled till the last plate was washed and dry, sat down and ate a well-earned meal.

As the feast progressed, a great visiting of friends took place. Old acquaintances were renewed and new friends made. And all was harmony and good fellowship, a fine example of true fellowship in the quiet companionship of our Native people.

The season of dancing was over for another year. The age-old custom would not die. The chiefs from Musqueam and Lummi rose during the feast and each in turn with true Indian oratory expressed to Chief Ritchie Malloway the gratitude of their people in having been invited to this great gathering. They spoke of it as the only custom of their ancestors which they had not lost—one which truly belongs to the Native people—a custom that they said *must not die*. Each as he concluded his remarks lifted his hands in an expression of sincerity, and in a like manner of simple acceptance Ritchie Malloway raised and lowered his hands.[1]

---

[1]The following description of a spririt dance was found among the Oliver Wells papers, dated February 1964.

The Native Dance

There are many fine things about the Native dance, and nothing which is not good. Here the Native people are at their best, here they gather in families to continue the tradition of their ancestors, and here the influence of the White man has been unable to break into Native tradition.

True, the young drummer, whose painted face does not hide the intensity of the purpose as he takes the beat from the dancer, may pause, hand his drum to a fellow-drummer, while he switches to the duty of a modern husband. A moment later he may appear bending over a month-old infant wrapped in a snow-white blanket in its mother's arms. The temperature of the baby's bottle is expertly tested on the bare arm, and as the father goes back to his drum, the baby sleeps. The sound of twenty drums and dozens of beating hands and sticks does not disturb this Native son, nor did the drummer lessen the strength of his beat as he again took up the drum and passed within touching distance of the infant, but now with a look of serious intensity on his face as another dancer became the focal point for all who watched and all who were responsible for the support given by the drums.

As the hours passed in an orderly procession of dancers, two strangers entered the hall and made their way rather boldly to a vantage point in the upper benches. They were not of the Native people, and the watchful eye of the responsible chiefs never left them. For a brief moment a bottle appeared. A single shout was heard above the drums, and a dancing staff bedecked with deer-hoof rattles was pointed at the intruding White men. In an instant a drummer broke from the dance floor and was accosting the strangers. A bottle was dropped, but it was promptly brought to light, and two White men felt the embarrassment of 200 accusing eyes. They left the hall. The drums never faltered. The dancer held by the power which controlled her movements did not know of the incident, which had preserved for her and others the right—sacred in their minds—to perform undisturbed by foreign influence.

5. Bob Joe—II

In 1918, then about 75 years of age, Chief William Sepass placed on record on a map, prepared by him with the assistance of E.A. Wells, items of historic interest concerning the Chilliwack River and the Native people of Chilliwack. In this interview Oliver goes through the two Sepass maps with Bob Joe with a view to consolidating the information in a map of his own.

Bob Joe at Tzeachten, 16 January 1964

WELLS: I'd like to record all I can about the names of the different streams up the Chilliwack River. This is a map which Billy Sepass made up, and if we start down at this Sumas end—it's not in proportion to the way everything is, like, but this, starting at Sumas, how do you say this word here?

JOE: Semáth. Now, this, Sumas River, there's a name for that.

WELLS: He has this "Sumatz Staala."

JOE: Yeah, Semáth Stó:lō.

WELLS: He has here for the Sumas Creek, he's got "Tat t lean." Do you know that word? There's another river somewhere down here. I think it's on the other side of Sumas Mountain. It's recorded in the Hudson Bay Company, when their first man come up the Fraser River, they sent them up to explore this country, and they said they went up the Sometz River, and then they come down the Sumas. Well, now here he marked in the Vedder River, which cut through later. Can you pronounce this name? It means "river changing its course."

JOE: Oh, what's that? Let's see. They have a name for that. Lhewá:lmel.

WELLS: O.K. Now, this Cultus Lake: "Sweeltsa."

JOE: Swí:lhcha.

WELLS: Good. Now, how about the little stream "Tsewely." can you say that?

JOE: Tṓtalō.

WELLS: Totalo? Where? Is that the little stream...?

JOE: Yeah, that comes by that hatchery, comes down off the hill.

WELLS: How do you say it again?

JOE: Stútalṓ.

WELLS: O.K. They have another stream marked here which comes in from the Leaven's property above Smith Falls. You and I went in there the other day. It looks to me like "Lochthleelz."

JOE: Yeah. That's got the same name as that Slhílhets'. That buried lake, you know.

WELLS: Yeah, that's right. Very good. Now, if we go on the other side of the Chilliwack River, we go up above Soowahlie, we come to the "Laaomchin Creek."

JOE: Yeah, Loyú:mthel.

WELLS: Good. Now, on the other side of the river, we come up to a stream that comes down from Ryder Lake.

JOE: T'ept'ṓp. That's the creek that runs by Bridge [Bailey], right by his house.[1]

WELLS: Yeah, not long ago they picked up a jade axe in there, a little jade hatchet that the Indians must have used up there. Wedge-like. "Tummahy Creek." How do you say Tamihi?

---

[1]Bridge Bailey's father, James Bailey, was an early settler in Sardis. Bridge (short for Bridgeman) ran pack-trains through the mountains around Chilliwack river valley. Oliver interviewed him on 3 December 1965 at his home at Ryder Lake (see footnote 3 to the John Wallace interview #20).

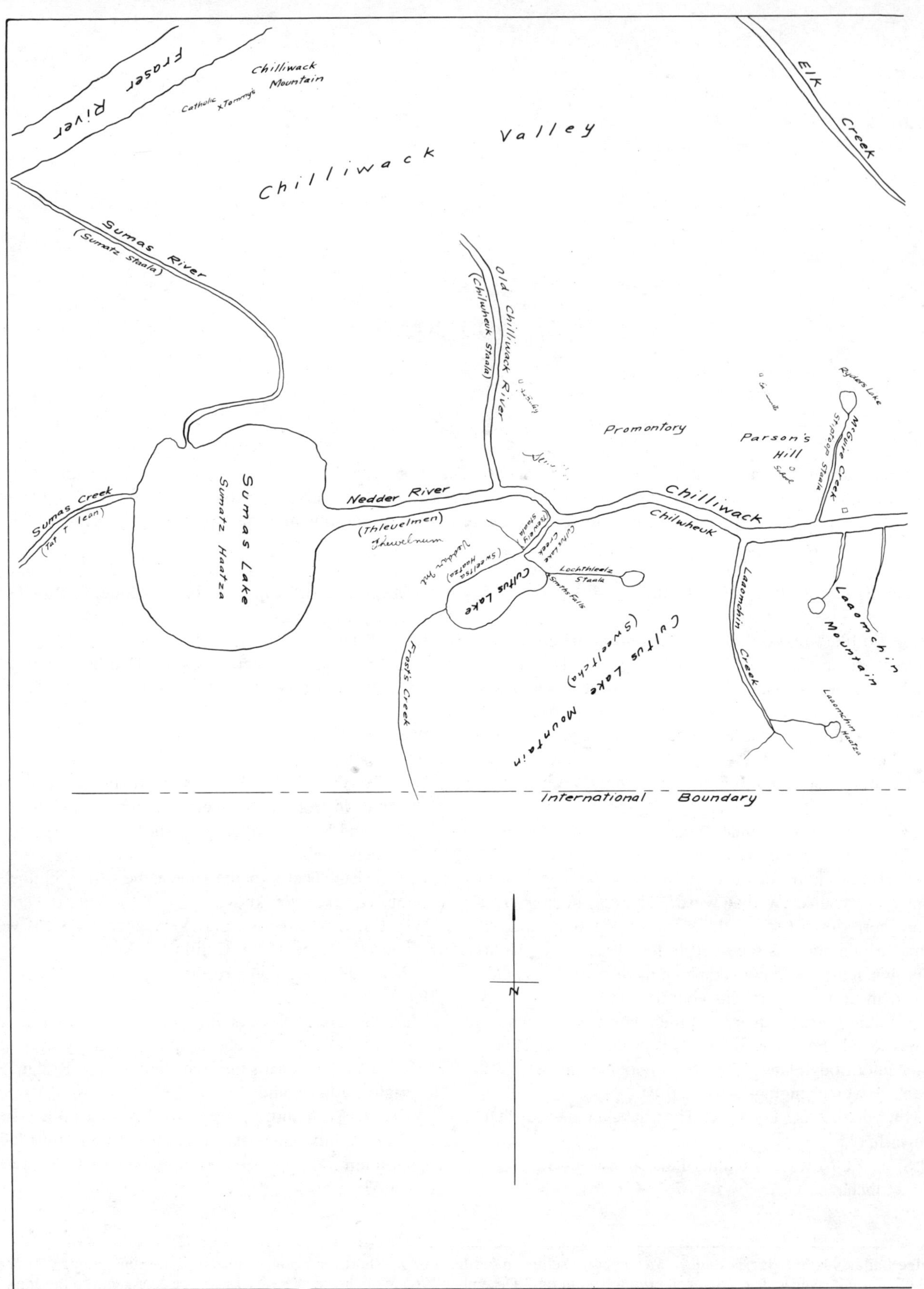
Fraser River
Chilliwack Mountain
Catholic
Chilliwack Valley
Elk Creek
Sumas River
(Sumatz Staala)
Old Chilliwack River
(Chilwheuk Staala)
Promontory
Parson's Hill
School
Ryders Lake
McGuire Creek
Sumas Lake
Sumatz Haatza
Sumas Creek
Nedder River
(Thlevelmen)
Chilliwack
Chilwheuk
Cultus Lake
Lochthleelz Staala
Smiths Falls
Cultus Lake Mountain
(Sweeltcha)
Frost's Creek
Laaomchin Creek
Laaomchin Mountain
Laaomchin Haatza
International Boundary
N

HOPE TRAIL
Silver Creek
Brown's Creek
HOPE TRAIL
Chilliwack Lake
(Chilwheuk Haatza)
Dolly Varden Mt.
Schweetz staala
Jones Lake
(Schweetz Haatza)
Dolly Varden Creek
Surveyors
Camp
Big Chief Mt
Big Chief Mine
Chilliwack Lake mt
Beaver Creek
Beaver Lake
(Sklaow Haatza)
Ford Lake
Silver Lake
(Laseescilp Haatza)
Ford mt
Ford Creek
Laseescilp Staala
Middle Creek
(Lyaaquaatz Staala)
Cheam Creek
(Squaap Staala)
Cheam Peak
Roland Jack's
Coal Mine
Silesia Mountain
Red Mountain
Elk Creek
Silesia Creek
(Silesia Staala)
Thurstons
Elk Mountain
Chief W Sepass
Skowkale Reserve
Sardis BC.
Tummahy Mountain
(Tumyahya Smealt)
Tummahy Lake
Tumyahya Haatza
River
Staala
Skookum
Mountain
Tummahy Creek
(Tumyahya Staala)
Elk Creek
Falls

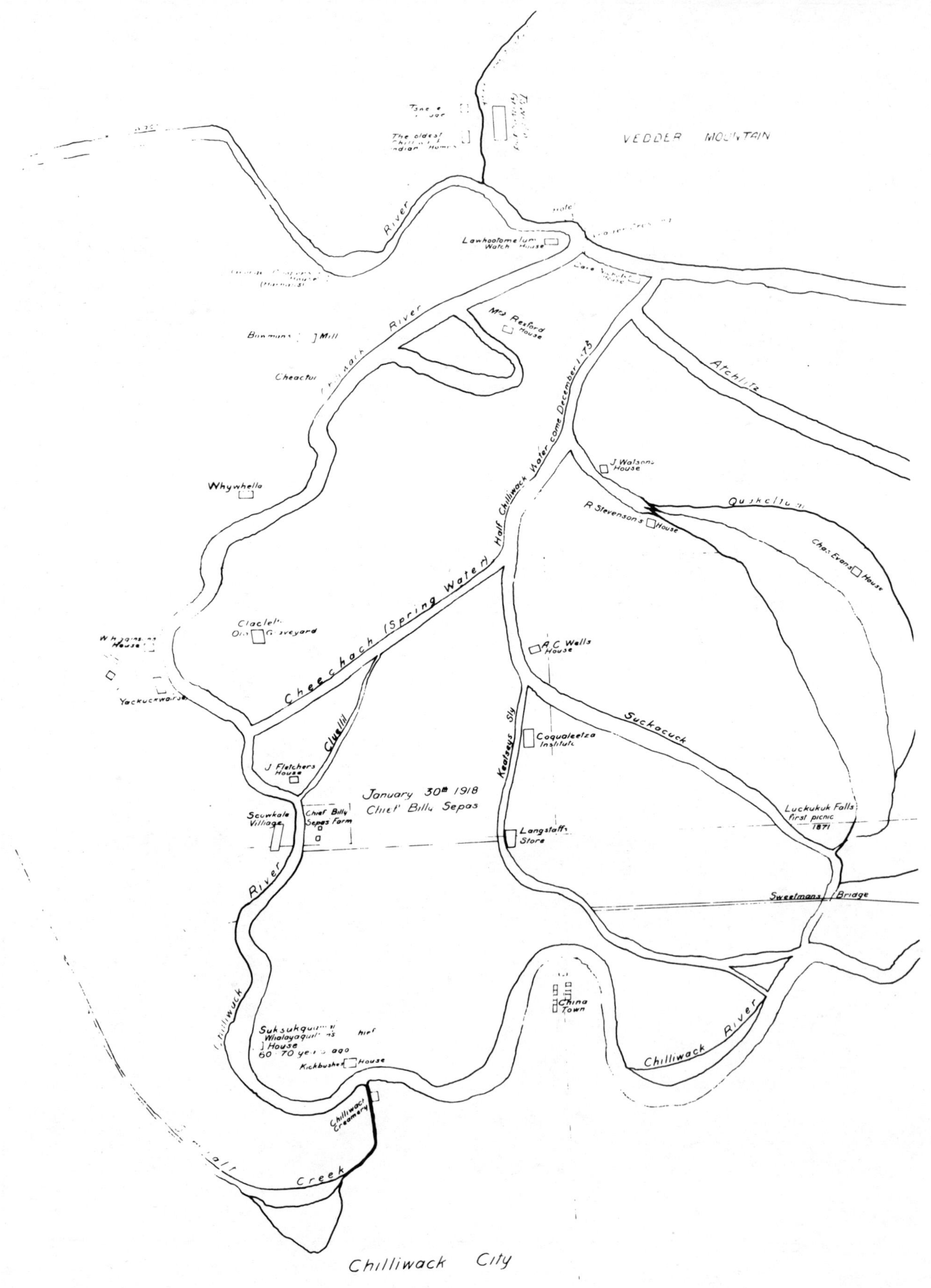
VEDDER MOUNTAIN
The oldest
River
Lawhootomelum
Watch House
Chilliwack River
Mrs Rexford House
Bowmans Mill
Cheactur
Atchilitz
Half Chilliwack Water come December 1-75
J Watsons House
R Stevensons House
Whywhella
Chas Evans House
Claclelk
Old Graveyard
Cheechach (Spring Water)
A C Wells House
Yackuckwairs
Kealseys Sly
Suckacuck
Coqualeetza Institute
Cluellil
J Fletchers House
January 30th 1918
Chief Billy Sepas
Scowkale Village
Chief Billy Sepas Farm
Langstaffs Store
Luckukuk Falls
first picnic
1871
River
Sweetmans Bridge
Chilliwack
China Town
Chilliwack River
Suksukquim
Whalayaquil
House
60 70 years ago
Kickbushes House
Chilliwack Creamery
Creek
Chilliwack City

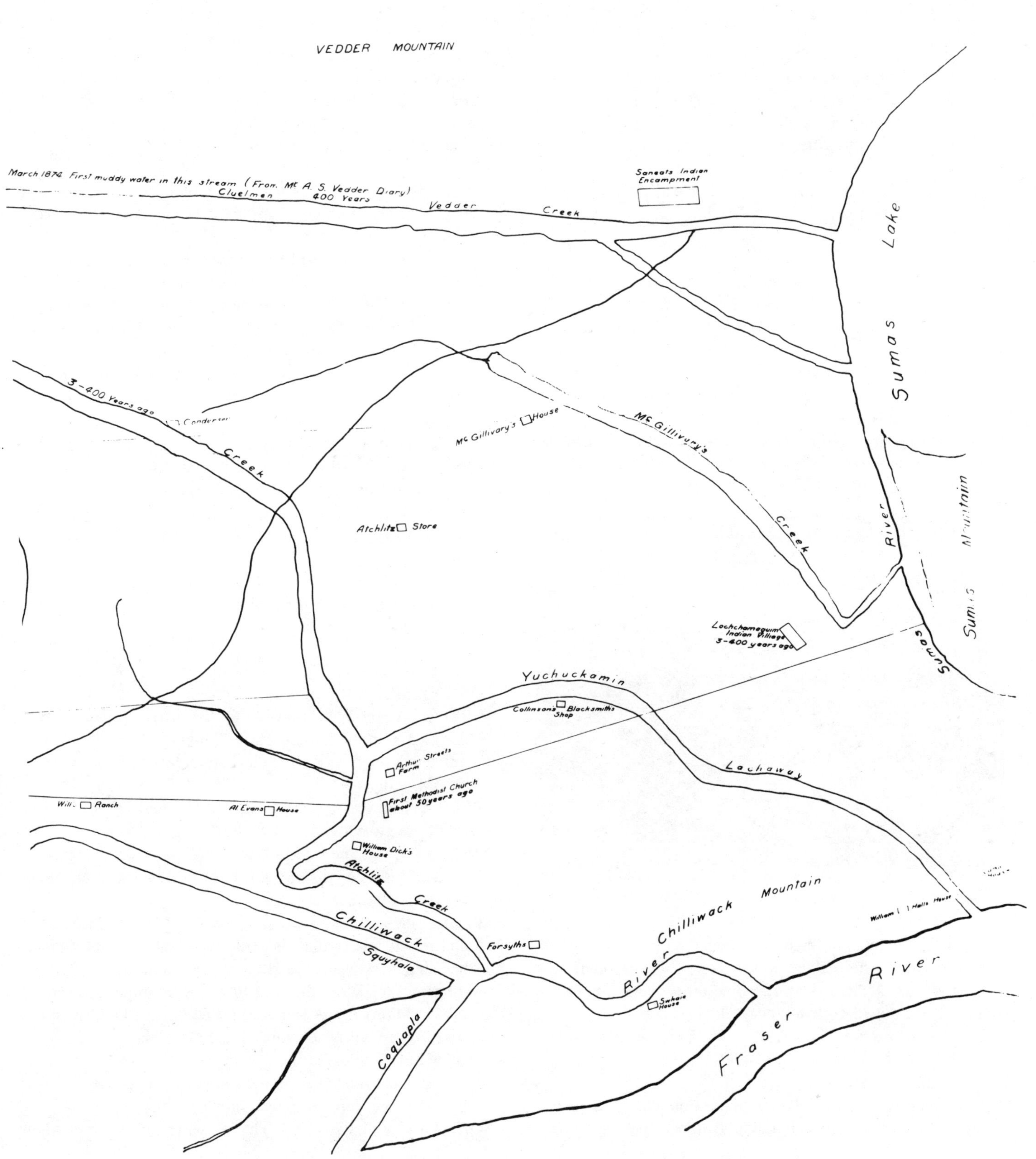
VEDDER MOUNTAIN
March 1874 First muddy water in this stream (From Mr A. S. Vedder Diary)
Cluelmen 400 Years
Vedder Creek
Saneats Indian Encampment
Sumas Lake
3-400 Years ago
Creek
McGillivary's House
McGillivary's Creek
Atchlitz Store
Sumas River
Sumas Mountain
Lochchamequim Indian Village 3-400 years ago
Yuchuckamin
Collinson's Blacksmiths Shop
Lachaway
Arthur Streets Farm
First Methodist Church about 50 years ago
Ranch
Al Evans House
William Dick's House
Atchlitz Creek
Chilliwack Mountain
Chilliwack
Squyhala
Forsyths
Chilliwack River
Swhaie House
Fraser River
Coquapla

JOE: T'amiyahó:y: that means "deformed."

WELLS: There's a little lake there, I guess. Below Selesse, where Anderson's place is, there's a stream comes in there. What's the name of that stream? Between Tamihi and Selesse?

JOE: Well, I don't know about—there's two little streams that is across the road there. Salmon runs up in there. Cohoes.

WELLS: We'll let it go now. How do you pronounce Selesse?

JOE: That's Selísi, that's all.

WELLS: Good. And when you get up further, they have a stream come in here. He calls it "Cheam Creek," but this must be—it's below Ford Creek. They call it Foley Creek now? He's got it here "Squaap Staalo." Do you know that one?

JOE: No, I don't.

WELLS: We'll check it on the other map and see. He has a little one here. It's the second stream down from the lake. On the north side. It comes down from a little lake, and Billy Sepass has it "Laseescilp Haatza." The same name for the stream. Then we come over here to Middle Creek. Have you got the Indian name for Middle Creek?

JOE: No. I had it.

WELLS: Can you see how it's written here? I don't know how to pronounce it: "Lyaaquaatz." That's Billy Sepass' idea.

This photograph of Chilliwack Lake from the air was taken by Casey Wells. The plane was piloted by Ron Wells, brother of Casey and Oliver.

JOE: Yeah. It must be right.

WELLS: Now, he called Jones Lake by the name of "Schweetz." There may be some other name for it.

JOE: That's outside our territory, Jones Lake.

WELLS: Now, this other, Chilliwack Lake, he just puts it "Chilwheuk."

JOE: Yeah, Sch'elxwíqw.

WELLS: He has a little lake up on the Boundary Line at the upper end of Chilliwack Lake. Beaver Lake, and Billy Sepass called it "Sklaow."

JOE: I don't know the Indian names for that.

•

WELLS: O.K. we'll go ahead now, and I have this other map which Billy Sepass made, and I want to ask you about some of the names on it. If we start down here where the Chilliwack River comes around past the Semmihault—Semmihault's an Indian word, is it?

JOE: Smiyólh.

WELLS: Good. Now, he has quite a bit here. The Kickbush house is here, and this chief's house would be about Albert Knight's farm, eh?

JOE: That's what you call Sékw'sekw'emá:y: "birch grove."

WELLS: Oh, "birch grove." And the name of that chief there, he's got it "Whalayaquilton." Do you know that?

JOE: I might get it after a while. (*Laughs.*) But the pronunciation's different from what's written.

WELLS: Yes. I see the Scowkale. Chief Sepass. Now here's these two creeks, now, "Cluellil." This is the one we were talking about a little while....

JOE: Yeah, that's Temélhem.

WELLS: This is what you give me for this one now, eh?

JOE: That's Thíthx̱, this one here.

WELLS: That's "Cheechach"?

JOE: Yeah. The church is over here some place, the Anglican Church.

WELLS: I see, yeah. Well, now, up here, opposite "Yackuckwairse"—how do you say Yakweakwioose?

JOE: Yeqwyeqwí:ws.

WELLS: Good. This is the area where that headquarters of the tribe was. It was up here further, was it?

JOE: Yeah.

WELLS: Yeah. Well, how about this little graveyard here?

JOE: That's on the Lapum place. This is supposed to be the grave that they found, that old Lapum found. This one here. That's... darn it....

WELLS: I've got it right here. "Whywhella."

JOE: X̱wóyx̱weyle. This was the lost grave.

WELLS: That's the one you told me about on that tape?

JOE: Yeah, that's what we got here in this graveyard now, what was there.

WELLS: Well, then, if we go up here we're at "Cheacton," and this is where that fish-trap was, eh? And the Indians had that first when the Hudson Bay come in too, according to Saul Wealick. And they had an interest in it, he thinks. I think it was Saul told me they had a fish-trap down where the Chilliwack joins the Fraser also.

JOE: Mm-humm.

WELLS: Can you give me the name of this house that was on the ridge here, this watchtower?

JOE: That's Shxwtiytós. That's where they had their

watchtower right on that point, that little bench up there.

WELLS: He's got a name here, "Lawhootomelum," "watch-house." Did you ever hear that?

JOE: I didn't hear that.

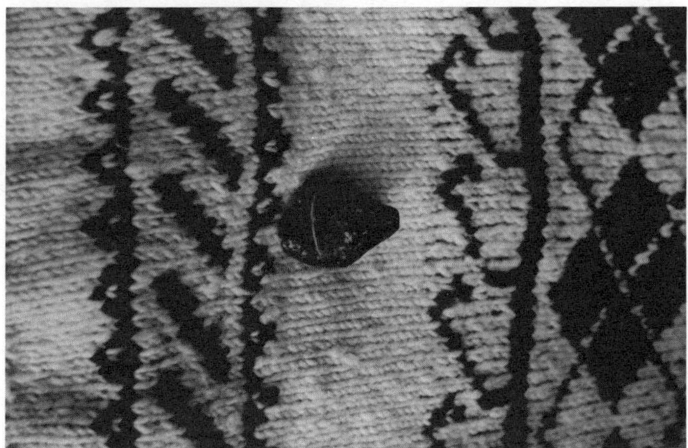

The bear's head "totem" picked up by Carl Wilson at Stee-tahs, photographed against the sweater knitted by Mrs Amy Cooper for Oliver Wells.

WELLS: Carl Wilson picked up a little bear's head there when they were doing some clearing, a small bear's head, a little carving, a very nice carving. It would be a totem, eh?

JOE: Yeah, it would be. Maybe they mean this here where that Thunder gulch is now. Darn... don't know the name to it. There was a hole right in the rock, and it's slanting, like this. And three of four, they go down it, and they say the rock is just as smooth as that leaf. Oh, I'll get the name of that after a while. One of the old fellows, he wanted to go down there; he had the dickens of a time getting out. The next time he went out there, a fellow we used to call Bill, Crazy Bill, he had a long rope. He tied it to a little tree there, and he went down. The further you go down there, he says, the air smells different.

WELLS: You have no records of an Indian village up on top here, where the old Bowman house was? Orion Bowman on top of the Promontory.

JOE: There were houses there, and after you passed the first slide, it's just a short ways from Albert Cooper's.

WELLS: Yes, but that's down near the river.

JOE: Some of them lived down by the river, and some of them lived up on top of the ridge there. It's the same people, but there were so many of them that they couldn't live all together. They had to move out to make room for the rest.

WELLS: You know where the Teskey trail come down—would that be the old trail?

JOE: Well, it could be. But we think, you see, that the slide there was larger than it is now.

WELLS: Now, Billy Sepass, he has these as "The oldest Chilliwack Indian homes," that's on the Soowahlie.

JOE: Mm-humm.

WELLS: Then he mentions this "Tswellie Graveyard" here. These streams down here now, past Watson's place and down through the Stevenson farm, sometimes they were streams, and maybe in early times they come too. Billy Sepass called this one "Quakeltum." Do you know that name?

JOE: No, I don't. Well, this old Chilliwack River it used to flow that way to the lake back here hundreds, maybe a thousand years ago. That's Lhewá:lmel.

WELLS: Yeah, we got that name on here. "Cluelmen." According to Billy Sepass, maybe "400 years."

JOE: It could be more, more than that.

WELLS: Now, there's one Indian village he marked here. I've got it mentioned in Crosby. When Crosby come in, he said he would go across Sumas Lake to this Indian village, and he named it. Sepass called it "Saneats." Is that it? Maybe there was another one?

JOE: Kw'ekw'e'íqw?

WELLS: No, no, wait a minute, that's—no... We'll look at that on the other map I made, because I've got the whole thing on that, you see. But now, I wanted to ask you about this house here, "Swhaie House." This island, there was a big island out here?

JOE: Shxwóy. Yeah, that's Shxwóy there.

WELLS: That became Skway Reserve, did it?

JOE: Yeah.

WELLS: How do you pronounce this, "Yuchuckamin"?

JOE: That must be McGillivray Creek, eh?

WELLS: No, McGillivray Creek's further up. This one come out past Arthur Street's house, Al Evans's house here. This is about the highway line here, see.

JOE: That would be the old Arnold place. There's another slough that goes in there, that comes out where old Catholic Tommy was. That's part of this river, you see. It kept moving down.

WELLS: Well, here is the name of where Barrow took up his home. You know Mr Barrow's house, the big white house? There's a ridge there. Sepass, he claimed that's "Lochchamaquim Indian Village 3-400 years ago."

JOE: Oh, that's Láx̲ewey [Lackaway], where old Barrow used to live. That territory: from Láx̲ewey to Maple Falls. This here is another tribe, Sumas, Kilgard today.

WELLS: O.K. This camp at the other end of Sumas Lake—"Saneats" they call them—they should be Sumas, eh?

JOE: Yeah, they're Sumas.

WELLS: O.K. We'll look at that other map now; I think we've got everything off of this one. This map I have here is one I'm having made up now. And when I get this finished, I want this to show the lands the Chilliwack Indians lived in, like. And I'd like to run a line—when we finish today, I'd like to run a line—maybe we should do it first—run a line around the Chilliwack Indians' homeland, so that when we finish this I just want to have the lakes and the rivers and the names that the Indians called them. And then the boundary line of the tribal territory. So I'll get a pencil and we'll put it in now, and then after that we'll talk about different places.

•

WELLS: And, Bob can you tell me any locations up here, up the Chilliwack River, where you know there's keekwilee holes? Bridge Bailey told me where there's one or two, and Jack Stevenson told me. Do you know?

JOE: No, I don't. But we were told that it must be above Anderson's flat. Jack Uslick, James and Fred Wealick—that's Dunc's father—they were out there hunting, so they camped. In the morning they worked back up on the Chilliwack River. Now there was a ledge, he said, the river's down there not very far.

WELLS: And this was above Anderson's flat?

JOE: Anderson's flat, on the north side of the river. So they were going further up, and Jack Uslick walked a long ways. He stopped; there was a lot of moss on this rock. So, "All right," he says, "Let's go." They had packs, and Jack made two or three steps, and down he went. And it go way up here, so he kicked around. Water in there. Well, they helped him out. He says, "What is it? It's all rock here, and all rock there." After they got him out, they scraped the moss off. The moss was that thick. After they got the moss off, a little stream, a little spring, there was water in it. Well, just out of curiosity they start to dig out this mud and leaves, and they found three big bowls, right in the virgin rock, where the old Indians at that time cooked their food.

WELLS: Is that right?

JOE: Drilled right into virgin rock. They went up there again and tried to locate that place, and they couldn't find it.

Oliver took this photograph of his brother Gordon exploring a keekwilee hole up the Chilliwack River.

WELLS: Well, you know, my brother Gordon knows that country pretty well now. He had cattle there, and it was all burned over, and he got over that country a lot. He told me that he found—look, I'll show you where it is here. You see these three marks on the map here? I had Gordon show me on this map. This is the north side of the river, and this is just about the country you're talkingabout. This is Selesse, and that's Middle Creek. Is that where those fellows were?

JOE: Yeah, it was below here, below this creek, but it's around here somewhere.

WELLS: Yeah, well, Gordon says he knows there's about three keekwilee holes here.

JOE: Well, there could be. That would be around where Allison used to live, across from Anderson.

6. Dan Milo—II

The following pages contain stories told by Dan Milo to Oliver Wells and transcribed by him from tapes which are lost. Knowing Oliver's usual practice, we can say that these stories appear in an almost, if not absolutely, verbatim form. In any case, they are too valuable to omit just because there is no way of checking the transcription.

One of the stories, "How the Sockeye Learned to Come up the Rivers," was included in *Myths and Legends of the STAW-loh Indians*, and we have reproduced some of Oliver's drawings that accompanied the story there. "The Story Teller" and "The Listener" were also included in that publication. The other two stories are printed here for the first time. The "SꝁWIYꝁway Mask" story is dated 31 January 1964 in Wells's typescript; all the others are dated July 1964, and were presumably obtained from Dan Milo in a session prior to the July 1964 interview at Edenbank Farm which is included here below.

THE STORY TELLER

Sloh-kwih-LAH-loh
(Better known as DAN MILO)
Born October 10, 1867
He sat at the table, near the window, at the close of day. His eyes no longer adjusted their vision to the lessening light. In the west, the clouds banked against the sunset parted momentarily, and the pale rose shafts of light lit up the bronzy tan of his weathered face; but he did not see the light, nor realize that evening had come and darkness had fallen. Sight had gone from those eyes in recent years and the light had gone from the world around him.

For a few moments he sat quietly, an intent look on his face as his mind swept back over the years—nearly one hundred of them—to the days of his youth, when he listened to the stories that the "old people" told, round the fire at even-tide. He was living in the days of long ago as he began telling the stories that his grandfather had told him. As he began, speaking in his native tongue, the scene he described became a reality. As the tale unfolded, the characters became as people; the animals of the woods and the birds of the air were brothers and sisters of the Native people.

With face uplifted as if to recapture the vision he sought to relate—one hand clasped to the head of his white cane, the other momemtarily resting on the table, now lifted in an intense expressive gesture or spread in quiet calm as if to indicate tranquil waters—his countenance reflected the mood of the story as it progressed, now calmly, now intent; and now and then a pleasant smile spread over his face.

SꝀWIY-ꝀWAY MASK

There is a story about a man who was diseased. This young man was up at a lake beyond Hope—KAW-kaw-wa is its Indian name. Well, he followed the creek and then he caught a cohoe; he butchered it and roasted it at a fire, like the Indians used to do.

After the fish was cooked he laid it on something ahead of him, and he sat right there watching that fish, cooked fish, roasted.

Well, the first thing you know a frog jumped from his nose—that was his disease—it jumped right into that cooked fish. He walked away from it; he went as far as the lake. He began to wonder. (The Indians back in those days said there were people down under the lake, that's where they lived.) Well, he thought himself that he'd jump into the lake. Well, he jumped right in. He kind of fainted—I guess he didn't know. He came to, just like he'd been sleeping. He was laying there, just where he had jumped from. The third time he jumped into the lake he run into a kind of cabin, the old old house like there used to be long ago—that's where he landed, on the top of the roof. Well, the people came out and took him down, took him right into this cabin down in the bottom of the lake; and there were a lot of little kids laying in bed, sick, real sick, down there. And these people asked him if he knowed anything about these kids' sickness—those kids have got a pain somewhere around the body. He looked at them and he could see that was his spit, when he was up there; so he went to work and just wiped that off and the kid got alright, didn't pain no more. So he done that to all those kids that were sick down there and they got all well.

Those days you know—that was just about the time the people used to go up to Yale to do that fishing, they dried fish up there—there was a beaver that was down there (at the bottom of the lake) with these people. When they began to think that those people (the family of the man) were home, the Beaver went up and he went to the place where the people were living. There was nobody home yet. The second time he went up, he saw that the people are home; so they deliver him from down there—down at the bottom of that lake—deliver him. He got pretty close to the house. Well, the people where he was told him to be careful not to go near the people because they would get the "fits." Well, he saw his little brother, small kid, and he called his little brother. My gosh, his little brother just come so far, and he got the "fits." They had to pack him in; but the man, he's got the medicine for anybody that gets the "fits" off him, you know. He gives them the medicine and they get all right. So they took his little brother in the house, and every one of them got the "fits," and he give them the stuff that cured them and they got all right.

The Story-Teller: Dan Milo.

Now, the people that were down there in the lake had told him: "You've got a sister. You tell your sister to come out to the lake and have a fish line, and have a feather for her bait." They told her to throw it in there, and she began to feel something pulling that line. She pulled it up, and it started to come out of the water, and by gosh it looked like a person, *and it started to sing right there*—the song she's going to use when she gets home. Well, the Indians used to have that kind of a dance they called SꝀWIY-ꝁway. They had a lots of feathers around their heads when they danced. She went home. It went the same way what his brother did when he got home from down in the lake there. So that's how that kind of a dance they call SꝀWIY-ꝁway got that round his head, you know, when he dances, and that's how they learned the song—from that girl they fish out with that feather.

Only, they say they have that long time ago, that SꝀWIY-ꝁway. There's a place down there pretty close to the Chilliwack Landing, that they call Skwiy-HAH-lah. That's where they used to have that kind of dance, years ago. Oh, I used to know a lot of Indian stories.

TWO-HEADED SERPENT—HOW IT HELPED THE PEOPLE DEFEAT THE COAST WARRIORS

Koh-KWA-puhl [Kwawkwawpilt]—that's where old Joe was Chief. There's a story there where that big court house was, there was a slough. That's where the Great Big Serpent swam around any place where there's water. Well, this man who lived at Koh-KWA-puhl ran into it; and this thing, this serpent, told the man how to kill him.

Well, they were making a great big house at Koh-KWA-puhl slough, a great big house. Probably you heard that the Indians from the coast used to come here to fight the STAW-loh Indians. Well, this man wanted to make a great big house where he can get something to kill those people. This big serpent seemed to show him how to do it. It's got a head both ends, and swims along the slough, back that way. Well, there's some kind of a grass that the Serpent told him would do it. He told the man how to kill him. "Chew it and then when I holler out, just throw it in my mouth, and you'll kill me." So he got that grass, and he swimmed out—cause this was a big slough you know—where that thing used to travel around. Well, when he got right

Oliver Wells's rendition of the "SEEL-kee of Koh-KWAH-puhl as described by Dan Milo, July 1964."

to it and grabbed around that serpent and it started to squeal and opened its mouth, he spit right into it. Then he left it. When he came back it was already dead; so he hauled it out of there, where it had said itself, "You just leave me there until I've rotted; then you can just pick out my ribs and bones and you burn that bone and use those ashes to paint the shape of that serpent." That's what he was going to put on his house. So he did. He marks where all those bones belong on that big timber that he's going to use. He pictured the shape of that serpent; then he burned the bones and he used the charcoal to paint that timber.

When he got all that painted—just the looks of that serpent—they put it on top of the door of that great big building at the Koh-KWA-puhl. Then when the people came to fight them nobody come out at all. When the Coast warriors tried to go in there they got the "fits" right there, and they died there. Pretty near finished them before they left.

HOW THE SOCKEYE LEARNED TO COME UP THE RIVERS

These people that were real Chilwheyuk Indians that came from up there towards Cultus Lake, well, these men come out and got all the fish they wanted; and they began to fish them very good and they forgot about their wives, you see. That's that story, and they were just having a good time with a lot of fish there, using it up themselves, and they never think about their wives. Well, there was a boy there—one man's son—he's got a mother that's at home up where the real Chilwheyuk Indians used to live up pretty close to Cultus Lake. Well, this boy began to think of his mother, and he got one whole fish and kind of cut it open and wrapped it up on his leg. Then he run for home. He got home, and he told his mother; he unwrapped that fish and give it to his mother, and then she feeds the other women some of that fish. Well, they began to get mad, those women, and they all say, "We'll fix them." Well, at their home, a woman is not supposed to do anything near the head of her husband's bed—it's no good for him; well, they began to work there, you know, and they began to feel it, those men that were down there where they had a fish-trap and catching lots of fish there. Well, one of them says, "I'll bet those women are going to fix us, that boy went home and they might be mad—well, they'll fix us some

"'We might become some kind of birds'—that's what one man said."

way.'' ''We might become some kind of birds''—that's what one man said. Well, you know how the river runs there, comes down this way and then turns at the short point there, well, they know they are coming; these men know they are coming. Well, one started to put a mark on each one to become a bird; and they were all different colors of birds. They hear them coming already, singing and dancing on two canoes. Well, they are getting pretty close to the site, you know. There was only two more not painted yet—the crow and sea-gull. Well, they had some white paint, you know, like what they used to have for their paint, and charcoal, you know. And the crow hasn't got no paint on yet, so it gets throwed on them. That's why the crow is all black. And the sea-gull white, real white. And just as soon as them women come in sight they all flew away.

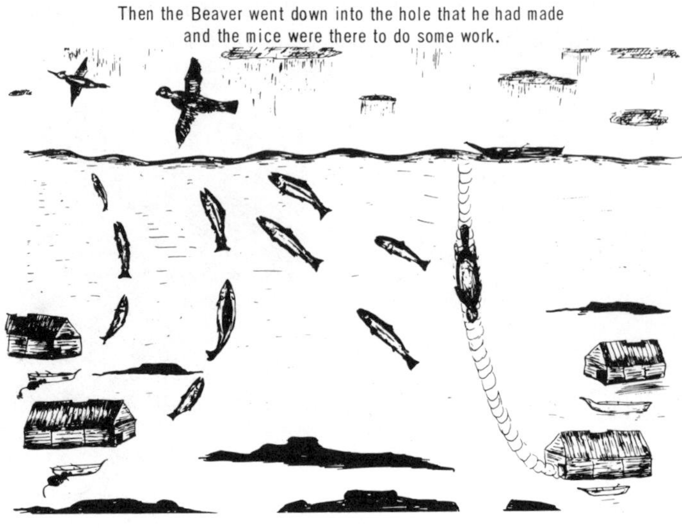
Then the Beaver went down into the hole that he had made and the mice were there to do some work.

Well, they went away up there pretty close to Laidlaw; they stopped and got together up there. ''I think we had better go to where all this fish come from.'' Well, there's a lot of different kind of fish comes in those days, you know, dog-salmon, cohoe, some different kind of fishes; but Sockeye they never did come out, they stayed at home, just like a person you know. Sockeye they stay at home. But these people know that the Sockeye has got a baby—''We'll steal that baby away and take it up the river, so the Sockeye will come into the Fraser River.'' So they began to plan that they will go to get the Sockeye's baby. Well, they were just like any person, you know; they got a canoe and went right out wherever the fish come from, them days. Well, they got pretty close to it, and they stopped there. And the beaver was there too. Then those pretty looking birds started to fly over where those different fishes were—those cohoe and sockeyes, spring salmon—and it was the beaver was the one that was going to take that baby away from there. He made a hole right into them to where the baby is, and then he went out to the mouth of the hole and was laying on its back. That's the beaver.

The Beaver picked up the baby and took it away from there.

And them days it's what the Indian says the Cohoes were the only ones that comes out here, you know, around the Fraser River. Well, the Cohoe says this: ''Somethings going to happen—this man is a smart man.'' Then they began to feel him, you know. The beaver was laying on its back on the water. Then that pretty looking bird came along, two of them; they started to chase after it. They forgot about the beaver, and they had to go away back behind where they are staying. Then the beaver went down and went into the hole that he had made and picked up that baby and took it away from there, took it over there to where those other bird peoples are. Well, one of those birds that did fly away there saw the beaver was already back now; so they flew back to their canoe. And the fish people come down—the beaver was gone. They went into their house and the Sockeye baby was gone. And the mice were there too, to do some work; they made hole in those fishes' canoes. The fish took up one canoe to get in, but it leaks—they couldn't travel. Just one canoe that was alright; so that's the one they used—that's the Sockeye—to chase after them. They come so far, and they just tip over and they swimmed along, the fish did.

The Sockeye chase after them.

So, with everything of the clothing of the baby, they come to the mouth of a river—like the mouth of the Chilliwack River, they put the best part of the baby's clothing in there—that was the baby's pillow, I think—nothing wrong with it. They went to another river like the Chehalis, and you can see, up at Harrison River, the fish up there are kind of a dirty-taste. You see, that's where they left the worst part of the Sockeye baby's clothing. They keep doing that until they get away up to about a mile away from the town of Yale—that's where they sunk the Sockeye baby. My father said he used to see it: "*pretty looking fish.*" But it was a rock there though. Oh, my father said, "When the water's low and clear, you can see that Sockeye down there."

That's where they sunk the Sockeye baby.

THE LISTENER

MRS SUSAN JOE
She had come to sell her basket; it was the last she would make. Her eyes had failed; her daughter had finished it for her. The daughter spoke for her mother who could not speak English well.

She had been born at Chee-AK-tel [Tzeachten], seventy years ago; but had lived away from her people for many years. "Would she like to hear Dan Milo tell one of the old stories?" "Dan Milo? Is he still alive?" "Yes, listen." From the tape recorder came the voice of Sloh-kwih-LAH-loh, Dan Milo. He was telling the story of the two bears that were sisters, SPAHTS and Kwayt-sh.ihl.

She bent forward when she heard his voice, her calm face sensitive to the feeling of response that held her tense. As the story began, in the language of the Ch.ihl.KWAY-uhk, which to her meant so much, she cupped her hand over her ear, to better catch the sensitive inflections of the voice, which translated to her the full meaning of the story. Instinctively she nodded gently, an approval of the unfolding theme. The story followed along a pleasant trail, long since lost in the legendary past. Then as the contrary forces came into the theme, gently she shook her head, as one of her ancestors might well have done in the dim distant past as the story teller then, as now, unfolded the same theme before the fire burning in the centre of the family SKUH-mel (pit-house). Unconsciously she followed the mood of the story and occasionally spoke quietly, as if to add her approval or join in disapproval, in sympathy with the mood of the moment, until at last the story ended."

Strangely enough, it was symbolic of her own story, ending thus: "And if any bone (meaning member) of the family go away, bring him back, that all the family may be buried together."

Dan Milo at Edenbank Farm, July 1964

WELLS: I'm very pleased to have you here again today, Dan, to do a bit of recording. It's good to have you come and give us some more stories.

MILO: Why, sure. I've got a very, very old story about the first Indian that was created, in a place, somewhere. It's a real good story.

WELLS: Yeah, let's have it. That'll be good.

MILO: But I'll tell you about the Wealick, Wilíléq; I think that's the best I can tell you first.

WELLS: The Wealick is a family...?

MILO: It's a family from the early days. The reason why it's called Tzeachten—ch'íyaq, that means "a fish-trap," Well, they used to have their trap in them days right there, put in front of that hall there. Well, that starts from about the Wealick.

WELLS: Would that fish-trap be there before the Hudson Bay people came?

MILO: Oh, yeah, a long time. Yeah. How they began to use the language that we speak now, those that speaks Indian, that's during the flood, after that flood, you know.

WELLS: I believe you told me this story one time before on another tape recording, Dan.

MILO: I believe I did, yeah.

WELLS: Today, could you give me that story about the Wealick, the early Wealick family?

MILO: Yeah, I'll do that. I have to speak Indian first?

WELLS: That'll be good.

MILO: Yeah, well, are you ready?

WELLS: Yeah. O.K.

[*Story in Halkomelem*]

WELLS: That's very good. Thanks very much. That should record very nicely. Can you tell me the story in English now?

MILO: Yeah, I will.

[FAMILY LEGEND]

My dear friends, whoever will be listening to this story of what they call today Wealick. That was the name of two brothers, and the older brother, he was called Wilí:léq, Wealick today.

Well, one day they got ready, Wealick and his younger brother, go hunting. That's all they do is hunting bear. And they start to walk the valley here, from Tzeachten. That's where the people used to live years and years ago. And on the way along this younger man, he began to think: ''I think my brother's going haywire. It don't seem to be him.'' On a little ways, he kind of turn his head a little bit, you know. And this Wealick, you know, his face is turned different, become a bear.

Well, later on, you know, they come to a great big cedar tree. And the Wealick, he made an awful noise and slapped the butt of the tree. He jumped up, climb up to a limb, and he set right there.

''My dear brother,'' he says to his brother, ''I'm going to leave you. But remember what we are doing, getting bear. You shall know my younger people, will be years from now. There will be a spot on the breast. That will be my children or grandchildren. And you know what we do; we always feed the other people. And if there's any bone goes away from home, tell the people to bring it back, and it will be buried together. That'll be Wealick's family.''

So, that's all that is told to his younger brother. He had to leave for home. Got home and told his people that his brother had become a bear. Then he told everything he said should be used for him. So I think that is all I can tell about them, the Wealicks.

WELLS: Thank you very much. That's a very good story, Dan.

MILO: Yeah. We'll start that ''Flood,'' eh? I'll speak Indian first, eh, same as the other one:

[*Story in Halkomelem*]

MILO: My dear friends, I'm speaking my own language. And now I'm going to speak the rest of the same story in English.

[THE FLOOD]

My dear friends, whoever will be listening to this story. I suppose you all know me. During the flood here in this valley, the whole place in the Fraser Valley was drownded—supposed to be drownded, at that time. Well, there was a man telling each one of his people: ''Build up a good canoe. There will be one mountain that's going to be clear—the top will be there, and that's where the people going to be saved, those that's going to have a canoe.'' But a lot of them people didn't believe that at all. ''There's a lot of high mountains; we can climb up there,'' that's what other people said.

Well, when the time comes, the flood started. They began to follow that Sumas Mountain. The Indian calls that mountain Kw'ekw'e'íqw. That was the name of the mountain that didn't go out of sight during that flood. Well, they got up to the top of the mountain, and they had a long rope that the Indians work, braided of some kind of a skin and trees, and they tie up themselves there. The story said there's three canoes went lost from there, that broked off and nobody knows where they went to.

For so many days they were up there; then the water began to come down. They got down, about halfway down, to the lower land. They stopped in a place, and there's a cave into the mountain. So they stay there, right there, to be dry. And they had that long rope coiled up inside the cave. And they stayed there, those people, stayed right there. They could see the lower land was dry. The grass began to get green. Then they began to come down. And that long rope and other stuffs that they had there, that's left there. Anybody can see that coil of rope inside the cave. Whoever will see it, it will be either good luck or bad luck, whoever will see the coil of rope and the stuffs that's left in there. And then they began to come down. They got down there, and the place was all dry.

Well, the story is that's why our language changes. The old Sts'elxwíqw language, what the White man calls Chilliwack, that all died out; and they began the language that we use today, Halkomelem. That's the end of that story.

WELLS: Very good, Dan. That's the story of the flood.
MILO: Yeah, the flood.
MILO: Well, I might tell you another story, about a black bear and a grizzly bear. They're supposed to be sisters. They both got childrens. Yeah. I might tell you that story too.
WELLS: Very good. Go ahead.
MILO: Are you ready?
WELLS: Yeah. Have it in your own language first.

[*Story Told in Halkomelem First*]

[BLACK BEAR AND GRIZZLY BEAR]

My dear friends, whoever will be listening to this story. In a place where there was a bear, black bear and a grizzly. The grizzly is supposed to be the oldest of the two. They were two sisters of them. The black one was younger than the grizzly. Well, every day these two womens goes out to do some hunting for what they eat. Well, one night she came home, and every one of the kids was sleeping. The daughter of the black bear was sleeping, and her brother, and her little kid. And the big girl, she spoke to her aunt: ''Where is my mother?'' ''Oh, she is going to stay there for the night. She'll be coming home later.'' Well, the girl knows very well that the grizzly killed her sister.

The next day she went away again, and they coaxed the bear's children, the girl and the boy, and took them out for a swim. Well, I tell you that the grizzly bear doesn't swim at all, can't swim. Well, all these children were drowned, the grizzly children were drowned. And these two, they went to work and picked up some rotten logs and laid them on these grizzly bear's children. Well, when the grizzly bear come home, all her children were in bed, and she tried to wake them up. No, they wouldn't move at all. She went there and picked them up, but they wasn't no children at all. It was rotten wood. And the black bear's children, they're gone.

So first thing in the morning the grizzly she followed them. They come to a place where there was a man working across the river, making a canoe. But they thought they'd climb a tree, the black bear's children. Well, the grizzly bear come along. Well, the girl says: ''Are you looking for your children?'' ''Yes. What have you done with them?'' ''Oh, I got them here. You lay down, down there, and I'll lower down your children.'' That's what the girl said. But this was the stuff from the trees; dust. ''You open your eyes wide. I'll lower down your children.'' She let it go, you know, and got it all over in her eye, and she got blinded. She couldn't see.

They come down. They hollered to that man that's making a canoe. That man come across, took them over. ''There's the grizzly is chasing after us. You must remember we don't want her to catch us. And you know that a grizzly cannot swim. You can drowned her for us.'' So this man he went to work and make a high seat for the grizzly to sit on. On their way across, about half ways over the river, he shook that tree, and the grizzly tumbled over, you know, and she got drownded.

And they just kept on going, the black bear's children. They come to a place, you know, and they make a fire for the night. And the little boy's got a cap on, and it's all on the older brother's way, you know. He got hold of his little brother's cap and throwed it in the fire. ''It's always in my way,'' that's what he said. So he throwed it in the fire. Just a minute, you know, the water began to rise from the river. By gosh, they had to run to get away from the water. They looked down there, and that boy was still sitting down there, and the fire's still on under the water. But they kept on a-going to be saved.

Well, that boy, he was there by himself. He saw a man come down the river, with a pole with a hook on it. He hooks the fish, and the kid, he see that man is doing some fishing. He just took a fish out. ''I'll go and fix him,'' this boy said. He jumped in the river and turned to be a nice pretty-looking fish, this boy did. Pretty soon that nice pretty-looking fish come along, and that man was ready. He set his hook there, and hooked the fish that's down there. Well, that kid he grabbed the hook before he hooked him, took him out of the water. And that kid he saw the club that he kill fish with. The kid, he kicked that stick, you know, that club. It went quite a long ways. Well, that kid, he went to work and he cut that hook, and he jumped in the river again. When that man come along, his hook was gone. He thought that was that fish took his hook away. So he had to go home. And that kid began to think: ''I'll go look for that guy that's doing the fishing.'' He had the hook with him. He come there, and ''Hello, grandpa,'' he says. ''You look to be sad.'' ''Oh, I lost my hook, sonny. I lost my hook. A fish took it away.'' ''Oh... here's your hook, grandpa. I found it.'' By gosh, that man is sure glad. ''Where do you stay, boy?'' ''I've got no home, grandpa. I got no home. I just wandered around.'' ''Oh, you stay with me.''

And one morning he went to that man's—he was outside doing some work—to fix up his bed, fix up his blanket. And there was a knot-hole laying under the blanket. That kid took it and throwed it in the fire. Pretty soon that man come in. ''Oh, my gosh, my wife must've went and got burnt.'' ''Is that your wife?'' this kid says. ''Yeah, that's my wife. I was the first man created here,'' that's what that man said to him. ''I was the first man created, and the Great Man forgot to leave me a wife. So that's why I didn't have any wife.'' ''Give me an axe; I'll get you a wife.'' So this man give him an axe, and he went out. And there's a nice tree, a birch; the next one is the alder. Cut them up, about the height of a person, and he split them and took it home, front of the man's home. Well, he holler at him, tell him to come out. ''I've brought you a wife. I am going to make a wife for you, whichever one of these sticks you want for your wife.'' ''I want it my colour.'' That's what the man said. ''That's the alder.'' ''Oh, alright. You go inside and I'll bring in your wife.'' Well, this boy, he went to work and made a nice pretty-looking girl, hair hanging down to her knees. Took her in the house. So he got a wife. Then he told that he was the first man created there, but the Man forgot to get him a wife. So, that's what the story says. The Indians had a man created in the first, like they do Adam and Eve. That's the end of the story, my friend.

WELLS: How did you call it? Soowahlie?

MILO: Th'ewálí. That's where the real Ts'elxwíqw [Chilliwack] Indians were living, right near the mountain. That's another part of that flood story.

[THE AVALANCHE]

After the real Ts'elxwíqw tribe used to live way up just about east from Cultus Lake, that's where the Ts'elxwíqw used to live, and they had—maybe I've told you about that before—one of them people that lives—, those Ts'elxwíqw Indans, he used to be a great one to go up the mountain to hunt, deer, things like that. Well, he run into a place where the skin cracked on the rock. Well, everytime he goes it's getting wider and wider. It got so he can't jump over it. Probably I told you about it.

WELLS: No, I didn't hear this one.

MILO: He couldn't jump over that crack. So when he got home he told his father and mother, ''I think this mountain's going to come down any time now. It used to be just a small crack when I first went up there, and now I can't jump over it.'' That was the east side of Cultus Lake, that's where the old Ts'elxwíqw tribe of Indians.

Well, he told, the father of this boy that goes out there to hunt, he told the people that the mountain's going to come down. They wouldn't believe him at all: ''I don't think a mountain will come down like that, all rock.'' So they moved away from there, this family, the father and mother of this young fellow that goes up there to hunt. They moved down to the creek that runs from Cultus Lake just about—, a little above the cemetery up there at Cultus Lake; that's where they went to.

Well, it wasn't long after they moved there, you seen that that mountain come down and bury those real Ts'elxwíqw Indians. So every one of them got buried, you see. Once in a while some people around there, you know, they hear them talking way inside the rock. (*Laughs.*)

WELLS: Did they have any totems of any kind?

MILO: I think they had. They built up a whole cedar tree. They cut it down from across the river, and crossed it over, and put it there at Vedder Crossing. Had it dugged. Well, every time it rains so much, you know, they had a crow on the end of that big long tree, when that's filled up, it began to sing, just like a crow.

WELLS: They carved one, eh? Would they use that for a water supply? No, they'd have lots of water without that.

MILO: Oh, yeah. That's just to make that crow.

WELLS: Make a noise, eh?

7. Edmund Joe Peters

On his first field trip to Seabird Island Reserve, near Agassiz, in August 1964, Oliver was interested mainly in going through the place-names of the Tait area, as given by Wilson Duff in *The Upper Stalo Indians of the Fraser River* (1952) pp. 30-34. We do not include that session here, except to note that Edmund Joe Peters gave his own version of the sxwaixwe mask legend in response to a question about village No. 14, which "is thought to be connected by a tunnel with Kawkawa Lake, and it is through this tunnel that the sxwaixwe mask and costume were brought to its first human owner" (Duff p. 33). Edmund Joe Peters responded with the following:

> A man went up to—he got all sores, you know—he went up to the lake, and he caught a fish; and the fish—well, after he cooked the fish, there's a frog come on his barbecue salmon, you know. Then he got all scabby, you know. And he went up there. He committed suicide. He jumped down the bluff. When he landed in the water he landed on a roof. They opened this roof. He went down in. And there they brought him—he was all sore, scabby—then after these people there went and got him fed this medicine to cure his scabs. And then they were supposed to bring him home, and they build this tunnel, through the lake. He was a strong doctor when they got home.

In his *Vocabulary of Native Words*, Oliver wrote the following tributes to Edmund Joe Peters and his wife Mary:

> Edmund Joe Peters was born at SKWAH-tehts, a village on the east bank of the Fraser River, at the north end of Seabird Island.
>
> His father's name was PAHTH-ee-ah-tihl, and Edmund, at seventy years of age, has a very clear memory of the knowledge passed on to him by the "old people"—language, legends, myths and stories of the river-people of the Tait tribe.
>
> As a young man he attended school at St Mary's, Mission, where he learned to speak English well. He has a naturally courteous and appreciative manner.
>
> He has a broad knowledge of the topography of the country, having worked for a number of years with Government survey crews in the Cascade Mountains.
>
> Edmund is now confined to bed with arthritis, but has contributed much to this effort. He maintains an active interest in family and community life. To him should go the credit of recognition of the old Native name of Maria Slough. It was known to the Indians as SK''AW'K'-ehl, meaning "going around a turn," as they did in coming into the slough from up the Fraser.
>
> Mrs Edmund Joe Peters was born at Puhk'l-CHOHL-thun (American Bar) in the Fraser Canyon. She had no formal education. It has been affectionately said of her, "She knows everything, she never went to school." This refers to the fact that she has a full knowledge of Native arts and crafts. Her fine work was given recognition by the Canadian Handicraft Guild when her basket won the prize for "the finest

basket in the Show,'' Montreal, 1964. In recording the language she assisted greatly in giving clarity to the pronunciation of numerals and village sites of the Canyon area.

Edmund Joe Peters (third from right) with survey crew, Chilliwack Lake, 1915.

For the background to this interview, Oliver's booklet, *Salish Weaving: Primitive and Modern*, may be consulted. The section entitled ''The Return of the Salish Loom'' is included at the end of the present volume, and contains further information on Mary Peters and her work.

Edmund Joe Peters and Mary Peters at Seabird Island, 16 September 1964

WELLS: I wanted to ask you about these pictues of these blankets, these museum pictures; and this one here is one I got from the London Museum. The diamond pattern is much like the one your wife makes.

PETERS: Yeah.

WELLS: But have you seen this type, this pattern?

PETERS: No, Oliver.

WELLS: No, this is a very old one.

PETERS: But people down here used to make it in. They took a wood, you know, brown wood, and they pounded and pounded, sit pounding, you know, till it gets soft, like.

WELLS: That's the way they work the cedar bark? Is it braided, or do they spin it together like wool?

PETERS: Well, they don't spin it; they just pick it, like that, you know.

WELLS: They make it almost look like wool. It's very fine. Now, these two with the curved bottoms, do you think they used them in this country too? They made them here?

PETERS: Oh, yeah.

WELLS: Would they call them dancing blankets? Dancing aprons?

PETERS: Yeah.
WELLS: What's the Indian name for them?
PETERS: Òtes te lhqw'á:y, etlh?
MRS PETERS: Lhqw'á:y.
WELLS: How do say it?
PETERS: Lheqw'à:y.
WELLS: Good. There's another small dancing apron that come on the front and went down underneath and come up behind. Mrs Cooper give me the name "stayuhp."
PETERS: Sthíyép.
WELLS: Is that a different one? That's not like this one, eh?
PETERS: Oh, it's the same as that. Sthíyép.
MRS PETERS: Á:'a. [Yes.]
WELLS: You see this picture here. Now this blanket was taken from near Yale, and it's mountain goat and dog hair. And it was taken from Yale about 130 years ago.

Salish weaving displayed at the British Museum, London, England. Photographed for Oliver by Allan Cecil Brooks.

PETERS: Well, it's swṓqw'elh.
WELLS: Is that the name of the blanket?
PETERS: Yeah.
MRS PETERS: Wetl'ó swás te p'q'élqel.
WELLS: Puhkuhlkuhl—that's mountain goat?
PETERS: Yeah, mountain goat.
WELLS: But these colors would be orange and yellow and black, all colors.
PETERS: Indian dyes.
WELLS: Indian dyes, yeah. Do you think you can make one like that some day?
PETERS: Oh, no.
WELLS: *(laughing)* Ah, I didn't ask you. I asked her.
MRS PETERS: *(laughing)* I think I make it like that.
WELLS: I think you could.
MRS PETERS: Yeah, use wool, yeah.
WELLS: Make your different colors, yeah. I'll make a picture of this in color some day. I got a colored picture at home.[1] I'll give you a colored picture, and maybe this winter some time you make it.
MRS PETERS: Oh, yeah.
PETERS: Oh, we'll make it, yeah. Out of wool, you know.
WELLS: Yeah, well, you make this one like this. It's all Salish, you see. Nobody else's got one like this.
PETERS: She's got to have the picture to copy it.
WELLS: Yeah, well, that's good. I'll make a colored picture of it, and then bring it to you, and you keep it, and then you can work from it. O.K. You see this picture here. I got this one from the Museum in Victoria. And this blanket was made down in Musqueam.
MRS PETERS: Oh.
WELLS: This arrow-point design. And these spindles, you see. The old people used those spindles. What's the name for these? What do you call a spindle?
MRS PETERS: Qáqelets'.
PETERS: Qáqelets'.
WELLS: Good. They used a sword, like, for pounding the wool. Do you know the name of that one?
PETERS: She don't know that one.
WELLS: I see. That's a good blanket, eh? I think they just used black and white in that one. This one is on—that's Mrs George Johnny, I think, making a big blanket. And

Mrs Harriet Johnny at Mission Indian Reserve 1, North Vancouver, 1928.

this one is Frank Charlie. I think this must be Frank Charlie, the man here. Do you know that family?
PETERS: No, I don't know, Oliver. I don't know that people from down there.

[1]This color photograph is reproduced on the inside front cover of the *Salish Weaving* booklet, with the caption: "A Rare Salish Blanket, Property of Museum of American Indian Heye Foundation N.Y. Originally obtained about 1850 by Joe Mackay of Hudson Bay Co. from the Chief of the Tsakuam band of Salish Indians at Yale, B.C." It was originally reproduced and discussed in William C. Orchard & George G. Heye *A Rare Salish Blanket* N.Y. Museum of the American Indian 1926.

WELLS: I sent wool over to Mrs Pat Charlie. I asked her if she knew the loom, the old loom, like your wife uses. And she said that she has one. They have one there. But she doesn't use it now, I don't think. That's goat-hair too, you see.

MRS PETERS: O kwá alétsa tthá?

PETERS: Where's this place?

WELLS: I think maybe at Nanaimo or Cowichan or somewhere along there.

PETERS: Must be the Cowichan.

WELLS: Or it might be Koksilah. When I went down to Vancouver on those Indian days in North Vancouver, I talked to this old man—he's 94 years old now—that's Chief Khahtsahlano. Well, somebody told me that this man had Indian religious training, he knew the Indian religion, like, the old ideas. I think he lives at Squamish now. Some day I'm going to go and see, and take a tape-recorder so that I can get it down on tape.

PETERS: Yeah, he'll tell you lots of things. He knows things from way back. I'm glad you showed me these, Oliver. Thank you.

WELLS: Yeah, it's a good picture too. He's got a good Salish head-band. And just one feather.[2] The Indians here they just use one or two feathers. They don't use a big head, like the Prairie Indians, eh?

PETERS: No, no.

The second of the photographs referred to by Oliver Wells. The man pictured is Frank Charlie from Musqueam.

WELLS: Just about come at the end of the tape. I'll turn it over.

•

WELLS: You were going to tell me a legend or story about Cheam Peak. Can you tell me now?

[MOUNTAIN GOAT LEGEND]

PETERS: Qwóqwellh.

MRS PETERS: Á':a. X̲ét'e swíweles a la akweláx la telí tthá te kw Chíyò:m Smá:lt, Lhílheqiy.

PETERS: A young fellow went up to hunt, up in Cheam. And he tracked a...

MRS PETERS: P'q'élqel.

PETERS: Goat, you know, mountain goat. And he comes to the lake there, little lake, and he seen two young womens sitting down there. They got selchí:m.

MRS PETERS: Qesu le kwú:tem.

PETERS: And they told him that he shouldn't be ashamed of us, and they took him, you see, took him...

MRS PETERS: Kwe le só:seqwt tl'e le xwe stó:les.

PETERS: The youngest one is the one that got him for his wife. And every time they want meat, when the guy goes out, and every bone, Oliver, every bone they eat, you know, they don't burn it, throw it in the lake, back.

MRS PETERS: Li te qó:.

PETERS: In the water. One time this young guy that was brought there...

MRS PETERS: Kwá:lxes tí te méqsels t'émches sth'ò:m.

PETERS: They hid a piece of the nose, you know, and this fellow went out, he come back, his nose was bleeding, and they asked him whoever hid the bone, you know, they wanted to give it to this guy, and he throwed it back in the water. Well, this guy got all right. That's the story, Oliver.

WELLS: Well, these two young women at the lake, were they like spirits? Were they the spirit of the hunting, the goat, or were they women, like?

PETERS: The spirit of the goat.

MRS PETERS: E théxwemet mestíyéxw yútl'òlèm e te p'q'élqel.

---

[2]Oliver is showing the photograph of August Jack Khahtsahlano he had just received from Major J.S. Matthews of the Vancouver City Archives. It is reproduced later in this volume (interview #12).

PETERS: When they go home to where they are, they were real people.

WELLS: Yeah, I see, yeah. But when this man saw them at the lake, they were the spirit of the goat.

PETERS: Then they were goats, yeah.

WELLS: Yeah, I get it. Now, Cheam, I noticed your wife says Cheam just like it was an Indian word

PETERS: Yeah, Chíyò:m.

WELLS: Well, did the Indians have...?

MRS PETERS: Lhílheqiy yalh te skwíxs tútl'o smà:lt.

PETERS: Lhílheqiy, the mountain's name.

WELLS: That's Cheam Peak, eh?

PETERS: Yeah.

WELLS: What does it mean?

PETERS: Well, I don't know the meaning. But, you know, many Cheam people are living, still living, that's their ancestor is that goat, you know.

WELLS: Oh, I see, yeah. Well, now, when you say Cheam, it refers to the people, not the mountain, eh?

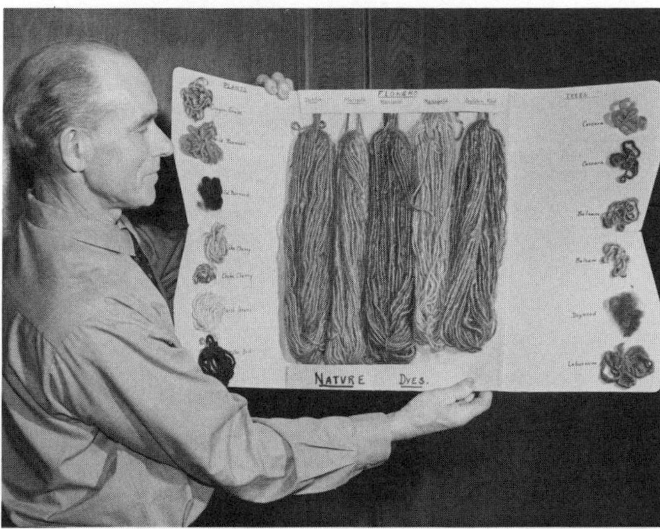

Oliver Wells exhibits Indian dyes made from natural sources. Photo: Gordon E. Whitaker, Beautiful B.C.

PETERS: Not the mountain.

WELLS: No, but the ancestor was the goat of the mountain? I see, yeah. And how do you say this name, this ancestor? You give it to me just now.

PETERS: Syewà:ls.

WELLS: And the Cheam refers to the people at the bottom of the mountain?

PETERS: Yeah. When the kids grow up, well, they send them—send them that man down with his kids, you see, send them home, and his wife too.

WELLS: And that was the beginning of the Cheam people?

PETERS: Yeah. But don't say that, Oliver, don't tell anybody. They won't like it, you see. (*Laughs.*)

•

WELLS: When I was on top of Elk Mountain, I got this lichen. Now, this one mostly grows up in the Interior, in the Thompson River country. But on top of Elk Mountain you find some things that are Interior-like, you know, about four thousand five hundred feet. And I brought this home, and I boiled it, and this is the colour I get. Isn't it a nice color, eh? This grows on the dead trees about...

MRS PETERS: Ō::, tl'ó t'we metu'álqel.

WELLS: What color do you call that in Indian?

MRS PETERS: Yellow, tsqwà:y.

PETERS: Let me see that.

WELLS: That's what it come from.

PETERS: Nice and yellow.

MRS PETERS: Oh, yeah.

WELLS: Some day you ask your friends up in the Interior, you ask them about this one, and maybe you can trade them some, trade something and get this for a color for your wool. When you make that nice blanket, why, I'll try to get you some of this, eh?

MRS PETERS: Oh, yeah.

WELLS: That'd make a good color.

MRS PETERS: Lí kw'e qéx̱ kw'e shxwólexwes ttha.

PETERS: You got lots of that?

Mary Peters with Oliver Wells.

WELLS: No. On Elk Mountain I only got about a hatful, and I looked all over all the trees on top of the mountain. And the only place it grows is on the dead trees. They stand up perfectly dry, you know. And out on a limb, just on a dry tree, you see a little piece like this, sometimes about twenty feet above the ground. But I'll try and get some more. But you know Shaw Springs, up on the Thompson, up near Ashcroft? Shaw Springs?

PETERS: No.

WELLS: Up in that country up there on a way, they grow this stuff; but it's yellow like that, right on the trees.

8. Harry Edwards

Oliver wrote of Chief Edwards in the *Vocabulary* pamphlet:

> Harry Edwards was born at Cheam in 1884, where he has lived his entire life except for a period of seven years, when as a youth he attended school at St Mary's Mission.
>
> He cleared land and commenced dairy farming. In 1917 he was one of the first members to join the Fraser Valley Milk Producers Association. He was a careful dairyman, and continued to ship the highest quality milk to that organization until he retired from dairying in 1950.
>
> For a period of forty years he was a much respected Chief of the Cheam people. Chief Edwards during these busy years greatly broadened his field of knowledge by subscribing to and being an appreciative reader of the *Readers Digest* and the *Chilliwack Progress*. For a period of years he had made available to him regularly, copies of the *National Geographic* magazine, which he greatly enjoyed.
>
> He now lives a pleasant retired life with his family at KWAWM-kuh-moos, a quiet spot known to the early Natives, at the upper end of Hope Slough, "place where the stones are covered with moss."

Harry Edwards at Edenbank Farm, 8 October 1964

WELLS: Mr Edwards, I'm glad to have you here today to talk to you on a number of things; and one thing I wanted to enquire was concerning the villages of the Pilalt people. And first of all I'd like to ask you—I understand that you were chief of the tribe at Cheam for some years—how long were you chief?

EDWARDS: About forty years.

WELLS: And do you still retain the title of chief, or has it passed on to someone else?

EDWARDS: It's passed on to Albert Douglas.

WELLS: But I imagine a good many of your friends still call you Chief Edwards.

EDWARDS: Well, just for friendship, you know, being I was a chief for such a long time. Well, I'm an old man now, and they still like to call me Chief.

WELLS: You are in good health. How old are you now, Mr Edwards?

EDWARDS: Eighty years.

WELLS: Well, that's very good. Did you live all your life at Cheam on the reserve?

EDWARDS: The only time I was away was while I was at school at St Mary's Mission. I spent seven years at St Mary's Mission school.

WELLS: You still retain some of your native language?

EDWARDS: Oh, yes. Not too much though, because I have nobody to talk with, you see, to use my language.

WELLS: Do I say Cheam correctly?

EDWARDS: Well, the Indian way of pronouncing it is Lexw-chíyò:m. "Where strawberries grow." It's still living up to its name; there's wild strawberries still growing plentiful around there.

WELLS: I see. That's interesting. I understand all these villages along the Fraser River, on both sides, at one time were Pilalt, from Cheam down to where the Chilliwack tribes were?

EDWARDS: Yes, so I understand.

WELLS: And do I say the word "Pilalt" correctly?

EDWARDS: Well, almost. Pelólhxw.

WELLS: Very good. Could you tell me just where these villages were on the other side of the river? There's one village in the Agassiz area.

Harry Edwards.

EDWARDS: It would be just about the edge of that new bridge they have there. In the Indian it's Siyét'a.

WELLS: Does it have a meaning?

EDWARDS: I couldn't say.

WELLS: No. Well, then, what other villages were there in that area?

EDWARDS: It's the only one that I have any knowledge of.

WELLS: There was a village mentioned by Peters: Skwahtehts. It was his home village. Now that's up on Seabird Island, is it? That's not Pilalt country anyway, is it?

EDWARDS: No, I hardly think so. They have a different name from there on up.

WELLS: There was another village, which is mentioned by Wilson Duff. It was known as "a fishing place," and it was "at the end of" the mountain, "where some people lived the year round." Bob Joe said "that there had been a fishing village at the mouth of the Mountain Slough at the west end of Agassiz, but was unable to give the name."[1] Can you remember the name of that village?

EDWARDS: Well, I know the fishing place. Lhí:lhkw'eleqs.

WELLS: Very good. That's the one that I wanted to get the name of. Was that on the Fraser River proper?

EDWARDS: Oh, yes. On the Fraser River proper. That's a fishing place all right, but I don't know if there was any village there. It's right at the bluff of the mountain where it went down to the river, you know. They used dip-nets there.

WELLS: There was another village which Wilson Duff mentions here, which I was trying to locate: a "large village on Hope Slough." It's now known as the "Chilliwack Indian Reserve Schelowat."

EDWARDS: Sx̱elá:wtxw. That's just across the slough there from the Melody Cafe.

WELLS: Oh, yeah, right at the end of the Annis Road. This would be an old established village, would it?

EDWARDS: Yes. The Indians lived there for nobody knows how long. They lived there when they were hit by an epidemic. And there was one man, you know, that thought he'd try and save his family. He went out and got ahold of a skunk. Killed the skunk and he cut it up. He put it all around his house, in every little crevice in his house, all around. Not one of his family took sick during that epidemic.

WELLS: Is that right? Well.

Harry Edwards at Cheam.

EDWARDS: It wiped out all of them. There were very few survivors, or so they say. I guess he had quite a lot of faith in that skunk there.

WELLS: Maybe it was strong enough to keep the people away that were sick! You mentioned when we were coming along there that there were a great many big cedar trees along there.

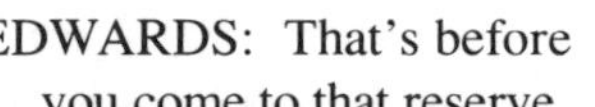

EDWARDS: That's before you come to that reserve. Yeah, they call it Salq'éywel: "a lot of cracked trees." There's one big tree now up there, it was hit by lightning, eh?

WELLS: I see, yeah. Well, if we come down around Hope Slough further, the next village, where some stone work has been dug up, is where the Gravelly Slough joins Hope Slough, but you don't have the name of that?

EDWARDS: No, I don't.

WELLS: They must have left there a great many years ago, eh?

EDWARDS: Well, I guess people were scattered all along, or, like, maybe they kept moving around here and there. They've been here for so long, nobody knows how long.

WELLS: At the west end of Little Mountain, where the quarry road is now, when that new school was built in there they dug up a lot of Indian artifacts, that was an early Pilalt village there, was it?

EDWARDS: Yes, the Indians kept a small reserve there. They called that place Sqwá:la [Skwahla].

WELLS: And where are those Indians now? Did they all die off, or where...?

EDWARDS: No, I don't think there's anybody living there, but the Stewart family out in Wellington Reserve there, they have an interest on that place.

WELLS: And the Pilalt people, their territory, did it extend still further down the Fraser from there?

EDWARDS: No, just as far as that reserve they call Qweqwe'ópelhp [Kwawkwawapilt].

---

[1]Wilson Duff's *The Upper Stalo Indians* is being quoted (p. 37). Bob Joe was an informant for Duff.

WELLS: That was Pilalt? Is there another reserve towards the Fraser from there? Skway?

EDWARDS: Yes, they call that Sexwá:y.

WELLS: And do you know the meaning of these words?

EDWARDS: Yes. The Qweqwe'ópelhp means "crab apple grove, wild crab apple grove." And Sexwá:y means "a place where they make canoes."

WELLS: Very good. Are you ready for tea?

•

WELLS: I wanted to ask you, Mr Edwards—you mentioned that you were brought up by one of the older people?

EDWARDS: I was orphaned quite young. I remember my father, but I don't remember my mother.

WELLS: In the early days most of the training of the younger people was undertaken by the older people, wasn't it?

EDWARDS: Mostly.

WELLS: And our local tribes here were not as warlike as Indians up the coast, were they? Were they trained or were they taught to be otherwise, or how?

EDWARDS: They trained themselves to just defend themselves. They never went out to raid other people. And they used to train the young ones, the children, to go up at night sometimes, stay away in the bush, you know, in case there was raid. So if there was raids, well, the children were away, you see, safe. They called that skwú:m, skwù:m; get the children to hide away for the night, in case there was a raid.

Harry Edwards at Cheam.

WELLS: I read about these raids in the Hudson Bay Journals, about 1827 to 1830. They give a record of these Kwakiutl people coming up, and they would tell the Hudson Bay people they were going to raid the Chilliwacks or the Pilalt, and then a day or two later, why, they would come down the river, and sometimes they had prisoners, and sometimes, once or twice, they got beaten. I think there's record of the Chilliwack people defeating them on the lower Chilliwack here in one raid. Do you have any record of the Pilalt defending against them when they...?

EDWARDS: No, but when those raiders were going back, you know, the local people knew how to use poisoned arrows. Any one of these raiders got wounded, well, they died from the poisoned arrows after they got home.

WELLS: Yeah, John Hall up here, he told me they got rattlesnake poison; they took it in exchange from the Thompson Indians.

EDWARDS: Oh, I wouldn't know. I don't know what it would be.

WELLS: You mentioned that you were dairying; you spent most of your life farming on your own farm?

EDWARDS: In 1950, sold my dairy cattle. My back got weak. I couldn't lift the 125 lb. cans any more, so I had to give up.

WELLS: You'd be farming then until you were about sixty-five. You did very well to stay with it that long. How many cows did you keep?

EDWARDS: I got up as high as twelve.

WELLS: Yeah. And you shipped your milk?

EDWARDS: It came to the creamery in Sardis. Fraser Valley Milk Producers Association.

WELLS: And how early did you join the Fraser Valley Milk Producers?

EDWARDS: 1917.

WELLS: Well, that would be among the very first. Farming on the reserve, did you have difficulty keeping up the standard of your milk? Did you ship grade A milk?

EDWARDS: Oh, yes, all the time. I never had any trouble with the quality, and I just had simple buildings, you know. But I was very careful in handling it.

WELLS: Did you have to take it out to the road?

EDWARDS: I had to take it out a little better than half a mile from the house every morning. When I first started, the milk wagon used to get to the stand at six o'clock in the morning. (*Laughs.*)

WELLS: How many acres did you have?

EDWARDS: Well, right now I have about—I've over fifty acres clear right now.

WELLS: Well, and it's rented now, is it?

EDWARDS: Oh, yes, yes.

•

WELLS: In some of the early records of the Catholic Church, there's reference to the early chiefs, and I believe one chief that was mentioned was Chief Alexis. Do I give that name correctly?

EDWARDS: Yes. He was my grandfather.

WELLS: And he was chief of the Cheam Reserve?

EDWARDS: Yeah, he worked for all the Fraser. At first, you know, when the places were reserved, they were very small. They just surveyed, you know, where they found a band of Indians. My grandfather wasn't satisfied with that. He kept going to Victoria to see the government. He wanted the reserves enlarged. So finally they consented, and told all the Indians where to pick out whatever lands they wanted. So each reserve picked out the extra land they wanted.

WELLS: Well, that was fortunate he made that effort. It would have made a big difference nowadays; it would have been impossible to do anything now.

EDWARDS: Oh, yes, he worked hard for it. The whole Fraser Valley Indians knew him well. They say he was very intelligent.

WELLS: He could see into the future a bit. Well, now, I went to the Catholic priest in New Westminster asking about the early information about the reserves up here, and on the wall in his studio at the church or the home there there was a needlepoint work done by a young woman by the name of Emily. It was a Biblical scene, quite large, and it was done in handwork, like the women do. And the name on the bottom of it was Emily. Do you have any recollection of that name, or anybody talking about...?

EDWARDS: Yes, I've heard that name. I knew the woman too; she lived up our way. She was brought up in the St Mary's Mission School, and they learnt a lot of that work there at that school. She belonged to what we call the Harris family now.

WELLS: He's chief on Seabird now, is he?

EDWARDS: No. Same name, but no relation. The one I know is living now in Chehalis. This Emily was his sister, William Harris's sister. He's about the same age as me. We were at school together anyway.

WELLS: Well, I'll have to talk to him some time, because the priest down at Westminster asked me to find out any information I could about this Emily.

•

WELLS: Where the old church is at Cheam, that's quite high, maybe thirty feet above the river, isn't it?

EDWARDS: Oh, well, all of that. The original village here in Cheam there was down on the lowland, what we call the bottom land. It was my old folks, the people that brought me up, they were the first ones to move up the hill. They were up on the hill already when the missionaries came.

WELLS: The river hadn't cut in so close on the old graveyard at that time, eh?

EDWARDS: Oh, no. This low land extended way out, covering that island, what is Park Island now. That was all mainland.

WELLS: And the Pilalt people, where did they do their hunting, the early people?

EDWARDS: Mostly on the Mount Cheam, I guess. They climbed the Mount Cheam to pick these blue huckleberries about the latter part of September and October. Yeah, that's where they used to get the wild goats.

WELLS: I have a goat hair blanket upstairs. I'm going to slip up and bring it down to you.

EDWARDS: I never saw one. The wool of the wild goats made the most expensive blankets, and the cheaper blanket they made it out of—well, they had a breed of dogs that was very woolly, so they shore them in the springtime, and they made cheaper blankets out of them. But the wild goat wool was the most expensive.

WELLS: Last year I was able to get some goat hair from the game wardens. Some goats were confiscated that were shot illegally up at Hedley, and Mrs Cooper found out about it, and so we were able to get these goats. And then Mrs Edmond Lorenzetto made this for me. And it's the same weave—see this, the old blanket weave? Now, then, this is an old goat hair blanket, likely a hundred years old. This is just a piece off the corner.

EDWARDS: Yes, this would be the first one I've ever seen. I've heard of them, but I've never seen one.

WELLS: This blanket was owned by Mrs August Jim, and she got it from her uncle; so it must be pretty old. And I managed to get it when their house was torn down. Why, it was thrown out, and somebody got ahold of it, and they took it home, and he had it in the garage under his car. And she told me I could have it for the Museum if I could get it, and I went to see this man and told him what I wanted it for. And I brought it home and washed it up, and I cut this off the corner that was all ragged. But we got about six feet square in the Museum in Chilliwack, so it'll always be there.

EDWARDS: Yes.

WELLS: But I kept this so I could—if I could find somebody to make one, they would get the weave, the same weave. And Mrs Lorenzetto, she did a good job there.

Goat hair blanket, 1830, donated by Mrs August Jim to the Chilliwack Museum.

EDWARDS: Oh, yes, yes. I hear that Mrs Gordon James is a good weaver.

WELLS: She's doing mostly spinning now. And making sweaters. She made the best sweater I sent East. And she spun the wool for this blanket, saddle-blanket. Now I had Mrs Peters, Edmund Joe Peters, she made this, on an old loom. The wool was spun by Mrs Gordon James—like, we paid her to spin the wool because Mrs Peters couldn't spin it. Her thing was broken. But this is dyed wool, which I dyed for her, and she worked in. But that's nice work, eh?

EDWARDS: Yes, you bet. Commercial wool?

WELLS: No, this is home-spun. I'm hopeful that we'll get quite a few people doing things like this again. It's too bad they ever stopped. I've been trying to find somebody that knows how to make string from grass like the old people did, you know. And there's string in the base of this, you see; I made this just twisting grass. I made enough for this, and she made some. But do you know anybody that knows how to make string from—?

Martha James of the Skwah Reserve, with the sweater she made for the "Indian Crafts To-day" Competition in Ottawa, May 1964.

EDWARDS: No.

WELLS: Nobody seems to know, and I can't even be sure to get the right grass any more.

EDWARDS: I understand that the people used to get the material from up country somewhere for making their fish-nets.

WELLS: Yeah, well, Mrs Cooper, when I went up with her I got some. It's the bark off a bush. They call it "Indian hemp," I think.

EDWARDS: I never saw the material myself, but I heard they used to get it up country. They called it méthelh.

WELLS: Mrs Cooper has that same word. I've got a few pieces of it down here; it stands about this high, and it's kind of a bush. They get the bark off it.

EDWARDS: Yeah, I'll be learning things from you that I never heard before. (*Laughs.*)

WELLS: For two or three years I've been working at this, you know. And I keep going back and getting older books all the time. And I've got some of the material which they got when they first come to the Indians. I sent to the British Museum, and I got pictures of the old blankets which the Hudson Bay people got, and they're really good, you know. It's amazing that the Indian people themselves, they don't know that they made these nice things.

EDWARDS: Yes, yes.

WELLS: When I went to visit Mrs August Jim, I made some tape recordings, and, well, we took her a little fruit or something, you know; and about the third time I was there she reached underneath the bed, and she pulled out a basket and in this basket she has several tump-lines. And she wanted to give me one; and I wouldn't take it for nothing, because she let me pick the one I wanted, and I gave her a couple of dollars for it or something. And then I went back afterwards and I bought two more from her because I wanted to make sure that I could get them into the Museum where they would be safe, like, you see. Because nobody knows anything about these any more.

Mrs August Jim carrying a basket by means of a tump-line.

EDWARDS: Pack straps.

WELLS: Yeah. She said this was a Lillooet design. It was not her design, but she made it. She made this about twenty-five years ago now. Isn't that nice?

EDWARDS: Yes, yes. It's a long time since I saw one.

WELLS: Mrs Bob Joe, she's the first one I've been able to get to make one; and she's making one today. She's working on it today. I took one of these up for her to look at, and she told me today the string I took wasn't right. This string was hop string that they'd used. She's got string they use for a fishing line. It's a little heavy, but it's doing the job.

EDWARDS: Yes, yes.

WELLS: In some of this stuff I was reading, there was an old chief at Yale. He was ninety years old a hundred years ago in 1858. This Jason Allard knew him as Taltalwheetza. You never heard of him, eh?

EDWARDS: Why, I would have; but then, you see, I don't remember these names any more.

WELLS: This old chief told him about the really bad winters they had before. It was so cold for so long that the deer come right down for food, and they found out it was warm on top of the keekwilee homes, and they would get right over top of 'em.

EDWARDS: Well, well. They call those keekwilee homes in the Indian language sqémél.

WELLS: You haven't got any chance of making some—? I've got Bob Joe making a long house now, just making it to scale, like, stand about this high, like. And he's making it out of split cedar stuff. An old legendary house up near Soowahlie was supposed to have the roof coming in this way instead of this way. They took the water out on a log, and caught it at the end. It's written in this book here; Wilson Duff, he and some other people too, they have stories of it from the Indians. So I asked Bob Joe if he would make it for me, and he's got it about half done. I thought if I could get it made it would be a good museum piece, like.

EDWARDS: Yes. I was wishing I'd get some of that Indian lumber. They had some for their drying sheds, you know. But then the old people'd get out of kindling, you know, they'd chop it up. I wished I had kept some.

•

WELLS: I've got notes here that I took from Simon Fraser's Journal,[2] and he was below Hope on the June 29th. He said: "The Indians in this quarter are fairer than those in the interior"—skin lighter complexion. And this is before the coming of the Whites at all, 1808. That's thirty years before there were any Whites in the country.

EDWARDS: Course, the interior people, they lived in the warmer drier climate, you know.

WELLS: Yeah. "Their skin and hair has a little reddish cast to it." You still see it some too, eh?

EDWARDS: I think so. They had a few real red-headed, even before the Whites came. I remember seeing one. They called him by his red head, Sísx̲eqw.

WELLS: Well, this Simon Fraser he refers to the rugs made of dog hair: "They have strips of different color crossing at right angles resembling that of a Scottish plaid." Well, the next day, on June 30th at eleven o'clock in the morning, he stopped "at a camp of four hundred souls." And at two o'clock in the afternoon, Indians who conducted him in the morning, they went back home again, and he "had to go get others with difficulty." They didn't want to go out on the coast, you know. And then he said: "After nine miles the river expanded into a lake, and here we saw seals and a large river coming in from the left, and a round Mountain ahead, which the natives called Shemotch."

EDWARDS: It's what they called Sumas. The Indian name was Sumáth.

WELLS: Yeah, good. And at that time apparently the ocean seals come up that far up the river.

EDWARDS: Well, the tidal waters came up there that far.

WELLS: Yeah, and at that time the river was just spread right out into Sumas Lake, I guess, in the spring. This was June, you see, end of June.

EDWARDS: Oh, yes, yes. I remember the time when the Sumas was all water.

WELLS: Yeah, well, even in my days—I think it was 1927 they dyked it.

EDWARDS: '22.

WELLS: '22? I was just thirteen years old then, but I can still remember. I went down there hunting one time with Carl Wilson; he was a couple of years older. When we went out from where Yarrow is, we were on the mud flats right away, and there was a lot of mud, and then the lake was out beyond.

Simon Fraser, he talks about these long houses, and they were sure long. On July the 1st they got going at four o'clock in the morning and at eight o'clock they arrived "at a large village." Now this'll be below Sumas.

EDWARDS: It might have been Matsqui. Máthexwi.

WELLS: Matsqui? Yeah. Do you know what the word means? I found out somewhere. It means: "Easy portage." And it meant that the Matsqui Indians could go into the Sumas or over into the Nooksack with the easy portage of the canoes at the head of the water courses, like. I found out that somewhere. But Simon Fraser said these houses of cedar planks, "the whole range is 640 feet long and sixty feet broad under one roof."

EDWARDS: That's a large house.

WELLS: Yeah, isn't it? And when they got down to Musqueam they were longer. And he wouldn't—these explorers, they were trained men, like. He wouldn't make any mistake in it.

EDWARDS: No, no.

WELLS: He said, "All the apartments, which are separated by partitions, are square, excepting the chief's which is ninety feet long. In this room the posts or pillars are nearly three feet in diameter at the base. In one of the posts is an oval opening answering for the purpose of a door through which to crawl in and out. Above, on the opposite side, are carved a human figure as large as life, and there are other figures imitating the beasts and the birds."

EDWARDS: Yes. That reminds me of the tribe too that was over on the Agassiz side, they were building a large house, too; and they got into some kind of a quarrel there. One party was always moving their posts. Well, the other party,

---

[2]Oliver is using notes that he made from *The Letters and Journals of Simon Fraser 1806-1808* edited by W. Kaye Lamb (Toronto: Macmillan 1960) pp. 101-104.

the other party'd move it back again. So they split up, they split up without going into a fight you know; they just split up. Part of them went up to Ohamil, and the other party moved over to what you call Cheam now.

WELLS: You were mentioning there—and I wanted to get it on the tape—about when they had the dredge, the drag lines there, digging for the railroad or the bridge, they came to timber down deep under the level of the land. That was just where the bridge crosses, is it?

EDWARDS: Not far from there. Timber. Been buried there for thousands of years, I suppose. There must have been some terrible eruptions, you know, in those times, because there were rocks there, rocks and timber, and places that had blue clay.

WELLS: Even at that depth, eh?

EDWARDS: Yes, it'd be about thirty feet from the top of the bank.

WELLS: Yeah, the old Fraser River sure changed its course a lot in that period of time. Takes away the land and sometimes builds it back; but mostly just takes it away.

EDWARDS: Yes.

WELLS: But did the Cheam people have an emblem? Like the Chilliwack people, I think, had the bear and maybe the beaver as family emblems. Did the Cheam people have a family emblem?

EDWARDS: Not that I know.

WELLS: According to some of these early writers, in these long houses each family marked his utensils with his emblem. If it was a bear, why, he'd maybe carve a bear's head on the handles and on the post.

EDWARDS: Well, I may have heard of that, you know, but I guess I've forgotten.

WELLS: Yeah, one of the things I like about interviewing you people that are Native people, if you don't know, why, you say you don't know; and you don't try to make a story out of something that you're not sure is true. That's very important, you know. I don't think our race is quite so good at that. They like to always be making the explanation.

EDWARDS: Add a little extra.

WELLS: Do you remember that in the days of the Hudson Bay people there was a man at Hope and maybe Yale by the name of Jason Allard?

EDWARDS: Allard. I've heard of him. I knew the man too, I think. He lived at Fort Langley.

WELLS: Yeah, that's right. Well, now, in some of the material that he wrote he spoke about an Indian prophet that used to be in the Hope area. "His teachings were a mixture of the Christian doctrine and Indian mythology and common sense. He had a strange parchment which he had found in a cairn on top of a mountain back of the Katz Landing." And Jason noted down a number of the prophet's sayings: "Indolence is the cause of a great many evils." "Do not be called a thief." "In accepting gifts from neighbors, exchange the gift with profit." "Be kind to the aged and those beneath you." "The Indian prophet was one of the finest Indians I have ever met," Jason stated. "He and his wife would bend down their heads to thank nature for the food they were about to consume." Have you ever heard of this Indian prophet?[3]

EDWARDS: No. No, I never.

WELLS: You see, he must have been ahead of the Hudson Bay people even. It's strange.

EDWARDS: Oh, yes, yes. Course, there's lots of things I don't remember, you know, a lot of things that I've heard that I've forgotten all about altogether.

WELLS: Yeah. Well, this has been—I appreciate having you come down and having this talk with you today, because there are not many people have been interviewed that are living among the Pilalt people, like. There hasn't been too much recorded on this. And with what information I've got from you, I think I can build up an area to show where the people lived. And I want to do the same for the Pilalt people as I did for the Chilliwack, and then the Tait people further up. And Sumas on this side. I haven't got much on the Sumas people yet, but I think there could be some quite good material got. And the Chehalis people are a little

---

[3]Jason Allard's recollections of the prophet are recorded by B.A. McKelvie in "Jason Allard: Fur Trader, Prince, & Gentleman" *B.C. Historical Quarterly* IX (October 1945) 250-251:

> Another recollection of those days was of Quitz-ka-nums, the Indian prophet. This Indian aroused a great spiritual revival among the natives along the Fraser. His teachings were a mixture of Christian doctrines, Indian mythology, and common sense. He had a strange parchment which he said he had found in a cairn on top of a mountain back of Katz Landing. Jason noted down a number of the prophet's sayings:—
>
> "Indolence is the cause of a great many evils."
>
> "Do not be called a thief."
>
> "In accepting gifts from neighbours exchange the gift with profit."
>
> "Be kind to the aged and those beneath you."
>
> "The Indian prophet was one of the finest Indians I ever met," Jason stated. "I will say of him that he was an intelligent man among his people. He was also a weather prophet. He had four wives. He and his wives would bend down their heads to thank Nature for the food they were about to consume. The parchment he had with Jewish (?) writing or heiroglyphics was picked up by him on the mountain back of Katz Landing near Hope.
>
> "When Father Fouquet, O.M.I., pioneer missionary, came on the scene he asked to see the parchment. He spat on it and cast it into the fire and told the men he was an imposter. Insulted by Father Fouquet and loss of his favourite wife, who eloped with a white man, was more than he could bear. He wasted away in distress, refused to eat and died."

off by themselves. If I can get this finished, and if it's so that the Indians are glad to have it done, why, after that maybe I can get the Chehalis people and the Lillooet. But the Chehalis people really belong to the Stalo tribes, don't they? And the Lillooet really belong to the Interior?

EDWARDS: Yes. From Port Douglas up they have their own language.

WELLS: And the people out at Mount Currie, Pemberton, do they talk our Halkomelem language?

EDWARDS: No, we can't understand. They have a different language altogether.

•

WELLS: Mr Edwards, you were just mentioning that you might be able to tell me some of the—one of the stories the older folks used to tell to their children.

EDWARDS: Yes, kind of come to my mind here, couple of—well, one story.

[MR MAGPIE AND MR CROW]

Mr Magpie and Mr Crow were neighbors. Well, Mr Magpie—well, the Indian word of that Magpie is Ál'al. They were neighbors, and they both had families. So Mr Magpie thought he'd go out for a hunt, took his little lunch with him, and his bows and arrows. Going along the foothills, going along the foothills, you know, just before you start to climb, he saw a deer rolling down, tumbling down. It landed on the flat ground, you know, and he went up to it with—his intention was to pull the arrows out carefully. He didn't want to break them. After he got them all out he set them on the ground, waited there for the hunter. Course, I don't know if he had a pack of cigarettes or something to pass away his time. But anyway he waited till the hunter came along. The hunter, seeing his arrows there were carefully put away, none of them broken, "Well, my friend," he says, "my friend, you can carry away the deer; take it home to your family. Seeing you were very careful with my arrows, you pack it up and get going." Well, Mr Magpie thanked him for it. The hunter told him: "It'll be light, it'll be light in beginning your journey, until you get pretty near home, and then it will begin to get heavy. You'll just barely get home," he said. "The weight'll be so heavy you'll just barely get home." And true enough, it was light when he started, but as he was getting pretty near home, you see, it begin to get heavy, heavier. He laid it down outside of his house, went in and told his wife about it, wife and children. They went out, you know, and saw the deer there. The wife got busy; butchered it up, cooked, had a good meal.

Well, Mr Crow seen that, you know; so he made up his mind he'd go hunting. Well, he go'ed along, walking along the foothills, you know; he seen a deer tumbling down. Now he went up to it, you know. You see, I don't know what kind of words he used, you know. He was displeased over this hunter, you know, getting ahead of him. He pulled the arrows out; he didn't care whether he broke them or not. Mr Crow was a rough-neck, you know; he wasn't very respectable, like. Well, anyway the hunter got down. He seen his arrows; they wasn't in very good shape. Anyway, he told Mr Crow he could take home that deer for your family. "At the beginning of your journey," he says, "home, it'll be heavy; it'll be heavy. But as you're getting nearer home, it'll keep getting lighter; till you get towards your house, it'll be no weight at all." Sure enough, he got to his house, threw it down, went in, told his wife about it, wife and children. They came out, looked around. They couldn't find no deer, see. She went inside, told Mr Crow about it. He came out, and all he could find, you know, was a pile of dead bark that he was carrying.

So the moral of that, you know, was, the old people told—well, you see, Mr Magpie, he was respectful, good-hearted; he respected his neighbors. He was very gentle. Mr Crow got punished for that, see; he was rough. He had no respect for other people. His pack here had turned into dead bark instead of deer meat. That was the end of that story.

9. Mrs Amy Cooper—II

Mrs Amy Cooper at Soowahlie, 24 November 1964

WELLS: There were quite a number of things I wanted to ask you today, and most of them were about the bridge and maybe Captain John and some of the old-timers. But someone mentioned the other day that there was a possibility that sometime soon they might try to rebuild one of their keekwilee homes that used to be at Soowahlie. They're located just beyond the church there, were they?

MRS COOPER: Yes.

WELLS: And these trees that are growing out of them now will have grown since they were used, I guess. I was there with John Wallace one day looking at these depressions near the church there, and one of these cedar trees that had been cut off, it has sixty rings. I think it's about sixty years old. Now, would that indicate some idea of how long since they were used?

MRS COOPER: It would be longer than that.

WELLS: What was the proper name in the Chilliwack language?

MRS. COOPER: Sqémél. "Keekwilee" is Chinook. My mother lived in one, and you know Mrs August Jim says she lived in one.

WELLS: Yeah, I remember she said so.

MRS COOPER: Mom says there used to be about thirty in one. That's all around. Then this pole right in the centre, and the pole was grooved in where your toes went in. You could climb up like cats. That's what she used to tell us.

WELLS: Well, I wonder who knows how to build one.

MRS COOPER: Oh no, there wouldn't be any. I don't think that Mrs August Jim would even know. But mother says there they used to lay on the bed there, and look up at the sky; and then when you couldn't see the sky, the firelights there would shine up on top there, and she says you could follow the way the timber is by just looking up there. And every morning, rain, shine, it doesn't matter what kind of weather it was, there was an old man there, the oldest man that was there, he had a vine maple switch. If you didn't get up and go out and get your bath... This vine maple switch was put over the fire, and it softened it, and that's what you got whipped with. And mother says there they ran up that ladder there like cats.

Soowahlie Band restoring a keekwilee pit house.

WELLS: Well, that's very similar to what old Dan Milo told me about when he was a boy. Even in later years, why, he still had to go and take a dip in Scowkale every morning.

MRS COOPER: Did John Wallace ever tell you the old man would take them down when the northeast was blowing? We had colder winters than we have now. When they got up and shook their hair there it was wrapped in icicles.

WELLS: Is that right?

MRS COOPER: I used to wonder if those kids there were going to get sick. They never got sick.

WELLS: No. Well, that's pretty good.

MRS COOPER: Oh, and then about these houses, those keekwilee houses right there, there's more than one up at Soowahlie there.

WELLS: Yeah, there seems to be four or five and maybe more there. John Wallace told me about quite a large one that, when his folks moved from the flat and moved over near Sweltzer Creek there, why, he said there was a large hole there that as a boy he used to slide down into it, and he took me and showed me where it is.

MRS COOPER: In where Sam's living now?

WELLS: Yeah, close to there. Between him and the stream there.

MRS COOPER: Well, that was one. That was one. Those people never associated with the Soowahlies.

WELLS: Is that right?

MRS COOPER: Yeah. They were Swí:lhcha. That's the name of the Lake, Swí:lhcha. They were separate people. There was a line there that they couldn't cross. And these people never talked to them. They never talked to these people. Not unless they had to. And you couldn't go and hunt on their side, and they couldn't hunt on your side.

WELLS: They would use Cultus Lake more, then, than the Soowahlie people, eh?

MRS COOPER: They kept to themselves, and there's very few of them left that belong there. They could just name, say, about three, I guess. Two or three. They weren't sociable people.

WELLS: When this Captain Wilson came into the valley on the Survey work, he describes riding over across the valley about where Andy's living now; he rode through the old trail they had—I imagine it would have been an Indian trail. And then he went on up to Cultus Lake or "Schweltza" Lake, and then they took a boat from there across to the Boundary Line where the party was. But he mentions the Indians as the Indians of "Schweltza." Now that would be these Indians living closer to the Lake, would it?

MRS COOPER: I don't know if they were known much, much around there, unless he just got them mixed up. See, the band there of Soowahlie is different from the Sweltzer. They were different people altogether.

WELLS: Yes, I see, yeah. He mentions this tribe having these little wild dogs, which they used to...

MRS COOPER: Make blankets with, yeah.

WELLS: As he describes them, the dogs were almost like a coyote. Now any other Indian blankets on the coast out further, they'd always describe the dogs as little white dogs; but the dogs at Sweltzer were different, or at Soowahlie.

MRS COOPER: Well, Mrs Catholic Tommy, Billy Sepass's sister, told me that they were grey. Grey with black in them. And then she told me there how she had to pluck them.

WELLS: Is that right?

MRS COOPER: Yeah, in the spring, you know, when they begin to molt, take off their winter wool? Well, they just knew what time. And she says that every time, she says, you pulled one, poor little doggy there would "week, week, week"; and then she says that she'd sing along with the dog there, she says. I don't know why I used to ask her all these questions!

WELLS: Yeah, well, it's a good thing you did.

MRS COOPER: You had to be a well-to-do person to own a dog in those days. Why I don't know, because I asked her why. She said it was just the rich people that owned them. And then they used them for blankets, and they used them for this little mat that they used around their body, in the front and the back.

WELLS: You told me the name of that the other day, I think.

MRS COOPER: Sthíyép.

WELLS: Is that like a little apron, was it?

MRS COOPER: Yeah, just like a little apron. And some wore it just in front; the higher class wore it on the back. And she says there those were long ones that went right under the body there, and went right through the belt again, you see, then flopped down in front, and flopped at the back

WELLS: And they were made from dog hair?

MRS COOPER: Yeah, they were made from dog hair. And others used this bulrush.

WELLS: To make the same garment?

MRS COOPER: Well, they made them in sort of a little skirt, from the belt almost to the knees.

WELLS: The early Chilliwacks, did they also use the skins of animals, like the little mountain beaver?

MRS COOPER: Oh, I think they used the small hide there for the children in the p'óth'es. Do you know what p'óth'es is?

WELLS: No.

MRS COOPER: Baby basket. I thought you knew that.

•

WELLS: I think you told me one time that the Indians, some of the Cultus Lake or Soowahlie Indians, were sun-worshippers originally?

MRS COOPER: Oh, yes.

WELLS: What is their name for their god, you might say. Was it something like "Khals"? What did he represent? Was the sun actually worshipped as the sun, like, was it?

MRS COOPER: Oh, yes. Everything there that they worshipped there, like their sun god, you see, that came to them as they were growing up. When they were always by themselves they'd go out in the woods and live by themselves for months, and they had nobody else but their god to live with, the spirit; because they say that there's three things, and one is the spirit, and the other is yourself, and the other is your shadow. Did you ever hear that?

WELLS: Well, that has some relation to what they think of death, doesn't it?

MRS COOPER: Yes. And they say those two that goes with you—the spirit that goes around with you that they go out and find, that finds them, that they meet, and they find one another, and then that goes to your body, to your mind, and it's always with you, and the thing that you can't lose is your shadow. The shadow has a lot to do with it too. It's very interesting to hear them tell it there. I can't tell it like how they tell it. But I used to sit there and listen to them. In Captain John's days there, there was always old people visiting him, and they'd start in about three o'clock, just when your sleep is good there, and you'd hear them talk and talk. And when you get up, they're asleep. But it was worth it if you knew that you had to, should listen there; it was worth listening to. Well, I used to wish them to shut up, but they wouldn't shut up, so you had to listen until you fell asleep again.

WELLS: You mentioned this little fish-weir that you made for catching trout.

MRS COOPER: What do you call them? Weirs? They were called kw'et'óxwel.

WELLS: And that was when they were made out of the hazel bush?

MRS COOPER: Yeah. They were made to catch the trout drifting downstream. They even knew what time the fish or the trout went up, and they knew what time it'll go back. Now, when I lived up there, at Soowahlie there, the fish would come up at night there. Whether they'd go to sleep or not I don't know, but they'd all quieten down and disappear. They'd all drift down again.

WELLS: Yeah, well, I've watched the salmon in front of our place in the Luckakuck. And we always had what they called "the deep hole." You remember where the Indians used to come to fish there?

MRS COOPER: Yeah, yeah.

WELLS: And at night they would run up from there on to the shallows about in front of our house, and they would be spawning in the night; but in the daytime the next morning they would drift back into the "deep hole" and wait for the night again.

MRS COOPER: Go to sleep.

WELLS: Yeah. Apparently the trout—would this weir be set in the spring? Likely at their spawning time?

MRS COOPER: Yeah, in the spring. Some of the boys went fishing there, and they went and told Mrs Willie Dick there that it was time to get out with the net or whatever you call it, the trout trap.

WELLS: Can you remember Mrs Willile Dick's Indian name?

MRS COOPER: She had an Indian name, and everybody knows it. All you've got to say is Kwóxwílhò:t, and everybody knows who you're talking about.

WELLS: Do you know what it means?

MRS COOPER: No, I don't, but all children, when they were small, if they got mad at the other one, they'd say, "Oh, you're Kwóxwílhò:t." (*Laughs.*) Nobody wanted to be called Kwóxwílhò:t.

WELLS: It would be interesting to know what the meaning of the word is.

MRS COOPER: No, I don't know the meaning; but when she was named that, they made a very big thing out of it. They lived at Katz, you see, and there's no road there, and so they made this time in one of those big long-houses over at Ohamil. And they had hundreds and hundreds of people there, when she came of age there, and she was named Kwóxwílhò:t. So that name was a big name. She didn't get that name for nothing there. Her father and mother gave away a lot of things for that. Big potlatch, when she was called Kwóxwílhò:t.

WELLS: That's very interesting. We read about these things in the early research work, like, and you get the general idea of 'em; but it makes it much closer to the Chilliwack people if you know certain people that it actually happened to them, like. I wanted to ask you more about the potlatch...

MRS COOPER: Well, I went to one in Deroche, and the Soowahlies were called, and I went.

WELLS: You had to have an invitation?

MRS COOPER: Oh yes, a special invitation, a party that went right up there and invited you, you know, and he went from house to house there. And we got down to Catholic Tommy's there—we would call that Sumas Landing. We got down there, and they put their horses out in old Catholic Tommy's field. There was quite a bunch of us, and how were we going to get across? All the canoes were taken across, the small canoes. Old Catholic Tommy, he says, "Well," he says, "here we use our big canoe." And that was a great big canoe, and you sat down as you're sitting down on a chair, and your feet almost dragged down to the bottom of the canoe. There were six of us that sat with ease on one seat, it was that big, that wide.

WELLS: Where was this canoe made?

MRS COOPER: I don't know where old Tommy got it from, but he had it. And we went across. And we got out from the slough there where he had it, where we all got in, and there was a knot-hole out.

WELLS: Oh?

MRS COOPER: We were almost to the Fraser when we found out the water was coming in. And Mrs Willie Dick there tore off her underskirt there, and she just tore them in lengths and filled that hole up, that knot-hole, just as we were going. Anyway we got across.

WELLS: Can you give me Catholic Tommy's name, his Indian name?

MRS COOPER: Thetá<u>x</u>. Well, we got across, and from there there was wagons there waiting over at Deroche. And we went up there, and this was a great big barn, and all round the edge there was hay, and each one had so much space as theirs. And they had beef there, and they had fish there, and they had everything you could think of. We must have cleaned out a store of all the goods there that they bought out of there. You didn't starve anyway. And you just laid there, the blankets over you, and had a good sound sleep there, and the fire going there at your feet, you know. This was in the winter, but there was no snow. And then on the last day, this is the potlatch now, the last day, where they got up on top of the roof there, and here was these pile of blankets. And they had to know how to throw it. And when they threw it, the blanket just sailed along, and you grabbed it. If you grabbed one, you could run with it and keep folding it up. But if you let it drag there, somebody could go there and just slice your blanket right in two. (*Laughs.*) What they want with half a blanket I don't know.

WELLS: Most of the gifts were blankets, were they?

MRS COOPER: Oh yes, yes. Oh, there was a lot of things there to exchange there. They'd go and give the dancer a stick, and when she got through dancing there, somebody would stand there, the announcer would announce what that stick meant. That stick meant maybe a horse, and this horse is to be given to a certain party. Well, maybe in that family there that this horse went to, well, maybe in time to come, maybe at the next big time there, an exchange, maybe give this other party a couple of cows or something like that, maybe it was a rifle or something like that. It was all in exchange, anyway.

WELLS: It's right up to the time of the White man's goods, fairly recent years. Was it Thompson Uslick put on the last potlatch at Tzeachten? Jack Stevenson and Clifford Pearson went to it one night.

MRS COOPER: I never was there when Clifford was there.

WELLS: Well, they would be just boys. They could hear it going on at Stevenson's, and so they rode across through Tzeachten on the trail, and they were stopped on the trail by the outposts. The guards were watching the trails. I think it was Thompson Uslick, and he got—it was after it was illegal—and he got thrown into jail for it afterwards.

•

WELLS: This old bridge picture we were looking at, I brought it along today for you to see again, and maybe you can tell me a little bit about how the Indians built it. Can you remember the Indians that worked on it?

MRS COOPER: Well, George Cooper and Harry Uslick and old man David were hewers.

WELLS: Who would be the overseer, like? Who would be in charge of the whole operation?

MRS COOPER: Well, I don't know. Those three men talked it over. Commodore did most of the teamwork. And August Sam and the one they call Jacob, they're brothers, they did all the climbing. And Commodore there with his team, as always he did the teamwork. And they hauled that poles down from Soowahlie there, drift it down the creek and down the river, down here, and the teams hauled it out. That was canoe work as well. And then when they worked at it, they started hauling the logs one by one, a short one that went so far, then the other one went on top of that, and that's how they'd build it, until they got to the long one, and they said that one was the dangerous one there in case it slipped after all their work. But they made it, and they put that long one right across, and then they put the planks on, and then they didn't really know how to make the framing. And then, I don't know whether it was the framing down at your place there that they copied.

A painting by A. L. Chambers of the first Vedder Bridge, built in 1891, almost entirely by local Native Indians.

WELLS: Yeah, well, just—I brought this picture up to show you today, and you can see by it that it's a similar type of framing on the bride that was put across the river at our place. Do you know what time this bridge was built across the river at our place?

MRS COOPER: I can remember as a child running over it.

WELLS: This picture is painted—it's dated 1907. But it would be maybe a few years old then. And the river at that time, by this picture it looks as if it was...

MRS COOPER: That's when that river went down around your place. It was after that the bridge was made there that it went down Sumas.

WELLS: I think it first went down there about 1873, and then I think in 1886 it was going both ways. I think it was 1887 that it came down to our place the first time. Do you think this bridge was built as early as that?

MRS COOPER: Must have been. And then it was quite a long time before they got the river road.

WELLS: Around the mountain.

MRS COOPER: Yeah, around the mountain, along the Sweltzer. And they had to do a lot of crib work there. The Indians did it all on their own. The Indian Department hardly did—if they did ask for help, all they got was $25.

WELLS: Captain John would be one of the ones most interested in getting this bridge constructed, I guess, according to Dan Milo.

MRS COOPER: Oh, yes. Yes. Oh, they worked together. Old Captain John was a real guy. Whatever he said there, it went. And if there was any trouble, he never put it in the police; he settled that out himself. Anything that went on he did it in such a nice way there you couldn't help but just do as he said.

WELLS: He did this as chief, like?

MRS COOPER: Yeah, as chief, and I think mostly as preaching.

WELLS: After he was converted to Crosby, why, he actually preached for Crosby, didn't he?

MRS COOPER: Oh yes. He used to go right up to Hope; and then he went across the Line there, he went across over to Goshen, any place, any church. As long as there was a United Church any place, he was there, always invited there to preach.

WELLS: At that time it would be the Methodists. You mentioned to me one day that some of the things he did, on the river, as a canoe man.

MRS COOPER: Well, that's how he got his name as "Captain" because, if anybody had to cross, he always depended on Captain John to get him over. That's how he got his name as "Captain."

WELLS: To get across the Chilliwack River here?

MRS COOPER: Yeah, or any place. They had a big sign on a cedar tree that used to grow there. They cut it down after Simpson there had that place. And they had a big sign there that if they wanted to cross there to get Captain John to cross them.

WELLS: There's one description, in Hudson Bay times, where the first American steamer was coming up the Fraser River, and it was the first steamer to go to Yale. They stopped at Fort Langley and asked for a pilot to take them up the river, and they gave them this Indian that was dressed in a blanket and barefoot. And he piloted them up to Yale alright. The ship got there, and that was the first steamer that had gone up the river. And when it come back, he said that he come back dressed in captain's uniform, and he was known as Captain John.

MRS COOPER: (*Laughs.*) I've never heard that.

WELLS: Do you think it would be the same man?

MRS COOPER: I don't know. I never heard that. Of course he didn't tell those things.

WELLS: This would be when he would be a comparatively young man. It would be about 1858.

MRS COOPER: You know he was a warrior in his teen age.

WELLS: He was, eh?

MRS COOPER: Yeah, went way out on the coast. He says he had two trips. After he was converted, he says, never again.

WELLS: Most of the warring was done the other way round. The coast people come in and raided the Chilliwack.

MRS COOPER: Yes, went right up there to Soowahlie. And Carl Wilson's was their lookout.

WELLS: The name of that point, Bob Joe calls it Steetahs.

MRS COOPER: Stiytós. Well, I knew that right there at the bridge is Stiytós. I didn't know that was the lookout though.

•

WELLS: You know, I found out recently, from the geological people, that during the ice age, the ice went out of the Chilliwack River before it went out of the Sumas valley. This happened as late as 5000 years ago. The Chilliwack River run through Cultus Lake and out into what is now the United States. It ran out that way. This may seem very strange, but it actually maybe is the background to some of the Indian legends.

MRS COOPER: Yes, I heard that. I heard that before.

WELLS: Where would you hear it from?

MRS COOPER: I heard it from the Indians talking. There was two Indians that came over from the American side, and there was one from Kilgard and there was Captain John; these four old men talked all night over that. They said it divided up somewhere in the States and came through Sumas prairie, out to the lake, and the other went down out to where that empties out at Bellingham, doesn't it?

WELLS: But there's some material which I read which indicates that at one time part of the Nooksack River came out through Sumas and went out with the Sumas River.

MRS COOPER: Well, yes, that was in what they were talking about, how everything has changed.

WELLS: Andy Commodore and I drove around, where that big maple flat is up there. Billy Sepass used to say he could show you the water line on the mountains on Cultus Lake. Well, Andy points to the rocks. He says, "Look, Oliver," he says, "that's water-washed rock, that's a river-washed rock right there, and how did the river ever run past this?" Well, I have maps now from the Geology Department and they show that all the soil around where Andy and I were, up there high, that soil was all put up there by the Chilliwack River. Apparently the river went out there at one time, likely when the ice give out. Some of the old history looks more real when you get the geology people to explain when the ice was retreating.

MRS COOPER: Harry Uslick used to say, if you look careful, he says, you could see where the avalanche came, he says, where it broke and came right down on the village. Well, there's another place up in Yale that was the same, and there was only one alive from that band of people; they happened to be all home but one when the avalanche came down there, and they all died. I heard Captain John tell that a lot of times; heard my grandmother Lorenzetto tell it. There'd be only one left.

WELLS: These legends are very interesting—this one you told me about when the menfolk went out to look for food, and they left the womenfolk, well, I got that story from Dan Milo, and this man Professor Hill-Tout he got it from Captain John about seventy-five years ago,[1] and old Dan Milo still tells it just the same as it was told then. And Professor Hill-Tout he didn't record the finishing of it, about when they went up near Ohamil, these birds stopped on an island, and the beaver come out, and the beaver said he would help them bring the sockeye, help them get food. And they went out, and they found the home of the sockeye and stole the baby, and brought it up the river. And Dan Milo gave me this story, which wasn't in the book. Then one of the Sepass poems, it's called "The Salmon Baby," it's almost exactly the same story as given by the Yale people, how when spring came the sockeye wasn't there, and they decided to go and find the sockeye, and the whole story is the same only the people in it are different. There's one legend—you may know this one too—about how the wren told the Chilliwack people how to build the cheeak, the fish-weir.

MRS COOPER: Sts'iyáq.

WELLS: Do you know that legend?

MRS COOPER: That bird's got a lot of stories. T'ámíya, the little wee one.

WELLS: Do you know any stories?

MRS COOPER: No, I don't know. But I know that was the one there that had it out with a spider there, that it could shoot up to the sun. They were all, all the animals and the insect, were planning how to reach the sun, just like everybody's planning to reach the moon today.

WELLS: Yeah. (*Laughs.*)

MRS COOPER: That was real good, but I don't know it. I didn't want to listen to it.

WELLS: No, these little wrens, these are very...

MRS COOPER: This little wren, they said that the little bird couldn't do it because she was so small. And she went straight up. But I don't know if she reached it. And then the spider says, "I can reach it." So the spider wove its web, and let the wind take it up, its web up. And in the summertime, you know, when you're looking at the sun there to see what time it is, you could see all this spider web in the air. So the spider waited for the wind to come, and then it went up on that. It went with the wind there, and then when it got to a certain place there, it would let its spider web down and catch hold of another one, and rest there, and go up. So I didn't find out who won, whether the bird won or whether the spider won. That was fables, and so I didn't pay much attention to it. But nighttime there, the old people they used to start telling the children that. They would tell stories till the kids went to sleep. They say that the Kilgard group had a lot of stories. At Kilgard they like mixing up together. All the young people'd go to one house, and they'd get the older one there to tell a story. And then they'd go to another house there the following night, and then they'd tell stories there. Whether they know stories now or not I don't know, but old Gus there, he knew the stories; and old Pete Silver he knew the stories.

The five generations of the Kelly family of Soowahlie. Francis Kelly is holding his great-great-grandson, David Kelly, born September 9, 1980. Behind them, left to right: Mike (David's great-grandfather), Marvin (father), Arthur (grandfather).

WELLS: What was Gus's other name?

MRS COOPER: They called him Commodore. He never did have a name.

WELLS: Who are the oldest people over there now?

MRS COOPER: Clarence Ned I guess'd be the oldest.

WELLS: The Kelly family's over there too, are they?

MRS COOPER: Francis got grandsons over there, Bob Kelly's children. Johnny Williams, that would be Mrs

[1]See Ralph Maud ed. *The Salish People: The Local Contribution of Charles Hill-Tout* (Vol. III The Mainland Halkomelem) Vancouver: Talon Books 1978, pp. 57-58. Norman Lerman collected four versions of this Coqualeetza story, from Bob Joe, Mrs Harry Uslick, Dan Milo, and Mrs Louis George. "This story appears to be restricted to the Chilliwack-Sardis area. . . . All the informants at Sardis related this tale first thus indicating that this was their most important folktale"—Lerman's M.A. thesis (1952) p. 166. Dan Milo tells it in interview #6 above, and Bob Joe in interview #10 below. Albert Louie refers to the story, connecting it to the discovery of the sxwó:yxwey mask, in the interview of 28 July 1965 (#14 below).

William Kelly's brother, just older than her, I think. Whether they got the stories or not I don't know.

WELLS: Well, I might try sometime. I was going down there to see if I could find any. I got a very nice story from the former Chief Edwards, up at Cheam. He told me the story of the Magpie and the Crow, and it had a moral to it at the end. But it was a very nice story, it was a nice kind of a bedtime story.

MRS COOPER: Uh-huh.

WELLS: And this legend about the fish going out to bring in the sockeye, I told that to my grandchildren, and they always want it again.

10. Bob Joe—III

Oliver Wells wrote the following thumb-nail sketch of Bob Joe for the Halkomelem *Vocabulary* pamphlet:

> Robert Joe was born at Tzeachten on December 16, 1884, and has lived there throughout his lifetime. It has been the home village of members of the tribe who are, like Bob, descendants of Wee-LAY-luq, one of the legendary heads of the Chilliwacks.
>
> Bob has always been a hale and hearty fellow well met. He has been a lover of sports, and did much to promote the game of soccer and other community projects. Few, except for his Native people who respect his knowledge, have known that Bob Joe is the historian of the Chilliwacks and has a knowledge of Sumas and Pilalt history.
>
> His formal schooling consisted of only three years at St Mary's Mission. He has since broadened his knowledge greatly by reading. He has a gift of language, whether speaking in his native tongue or in English. He was, as a young lad, interested in and mindful of the history of his people. His interest brought instruction from James Michell and other elders, who expressed to him the belief that some day people would ask him concerning their early history.
>
> During the past twenty-five years, Bob has been frequently interviewed by representatives of various universities and by research workers, who sought his knowledge of history. Wilson Duff of the Provincial Museum used Bob as an informant during the production of his *Upper Stalo Indians* publication. Bob has done much, likely more than any other, to preserve the history of the Native people. His knowledge is encyclopedic; his ability to translate English into Halkomelem is phenomenal.

Bob Joe died in Chilliwack Hospital 1 August 1970.

Bob Joe at Tzeachten, 5 December 1964, with Mrs Joe and Casey Wells present

WELLS: We come up today, Bob, to see if we could get you to give us some of the Chilliwack language. And I have a list of words here, and I want to ask you these different things. And we'll just take one at a time, and if you don't have it, well, we'll just go on to the next one. Have you got a word for "north"?

JOE: "North." Not "north" but just for the wind: sótets.

WELLS: That's "north wind"? How about the south wind?

JOE: It's schéxwem. No, that's west. West wind: schéxwem.

WELLS: Very good. Have you got a word for "the east"?

JOE: No, I don't recall any.

WELLS: O.K. And you wouldn't have them for NE or SW?

JOE: No. No.

WELLS: O.K. For the sky?

JOE: Swàyèl.

WELLS: For a cloud?

JOE: Shxw'áthetel, "cloud."

WELLS: And for the horizon?

JOE: It's practically the same word, swàyèl, te swàyèl. That covers the horizon of the face of the earth.

WELLS: The next word, Bob, is "snow." A word for snow?

JOE: Máqa.

WELLS: For hail?

JOE: Hail...?

WELLS: S'kohkwakawss...?

Bob Joe making a model of a long-house.

JOE: Skw'ekw'xwós... small little round, yes.

WELLS: You say it again, Bob, so we got it for sure.

JOE: Skw'ekw'xwós.

WELLS: O.K. The word for ice?

JOE: Spí:w.

WELLS: And the word for icicle?

JOE: Icicle? No, I don't recall that. There is a name for that.

WELLS: I think I can give you the word for "water" but I'm not sure: kaw?

JOE: Qá:, that's "water."

WELLS: Yeah, good. And waterfall?

JOE: The "fall" in the old translation of the Chilliwack language, that's "swirling waters." Swirling waters, or falling waters, qó: me chá:lq.

WELLS: How do you say it again?

JOE: Chá:lq qó:.

WELLS: Tsehlk, "fall," and then the word "kaw" that refers to the water.

JOE: Yeah. That's about as near as I can come to it.

WELLS: The word for rain?

JOE: Slheméxw.

WELLS: Thunder?

JOE: Shxwexwó:s.

WELLS: And in lots of the legends there's a Thunderbird. Do you know the name for that? Or do the Chilliwack people have that?

JOE: Now, Thunderbird, it's quite a bit of translation in that. Some thinks, you see, that the Thunderbird is a bird, and other thinks it's just something like a little animal. Some thinks, you see, that thunder is caused by a certain amount of atmosphere in the wind. When two currents meet, then you hear that noise. And another translation of it: there's a kind of a rock or stone or whatever it is. You'll notice on some trees where the thunder's struck, well, that comes around, and they's supposed to've dug that at the foot of the trees, and they come across with a large piece of plate lying in the ground. That's what caused the bark to fall off from this tree. And other times when that tree is struck, from the very top there's a split at the top of the tree caused by this here.

WELLS: Now, over on the Hope Slough there's a place over there, Mr Edwards says it was called—the name came from "cracked trees." I don't know whether you'd have that or not.

JOE: No.

WELLS: The word for thunder—you gave me that. Do you have a word for Thunderbird or not?

JOE: Well, the only name of that is shxwexwó:s.

WELLS: O.K. How about lightning?

JOE: I don't quite remember that word. The nearest you can come to "lightning," this x̱éléq't te shxwexwó:s—just like you're opening your eyes, that's the lightning.

WELLS: That's a hard one. But the idea is that you are opening your eyes, and that's just like the lightning flashing.

JOE: Yeah. Yeah, that causes the lightning.

WELLS: Do you think you're going to be able to say these words, Casey?

CASEY: Yeah.

WELLS: O.K. Mrs Cooper started to tell me about a story—I asked her some of these bedtime stories the Indians used to tell, you know. I asked her about this little wren called tammeeah. It's the winter wren, little fellow.

JOE: T'ámiya. Yeah, they're little birds, small ones.

WELLS: That sounds almost the same as Tamihi, doesn't it? Do you say it almost the same?

Casey Wells.

JOE: T'ámiya. T'amiyehá:y, that's Tamihi.

WELLS: It's almost the same with a "hi" on the end.

JOE: Almost the same. Just a little different.

WELLS: Well, she told me there's a little story about this little wren and the spider. The animals and birds were talking about who could go to the sun I think it was, or to the sky, just like the White people now are trying to get to the moon. But these two were trying to get to the sky, and the spider said he would try to beat the wren in a race to the sun. But she couldn't remember the story. Have you heard of that story?

JOE: No. I guess I didn't listen close enough.

WELLS: No, I guess these stories were in different families. They each had their own stories, eh?

JOE: Yeah. There is a story about that little wren. He was supposed to be a great hunter at that time.

CASEY: Mosquito—that's the name of that warrior at Kilgard.

JOE: Qwá:l. Yeah, an old warrior.

CASEY: Do you know any stories about him, Bob? I just heard a little of how he used to maybe lead a party down to pay these Cowichans back for what they did up here. I wonder if there's any stories about that.

JOE: Well, Qwá:l was a great warrior, and some of his descendants are still alive today. That's part of the Commodore family.

CASEY: Are they?

JOE: Yeah. During that time when they had some differences between tribes here and there, well, one time somewheres down around Comox, somewheres in there, a big house right close to the salt water, the sea, and well-fortified. And this Qwá:l and his army, if you call it, they couldn't get in. So they figured and figured, "How are we going to get in there?" At that time there was no shovels. Well, they started digging. And they're digging and they had to go three or four feet in the earth, gravel and everything. Well, this Qwá:l he went under that.

WELLS: He did, eh? They'd go right in and fight on the inside.

JOE: Now, when he come out there wasn't a scratch on him, but there was blood all over him. And another time—.

CASEY: (*Laughing.*) Gee, he was a real fighter.

JOE: Another time they went to another place, and they couldn't get into this fort. There was a great big cedar tree leaning right over this house. The roof was made out of logs, great big logs. And just like on a side hill, you know, there's a lot of rocks, they started throwing the rocks around right on the roof. And they started to chop, and they're hacking this tree. Well, when the rocks got so heavy on the roof it was about time for this big cedar tree to fall, well, Qwá:l he says, "If they're a woman or child, help them out. Don't hurt them. We're after the men." Well, when a man comes out, they got him by the hair or his head comes off. And every man that is supposed to be brave might have four or five heads, and another man there he couldn't do that. Well, one of the warriors there had half a dozen heads—he sneaks around and takes one head. (*Laughs.*)

WELLS: (*Laughing*) On the Prairies they scalped them, but here they took the head right off?

JOE: Yeah, they took the head off, yeah. There were times when they were coming back home some place on them islands, and there's young fir trees here on the shore; and tip the top of a tree and put the heads right on there, facing where the warriors came from, maybe fifty or sixty heads up on the top of the little trees.

WELLS: It'd be a tough-looking sight. The Hudson Bay people they described one of these raids that come up from the coast, they come up to raid the Chilliwacks or the Pilalt; and when they came back down the river they had a head on the top of the canoe, on the front of the canoe, somebody they killed. Well, that makes it interesting; we got a lot off that mosquito, Bob. (*Laughter.*)

CASEY: Maybe we'll get some more. Bob got some real old stories in him. How would they tell the people in the valley that there was strangers coming and they'd better be careful? Maybe the man up on Steetahs could see them coming, but the people there couldn't see them coming. Would he build a fire for smoke, or would he put a white...?

[WAR STORY]

JOE: Well, in one particular case there was over ten war canoes came, came up. And at this time, when the war canoes came in, there was heavy timber then, large cedar and fir trees. So those young boys or teenagers, they roamed from here to there, and they were down here by Kickbush, and they call them Sekw'sekw'emá:y, that's birch. And they had these big canoes, and about that time the river was low. Well, they couldn't come no further. Well, these teenagers they were hiding in the bank and watching. "Gees, they must come from quite a ways. We'll go up and tell our people." They beat it up, ran all the ways from there till they got to round the Vedder Crossing. They told about them. "Well, all right," he says, "you boys stay here." And they send older men down. "You go down," he says, "and I think they're up to some mischief. They're going to cause us trouble." They come down. I think there was ten canoes, large canoes. There'd be fifteen to twenty men in one canoe. They smashed all those canoes. And they must have left one smaller canoe further down the river. These young men didn't see that one. Well, when they got up here there was an awful slaughter, yeah. The ones that got away, they come down to where their canoe was. Everything was smashed. There was just a few of them got home in this small canoe. Well, they found them in a cedar tree, hollow cedar tree, four or five here, four or five there. And a mother there has a baby, and a string pole, and the baby in there. They wake up and there's a warrior from the coast there, treadling the baby. Well, they knock him on the head, and throw him in the river. Well, from that time on they never came back. It was a little too much for them.

WELLS: Yeah. Very good. We'd better go ahead with these words. A moth, has it got a name? Like a butterfly, only a moth instead.

JOE: A moth. Well, the nearest I come down to—some of them call that spopeleqwíth'a, "a little ghost."

WELLS: Oh, is that right? There'd be stories about it then?

JOE: Yeah, there's lots of stories about that. That's the moth, you see, the big ones and little ones.

WELLS: Snake? And are the snakes all the same—?

JOE: Álhqey. All the same word.

WELLS: Yeah, we just had small snakes here. Have you got the name for the rattlesnake? They don't have it in Chilliwack, eh?

The ceremonial bowl referred to as a rattlesnake bowl by Oliver Wells.

JOE: Not here. They have a name for it, but at that time, even now, there is no rattlesnakes around.

CASEY: Did they not trade with the Thompson Indians for rattlesnake poison sometimes?

JOE: Yes, rattlesnake poison was used by some tribes. They'd kill a snake, and take that stuff, and they'd just smear it on the end of an arrow. Well, when one is hit, the liquid that's dried or as soon as it gets in the arrow, it'd be the same effect as if the rattlesnake bit you. You'd swell.

WELLS: In the Museum we have a bowl which was picked up, I think it was picked up down near Matsqui somewhere, and it's a carved figure like, and then there's a snake on it, and this must be a rattlesnake because it's got the diamonds on it. And it's kind of round the edge of the bowl. And we wondered why this could be here in the low country because there's no rattlesnakes down here. Do you think there'd be any chance that they would use this bowl for a rattlesnake poison, and mark it that way?

JOE: It could be used for that. That could have been taken from the Interior.

WELLS: When they dipped these arrows in a bowl, they'd have to be pretty careful.

JOE: Oh, very careful. I don't know how they kept their poison when there was no bottle or cans. It could have been dried.

CASEY: I keep running Bob off the track here.

WELLS: That's O.K. The best time to get things is when you get a chance to get them.

•

WELLS: I got the names of the different salmon from you before, I think, the different fish. I'll try to—Casey, you come and try to say these.

CASEY: Yeah, check me out.

WELLS: And see if Bob can... You see, these up here are what we translated from Wilson Duff, and these here are what Bob Joe gave us last time. So that this is the spring salmon here, and this is what Bob give us last time.

CASEY: Skawkum.

WELLS: That's what you give us. Get this one for Bob now. What salmon is this, Bob? Skawkum.

JOE: Sth'óqwi?

WELLS: No, skawkum, skawkum. What's your word for spring salmon?

JOE: Tl'élxxel, spring salmon.

WELLS: What is it?

JOE: Tl'élxxel.

WELLS: What is your word for sockeye?

JOE: Sthéqi.

WELLS: For coho?

JOE: Kwőxweth, that's coho.

WELLS: O.K. Now, if it's any kind of salmon.

JOE: Sth'óqwi; sth'óqwi means salmon.

WELLS: O.K. And the word for—Casey, you try this one, the word for trout.

CASEY: Kwesits.

JOE: Qw'esíts.

WELLS: Casey had it just about right, eh?

JOE: Yeah, yeah.

WELLS: Very good. Wilson Duff has a word here for oolichans.

JOE: Swíwe, oolichans.

WELLS: On Sumas there used to be a great migration of fish come up the streams, and before the White people came the Indians went there in great numbers. I have a description, but this naturalist he called them "round fish."[1] What fish would this be?

JOE: Oh, that could be—I didn't know that they came up that way, but they went up other creeks—That could be q'óxel.

---

[1]Oliver typed out the following passage from J.K. Lord's *The Naturalist in British Columbia* (London 1866), one of his favourite books:

The Round Fish: (Coregonus quadrilaleralis)

One may journey a long way to witness a prettier or more picturesque sight than Round-fish harvesting on the Sumass prairie. The prairie bright and lovely, the grass fresh green and waving lazily, various wild flowers peeping

They come in schools. They are about that large, full of bones, small bones, q'óx̱el.

WELLS: That's likely the ones that they described. They went to camp beside the Sumas River in the days when they had slaves, and they said the slaves and everybody was there having a big time, throwing them out by the thousands.

Bob Joe at Ee-AY-thel on Chilliwack Lake Road.

JOE: Yeah, that's right. The q'óx̱el come up on the Sumas River and then up on the old Chilliwack River. They still come up yet.

WELLS: They're kind of a shiny colour when they first come up, are they?

JOE: Yeah.

WELLS: Just like silver, like. And kind of greenish on top. Yeah, well, I'd pick a few of those in the Luckakuck when I was trapping in the Luckakuck there.

JOE: Yeah, they come up there.

WELLS: Now, have you got a name for the cut-throat trout? That's the one with a orange gash on the both sides here. I got old Mrs August Jim up there, she gave me s'pawltsah.

JOE: If you mean them little trout that's supposed to hatch when the berry drops into the water, we call it sp'íp'ehath'. You know them little blue berries that grows over creeks, well, the berry's supposed when they drop into water they come to life as a little trout.

WELLS: O.K. And the word for sturgeon.

JOE: That's skwó:wech. You know, there's another fish—you know these lizards, water lizards, well, they turn into trout. Their fins, the arms of this water lizard—.

WELLS: It wouldn't be an eel, like eh?

JOE: No, it's not the eel. At times the fish forms in by the tail first, and the head is still animal or however you call it. Well, when you can see the head and the mouth of that little trout hasn't turned into a fish yet, it's not fit to eat. So we were told. (*Laughs.*)

WELLS: That's an old Indian belief?

JOE: Yeah, that's an old... yeah.

WELLS: O.K. Now I've got some birds here. What's the name for a bird, any bird?

JOE: Bird, mó:qw means the big bird, hemóqw means the small bird.

WELLS: And the raven—not the crow but the raven, the big fellow with whiskers underneath his chin.

JOE: There is a name for that, the raven...

WELLS: Do they have any legends about the raven? Up the coast they used it on their totems a lot, you know. But did the Chilliwack people have any stories about the raven, like, legendary stories?

JOE: Yeah, there is. There isn't one on that big black crow.

WELLS: Have you got the word for crow?

JOE: Spò:l.

WELLS: Mr Edwards, he gave me a nice little story about the Magpie and the Crow. The Magpie he looked after the arrow and didn't break it, and he kept it for the hunter. When the hunter come down he give him the arrow, and then the story is that he gave him the meat, I think, and he carried it home, and when he was starting out it didn't weigh very heavy, and he got home with it, and he had good meat. Well, the Crow come along and he did the same; but when the game come tumbling down he was mad at the hunter, and he broke the arrow. And so when the hunter come down he gave him meat, but by the time he got home it got lighter and lighter and lighter, and when he got home he took off his pack, and there was nothing but dried bark in it. Have you heard that story before?

JOE: Yeah, I heard it.

---

coyly out from their cosy hiding places, seem making the most of the summer a fresh, joyous hilarity everywhere, pervading even the Indians, whose lodges in great numbers lie scattered about. From the edges of the pine forest where the little streams come out from the dark shadow into the sunshine, up to the lake, the prairie was like a fair. Indians old and young, chiefs, braves, squaws, children, and slaves, were alike busy in capturing the round-fish, that were swarming up the streams in thousands, so thick were they that baits and traps were thrown aside and hands, baskets and little nets and wooden bowls did the work; it was only requisite to stand in the stream and bale out the fish. Thousands were drying—thousands had been eaten, and many more were wasting and decaying on the bank. Round-fish are cured by splitting and sun-drying precisely in the same manner as salmon.

[BLUEJAY STORY]

Well, there's another one. Now T'ámiya, this is that great hunter, the little wren. Now, the grandmother is Kwà:y. The hunter T'ámiya went out. He got a great big deer. The deer was fat. And the old grandmother she sure wanted some of that fat. Well, the hunter T'ámiya he goes and gets his knife and cuts a piece of the fat off and gives it to his grandmother. And she wants some more. Well, the hunter T'ámiya, he was getting tired of this, and he reaches back and got a bone, got a bone and put it in this fat, and gave it to his grandmother. And she got choked on that, choked on that, and finally that bone come out on top of the grandmother's head. See the little crown on the bluejay?

WELLS: The crown on the bluejay. O.K. (*Laughs.*) That's very nice. I like to get these little stories down. Some day I hope to get about twenty of them, and then I'll make a little book of them. And they're good little stories for children, you know.

[THE SOCKEYE LEGEND]

JOE: Yeah, there's quite a bit of story about the crow, the beaver, the seagull. Now, years ago there were salmon that come up on the Fraser, but no sockeye. Now this is supposed to've happened. They lived here around Th'ewáli [Soowahlie], around where that little church is there, a large village. About that time the river went this way, followed that. And going into Chilliwack here, there you notice a large ditch where you go over the dike.

CASEY: Yeah.

JOE: He put his trap in there. And the only thing he caught were bullheads. So the woman-folks living at home, they were almost starving. No salmon. Well, they got angry at their husbands. Just about that time a little boy thought about his mother. He took the salmon eggs and tied it on his legs, and he started to run up. When the boy got home, they asked him, "How is your father?" "Oh, they eat a lot of salmon down there." And they got in their canoes and they come down. And there were the pillows. They took with them all them, and with all those pillows were just clubs, sticks. And they got down there, and that's when the beaver, the seagull and other birds was transformed into birds or animals.

WELLS: I see, yeah.

JOE: So the beaver says, "We'll go down and get sthéqi that's supposed to be down here some place." Then they went down. And the woodpecker, one with the red head and the other one, well, they got up in the air and they started to fighting one another, just flying around, you know. And they'd get down on the ground, flop around. Now the parents of the sockeye, they come there and want to catch them. And one of them says, "Here," he says, "that one is sick." They looked at him, and "I know him," he says. "He's very tricky; he's foxy. He must be up here for some reason of some kind." Well, while they were talking like that, these two woodpeckers got up pretty close to them, and they started to follow these two birds. Just about that time, the beaver he looked around. He saw the baby there, baby sockeye. He picks him up and put it in his canoe. That's when the mice and the rat, they gnawed holes in their canoes. Well, when they come back, the baby sockeye is gone. And they gave chase to the beaver. The others, when they got their canoes in the water, the water filled up right in the canoe. And instead of the beaver using his paddle flatways, he had it in edgeways. Well then, the chum or dog-salmon hollered at him, "Use your paddle the other way; use it flat." Well, beaver he got his stroke then. They left it. Well, they come down to Kwíkwetl'em [Coquitlam]. They took one of the diapers off and chucked it overboard. And on the Harrison Mills, or Harrison River, right along, well, the diaper that they threw off on Harrison River was the one right next to the body of this baby sockeye. So if you had a sore on any part of your body, well, when the salmon came up there first, then, if you wet that, that sore or whatever would get worse. Well, they kept a-going. They got up to Yale. And they threw the baby overboard there, and as soon as it touched the water, you see the tail of the sockeye there.

WELLS: I see. Very good.

JOE: That's a part of the story. It's a long story.

WELLS: I often wondered why that channel was dug there just the other side of the dike. The beaver dug it.

JOE: The beaver done that.

WELLS: What did they call what we call the diapers for the

baby, what did the Indians call it?
JOE: Sqelá:lh, sqelá:lh.
WELLS: Is it made out of cedar bark or moss?
JOE: Made out of cedar bark or nettles bark.
WELLS: Oh, is that right?
JOE: They take these nettles, and they maul it out just as fine as anything.
WELLS: Yeah. I've got a lot of nettles put away at home, hoping to find somebody that could work them into fibre.
JOE: Yeah, that was made for clothes also, where the main party of the family wasn't a very good hunter, see. The hunters they made their clothes out of bear fur or whatever.
WELLS: Skins. Very good. One story sometimes brings another. (*Laughter.*) I think there's lots of stories about those little owls, we call it the pygmy owl. Have you got a name for that?
JOE: There's just one name really: spòpeleqwíth'a, that's "small ghost."
WELLS: Small ghost? I'm glad to get that name of the pygmy owl. Over where Unsworth lives, they dug up quite a few things on the Unsworth farm; and one of the things they dug up was a bowl, and the outside is shaped just like a pygmy owl. It's an owl-bowl, like; two big round eyes in front, and the beak, and the wings on the side, and then the tail kind of hangs down. And I just wondered what—that must have been the Chilliwacks...?
JOE: Yes, it must have been the Chilliwack.
WELLS: Well, shall I go ahead with another shot of these words? If you say that they sang a song, have you got a word for a song?
JOE: St'ílém is "song," and t'ít'elem is "singing."
WELLS: O.K. Have you got a word for dance?
JOE: Qw'yélex.
WELLS: And a word for mask, any mask?

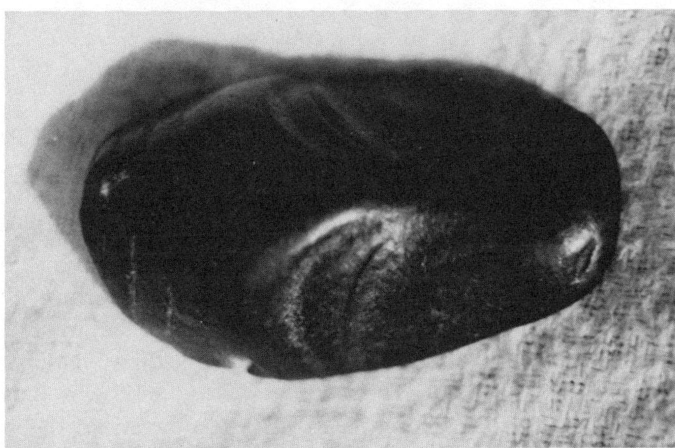

The "mask" owned by Stan Arnold, found near McGillivray property at Atchelitz. It is "likely" soapstone, and measures 1½" by ¾".

JOE: Sleqómét, a mask.
WELLS: Stan Arnold has a mask which is different than any mask I ever saw before, and I was going to ask you to see if you could tell me anything about it. It's only about two inches tall and about an inch wide. It was picked up on this side of Sumas in the Atchelitz country there, right near the old McGillivray place.
JOE: That could mean what they call the sx̱wó:yx̱wey.
WELLS: Well, I think I've got the sxwaixwe story. But this mask doesn't have those protruding eyes and anything on top. It's just smooth, almost like a duck's beak.
JOE: They call them "artists" at the present time. It wasn't everybody that saw that mask, just at certain times. So, from what this artist imagined that mask looked like, that's how he carved it. So the mask became a little different, and today there's a few on Vancouver Island, and it's different from the original mask that was taken from Q'áwq'ewe Lake that's above Hope.
WELLS: Kawkawa? What we call Kawkawa?
JOE: Yeah, Q'áwq'ewe. Yeah, on the side on that bluff, maybe you've saw a tree, a fir tree close to the bluff. Now that's supposed to be suicide bluff. In that lake is where they got this mask.
WELLS: Yeah, I think I got that story in Wilson Duff's material. I think you maybe gave it to Wilson Duff a long time ago.
JOE: More or less, yeah.
WELLS: Sometime, I've got a picture of this little mask and I'll bring it and show it to you, the picture, some day. And you might get some idea from it. I think it's a different one.
JOE: Yeah, do. I've never saw the original mask. They had one around here, they say. But when the Catholic religion came in, they forbid the Indians to use that or show it. Well, when the priest came up, they had a hole dug in the ground, and they hid that. They buried it. Well, as time went on the old priest got ahold of that mask. Well, it must have been some part he used. (*Laughter.*)
WELLS: Yeah, that's right. How about the name of the gambling sticks, the sticks they used for gambling?
JOE: They call them slehál, that's all.
WELLS: Just called slehhahl sticks. And there's a name, I think, for the winter dance, the winter dancing season, like. You say a certain season is coming, the dancing season. What do you call it? Smaytla?
JOE: Smílha, smímelha. There's a season for that, you see, in the winter parts of the year. Or mímelha, that's when they're in action, you see.
WELLS: And the spirit songs? Syoowen?
JOE: That's syúwel. You take an Indian dancer, now. He doesn't compose the song himself. He gets that from some place. There wasn't two songs at that time that sounded alike; all a little different. How come that? Too deep for me, that. (*Laughs.*)
WELLS: There's what they call a "burning song,"—when would they sing that, when they were going to burn

somebody's house, or when a house was being burned or something?

JOE: No, you see, that's a custom years ago. It's being carried in places, even here, to tell you a matter of truth. Someone dies, you see, a friend. Well, after six days you take the clothes of this person or whatever, a grown-up or a baby, and then you burn that. You burn some food also around the fire.

WELLS: And that's when you sing this song, eh? And how do you call it?

JOE: Heywí:leqw. Or it's called shyiwí:l. Oh, it was at that time, when it wasn't used right, that maybe you'd go nuts, you'd go crazy. You could take your own life.

WELLS: I think on that old map of Billy Sepass's he showed a village about where the Higginson farm is, and he called this Whyweela.

JOE: Oh, that's down here where the Anglican church is: X̲wóyx̲weyla.

CASEY: What's the "lah"?

JOE: X̲wóyx̲weyla is the name of this place where this village was.

CASEY: But you said Skwiy-kway-lah. Now, does "lah" mean "the place"?

JOE: Yeah, that means the place.

CASEY: "The place," eh? "Lah."

JOE: Yeah, the name of the place.

CASEY: You were right, Oliver.

WELLS: Yeah, I noticed that quite a few times we get a word, it's got the word "lah" at the end of it. And when that's there, does that mean it means "the place of"?

JOE: Yeah, that's it, yeah.

WELLS: I see, yeah.

JOE: You know, that Sx̲wóyx̲weyla were one of the villages where at the time, well, just as it is now, people pass away, they die off. Well, about that time people were dying off, and one of the leaders and his sister died. That was before shovels, and they made a large box to put their dead in there; and it was just sat on the ground some place. Well, as time went on, a man by the name of Lapum was clearing land there...

CASEY: Yeah.

JOE: Pulling stumps out. Under a great big cedar or cottonwood he came across a bunch of bones piled up. Well, he left his team or whatever he had, went to the old chief called T'íxwelátsa, that's Chief Louie's father, and Chief Louie's mother was alive then. They told the chief about this bone. He says, "No, I don't know," he says. But his wife says, "Let us go up here," she says, "and ask the old lady." Her name was Sally.

WELLS: Do you get her name in Indian?

JOE: She was very old, yeah. They went up there and they told her. They had to talk kind of loud. Her hearing was about weared out. She says, "Yes, I heard about that. And if it's the one," she said, "that was lost long ago, lhíth [long ago]; you'll find it's on the left arm: sqw'ól—that means copper or brass—six bracelets on the left arm. And the sister, if it's the one, you'll find her hair braided in two, two parts, and in the braids you'll find the sqw'ól—that's brass or copper." They went and they took these bones. Sure enough, they found that. Now we figured about, oh, I'm not sure what, four or five thousand years ago.

WELLS: Yeah, a long time.

JOE: Well, we moved them. The hair was just about that long, and it was about that large. I couldn't get my hand around it. And I took a piece of that brass or copper. It was about as thin as that paper, and pliable. Wherever they got that from no one knows.

WELLS: That's pretty good. I think I got quite a bit of that story on a tape before; but you gave me some names on this time that I didn't get last time. I'm glad to get those Indian names. Did Sally have an Indian name that you could remember?

JOE: Sally. No, I couldn't remember it.

WELLS: I got some more words here that go with the dance business, I guess. When there's a dance on, there's one man, maybe the official, has he got a name?

JOE: The official, that may be one or two. They done the talking, announcing, or whatever was to do: ye qwóqwel, the speakers.

WELLS: Yeah. Well, then, what's the word for a fortune-teller?

JOE: Fortune-teller? Yeah, yewí:lmet, I guess.

WELLS: That would be different...

JOE: Syṓ:we, syṓ:we.

WELLS: Yeah, that's the one that Wilson Duff has here. And "the soul." You talk about a man's soul, his inside spirit, what...?

JOE: Shxwelí, shxwelí, your soul.

WELLS: O.K. And these supernatural creatures, we call them slalakum?

JOE: Stl'áléqem.

WELLS: Just about the same, eh?

CASEY: Shlah-lah-kum.

WELLS: O.K. And the ghost?

JOE: Spoleqwíth'a, a ghost. You know them little owls, well, they call them spopeleqwíth'a. That "ghost" word is still in the Bible, the Ghost, the Holy Ghost. So they figured it was a little bird, just like an owl, something like that. (*Laughs.*) Nobody ever saw it.

WELLS: Yeah, I get the idea. This little pygmy owl, you never see it because it just comes out late in the evening, doesn't it?

JOE: Yeah, that's right.

WELLS: And so that's why they say this little owl is the same as the ghost—I mean, it had the same name.

JOE: Yeah, the Holy Ghost, yeah. (*Laughs.*)

WELLS: O.K. In one of the legends there's a story about the cannibal woman that was hard on the little children. She got them to come to her, and then she would kill them. Do you know the name of that?

JOE: No, I don't.

WELLS: A double-headed creature that you and Dan Milo both talk about down in the swamps down here near Chilliwack, you gave us the name of that...

JOE: Oh, that sílhqey, yeah.

WELLS: Yeah, well, now, look, this young fellow over here, he's doing a pretty good carving, young Currie—at least he comes from Mount Currie. His father did; his mother was Tzeachten, I think. Do you know the man I mean, young fellow? Anyway he was over to my place once or twice, and he's doing some pretty good carving of things, and he's trying to find something to carve. And I asked him if he'd come and talk to you about this seelkee. And maybe he could carve one with your help. And I think that if we could once get one carved, maybe make it about as big as this thing, and make one that would be the model of what it was like, you know, then I think it would be altogether Chilliwack, you see. Just like the Okanagan, they talk about their Ogopogo, this would be a Chilliwack seelkee.

JOE: Well, where does this fellow live?

WELLS: He's living now near the Atchelitz, near the Anglican Church. His stepmother is this old Mrs Susan Joe. You know Susan Joe?

JOE: Oh, yeah.

WELLS: Well, she comes and lives with him part time, I think. She's down at Mission. I think his name's Currie.

JOE: Oh, Johnny Currie?

WELLS: Yeah. He's hurt one hand lately; it won't work very good.

JOE: That'd be Johnny.

WELLS: Yeah, well, he's trying to do some carving, and he's quite good at carving little canoes; but I think he's good enough carving he could carve this seelkee if somebody told him what it looked like, you know.

JOE: Yeah.

WELLS: In something that Wilson Duff wrote we read about a skin they used for determining the weather, and this man was a weather man, and he had a skin stretched. Did you ever know anything about that?

JOE: No.

WELLS: I think he must have got it from the River people, and it's on the Fraser River somewhere. And then there was supposed to be a stone statue down in Sumas.

JOE: Oh, you mean that on Sumas Mountain?

WELLS: No, but it might have been on Sumas Mountain, I don't know. This stone was supposed to be the Transformer. He transformed a woman and a man into stone. It's an old legend. Do you know that?

JOE: No. It's supposed to happen in several places. And one's supposed to happen across Yale. A man is there in virgin rock, and his canoe is there. And the man's wife, this man that is supposed to come down at that time took this woman and threw her in the river. Well, this time of year you see the water boiling where this woman is supposed to be at. And it is supposed to happen up here in Harrison Lake, where this stone going about that high has the head, no nose, no ears, no arms. It's when they transferred him into rock, took his arms and threw them away. Well, that stone is still there at Harrison Lake; it's on this side. And as they tell it even now, if you say some words just to abuse on this rock, heavy winds are going to come. Whether it'll happen now, we don't know; but we can go up and try it. (*Laughs.*)[2]

WELLS: Is there a Qwehqwahls or something like that?

JOE: No.

WELLS: I noticed in the *Sepass Poems*, Sepass I think he refers to it as "Haals." Is there no word like that in your...?

JOE: No. No.

WELLS: I think quite a bit of the background of Sepass was Thompson and down in the Columbia River country, where his people came from originally.

JOE: Yeah, Billy Sepass's father come from around Swelús, that's Merritt; but the mother was from Scowkale. Well, in some of Billy's...

WELLS: Poems...

JOE: What he translated gets mixed up for what happened up Swelús, that's up in Merritt, with happenings down here.

WELLS: Yeah, I see, yeah.

JOE: Because but it wasn't only him that told it. It was other people older than Sepass that told how these things happened, you see.

WELLS: Yeah, and he would pass this on.

JOE: Yeah, yeah, and get kind of the words mixed up here and there. You know how mistakes is made, easily made.

•

WELLS: I think I got the word for "blood" from you before.

JOE: Sthá thiyel.

WELLS: How about the word for medicine?

JOE: St'élméxw.

WELLS: And the medicine-man, there's three kinds, eh? You

---

[2]This rock on the west side of Harrison Lake is commonly referred to as Doctor's Point. The word for the Transformer X̲á:ls (speaking of one); X̲ex̲á:ls (speaking of four of them) was, of course, well-known to Bob Joe, who must have misunderstood Oliver's attempt to say the word.

gave them to me before one time, Bob.

JOE: That'll mean a shxwlá:m.

WELLS: That's right. That's one, and the other one?

JOE: Yewí:lmet.

WELLS: Yeah, and what's the other one?

JOE: Shyewíl.

WELLS: Yeah, O.K. And a medicine-song? I've got some of old Tommy, Catholic Tommy's songs on the tape recorder now.[3] I'll have to bring them up and play them to you sometime. What would you call them, these songs?

JOE: Well, a song, unless it's called yewí:leqw.

WELLS: O.K. Well, we just about finished. I think your wife wants to get working on the supper, do you? Are we in your road?

MRS JOE: No, it's O.K.

WELLS: Just a few minutes more and I'll get all the names, I think. "My son"?

JOE: L mél:a.

WELLS: "My father"?

JOE: L mà:l.

WELLS: "My son's son; grandson"?

JOE: L íméth.

WELLS: And "granddaughter"?

Catholic Tommy, photographed by Frances Densmore in the Chilliwack hop fields in September 1926.

JOE: Íméth; it's the same.

WELLS: "My mother"?

JOE: L t'à:l.

WELLS: "My wife"?

JOE: Stó:les.

WELLS: "My husband?"

JOE: L swáqeth.

WELLS: The male organ, or your penis?

JOE: Sxéle. (*Laughs.*)

WELLS: A female organ?

JOE: Oh, I don't quite get that one. (*Laughs.*)

WELLS: O.K. what's the word for a family?

JOE: A family means thel mámele.

WELLS: Have you got a name for the Indian people, all the people together?

JOE: Ó:wqw'elmexw. That'll mean a bunch of people, you see.

WELLS: Gosh, you're a good one, but I don't see how you remember all this stuff. I think we got enough words down now so that if anybody wants to read them afterwards, after we get them all listed, why, I think we can work them in this new system that Casey and I have worked, so that the young people, if they want to try to get them...

Mrs Bob Joe.

JOE: Yeah.

WELLS: Why, it'll be a start anyway. And if they want to learn it better they talk to somebody that knows maybe.

JOE: Maybe. We had a couple here a little—but they weren't man and wife.

WELLS: Harris?

JOE: One was an American. Well, they were both American. Anyway, one was Hawaiian, a young lady. They come University of Washington.

WELLS: Yeah, well, now, that's Harris, I think. He was a nice young fellow.[4]

---

[3]Oliver had just purchased from the Library of Congress, Music Division Archive of Folk Song, a duplicate reel of Frances Densmore's recordings of songs made in the hop-picking camps near Chilliwack in September 1926. In her *Music of the Indians of British Columbia* (Washington D.C.: Smithsonian Institution 1943) Frances Densmore introduces Catholic Tommy's songs as follows, pp. 17-18:

> Tasalt is commonly known as Catholic Tommy. The name Tasalt is inherited from a remote past and he does not know its meaning. In manner and mode of life he is quiet. H. Harding, Chief of Municipal Police in Chilliwack, has a wide and intimate acquaintance with Indians throughout the region, but did not know that Tasalt treated the sick, until the present material was obtained. Although living in the hop-picker's camp, Tasalt was not in one of the communal houses. Instead, he lived in a shack located in the rear of a building on the edge of the camp (pl.7, fig. 1). It seemed scarcely a habitation for a human being, even as a temporary abode, but it had the advantange of privacy. Tasalt's wife is a cripple, lying on a rough wooden bunk while he is absent at work. The roof is low and little light enters the place, yet in these surroundings the writer found this interesting medicine man.
>
> When the purpose of the present work had been explained to Tasalt, he said that he would record his songs for the treatment of smallpox, fever, palsy, hemorrhage from the lungs, and pneumonia. Five songs were recorded, and it was supposed the entire series had been obtained, so the subject of inquiry was changed. About a week later, Tasalt returned, and said that he did not record the song for the treatment of pneumonia and wished to record it in order to fulfill his promise.

[4]Oliver wrote on p.5 of *A Vocabulary of Native Words in the Halkomelem Language*:

> In 1962 I had two interesting discussions with Jim Harris, a trained linguist from the University of Washington,

JOE: Yeah, a nice young man and a young lady. You can contact them; maybe you compare with what they got, you see.

WELLS: That's what I tried to, Joe. A few months ago I wrote down to the University of Washington, and I asked them about this man Harris. He came to my house, and he was very interested in what we were doing. And he asked me to do all the recording we could, and he would help us on it. Well, when I wrote to them next time they said Harris had gone to Japan or Indonesia. And they said he'd be away for a couple of years. But he was a good young fellow, and he had a good way about him.

JOE: Oh, yes. When they were here the young lady was going on vacation; she was going back to Hawaii. When she got back she sent a card over here. We haven't saw them since.

WELLS: No, well, if they come up again I'll sure bring them over.

JOE: Yeah. There was another man; I've all forgot his name now. I must have his address some place. He was from UBC. He was a art and craft of some kind.

WELLS: I don't know who he'd be. This man, Mr Wilson Duff, you talked to him before, I guess, eh?

JOE: Oh, yes, many times.

WELLS: You helped fill up that book, because he used you as an authority on lots of things. I talked to him in Victoria lately.

JOE: There's quite a few people that comes here for one purpose or another.[5]

> who was doing considerable research work on the native language of the Chilliwack tribe. I asked my brother Casey Wells to sit in on the interview. Subsequently, Casey and I gradually built up the idea that it should be possible to write down Indian words in such a manner that they would be pronounced correctly without the necessity of using phonetic characters which are not usually understood by the average reader, nor can they be produced in ordinary type. From this point on I undertook tape-recording of the native language, and Casey developed and established the Practical Phonetic System.

Harris's fieldwork in Chilliwack resulted in an M.A. thesis, Jimmy Gene Harris *The Phonology of Chilliwack Halkomelem* (Seattle: University of Washington 1966), where he lists Dan Milo as his chief informant.

[5]Marian Smith used Bob Joe as an informant in 1938-39—see, for instance, her "The Nooksack, the Chilliwack, and the Middle Fraser" *Pacific Northwest Quarterly* 41 (October 1950) 331. Duff in his *The Upper Stalo Indians* (1952) p. 9 says of Bob Joe:

> R.J.—Robert Joe, who is nearing 70, was my only Chilliwack informant, and I relied largely on him for information on Pilalt and down-river tribes as well. He lives on the Tzeachten Reserve at Sardis, near Chilliwack. His father and grandfather were Chilliwack, his mother Pilalt. A good informant, he was careful with his phrasings and stayed with a topic until he felt it had been exhausted. This may reflect his earlier experience as an ethnographic informant, notably for Marian Smith. Bob has spent some time in the Nooksack area, which may have affected some of the information he gave. His chief fault was a slight tendency to apply modern interpretations to his information.
>
> Mrs Joe, who is over 80, was present at most of our interviews, and often added good information. She could have added considerably more had she been in better health and had she not felt that Bob was the spokesman of the family.

The same summer that Duff was in Chilliwack, 1950, a young student from the University of Washington came up to collect stories from Bob Joe (and also from Harry Uslick in this, the year before he died). Norman Lerman gives the following account in the Preface to his M.A. thesis *An Analysis of Folktales of Lower Fraser Indians, British Columbia* (Seattle: University of Washington 1952), information summarized later in his introduction to *Legends of the River People* ed. Betty Keller (Vancouver: November House 1976) p. 6.

> The informants were Mr and Mrs Harry Uslick, and Mr Bob Joe. Harry Uslick was born in Sardis in 1871, lived there all his life, and died in 1951. His wife was born in 1874. In the old Indian culture Mr Uslick was a woodworker and was, therefore, a respected specialist craftsman. He had been reared in the traditions of the old Indian culture and could speak almost no English. Due to age, he was totally blind and partially deaf. His wife, also a Sardis native, spoke quite good English, which she had learned at a Methodist mission school in Sardis. The presiding minister of this mission, had, according to the informant, considerable respect for the Indian culture and did not force his flock to abandon it. Mrs Uslick acted as an interpreter for her husband. The two talked about the tales every evening, and Mr Uslick occasionally corrected his wife, or made comments during her telling of the stories. The presence of their grandson during the author's daily visits heightened the Uslick's interest and enjoyment in relating the folklore. They were eager to have him know the stories and perhaps tell them to his progeny. It is difficult to distinguish which tales and motifs came from Harry Uslick and which came from his wife. Since communication with Mr Uslick was almost impossible, all the material has been attributed to Mrs Uslick. Harry Uslick was well-known as a story-teller, and his wife had undoubtedly heard all his tales before. To his stock of stories she probably added some of her own tales. All were noted in her own manner of presentation.
>
> Bob Joe was born in 1873 in Sardis, and is still an active man. When not working on his farm, he seeks labouring jobs with neighboring White farmers. He reads a Vancouver newspaper daily, and has a number of religious tracts in his home. He is a worker in the local movement for the recognition of Indian rights by the Canadian government. He is the only informant used by the author who had previously worked with an anthropologist. Dr Marian Smith of Columbia University had done field work with him in 1938. Bob Joe consulted his wife during the telling of most of his tales. This is probably another instance of the pooling of stories by a man and his wife, so that it is difficult to tell who is the true carrier of the tale.

Epilogue to Part II

Only a small percentage of the linguistic work Oliver did with his informants on the tapes has been presented in the selections here. A long session with Dan Milo on the Halkomelem language (4 December 1964) has been entirely omitted. Hopefully, enough has been included to indicate Oliver's great devotion to the language and his persistence in making sure a great deal of it will be preserved for all time on tape, some of it in a rare natural conversation setting. The publication in 1965 of *A Vocabulary of Native Words in the Halkomelem Language* was a milepost. Oliver's Preface to this small but important pamphlet is given in full:

During a lifetime of close association with our Native people, I have had many opportunities to hear them speak in their own language. As a young lad, a common sight at our home was a team and wagon coming up the driveway; an older Indian on the driver's seat, and three or four dogs holding close under the wagon, seeking the protection created by the heavy wagon wheels crunching the gravel all around them. My father would meet them at the garden gate; a friendly visit in the language they knew in common, Chinook, would be followed by the business of the occasion. While the men discussed the deal, the women, comfortably seated in a bed of hay on the floor of the wagon box, would discuss amongst themselves the merits of the deal which was frequently referred to them for their appraisal of its worth. Then for a period, the native Halkomelem language flowed freely. The niceties of expression of which it was capable, I am afraid, were lost to me then, for I can best remember the description my brother had for the sound of the language in his youthful ears—"it sounded like they had a mouthful of saliva and couldn't spit."

In 1962 in company with Mrs Cooper, a life-long friend of the family, I drove to Ohamil to visit Mrs August Jim. Having made arrangements on an earlier visit, our conversation with her was tape-recorded. Her voice, her manner of speech, and her accent, have been unspoiled by the use of the English language, which she never learned to speak. This tape recording will be a permanent record of a language and a manner of speech which is quickly passing from its native land. We cannot hope to retain the language as it was once spoken. We may, however, preserve the basis of it, and this little volume is an effort to record it in ordinary print *as it was originally spoken*.

During recent years, I have tape-recorded interviews with a number of our older Native people in an effort to obtain material for publication which is relevant to the early history of "The Chilliwacks and their Neighbors." These interviews have been a revelation to me of the quiet dignity, modesty and sincerity of our Native people. There was a total absence of ill-chosen words or idle gossip or of any attempt to create a false impression. They had an honest desire to present a true representation of their people and the life they formerly lived.

Interest in writing or reading early Native history lies in the ability to set down in print or to read Native words in such a manner that their original pronunciation is preserved. This is especially true because so many of these words were originally created because of the meaning they carry. Because of this, I have spent considerable time and expense in compiling a vocabulary of Halkomelem words, a portion of which is here published, as a source of reference material from which to work. Much that is of interest in Native culture *is lost with the passing of a language*. This little vocabulary is published in the hope that it will stimulate interest in and help to preserve the Halkomelem language.

Oliver N. Wells.
Edenbank Farm, Sardis, B.C.
January 5, 1965

PART III

OUT FROM CHILLIWACK

Oliver Wells began to expand his ethnographic work into the areas of the Chilliwacks' neighbors, chiefly the Nooksack, the Matsqui, the Tait, and the Squamish. His most conspicuous success was in interviewing August Jack Khahtsahlano and publishing the results in a timely booklet, *Squamish Legends* (1961), just prior to August Jack's death.

However, Oliver's primary concern was always for the homeland of the Chilliwacks, which he felt was centered at Vedder Crossing and the Soowahlie Reserve, so well represented by Mrs Amy Cooper and John Wallace, and the posthumous presence of the patriarch, Captain John. We print below the typescript in which Oliver Wells gathered from all sources, chiefly the autobiographical narrative he cites, the fact and fiction surrounding this historical character, Captain John.

''Capt John''—a Biography

SWA-lihs—This name is almost legendary among the Ch.ihl-KWAY-uhk tribe. It was stamped on the pages of history by the exploits, accomplishments and character of one of the family, who became known as ''Capt John.''

The writer has in his possession a copyrighted manuscript published in 1898, entitled, ''The Conversion of Capt John,'' as narrated by himself and translated by Rev W.H. Barraclough B.A. at Coqualeetza. Excerpts from this manuscript are here given:[1]

> Capt John said, when he was a very small boy, he, like all the other Indians of that time, contented himself with wearing no apparel whatsoever. He remembered the first time he ever wore clothes. He was quite a large boy. He had got a coat from a White man at Fort Langley, this being the nearest White settlement at that time.
>
> As he grew older, the height of his ambition was to be a great and mighty chief. He made all his energies concentrate themselves on the attainment of this object. For a long time he got all the nice things he could, clothes, blankets etc., and stored them away until he had enough merchandise accumulated to enable him to give a great ''potlach'' to which he could invite all the Indians of his and other tribes, in the meantime living as economically as he could.
>
> At last the time came when he sent his invitations and Indians from far and near came to enjoy the festivities of the great occasion. He then climbed to the top of the house and sat astride the roof gable and the Indians below pronounced him to be a very, very fine fellow. This, he says, caused him to become very proud and high-minded and only added vim to his already insatiable ambition.
>
> Then other chiefs, hearing of his great popularity, and realizing what a good thing it would be for themselves to have such a celebrated chief as their guest at their ''potlatch,'' invited him here and there to their festivals, until at last he became head chief of all the tribes of the lower valley.
>
> He said it was about this time that the Caribou Gold excitement started, and he used his canoe to ferry White men across the Fraser from Yale. The White men offered him money, but he had never seen silver or gold and at first he refused to accept it as payment for his services, much preferring an old hat, or shirt to the White man's coin. Finally, however, he began to accept money, being in ignorance of its value as a means of exchange. He said that Sally Ann, his klootchman, thought it must be some good, though; and so he put it away in a bag and kept adding to this until he accumulated about $2,000 in coin.
>
> About this time he was taught by a White man how to drink liquor—a little at a time—so that it made him ''feel good inside.'' Instead of the taste being disgusting to him as it was at first, he was told, ''You will then want to take some more until finally, you will grow very, very fond of it.'' From this time on, the habit grew on him, until at last he could not give it up. He became so anxious to get whiskey that he would give very large sums of money for very small quantities of the liquor. This continued

[1]The manuscript can now be consulted at the Chilliwack Museum.

for some time, until he began to realize that if he did not stop drinking altogether, he would lose all his self-respect as as well as the respect of all the Indians around him.

About 1869, Capt John met the Methodist missionary, Rev. Thomas Crosby, who spoke the Halkomelem Language. With the help given to him by Crosby, he was able to overthrow the grip that liquor had

Capt John, from the photograph album of Margaret Smith Wells, the second Mrs E. A. Wells, who came from Nova Scotia in 1893 to be a missionary teacher at Coqualeetza Indian School.

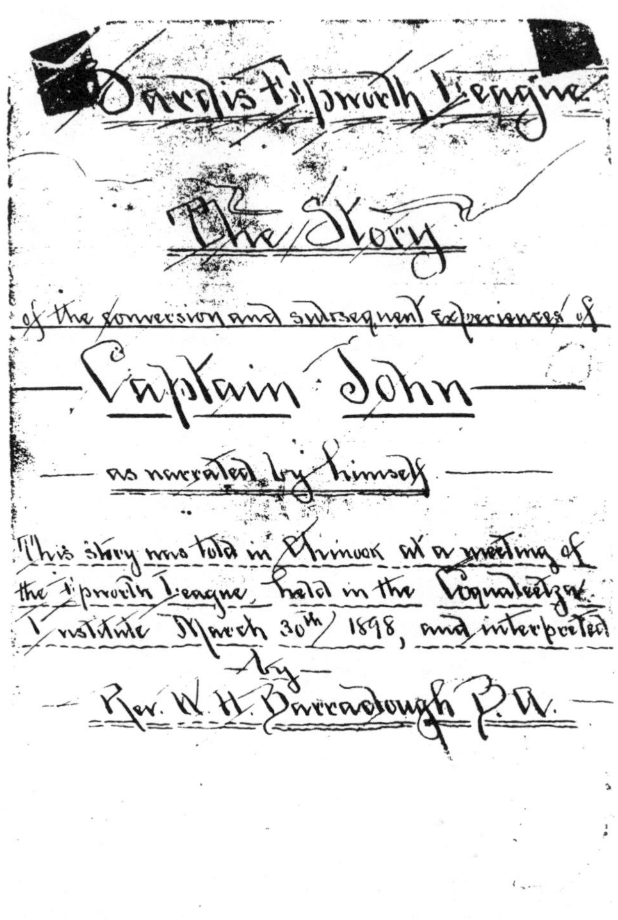

Sardis Epworth League

The Story

of the conversion and subsequent experiences of

Captain John

as narrated by himself

This story was told in Chinook at a meeting of the Epworth League, held in the Coqualeetza Institute March 30th 1898, and interpreted by

Rev. W. H. Barraclough B.A.

Reproduction of the title page of the manuscript by Rev W. H. Barraclough of Capt John's life story, told by him in Chinook Jargon at an Epworth League meeting on 30 March 1898. The manuscript was donated to the Chilliwack Museum.

on him. With the establishment of the Church at Soo-WA-lay, near which he built his home in 1870, Capt John became a power for Christianity and for thirty years worked as a lay-preacher among his own people.

The life-story of SWA-lihs would fill a book. He was likely born about 1810—at a time when the Gulf Island tribes were making periodic raids on the STAW-loh Indians, to plunder and take slaves. As a young man, he was known as SPEEL-seht. His uncle, S'PAHK'-tuhl, was the war-chief of the Soo-WA-lay and on at least two raids SPEEL-seht accompanied the old chief on reprisal raids which took them out across the Gulf waters. He became recognized as a great canoe-man and was head of a crew freighting on the Fraser for the H.B.Co.

In 1858, when the American steamer, "Surprise" tied up at Fort Langley and asked for a pilot to take the ship up the Fraser to Yale, the factor at the fort gave the Captain of the "Surprise" an Indian, barefooted and wrapped only in a blanket. SPEEL-seht guided the "Surprise" safely up the river to Yale and return—the first steamer to reach Yale. SPEEL-seht returned wearing a Captain's uniform and with a pilot's wages in gold in his pockets. Henceforth he was known as "Capt John."[2] With the gold-rush providing unlimited opportunities for gaining wealth with the use of his canoe, Capt John established a ferry service across Cultus Lake and at Vedder Crossing.

When the Suspension Bridge at Alexandria was under construction, Capt John with his helmsman, Big Jim, took the contract to deliver the cable. Using two large canoes, they built a plank deck between them and on this the great coils of cable were taken up the Fraser River by powerful crews bent on pitting their skill and strength against the Fraser.

At home among his people, when he had become their see-AHM, he was much respected. He was their guide and counsellor and "master" as a father would be. When the Boundary Commission was hiring the Native people, among those working for them were slaves who belonged to the head men of the Ch.ihl-K̶WAY-uhk tribe. When payday came, the owner of the slaves collected the wages.[3]

When Captain John accepted Christianity he no longer accompanied the war parties on their reprisal raids and his slaves were given their freedom. In his later years he was known for the strength of his faith, the power of his sermons, and the kindliness of his heart, as he drove with team and wagon to the homes of his tribe, with freshly caught salmon that all might share with him that which was his to give. The name SWA-lihs signifies "getting rich."

Capt John was interviewed by Charles Hill-Tout about 1895, and much of the early history and language of the Ch.ihl-K̶WAY-uhk people was preserved because of his knowledge.[4]

Scowkale Methodist Church and congregation, c. 1900. Capt John stands on left. From the photograph album of Margaret Smith Wells.

---

[2]As indicated by Oliver's workbook, the story of the piloting of the "Surprise" was told by Denys Nelson on p. 24 of *Fort Langley 1827-1927*, issued by the Art, Historical and Scientific Association of Vancouver in July 1927. But is this Capt John the same man as Capt John of Soowahlie? The Barraclough manuscript has him getting a coat at Fort Langley when a boy and when still young becoming chief at Soowahlie. If it is the same man, we are asked to see him barefoot and in a blanket in 1858, aged 48, earning his first "cloth suit with a white hat and calfskin boots" by taking the "Surprise" up to Yale, "the proudest Indian in the valley" (p. 24). On 24 November 1964 (interview #9) Oliver told Mrs Cooper the story of the piloting, and she replied, "I never heard of that." Oliver asked, "Do you think it would be the same man?" Mrs Cooper said, "I don't know. I never heard of that. Of course he didn't tell those things." Our cautious conclusion might be that Capt John's life story has taken on mythic proportions.

[3]Oliver had a xerox copy of the 1866 Report of Capt. Wilson of the Boundary Commission, which included the following comment on slavery:

> A Chilukweyk Indian, whose slave was employed for several months by the Commission, pocketed a large sum in this way; the money was of course paid to the slave, but his master was always near at hand on pay-day to look after the dollars (p. 290).

[4]"The Indians most useful to me in my studies of the Chilliwack were Captain John, chief of the Soowahlie sept; his son-in-law, Commodore, and David Selaketen of Cultus Lake"—p. 59 of Ralph Maud ed. *The Salish People: The Local Contribution of Charles Hill-Tout* (1978) Vol. III: The Mainland Halkomelem.

11. Mrs Amy Cooper—III

Mrs Amy Cooper at Soowahlie, 3 July 1965

WELLS: I'd like to ask you a number of questions today, Mrs Cooper. And one of the things I would like to learn more about are the fish runs that used to be in the Chilliwack River before the White man came and up until the White man's influence maybe cut down on some of the runs of the fish that were in the river. If you were starting at this time of the year, what fish would be in the river now?

MRS COOPER: It'd be the spring salmon.

WELLS: And would they run for two or three weeks?

MRS COOPER: Oh, they run by the month. They'd be the spring salmon there would run all spring till summer; and then in June there'd be the June sockeye that'd come up. That goes up to Chilliwack Lake. There's three kind of sockeye that came up our river, the Chilliwack River, and then the one that goes up to Cultus Lake—there's two kind that goes up there. There's one that goes up Cultus Lake in August, and then there's the other one that goes in September, and those are the long skinny ones there. They're not near as fresh as the ones that comes in August, really beautiful fish.

WELLS: And do these run in great numbers?

MRS COOPER: Yes, for a week or so.

WELLS: In June, how would they take them?

MRS COOPER: They just took them fresh, with the nets.

WELLS: During July would there be any particular run of fish?

MRS COOPER: Well, it'd be June-July, and then that one that goes up in August up to the Lake. And then in September the sockeye, the long skinny ones, the wormy ones, goes up there. They didn't eat much of that. The skin gets red. That comes up with the dog salmon; and these humpies come up. I can't tell you which comes first. I think the humpies come first and then the dogs come. After they get that all smoked there, then the steelhead comes in the winter; as soon as it gets cold the steelhead come up. And they used to have plenty of that. They didn't smoke that. They ate the steelhead fresh, and they didn't get any more than what they wanted, what they needed.

Amy Cooper and Albert Cooper.

WELLS: How about the coho?

MRS COOPER: Oh yes, the cohos came after the sockeye. I forgot about them.

WELLS: That'd be October. Did the Indians live on trout to any extent in the river?

MRS COOPER: Any time of the year. You know when I lived there near that little church? About eleven o'clock the kids would come in and ask if I wanted any fish, and they'd say, "Take it." And it didn't matter what kind of a rod they had, didn't matter what kind of a line they had. If they had one little hook! And you know what they used to do, they used to set a match to my needles, and crook that. That's what they used for their hooks, because they didn't have any hooks. And that's what they used to catch the trout with. I used to tell them, "Don't bring any more than four now."

The church at Soowahlie.

WELLS: Would they heat your needles with a match?

MRS COOPER: Heat your needle, and then keep turning it while it was hot. If the needle broke, well, it broke. It was no more good. But if they got a hook and hooked somebody, that was just too bad.

WELLS: Then there was a little fish called the kokanee, did the Indians make use of these fish too?

MRS COOPER: No, because they had plenty here. And the fish, the sockeye they dried, they dried it up the river, Fraser River. They didn't use the fish up here.

WELLS: Not for drying.

MRS COOPER: No, they were too fat.

WELLS: But when they wanted to dry sockeye they went to Yale.

MRS COOPER: They dried all the sockeye, and all the sockeye they salted, they salted at the Fraser River. If they were to dry these up here, they were so fat when they came up in the early summer that the dried ones would go sour. And it's the same if they were salted.

WELLS: Well, now we're coming into the time when they salted salmon; this would be for the Hudson Bay Company. Did the Hudson Bay supply them with barrels or what?

MRS COOPER: They got the hoops—I think they were the hazel bushes and the small vine maple—they brought that down to Langley. And the staves were made down there; and they made the staves, and gave the Indians the barrels. And they brought them up, and they taught them how to do it at first. And it all spoilt, you see, didn't reach England.

WELLS: When the settlers came, someone told me that the Indians helped the settlers put up salt fish. Would this be for their own use, would it?

MRS COOPER: That's for their own use. I believe every old time settler there got the Indians to salt them a barrel of fish. They supplied the barrel like the Hudson Bay did. Because once they got in the snow, Chilliwack was too far for them to get out. Because we did have snow! In those days, a lot more snow than they have today.

WELLS: I have a picture which I got up at the canyon the other day of one of these fish-drying racks. And I think it's the Lorenzetto rack.

A postcard bought by Oliver Wells at Barry's General Store in Yale. It shows Adeline (Delina) Lorenzetto and Edmund Lorenzetto at their fish-drying rack.

MRS COOPER: That's Delina.

WELLS: Is that Delina cleaning fish?

MRS COOPER: That's Delina. Yeah, I've got pictures of them.

WELLS: Is that Joe [Lorenzetto] standing beside the rack?

MRS COOPER: No, that his father.

WELLS: Oh, is that Joe's father, eh? Would that rack be used by that same family?

MRS COOPER: Always. They put it down on account of the wind there in case the wind blows it or the snow there breaks it down. And nobody touched it. The next spring there, year after year, they go back and use the same boards. Nobody used to bother it. Not like today.

WELLS: Yeah, they would put a cache of fish in the trees even, after they've dried it, and leave it, and nobody would steal it.

MRS COOPER: No, nobody'd steal it. Everybody there, if they didn't know whose it was they wouldn't touch it.

WELLS: One other thing I was going to ask you about: were the eagles numerous in the valley here along the Chilliwack?

MRS COOPER: Oh, yes. The Golden didn't come down as often as the Baldhead. And then there was the ospreys, which we call the fish-hawks. There was a lot of them.

WELLS: Did the Bald Eagles feed on the fish as they were running?

MRS COOPER: No. No. And the osprey there just got the

suckers. Did you ever see them catch a sucker?

WELLS: I've watched them up different lakes, at Chilliwack Lake and Loon Lake.

MRS COOPER: Right there around the old church there used to be thick there. And up at Andy's, they had a great big nest up there on a stump. I've watched them build their nest, and watched the young ones grow. Watched them fight the eagles away. I don't know what the the eagles wanted with their babies. Maybe he ate them, who knows?

WELLS: Maybe the eagle wanted the fish they brought to the babies?

MRS COOPER: No, it was the little ones.

WELLS: But the ospreys would fight the eagles off?

MRS COOPER: Oh yes, they're far quicker. And the eagle would turn right around on its back to grab the osprey.

WELLS: Is that right? I remember Alan Brooks described an eagle and another bird fighting, and he would refer to the fact that they would turn over and put their talons up.[1]

MRS COOPER: Yeah, and kids has often taken a string and tied it on one big feather, you know, and then they'd swing it around like that; well, that's what it sounded like. It sounded just like a truck coming. We, the dog and I, got off the road, and we looked up. We never saw no truck coming. We looked up and here it was up in the air, the eagle on its back. The eagle was slow though.

WELLS: Jack McCutcheon, he referred to the fact that there were about thirty pair nesting along when the telegraph line come through. He would go with his father along the telegraph line, along Vedder Mountain.[2] Well, now, to what extent did the Indians use the eagle feathers?

MRS COOPER: They used the down for dancing. They'd oil their hair and the down would stay on, and they'd have a mass of white feathers on their hair, and while they were dancing there the feathers'd be flying off like that, you know. And sometimes there they would fly over to the fire, the open fire, and you'd see the feathers going, circling up.

WELLS: And this would be eagle down?

MRS COOPER: They never killed an eagle unless they wanted the down and the feathers. And they did use the feathers before the White man came, to put in their hair. And I just forgot how it was fixed. The feathers were counted. Certain number of feathers there was put on the man's head and certain number of feathers was put on the woman's head when she wore the feathers.

WELLS: Would they wear them in a band?

MRS COOPER: Yeah, they had the band. But they didn't make those what you see today there, that feather head-gear there with the long tail. I never heard of that. That's from the Prairies.

WELLS: The head-band which they would use, would it be braided or what? How would the Salish people here make their head-bands, do you remember?

MRS COOPER: I saw one, and I fixed one up, but I can't tell you how the old one was. I used buckskin, and it's two layers of it where the feathers go in, you see. Well, I didn't do it the way the Indians did it. I used a sewing machine. And these feathers that were on it was all painted.

WELLS: But the feathers on the headdress would be painted to suit the occasion, like, would they?

MRS COOPER: Oh, I didn't see that at any of the dances. No, just what I heard. And I didn't know enough about it at that time there to ask the old people the questions that I would have liked to ask.

WELLS: Can you tell me if the Chilliwack Indians had much thought about the stars, and did they have names for, like we call it, the "Big Dipper" and the "Little Dipper."

MRS COOPER: Yes. But I can't tell you.

WELLS: Billy Sepass he had quite a bit of this in his mind, didn't he?

MRS COOPER: Yes.

WELLS: Is there any Indian living now that would know anything about that?

MRS COOPER: I don't think it. My Granny Lorenzetto there she could tell you about the stars just like—well, that's what her husband was; and he used to tell her, and she used to tell him what the Indians said. What the two of them put together I don't know.

WELLS: Yeah, it would be a very interesting part of Indian lore.

MRS COOPER: They spent a lot of time on the stars. They knew all what you know about stars, like Mars and all that, you know. They had names for them.

WELLS: Did they? I've only found one name, but it's in this work of Hill-Tout's. He gives the name for the Big Dipper.

MRS COOPER: What did he say?

WELLS: I'll have to look it up some time for you, and we'll talk about it again maybe. Some time I'm going to go and try to have a talk with old Chief Khahtsahlano, August Jack Khahtsahlano.

MRS COOPER: Is August Jack still alive?

WELLS: Yes. And he's quite good in his intelligence, like. He hasn't failed at all. He would know, wouldn't he? I sent him one of my little books about a week ago. I don't think he reads or writes himself. But he's living with a grand-daughter at Squamish. And I talked to his half-brother, Dominic Charlie, at North Vancouver. And I asked him if I could come and talk to him some time about the Indian religion and these things, and he said he didn't know maybe

[1]This was probably mentioned in personal conversation. Allan Brooks was a regular visitor to Edenbank Farm. Oliver owned Brooks's compilation, "Birds of the Chilliwack District, B.C."—pages from *Auk* 34 (January 1917) 28-50.

[2]Jack McCutcheon was the son of John McCutcheon, the first postmaster of Chilliwack, who supervised the installation of the telegraph service in the 1860s.

as much as August Jack would because he's quite a bit older. Dominic Charlie's seventy-nine I think he said he was. But, anyway, he said he would talk with me.

MRS COOPER: You haven't gone to see Mrs Jansen?

WELLS: No, I'm always going, and I never do.

MRS COOPER: According to her grand-niece, she says she's still in good mind and knows a lot.

WELLS: Can you tell me about where she would be?

MRS COOPER: No, all I know she's at Deroche. I guess you could easily find out from the store.

•

WELLS: Here I've got the story of Captain John's conversion, and this was Rev Barraclough's writing in 1898 at Coqualeetza.

MRS COOPER: Yes, he used to lecture at Coqualeetza.

WELLS: He spoke to the Epworth League.

MRS COOPER: Yes, and Miss Smith and Miss Burpee used to write it down as fast as they could and then make it into one when they were through.

WELLS: And apparently Captain John spoke in Chinook when he gave this address, and Rev Barraclough translated it. And he tells here about—he starts off when he was a boy, and he remembers the first time he ever wore clothes. He was quite a large boy and he had got a coat from a White man at Fort Langley, "this being the nearest White settlement at the time." And then it tells of his ambition to become a wealthy Indian; and after he grew older he gathered materials and put on potlatches.

MRS COOPER: And got three wives.

WELLS: And got three wives, eh? Did he?

MRS COOPER: Yeah.

WELLS: "Then," it says here, "then other chiefs hearing of his great popularity, and reasoning that it would be a good thing for themselves to have such a celebrated chief as their guest at the potlatch invited him here and there to their festivals, until at last he became head chief of all the tribes in the lower valley." And then he refers to the gathering the gold coin at the time of the gold rush, and he collected, kept adding to this until he had accumulated about $2000 in coin. And he speaks about the White man's introducing him to fire-water and how he got taking this; and then he finally—the interesting part about this is when A.C. Wells took him to Crosby, and then there was a certain amount of friction, I guess, whether the Catholics would lose him and whether he'd go to the Protestants or not. And one of the priests came, and they had quite a debate. Captain John he matched him in wits, you know, and he got the friendship of this priest by matching him in his wits.

MRS COOPER: It'd be Father Chirouse then. He often spoke of Father Chirouse.

WELLS: Well, I guess, for a period Captain John would be Catholic?

MRS COOPER: They all started Catholics. Before Crosby came, they were all Catholics. My mother was a Catholic.

WELLS: And then I noticed in Crosby's book, he referred to I think it was the chief before Billy Sepass, he referred to this chief, and all his tribe came with him, came over to the Protestant. But here he—"Not long after this he met a priest at a home of a friend of his who had just died at Squiala. The priest did not know who the old chief was. He was telling all in the house, no doubt to comfort them, that Salmon—that was the man that died—had gone to hell where all bad men go because he was a Methodist. If they wanted to go to heaven they must belong to the Catholic Church and wear the crucifix which the priest would give them. The crucifix could save them from their sins, and that alone. Captain John listened attentively until the priest had finished, and not saying a word. But when the priest got through he sarcastically remarked it must be nice to belong to a church in which you could do as you liked and then ask for forgiveness for your sins and then go and repeat the offence as often as it suited your convenience, and finally get your reward in heaven. He then got up and left the house."

But later he had a dialogue here with another priest. "It was not long after this that this priest met Captain John in a house at Skowkale. After dinner he asked the chief to go for a walk with him. He readily assented. He soon asked Captain John if he would listen to him, and he asked to talk to him for a while on a religious subject. Captain John said, 'Yes,' and the priest proceeded, 'Do you see my hand?' Captain John said, 'Yes.' He then asked again, 'Do you see my hand?' Captain John assured him that he saw his hand. 'Well,' said the priest. 'Do you see that on my hand are five fingers, and that the middle one reaches way out beyond the other four?' Captain John said he noticed that that was the case. 'Well,' said the priest, 'that middle finger is me and my church. Only those who belong to my church can go to heaven. My church is above all the other churches, and by it alone men can be saved from their sins.' Captain John then replied: 'Do you see my hand?' The priest said, 'Yes.' After he asked him again 'Do you see my hand?' again the priest replied in the affirmative. 'Well,' said the Chief, 'do you see that on my hand are five fingers and that the middle one reaches out far beyond the other four?' The priest said, 'Yes.' 'Well,' said the Indian, 'that middle finger is Jesus Christ. It is only by him that men can go to heaven. Your church or any other church cannot save men from their sins. Christ is the head of the church, and He alone can forgive men for their sins.' "

MRS COOPER: Well, that's an answer!

WELLS: "Then the priest wanted to know more about this Christ of whom the Chief spoke, and Captain John told him all that he knew and what He had done for him. When he had finished, the priest told him that he believed that what he said was true, and that he wanted to be like Christ. He continued: 'I want you to watch my people while I am away. I will be your friend. I will watch your friends for you.' The priest's desire to be friendly was so evidently well-meant that he and Captain John became friends, and when he went away he promised Captain John that he would always be his friend, and that he would be good himself.''

MRS COOPER: Pretty good.

WELLS: That's pretty good.

MRS COOPER: It couldn't be better.

WELLS: No.

•

WELLS: I wanted to ask you what Indians worked on the Boundary Survey. Can you give me the names of the Indians?

MRS COOPER: John Wallace's father, Dr George they called him. His Indian name was Xe'ílhatel. He worked on the Line there.

WELLS: Very good. Who else worked there?

MRS COOPER: Edmund Peters' grand-uncle—or grand-father, I don't know. I can't tell you what his name was.

WELLS: Did old Captain John?

MRS COOPER: No. Just those two that I know of that old George told me about.

WELLS: There's some mention in the Boundary Line Reports that the Chilliwacks had slaves at the time, and one of the men that worked on the Boundary Line collected for his slaves when they worked.

MRS COOPER: Oh, I wouldn't know that.

WELLS: You wouldn't know who it was?

MRS COOPER: Thank goodness I wasn't a slave. (*Laughs.*)

WELLS: This is quite interesting, isn't it?

MRS COOPER: I don't know who had the slave. Do you?

WELLS: No, it doesn't say who.

MRS COOPER: Oh.

12. August Jack Khahtsahlano—I

Oliver Wells corresponded with Major J.S. Matthews, City Archivist of Vancouver, who sent him the photograph of August Jack Khahtsahlano reproduced here. The caption in Matthews's hand reads as follows:

> Son of Khaytulk, or "Supple Jack" of Chaythoos, and grandson of Chief Khahtsahlanogh (no European name) in whose honour the suburb of Kitsilano, Vancouver, is named. On 12th February, 1879, he was baptized by Rev Father N. Gregane, as "Auguste fils de Shinaotset and de Menatlot, Squamishs, baptise l'âge d'environ 16 mois le 12, Février, 1879." August stated 16th July, 1946: "Auguste!! that's me. When I little boy they call me "Menatlot," (pronounced men-at-el-ot). But priest make mistake. My father Khay-tulk, he die day I was born. Qwy-what, my mother, marry Chinoatset (usually spelled Chinalset, i.e., "Jericho Charlie", a very good man), whose first wife was Menatelot." The original baptismal certificate is in City Archives, deposited by August. August was born at the vanished Indian village of Shaug (False Creek Indian Reserve) in a lodge directly below the present Burrard Bridge. At this Squamish village, in the big long lodge of Toe-who-quam-kee and by Squamish rite, in the presence of a large assemblage of his tribe and visiting Indians from Musqueam, Nanaimo, Sechelt and Ustlawn (North Vancouver) the patronymic of his grandfather, "Khaht-sah-lah-nogh", was conferred upon him with ceremony by a Squamish patriarch, and that of Kaytulk, their father, upon his brother, Willie. They were both young men, and August, having acquired wealth by working in a nearby sawmill, returned the compliment by giving a potlatch, at which he distributed to the assembled guests, men, women, and children, over one hundred blankets, and other valuables, and also provided a feast. It took place before about 1900. See "Early Vancouver", Vol. 4, page 10, Matthews. On 29 August 1938, by deed poll, deposited at Division of Vital Statistics, Victoria, and also City Archives, Vancouver, Mr Khahtsahlano renounced the surname of Jack, by which he had been known, and assumed the name of August Jack Khahtsahlano. North American Productions Ltd. photo. Presented December 1947, by Mrs. Masie Armytage-Moore, Vancouver. It appeared as a full front page illustration in the Indian monthly newspaper, "Native Voice", Vol. 1, No. 5, April, 1947. August is a wise man, a courteous gentleman, and a natural historian.
>
> CITY ARCHIVES/JSM.

Oliver made contact with August Jack through Charles Chamberlain of the Tomahawk Cafe in North Vancouver, where August Jack's carvings were on display and could be purchased. Mrs Wells remembers that Mr Chamberlain warned them "that if Chief August thought Oliver's interest was merely personal he would not cooperate." "So we drove to Squamish and visited August Jack. No trouble August Jack took Oliver to his heart. He and Mary Ann, his wife, came out to meet me. Oliver took their pictures, and a date was made to return with the tape-recorder. That was a very happy recording day for Oliver."

This interview, Oliver's first ethnographic venture outside the Chilliwack area, took place on 9 July 1965 at the ancestral home of August Jack's mother, Yekwaupsum Indian Reserve (No. 18), north of the town of Squamish.

August Jack Khahtsahlano, 1946.

Son of Khaytulk, or "Supple Jack," of Chaythoos, and grandson of Chief Khahtsahlanogh (no European name), in whose honor the suburb of Kitsilano, Vancouver, is named. On 12th February, 1879, he was baptised by Rev. Father N. Gregone, as "Auguste, fils de Shinaotset & de Menatlot, Squamishs, baptisé l'age d'environ 16 mois le 12 Fevrier, 1879". August stated, 16th July 1940:- "Auguste!! that's me. When I little boy they call me "Menatlot", (pronounced Men-at-el-ot). But priest make mistake. My father Khay-tulk; he die day I was born. Qwy-what, my mother, marry Shinaotset (usually spelled Chinalset, i.e., "Jericho Charlie," a very good man), whose first wife was Menatelot". The original baptismal certificate is in City Archives, deposited by August. "August was born at the vanished Indian ville of Snauq (False Creek Indian Reserve) in a lodge directly below the present Burrard Bridge." At this Squmish village, in the big long lodge of Toe-who-quam-kee and by Squamish rite, in the presence of a large assemblage of his tribe and visiting Indians from Musqueam, Nanaimo, Sechelt, and Ustlawn (North Vancouver) the patronymic of his grandfather, "Khaht-sah-lah-nogh, was confered upon him with ceremony by a Squamish patriarch, and that of Khaytulk, their father, upon his brother Willie. They were both young men, and August, having acquired wealth by working in a nearby sawmill, returned the compliment by giving a potlatch, at which he distributed to the assembled guests, men, women and children, over one hundred blankets, and other valuables, and also provided a feast. It took place before about 1900. See "Early Vancouver," Vol. four, page 10. Matthews. On 26 Aug. 1938, by deed poll, deposited at Division of Vital Statistics, Victoria, and also City Archives, Vancouver, Mr Khahtsahlano renounced the surname of Jack, by which he had been known, and assumed the name of August Jack Khahtsahlano. North American Productions Ltd photo. Presented Dec. 1947, by Mrs Masie Armytage-Moore, Vancouver. It appeared as a full front page illustration in the Indian monthly newspaper, "Native Voice", Vol. 1, No. 5, April 1947. August is a wise man, a courteous gentleman, and a natural historian. City Archives. J.S.M.

August Jack Khahtsahlano.

August Jack Khahtsahlano at Squamish, 9 July 1965

WELLS: Does the Kitsilano district take its name from you, your name?

JACK: Yeah, from my grandfather's. My grandfather used to stay there, making canoes. Good cedar, lots of good cedar. And he stays there to make canoes.

WELLS: I see. What was his name?

JACK: X̱áts'lánexw.[1]

WELLS: And your mother's people, was she of the same village, same tribe?

JACK: No, not this. We don't live there, no. After we moved from Jericho, when I come a boy, we moved down to this place in Kitsilano. Yeah, we call that Sḵw'áyus. And then, when my grandfather was staying, well, then they said it's X̱áts'lánexw, and they couldn't catch it right, and they say Kitsilano.

WELLS: What year were you born?

JACK: Oh, let's see, I'm 97 now.

WELLS: You'd be born 1868 about. That's quite a long time. Not many of us will live that long. I was looking up about the history of the Chilliwack Indians, and when I read the old history it talks about them being very like the Nooksack. And I was reading in some very old books, and it said the Nooksack name means "mountain men." Is this right? Do you know the name Nooksack, what it means?

JACK: Nooksack? Well, I heard that the Nooksack was—when this country was flooded, and those fellows, they got loose from the big mountain up here, up at Squamish.

WELLS: What's the name of the mountain?

JACK: Nch'ḵaỷ. A great big mountain. [Mt Garibaldi.] And they say they got loose, and they head for Mount Baker. They go that way. The current was going south. They come in that, and when the river go down, well, they stay up there. It's the same language as us, a little bit different.

WELLS: When the old people were keeping the history of the tribe, how did they keep the history? They got no books.

JACK: It's all in the mind, in the head. No book, no nothing. Same as me, you know. I can't read, and I don't know books.

WELLS: They never sent you to school at all?

JACK: Well, I got a chance to go to school, but nobody to look after my mother. The old man died, and she was all alone. And that time I was wanted to go to school, she says, "Well, you can't go. Nobody'll look after me."

WELLS: You speak very good English for one that doesn't go to school.

JACK: Well, I've been amongst the Whites, you know, since I was a boy.

WELLS: Well, when the people talked to you about religion, before we had the White man's religion—when I talked to Bob Joe, I talked to him about the word for chief and he says "seeahm"; and then he says there's another word, "cheechel seeahm." This is "the big high chief," like a god.

JACK: That's a god, chilh siỷáṁ.

WELLS: Did the Indians worship this the same as we worship now? When you become Christian, why, we think we have the God to worship, like.

JACK: Yeah, much the same. When you believe, you're all right, you'll get what you want. But before the White peoples come, we had our, like, church, just about the middle of the Squamish there, up there they call 'em Yekw'ts. The saltwater peoples go up there, and the peoples from above come down—all meet in that one church. Everybody got his own language and his own grub, and they just trade, like.

WELLS: They would have ceremonies, would they, like a program?

JACK: Yeah, then they have just some kind of a dancing. And they prayed for something, for maybe apples, maybe cherries, or anything like that. Us peoples here, we see the priests coming down in the hop yard, and one fellow says, "They think we're just starting to learn, but we know how the church is before, before the White peoples came to this country."

WELLS: Our people, we didn't believe it when we come. My grandfather was Protestant, and my father, and I'm Protestant, and Crosby came in the Chilliwacks, and most of the Indians before this had the priests. Well, my grandfather was a friend of Crosby, so I know the Protestant Indians quite well, you see. But when these men came, why, all the missionaries they tried to tell the Indians about God and the High Spirit, and the Indians already had their—the White man thought he had something new, but the Indians already had it.

JACK: (*Laughs.*) That's right. We know it before, before the Whites come.

WELLS: Did you know Capt John from Cultus Lake, from Soowahlie?

JACK: Well, I heard the name.

WELLS: I talked to Major Matthews some, and he told me that you visited him frequently and he puts down a lot of history that you gave him. He writes it down. He is making sure they have a good place to put it before he gives it to 'em. He doesn't want it burned up.

JACK: He has got it all in books.[2]

---

[1]The spellings of the Squamish words in the August Jack and Dominic Charlie interviews have been provided by Randy Bouchard in the orthography of the B.C. Indian Language Project.

[2] "Commencing about 1932 we had frequent conversations. Invariably I put down what he said in his own words the day he said it, and frequently read back to him what I had typed, and he corrected or added"—Major Matthews, p. 3 of *Conversations with Khahtsahlano 1932-1954*. This compilation of the typescripts, though completed in 1955, was not published by the Vancouver City Archives until 1969.

WELLS: Yes, that's good. I have marked down two or three questions I was going to ask you about, and I don't want to forget them maybe. Oh, I was going to ask you about the names of the different dances. This skwiykway dance, this was a dance where they used that big mask, eh?

This photograph of August Jack wearing his grandfather's dancing mask was sent to Oliver Wells by Major Matthews.

JACK: It's a ceremonial mask. For birth, first child born, they use the sx̲wáyx̲wi mask, and somebody died they use that sx̲wáyx̲wi again. I just figure there's lots of ways to use it. Us now, we got them tied up; nobody use it.

WELLS: I see. Just to look at.

JACK: Yeah. I got my son, he belongs to our tribe, and my nephew Alvie Andrew, I gave him the sx̲wáyx̲wi like this one. Well, they can't use it, yet. They got to have everything, from the feet up.

WELLS: I see. They need the full dress.

JACK: We couldn't get the feathers. They are supposed to be goose feathers, because they're stronger than the others.

WELLS: Well, I raise Canada geese at home. I'll have to bring you down one.

JACK: When you pluck them, you have to save me lots. There's three tiers goes around your blankets.

WELLS: Do you want the small downy feathers or the big ones?

JACK: Oh, the big ones, the wings and the tail.

WELLS: My grandchildren they go and pick them up, you know. Yeah, I have about forty Canada geese. I keep them just to look at, nice, you know. Some time I'll bring you a bunch of feathers.

JACK: I don't know what kind of worms eat it up—in the trunk all the time, never moved.

WELLS: Did the Squamish people have a sweat dance?

JACK: No, just one dance, just the same as the Chilliwack.[3] When they first start to dance, they get after this man, everybody, twelve maybe, five, six, all jumping together. And then they—you know what they do, they take him, and he's fainted, he can't do nothing. He's fainted, but they put him on a bed. Of course they got the beds all fixed for him. They put him in there, and cover him up with blankets, maybe four or five blankets. They got two young fellows go on the side to hold the blankets. Pretty soon he start to talk. Then he start to sing his own song. We call them syéwen.

WELLS: That's his song.

JACK: Yeah. That's his song. He dances.

WELLS: Does he get up then and begin to dance?

JACK: Yeah. He get up. Four days they keep him and then they put him in a corner, put him in a corner where he can't move, you know, it's right in the corner. And they set eight buckets of cold water, eight buckets, well, just about hot water. Just pour that in to him. When he's finished, some of them fainted, and they take him out, change him, put new clothes on him, heavy clothes, cause they can't take them off. After he start dancing, he keep that on all the time.

WELLS: They have to be pretty tough!

JACK: Oh, they give me overalls when I first start dancing myself, yeah, overalls, tough stuff. I run... *[break in tape]* After it gets finished, after I get out of that water, they say, "Away you go." Then we go outside and have to start to run, way up in the bush, there where everything is—there is a lot of stuff there's sharp, you know—go way up and get in the tree and sit to listen. That's a good song. I sing that song. And those who left behind, they know the song. Then you turn back, turn back in the house, dance two, three times round the fire—one fellow always hold you in the back—and then they put you in your bed and sit down.

WELLS: That's pretty rugged. This idea of getting your song, Mrs Cooper or someone told me, but I went to the dance at Tzeachten. They had a big dance here last year and the year before. The White people don't go, but I know Ritchie Malloway pretty well, and so I phoned up to Ritchie and I said, "All right if I go up to the dance?" And nobody

[3]Khahtsahlano is now talking about the "spirit dance" and some of the procedures of initiation.

knows it's on, but I heard it was on, so I said, "All right if I go up to the dance?" "Oh" he says, "as long as you don't bring anybody with you." So I go up. Oh, there were a lot of people there, 350 altogether, men, women and children. And just a small hall, you know. And they had the dancers from, oh, there were seven tribes there, I think, from Lummi and all around. And the last time they had three girls from Lummi that they dressed in the special dress; they were just the beginners, like, the first time to dance.

JACK: Yeah, they were what they call a "green's hat."

WELLS: One man, when his song would come, why, then he'd start his song and the drums then come over to him, and they'd pick up his beat, and then he'd go and dance. And then when he's finished, another one he would start his song and the drums would go over to him, and they'd pick up his song, and he'd dance.

JACK: Oh, yes, a great thing, you know!

WELLS: Yeah, it is. It takes a good strong will power to get your song the first time.

JACK: Yeah. The first time you hear it, you remember right away. Like me, I belong to the dancers, and I heard the song. I know right away. Like, you fellows, you don't make your own song. But us Indians, we got our own song. Sometimes I got three or four, keep changing around, like. Next time I go dance I use the other song. That's the way. We can't use it all at once.

WELLS: In the Indian religion before the White man came, it goes just the Indian and then the Great Spirit, eh? Nobody in between? Or did you have the priest?

JACK: They got what they call a minister. This man goes way up in the woods, way back, and he was finished skinning a mountain goat, and he got tired, worn out. And he's gotten in a fire, and he was lying down. When he was lying down, somebody came; somebody came and talked to him, asked him, "Are you awake?" The fellow says, "I must have been sleeping a long time. Yes, now I'm waked now." He turned round; he seen this, somebody like that, on the other side of the fire, and he says, "When you get down to your place down on the reserve, you teach the peoples this here." It's all written, I guess, or something. I didn't see it, but that's what they told me. "You teach the Indians down there." He did. He roll 'em up and put 'em inside a hide so it wouldn't break. He come down. When he got down, he told his friends, "It's up there what they call Yelhíxw." (They call it Ashlu now, way up.) "Next Sunday"—how they know it's Sunday? "Sunday, it's six days from today. You go down to Yekw'ts." That's the first camp, and the people from here up, these people all come down. This man he got this thing; I think it is what they call the Ten Commandments. I think that's what it is.

WELLS: Same idea.

JACK: I just guess, you know. I didn't know if it is true. He's got a good mask; he put that on. "Now this is what you got to learn." So he learned the peoples how to start a church in his own language.

WELLS: This is before the White people come?

JACK: Way before the White people, yeah. I don't know how long before. I seen that roll when we was fixing the graveyard. They got him in a corner, but they wouldn't show it to us. "I want to see it." But the old man says, "No, you can't, you can't see this, it's Ten Commandments."

WELLS: This man, Jason Allard, used to be at Yale, he told about this, how the prophets in the mountain come down with a scroll. But this is the first time I hear the story, the full story, like. What do you call a prophet in your language?

JACK: This man his name was Sye<u>x</u>wáltn. That's his name.

•

WELLS: I wanted to ask you—some things were very important among the Coast Salish Indians; and the cedar tree, do they treat the cedar tree like a special friend?

JACK: That's the only friend we got is the cedar. (*Laughs.*)

WELLS: Well, then, the eagle, how about the eagle, was it a special bird among the Squamish?

JACK: Yes, a special bird, the Thunderbird, what we call Thunderbird.

[THUNDERBIRD LEGEND]

When the flood was on, it go down. And one man, I don't know how he got away, he came down up there at the Cheakamus River. Well, he was walking down. Mud was that thick. "Well," he says, "no use me alive, 'cause all my friends all gone." He was going along, walking down, and the bird's come, on his back. The bird's flying, you know, and he taps him on the back. And he says, "Well, my man, what you think, it's not right. You got to live, you got to make house, you got to make something that you can get your grub, make it yourself." He says, "Well, I don't know how to make it. I can make the house." He got sharp stone, and hit the cedar, and he makes the house. This bird, he says, "I'll come down certain days to keep you company." It's a Thunderbird. First he come in there, he trapped the salmon. Nice friend of his. "Here is your food. It will last you a couple of days." [*break in tape*] He stay there for a couple of months. That was a long time ago.

WELLS: Time when the sea serpent came?

JACK: Yeah, it's come down one end on this end and the other end on the other side.

WELLS: He was that big, eh?

JACK: It was three miles long. Nobody go over; if you want to go to town, go to Capilano, you got to go round this way, walk in the bush.

WELLS: They were afraid of the sea serpent?

JACK: Oh, the serpent, you get close, you get all twist around.

WELLS: It had a bad effect on you if you get close to it?

JACK: All twist, just like something.

"The Sea-Serpent of Howe Sound"—an illustration by Oliver Wells for Squamish Legends *(but not finally used).*

[SEA SERPENT STORY]

This man and woman just get married, like today, and the sea serpent started to go up. And this old man he says, "If you was man enough you'd follow that serpent. He's gone now." The man he says, "I'll be only two days, I'll be just two days up," he tells his wife. He's gone, and he followed—he don't get close, keep away. So the serpent was going, to try this lake here, try all the lakes. Three miles is pretty long. But he keep away, and danced the Indian way, and he want to come in a doctor, like, danced nighttime. And he wants to find out what the sea serpent what it's like. He wants to find out. He keep on, keep on. He gets a little closer. He was out there ten years! When the serpent get in the big lake some ways up here, go down, and he says the serpent told him, "You got pitch stick, make it sharp, about so long. Make three; one on the head, one in the middle, and one on the other head." It's got two heads, you know. So he done that. And four years he was waiting, waiting for that to get rot. The lake was dry, high dry, and he go around, and he go around. He pick out a bone just like a bat. "I guess this'll be all right. I can use it." When he got off the lake, the lake starts to come up, and it's covered. Then he come down, down to Squamish. People from way up high come down there. He had got this thing hidden; he's got a cover for it. When he get in there, the peoples come, he took that out, and he start to lift them up like that, everybody get started twist and twist, all over, everybody. And then he got the medicine for it. He got the medicine, and he go to spread it over all these. They get up. He's finished there, and they're all right. He do that all along from way up down there.

WELLS: Yeah. That is a very interesting old legend, like. That's the double-headed serpent here? I got my camera here; before I go I should photograph it to go with your story.

JACK: Yeah, that's the serpent, and this is the sx̱wáyx̱wi.

[THE STORY OF THE MASK]

There was a fellow there was making canoe down at they call it Lumberman's Arch, that's in Stanley Park. That's how it come to name X̱wáy̓x̱way, cause that's where the sx̱wáyx̱wi come. But this fellow was making canoe, and when the tree split he seen something flew down. He went there, and looked at it. He says, "Well, that's funny. How did that thing go inside the tree?" He take off his what you call it cape—the old men always had a cape—and he wrapped it up with a cape, took 'em down, took 'em home. And he tell his wife, "I got something here. Nobody can touch it." It took him two days to make a box. I think they lace it; it's laced. He make a box, just put the sx̱wáyx̱wi. That sx̱wáyx̱wi is eighteen inches long, and it is about twelve, a little bigger than twelve wide. Well, that's where he got that sx̱wáyx̱wi. Sx̱wáyx̱wi is just a luck, like. We still got it. I got it myself. It's in a trunk here, in a box.

WELLS: Did the Indians know the stars? Did they call the stars by different names?

JACK: Oh, yeah, they got names for pretty near every star.

WELLS: Does anybody know these names now?

JACK: Oh, no.

WELLS: I can't find it in the books, but I can remember old Billy Sepass, old Chief Sepass of Skowkale, I can remember him. He thought about the stars and talked about the stars.

JACK: My old man, my step-father, sometimes we'd be outside, and we'd look up, and he named the stars. He named all the stars. "That's a new one," he says. "We never seen that before."

WELLS: That's too bad we lose all the Indian names for them. Did you ever know the man by the name of Hill-Tout? He used to live at Abbotsford, I think. This man Hill-Tout wrote down a lot of the history and he gave the names of one or two of the stars. He gave the Halkomelem name, like, but not many of them. You don't know anybody that would know them, eh?

JACK: I think I'm the oldest of the whole bunch of people.

WELLS: You think of it, and maybe talk to your wife about it, and maybe if you look at a map of the stars, it may be another time sometime I come you might be able to remember them, you know. When we don't talk about them, we forget.

JACK: I can't see very far. I can't see the stars. I'm a blind man.

WELLS: You keep pretty good for your age. How about the raven, was he an important bird?

JACK: Well, he's our messenger.

WELLS: What's the name for him?

JACK: Sḵewḵ'.

WELLS: Very good.

JACK: He'll always tell you somebody get hurt, not here, maybe from long ways, somebody get hurt, he come around. "Kwok, kwok." But we don't understand him. Some peoples does, some of our own peoples they know what he's saying. Old peoples they say, "That Raven says

August Jack posing with his carving of the mythological two-headed serpent sínulhḵay. He was eighty-eight years old in 1965 when Oliver Wells took this photograph.

there is a big meeting,'' White man's meeting, 'cause Indians never care for meeting. They just get together, that's all. When they get together, well, they good mind look after the people, they keep them—some of them stay three days, two days, and then they bring out the blankets up on top here. They build a scaffold, they fill it up with blankets and they call the names, all the names of different peoples, different countries. I don't know how they can do it. Some body tell him his name, his name. That's what they call a potlatch. I remember when I was a boy down at Jericho Beach there, they got a thousand feet long a house. And they got some attached to it too. That's the biggest house they built, my stepfather. When the White people come there they took them shakes off and put them in the gun boat. They take them to England, I guess.

WELLS: Take them over there, a museum, I guess. I asked Bob Joe to make me a house, a small one, you know, like they used to make. He's got it all made now, except tying it together. Well, I think I better not tire you too much. I think I better play you a record. Thank you very much for all this information on the tape. I think I got your name on the first of the tape, but I better get it again. You are Chief...

JACK: X̲áts'lánexw.

WELLS: And your wife's name, I should have it in here too.

JACK: Swenámya.

WELLS: Dan Milo is about the same age as you are. Do you know Dan Milo?

JACK: No.

WELLS: I talked to him a lot about the Chilliwack history. He moved around the country quite a bit, you know. He is pretty good. He knows lots about the history, the different names of the different salmon, and all these different things. I get the Chilliwack words from him and Bob Joe, and Mrs Cooper. Do you know Mrs Cooper?

JACK: Yeah, I think I heard her name.

WELLS: She was Mrs Commodore at one time. Her parents lived up at Ohamil, just below Hope, up on the river. She helped me out a lot with the Chilliwack history.

13. P. R. Jeffcott

The following newspaper clipping was found in Oliver Wells's papers, taken from the *Record* (Bellingham) 8 January 1969:

P.R. JEFFCOTT, CO. HISTORIAN, DIES SATURDAY

By The Publisher

Further proof that the era of Whatcom County pioneers is fast passing, became evident again this week when it was announced that Percival R. Jeffcott, 92, the county's outstanding historian, died Saturday.

Author of four historical books on the county, Mr Jeffcott's death removes a former beloved early day school teacher, farmer, and in latter years, historian of wide renown. We admired this man who spent years in research, who traveled extensively to get facts or to substantiate what he thought were facts, who wrote letters to many parts of the world seeking information for his books. He talked to scores of former residents and relatives of early day settlers, his books being a true picture of the "good old days."

Jeffcott will be known always as one of this county's outstanding historians. He was author first of "Nooksack Trails and Tales," then wrote about the colorful character, Blanket Bill Jarman; and lastly, "The Mount Baker Gold Rush," or "Chechaco and Sourdough." He edited the late Emmett Hawley's notes and completed his book called "Skqee Mus."

Born in Ohio in 1876, Mr Jeffcott traveled with his mother to San Francisco when six months old. Mrs Jeffcott was ill all the way when they traveled by boat from San Francisco to Portland, where they were reunited with her husband. He attended Portland schools, and after passing the teachers' examination, later attended Eastern State Normal School where he received a teachers' life certificate.

In 1899 he applied for four jobs, accepting one at Pleasant Valley. It was here that he met his wife, Rebecca Tarte, being married in 1900. Later he taught at the Ferndale Central School, at Custer, and then at Evergreen. His hearing caused his retirement to his farm after around 25 years of teaching here.

P.R. Jeffcott at Ferndale, Washington, 12 July 1965

WELLS: Mr Jeffcott, I know you've been a long-time resident in this area; how long have you lived here?

JEFFCOTT: I came in 1899, the last year of the last century. I came here for the purpose of teaching school. That's my early work, and I taught school the first year at Pleasant Valley over near Birch Bay, and the next year I went to Ferndale, and was principal there for six years. And then

I was also principal over at Custer for about ten years all told, at different times. After I had been here a year or two, I got the notion into my head that I would like to have a piece of land, and I looked around and I found this location where my present home is, and bought it from an old German who had taken it up before. It was all marsh land.

WELLS: What started your interest particularly in the Indians of the area, do you remember?

JEFFCOTT: Well, I don't know. As a boy, I had a friend who lived on Sauvie's Island [near Portland, Oregon], and that was the site of the Multnomah Indians, who were one of the big tribes in the Willamette Valley in the early days; and there were many arrowheads down there, and this chum and I made quite a collection, probably a hundred or more that we collected there. That was what started me on it, and when I came up here I always kept my eye open for relics of the Indian tribes.

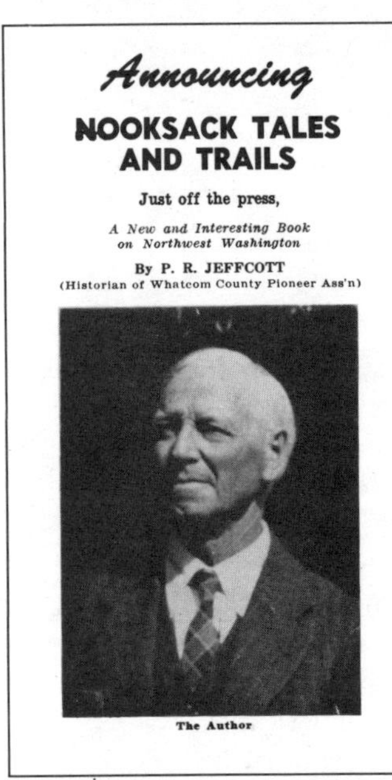

P. R. Jeffcott.

WELLS: Your interest in Indians has continued through quite a portion of your life. How old are you now, Mr Jeffcott?

JEFFCOTT: I'm 89.

WELLS: Eighty-nine! I'm glad to see you're so hale and hearty.

JEFFCOTT: I am one of two members living of a family of ten, old pioneers in and around Portland, Oregon; and we came from the East, from Ohio in 1876.

WELLS: Your farm is located on what could have been an Indian campground at one time. Would the Indians come here to hunt the marsh?

JEFFCOTT: Well, they didn't at that time; they had formerly done so, and they had left their marks, which I could interpret very easily.

WELLS: What would they hunt in this area?

JEFFCOTT: They were hunting evidently for elk. They might have hunted for beaver also—there were beaver in the marsh, lots of beaver—no doubt trapped for the Hudson Bay Company and sold their pelts either to Fort Langley or to the early settlers at Lynden.

WELLS: I noticed in some of the old Hudson Bay records at Fort Langley as early as 1830 they recorded the Nooksacks had been in with furs.

JEFFCOTT: In about 1832 the records of Fort Langley speak of visitors from the Skagits going up there; and when they went back they went by the eastern trail along the foot of Mt Baker, they said. Evidently they went through the Columbia Valley and up the South Fork and crossed over onto the Samish and down the Samish and over the divide to the Skagit. The Hudson Bay Company had a station over here on Ten-mile Creek at a very early date, and that station was there and the buildings were there when the first Whites settled at The Crossing, or Everson, as we call it today, and at Lynden, both of them.

WELLS: Did you find evidence of elk on you place here?

JEFFCOTT: Yes, I found two skeletons of elk in the marsh here, and I found individual pieces of horns beside that.

WELLS: Well, that's pretty concrete evidence.

JEFFCOTT: Oh, there was no question about it. There was the ashes and the charcoal of their fires there, and on their trail going across the marsh here I ploughed up a number of good-sized boulders right on top of the peat, and they couldn't have gotten there any other way excepting it's being carried. You see, the Indians carried those to cook with. They heat them and use them for cooking in their pots.

WELLS: What trails ran through this immediate area where you are now?

JEFFCOTT: Well, there was the trail from Lynden to Birch Bay, and suddenly it branched off and a branch went to Semiahmoo also. But the Indians up here, the Nooksacks, yearly visited the bay to dig clams and dry them for winter's use.

WELLS: In your searching for the early history of the Nooksacks, I'm interested in it and came over to talk with you on the subject because I'm searching into the history of the Chilliwacks, and I find the early Chilliwacks' history is very close to the Nooksacks'; and recently I've been getting back into the earliest records of the village sites and the names of the streams up in the upper branches of the Chilliwack, and the Nooksack tributaries come right up into the same country, and then we have several low passes. What have you found in your research as to the origin of the Nooksacks? Do you know where the tribe actually originated?

JEFFCOTT: The tribe? There is no definite information. There is surmises and guesses, but there is no definite—but indications point, at least they do to me personally, to a common origin with the Chilliwack Indians and the Matsquis.

WELLS: This is something the same feeling that the older Chilliwack Indians have. And there is always quite a bit of interchange in visiting, even in comparatively recent years. I should record the fact that you've written several books on history. Can you tell me off-hand what they are?

JEFFCOTT: The first book that I published was Mr Hawley's

book, *Pioneer Days on the Nooksack*.[1] It was his memoirs. He wrote most of it, but he had no education beyond the fourth grade. He couldn't handle the work himself, and he was eighty-three years of age at the time that I came to connect up with him, and he couldn't find anybody to help him. He had two hundred dollars that he said he would put into it, but that was all he could scrape up for the purpose. So I told him that I would take it over, providing his children would give me a written release to their rights to it. So I had no trouble with it whatever.

The second book that I wrote was *Nooksack Tales and Trails*. In 1949 I published that. It was rather a pretentious affair that grew and grew, and it seemed that it had no end, but I finally decided to cut it off, and possibly publish a second volume; but I have never done it, although I could very easily. I have the material, but it's quite a job.

WELLS: It's a wonderful historic record and contains a tremendous amount of material, and I was particularly interested in the first two chapters because—.

JEFFCOTT: Well, the first two chapters are really an important part of it. I had the material; I had the only file in existence of *The Northern Light*, which was published during the time the Boundary Survey was being made and during the time of the gold rush on the Fraser River, a weekly paper published in Bellingham. And I had the only file that there was in existence. It belonged to the *Bellingham Herald* down there at Bellingham, and I went in to see the editor to see if I could look it over, and he says, "Sure," and he got it for me. And I saw at once that it was a valuable document, and I told the editor. When I'd gotten through the first day of looking over it, I didn't get very far in copying, and he says, "Well, Mr Jeffcott," he says, "take it home with you, and use your own time." "Well," I says, "Mr Carver, you're a foolish man, if I do say so," I says. "There is one of the most valuable records that we have in existence, and," I says, "to let a stranger come in here and borrow it is a very foolish thing to do. But," I says, "I appreciate your confidence." And I says, "If you stick to that suggestion I shall certainly accept it and see that it comes back. But," I says, "one

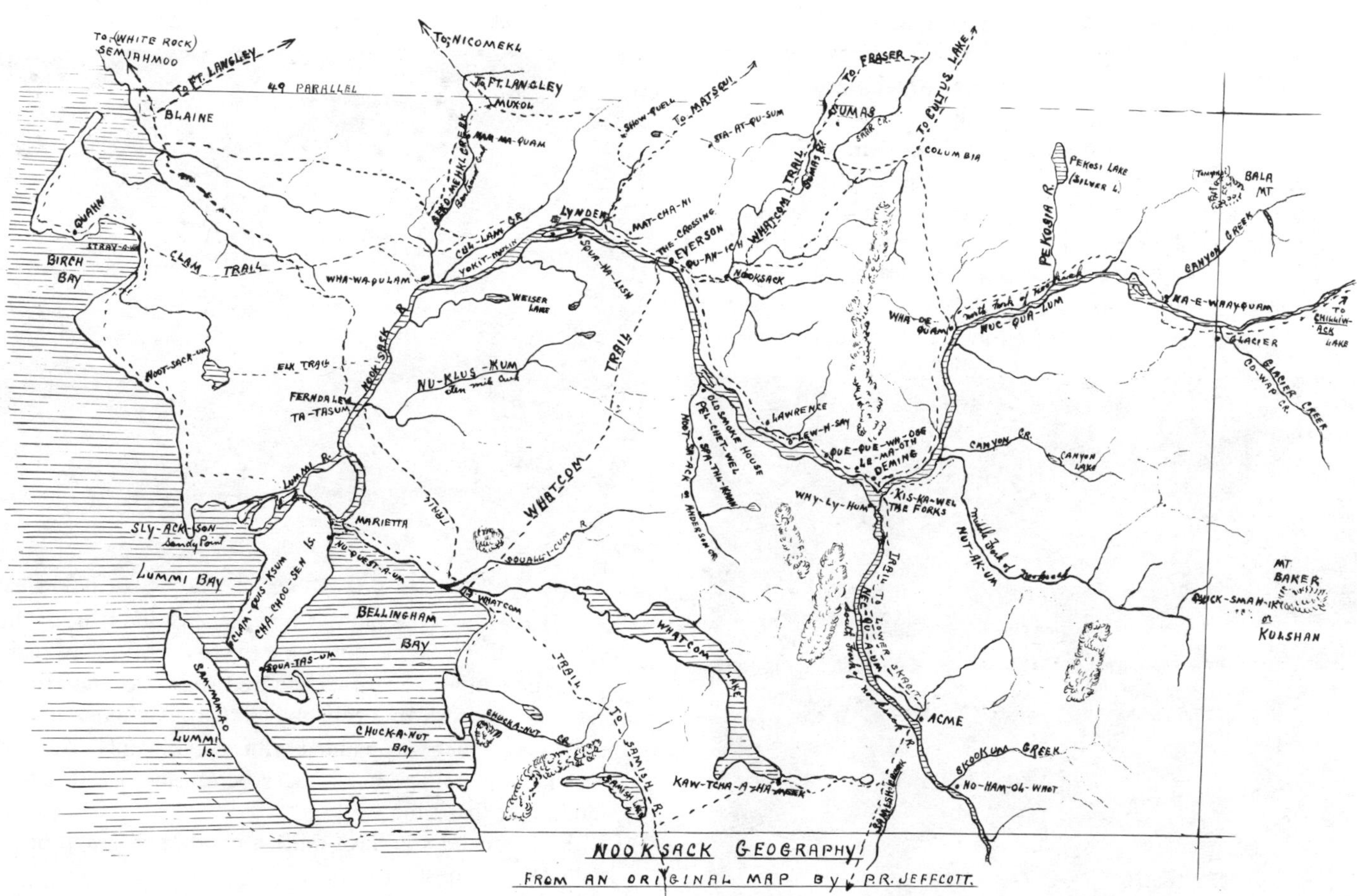

Oliver Wells's rendering of a map by P. R. Jeffcott.

[1]R.E. Hawley *Skqee Mus or Pioneer Days on the Nooksack* (1945).

of the first things I'm going to do is to photograph the whole thing right through and make a special copy for myself and one or two for particular friends of mine.''

WELLS: Well, that's very good.

JEFFCOTT: I made one for the B.C. Archives at Victoria. Mr Ireland, I gave him a copy. He was very appreciative of it.

WELLS: Yes, he would be.

JEFFCOTT: And it was the only record we had of the gold-rush that was complete, and virtually the whole thing is in this chapter of the Gold Rush and the Boundary Survey.

WELLS: You have a very fine list of the Indian villages here in this book in connection with the Nooksack tribe, and I wondered if I could get you to read this list, so I would get the pronunciations of the names.

JEFFCOTT: I will read them and give the pronunciations as the Indians gave them to me, and tell you what they mean, and what they are, and where they are.

WELLS: That's just fine. This would be very valuable.

JEFFCOTT: All right, are you ready? I'll begin with the first one is Squa-ha-lish, the name of the Nooksack village at the present site of Lynden, on the Nooksack River.[2] I don't know what the name means for that particular one, however. The next is Nec-qu-a-um, which means ''clear water,'' and was the Nooksack designation for the present-day South Fork of the Nooksack. The next one is Nuc-qua-lum, means ''dog salmon,'' and was applied by the Nooksacks to the North Fork of the Nooksack because the dog salmon only passed up that branch. Nut-ak-um ''muddy waters,'' so applied to the Middle Fork of the Nooksack. Being a glacial stream, it's nearly always muddy. Noot-sa-ack, probably a constructive form of Nooksack, the name

This and the following two photographs were taken by P. R. Jeffcott at ''the old smokehouse near the mouth of Anderson Creek.''

of the present-day Anderson Creek, so-called because there were many ferns drooping on its banks.

WELLS: Ah, that's very nice; that's the Indian name for it.

JEFFCOTT: Pop-a-ho-my, meaning ''A crossing place connecting two trails,'' called by the early Whites ''The Crossing,'' or ''Nooksack Crossing.'' You know where that is?

WELLS: Yes, I think I have a feeling.

JEFFCOTT: Pel-chet-whel Ne-wh-sa-ack, literally ''Nooksack Prairie,'' was a part of the Goshen District. ''In the early days, there was a prairie there, long since washed away by the Nooksack.''

WELLS: I think we should have a record of this story about this old smoke-house.

JEFFCOTT: Yeah, all right. The Nooksack has a habit at that point of changing its channels often, and it originally stood on the east side of the river, and then the river moved in and flowed on the west side of the smoke-house for a while, and then later it moved back to the east side again, and at the time it was pulled down, which was some years ago, it was located on the west side of the river. And yet it had all those changes eithout ever moving itself at all.

WELLS: That's quite interesting.

JEFFCOTT: It was the old meeting place of the tribes. The old Indian that took me through it the first time many years ago claimed it was over two hundred years old, but I think that was overdrawn probably. It had one post in the smokehouse that was painted with native paints. He said that that was in the smoke-house before the one that was standing at that time.

WELLS: I noticed you have quite a good photograph of it; it shows the construction.

JEFFCOTT: It was well-preserved when I was there, and I took pictures of it. The next is Lew-h-say—that middle

---

[2]Jeffcott is reading from pp. 54-57 of his *Nooksack Tales and Trails* (Ferndale, Washington, 1949).

syllable is really a breathing, hah! Lew-h-say: it meant "steelhead salmon" or "steelhead trout," and was in the Lawrence District and at the present time is known as Smith Creek. The steelheads always ran up that creek. Le-ma-oth, "taking salt water away" is the meaning. There is an odd legend regarding that, which indicates there is more or less truth in it also. The old lady who told me about it said it meant "where the salt water stopped," and she went on to explain that at one time the bay came that far up the river.

WELLS: Well, that's very interesting. They know now that the gulf came up as far as Yale in our area, you know.

JEFFCOTT: And undoubtedlly there is some truth in it because we find clam shells and petrified clams up in that section even today. I have found them myself way up on Church Mountain.

WELLS: What would the elevation be up at this place, this last place you mentioned?

JEFFCOTT: Well, the elevation of Le-ma-oth would not be over, probably, oh, seventy-five to a hundred feet.

WELLS: Yeah, just about like Vedder Crossing. Yeah, very good. Just here, could we break in to this question of how far did the Lummis come? I noticed in your history you refer to the fact that possibly one tribe moved the other back, did they?

JEFFCOTT: The Lummis had supervision of the Nooksack Valley up to Barrett Lake.

WELLS: I see. Had they always? Did the Nooksack originally control the river to the mouth or—?

JEFFCOTT: They seemed to have done. But there was an understanding of some kind between the two tribes that the Nooksacks had the right to navigate to the mouth of the river. At least from the earliest period of the White man that was true, anyway. Nu-quesk-a-um "many snakes," the original name of the Lummi village. There were lots of snakes. Old Chief Martin told me that before he died. What-com means "noisy waters" or "noisy all the time," and was the designation, the Native designation, for Whatcom Falls in Whatcom Creek in Bellingham.

WELLS: This name Whatcom is still pronounced very similar to the original Indian pronunciation, isn't it?

JEFFCOTT: It is supposed to be the Indian pronunication, yes. Sa-mam-a-o means "high mountain," the Lummi's name for Lummi Island. Squa-tas-um, "always covered with water," is what we now call today the Portage. Point Francis is really an Island at the present time, but at one time there was a little isthmus that connected the mainland with that island, and a big high water and storm washed out that; and now it's covered with water at high tide, but it's out of water at low tide; but you could make a portage across there with an automobile even at the present time. Strav-a-wa, "many clams." Because of the may bi-valves found there, Birch Bay was so called. Nook-sack-um, the Lummi name for Cherry Point.

Se-ko-mehkl—we call it Bertrand Creek—flows south from British Columbia. It rises right near Aldergrove and flows south into the Nooksack about six miles below the boundary. Chilo-we-yuek—now we're getting home! I don't know whether I pronounce that correct. Chilo-we-yuek. Chilliwack River, now in its lower course the Vedder, it's still called the Chilliwack above, isn't it?

WELLS: Yes, that's right.

JEFFCOTT: Rises near Hannigan Pass, in fact one branch of it rises right at Hannigan Pass, and flows through Chilliwack Lake.

WELLS: The closest I can come to it through the older Indians that are alive now, and also trying to get Hill-Tout's phonetic translation, is Ch.ihl-kway-uhk.

JEFFCOTT: Just two syllables?

WELLS: No, three. Ch.ihl-kway-uhk.

JEFFCOTT: Oh, a White man can't pronounce it.

WELLS: No, that's right.

JEFFCOTT: But I took the spelling and pronounciation from the Boundary Survey. They got it from the Natives.

WELLS: Yeah, that's right. Their words are as close as you can get almost to it.

JEFFCOTT: The next is Swehl-tcha, Cultus Lake. I think it should be three syllables; I've got it two here.

WELLS: No, I think it's two: Sweltzer, they just generally put it.

JEFFCOTT: I don't know whether you know or not, but the Whatcom Trail had two routes by Sumas Lake.

WELLS: Well, I'm never sure on these, and I'd like to get them down.

JEFFCOTT: One followed the shore line approximately of the Lake at the foot of the mountain clear to the "crossing" of the Chilliwack, "Tiytó:s" or whatever you called it. And the other, east of Sumas city is a low place in the mountainside.

WELLS: I noticed that coming down.

JEFFCOTT: The trail branched there and went over into Columbia Valley and then down to Swehl-tcha or Cultus Lake, and then to the crossing in the river. During the Gold Rush both trails were used. Old Captain Roeder—in 1862 Captain Roeder from Bellingham Bay drove a herd of cattle up to the Cariboo, and he started a store up there.

WELLS: What route did he take?

JEFFCOTT: He took them that way. He took them through into Columbia Valley, and then down by the Lake, and then he drove them up as far as Hope, and then he went over the old trail, you know where Anderson Creek comes into the Fraser, up near Boston Bar?

WELLS: The old Hudson Bay trail.

JEFFCOTT: It comes in straight, but it bends, and its headwaters are only a few miles from Hope, and there was an Indian trail through there, and the Hudson Bay Company used it in their early days. But he used that route to drive that herd of cattle, and he drove them up to the present site of Lytton, and he swam them across the river across the Thompson there, and took the trail up over the mountains there to the Hat Creek headwaters, and down Hat Creek, and hit the old Cariboo Trail.

WELLS: It's amazing, isn't it, where they took cattle? Until I read your book I didn't know that this cattle drive ever took place.

JEFFCOTT: Oh, there were several cattle drives. He drove two sets: one he took to Miller's Landing, the old steamboat landing there at the mouth of the Chilliwack. They called it in the Gold Rush days "Miller's Landing."

WELLS: Yeah, well, that's right. He was a settler there. That was his home.

Jeffcott's caption to this photograph in the unpublished typescript of his book The Nooksack Indians *(1964): "Mrs Lottie (Sulkanum) Tom at her work. Was a worthy Tyee of the Tribe and help to the writer in former years."*

JEFFCOTT: He took the second one there, and put them on board the steamer, and took them up to Yale.

WELLS: Who were your best informants of the older Indians?

JEFFCOTT: The old Nooksacks are all gone. I've got pictures in here. The old Indian Jim, Chief Yel-o-kan-um. Mrs Lottie Tom, I got a lot of information through her. She's gone too. I got a picture somewhere here of the last Chief, Swanaset. Here is the Indian cemetery at Worthen on the other side of Lynden. Vandals went through that cemetery and knocked all of the headstones every-which-way. I set up most of them, but there's some of them, they smashed them all up.

WELLS: Too bad.

JEFFCOTT: That's Indian Jim's stone.

WELLS: I noticed in one of the books you described the lament of the family that had to leave their land when the White people surveyed the property.

JEFFCOTT: Yeah. Soon after Jim Bertrand went on to the Se-ko-mehkl up here, there was another fellow that took up a claim also, right where Skaleel, the old Chief on the upper Bertrand Creek, had his village; and he ordered him off. And he wouldn't go, and so he finally brought influence to bear, and said if they didn't go they'd bring soldiers in.

The grave of Indian Jim and some of his relatives. From P. R. Jeffcott's Nooksack Tales and Trails.

And that scared them, and Skaleel and his few tribesmen picked up their-- what little belongings they had, and went across the Line. What became of them I don't know, but Mrs Bertrand's daughter told me the story, and she said that, as they went, they could hear them weeping and howling, and said you could hear them for a mile or more. The last they heard of them, they were across the Line, but they said they could still hear them, the women weeping and howling, and the men.

WELLS: Quite a sad departure. Quite a sad departure.

JEFFCOTT: It was their old ancestral home. They had to have been there—we don't know anything about how long they had been. But Skaleel, Hawley said he claimed to be well over a hundred, and his son was an old, old man. He said that Skaleel was just nothing but skin and bone. He never wore any clothes. He just had a sort of a blanket made out of an old flour sack that he threw over his shoulder, and that's all he wore. He used to come to the store, his mother's store there at Lynden in the early day.

WELLS: Well, you've gathered a wonderful history for me.

JEFFCOTT: I think you would enjoy reading this.

WELLS: Yes. Some time, if you don't mind, I'll come again and just sit down and read through it.[3]

JEFFCOTT: Could you get over again?

WELLS: Oh, yes. It's only about three-quarters of an hour actually from our place. I'll drop you a line some day when I think I can come again. I've got my first crop of haying in.

---

[3]Oliver later obtained a photocopy of Jeffcott's unpublished typescript, *The Nooksack Indians: A Brief History of the Tribe* (1964).

14. Albert Louie

Albert Louie was one of Oliver Wells's most valuable informants, though the quality of the tape-recording makes for difficult listening.

Oliver did not write out a biographical sketch of Chief Louie, but the tape transcription itself provides much personal background information.

Albert Louie at Yakweakwioose, 28 July 1965

WELLS: You were Chief here for a while, weren't you?

LOUIE: Oh, yes, it was ten or fifteen years, you know. My grandfather was an early chief. I told you his name is registered in Ottawa. Tíxwelátsa is his Indian name.

WELLS: Oh, yeah, how do you say it?

LOUIE: Tíxwelátsa. It's written in Ottawa, Andy Paull said. We had some case work on, and he asked Parliament. He found the name of them all. They asked, "Who's this X̲elálhten?" "That's Chief Sepass' uncle, that old fellow there." They owned this Yakweakwioos, and the land they picked up here at Tzeachten, and the land they picked up, 160 acres here, you know, where the pasture is. They was given it by Commissioner Sproat in the early days. He was the first fellow come along. And he wasn't the Governor, but he would give the Indians land. And he gave Queen's Island across Deroche, they had two thousand acres. And that Sx̲eláwtxw [Schelowat] is in Rosedale. Sx̲eláwtxw means "write"—that's the name of the house, picture, the totem-pole, you know, that's Sx̲eláwtxw.

WELLS: Oh, I see, yeah.

LOUIE: Sx̲eláwtxw: it means you color something, you know. It had colors in it. They had smoke-house there. And there's that smoke-house I was telling you Qoqó:láx̲el, and that's another smoke-house.

WELLS: Now, when you say it's a smoke-house, you mean this is a big house where people lived.

LOUIE: Yeah, that's a big house, yeah. There's the family, the tribe and band, all in one place.

WELLS: And there was one here at Yakweakwioose?

LOUIE: Yeah, and in other places.

WELLS: Was there one at Tzeachten?

LOUIE: No. None in Tzeachten. Tzeachten just moved there later. They had one at Cultus Lake. That's Qoqó:láx̲el, I was telling you. That crow nose, you know, it holds the water up, you know. Qoqó:láx̲el.

WELLS: The "qo" is—?

LOUIE: "Qó" means water. Because that thing holds water for seven or eight days, before they let it out on this crow's nose. And that thing rolls around, sounds like a big raven, you know. (*Laughs.*)

WELLS: That's very good. And this was just above where the Vedder Bridge is now, eh?

LOUIE: It's right there where Simpson's store is. There was no White settlement in those days. Just Indians. When the settlement come, you know, they moved up towards the Lake, towards Th'ewálí [Soowahlie]. Captain—well, it's the people older than Captain John, people older than that, really. My dad knows all their names.

WELLS: This David, he was one of the men that was here when the White settlers come, was he?

LOUIE: Oh, yeah, he worked for your dad, didn't he?

WELLS: My grandfather.

LOUIE: Yeah, your grandfather, I guess. That's how he learnt how to talk English. He was good talking in English, you know. That's where he learnt his talk. Great fellow to talk, you know; but he got no education. David never went to school. But he had a big family. They all died but one of them. The one living just went ahead and married Ed Mussell. They got a boy there now living today, Stan Mussell, about where Francis Kelly lives.

WELLS: Yeah, I was talking to Stan one day, and I was asking him about when the people went into the mountains to pick berries, and trying to find out what I could about the

Albert Louie.

early history, and he told me that one time one of the early Indian women was up on the mountains here and apparently a band of Thompson or Skagit Indians come over, and she got an arrow in her leg when she come home.

LOUIE: Oh, well, they were fighting in those days, you know; didn't agree together, different tribes, didn't know each other, you know.

WELLS: But the Chilliwack people would all be one people, like?

LOUIE: Oh, yes. That's all one. That's from mouth of river right up to Yale. They call it the Lower Stó:lo tribe. Stó:lo means Fraser River, you see. And talked the same language. After you've passed there, further up towards Lytton, then begins the Thompson language. After you passed Ashcroft, Cache Creek, they talk the Shuswap language right up to Kamloops.

WELLS: Did your father have an Indian name?

LOUIE: Yeah, Qw'otíseltel; that's his Indian name. I didn't have any name myself.

WELLS: Was your father a chief here at all?

Oliver Wells re-photographed this postcard of "Dr Bob," and wrote the following thumbnail sketch in his workbook: "Dr. Bob—maternal grandfather of Albert Louie. He was a medicine man of the tribe at the time of the first White settlement. His nickname was Kleh-EH-mihl Bob, or Mussel Bob, so named because he developed as a long-distance runner. When the steamer on the Fraser River pulled away from the dock at Sumas without taking him aboard, he started on the run for Hope—a distance of 30 miles—and arrived there in time to thumb his nose at the Captain when the steamer arrived there. Dr Bob was photographed by Rev Barraclough in 1894 at over 100 years of age. As a boy, he saw Simon Fraser in 1808." (Information from Albert Louie, in tape no longer extant.)

LOUIE: He was a chief up till he died, like Sepass. When he died nobody's the chief here, and we had the whole church up, and Frank Roberts and Dan Milo says, "Oh, you'd better take the old man's place," they says. So I says, "All right." And the priest agreed, and we wrote the Indian Department, and it went to Ottawa.

WELLS: You mentioned an uncle of yours—was he down at Kwawkwawapilt?

LOUIE: Yeah. He was Pat Joe. My grandfather was from down there too. Chief Joe Qwōqwe'ópelhp. Then Pat Joe, his son—he had only one son, and he was a brother and sister to my mother, you know. He raised me when my mother died.

WELLS: Do I say Koh-kwah-puhl...?

LOUIE: That's right, Qwōqwe'ópelhp. That means that they had a lot of them crab apple trees around there, you know. There's still lots down here, down near Chinatown here. When I was a kid, oh, there used to be lots of them, grouse eating them. S<u>x</u>wóyehàlè [Squiala] means—there's a little pond right there, and they call that little pond <u>X</u>wō<u>x</u>wá:ya, because that's a fly. I've seen them swimming in the water that deep. It was way in the bottom, clear water. My grandfather told me. "Don't go there. It's bad. If they ever bite you, well, they'll kill you, you see." Well, I used to shoot duck in there. While I was wading there I seen them things, oh, bigger than my hand, like. They're like flies, but they were crawling around. It's called X̲wiyá:ya—not a big pond, just about near the church. It wasn't deep; you could walk right across it. My grandfather told me, "That's kind of a bad thing; don't go there."

A double-headed Snake - "They made it on a 3 ft. wide post. The one head pointed down and the other up. The middle was round like a tub. It was like a big snake only the head was like a horse's head - long and smooth - a long mouth - long ears like a horse's - it's got a nose and teeth in its mouth, like an alligator. They had it painted, lots of red Indian paint - on the eyes - the ears were long like a horse's, only they were feathers."

"This *SEEL-kee was seen by two brothers who were searching for their "power" to be Indian doctors, down at *koh-KWAH-puhl. They saw it in a pond they used to call *qoh-QIY-ah; it was down behind where the Chilliwack Exhibition Grounds are now."

"My grandfather told me not to go there when shooting ducks - you keep away - Indian ways you know - when you see it - you pull your hair out of your head - like that - and blow it at him - and when you do that you are hurting him, - but when you see him, don't turn around, or if you do, you are going to twist all up. That's what my grandfather told me."

Illustration and Albert Louie's commentary from Oliver N. Wells, Myths and Legends of the Stawloh Indians *(1970).*

And he told me another little pond, "Don't go there—there's a big snake there, a snake there with two heads on." He says, "Don't go there. If you ever see it," he says, "you just twist around like that and you die from it."

WELLS: Yeah, I think Dan Milo told me about this one.

LOUIE: They call it sí:lhqey. It's got a head on him like that; long mouth; and it got—I see'd a picture. It's got long ears like a horse, like a horse's ears. It's got a nose, and it's got teeth in it like an alligator, you know.

WELLS: Do you know the story?

LOUIE: Well, I seen it once, but it was not so big, about that size. I was hunting, and I seen the thing way in the deep water. My god, his eyes just like fire. My god, I see that

Chief Joe was hunting at a big pond, south of Little Mountain, east of Chilliwack City, near where Prest Road is now.

"He heard this thing flying - it came right down into that lake - just like a duck - when he got to that lake he found out it wasn't a duck. He said it was just like a big tub floating, and while he was watching its head came up and started talking. It talked like a duck - like a Mallard. It was not long before another head came up - he had two heads - and how that thing could fly I don't know; but the Indian said that thing could fly from lake to lake. I don't understand, but that's a great thing you know:but if you tell a white man he wouldn't believe it, you know, but my grandfather, Chief Joe of *koh-KWAH-puhl, he saw it twice, it came right over him and it came down on to the lake just like a boat. He said it was just like a tub - then one head came up and it started talking - then the other head came up - like a duck's head on a long neck."

"That's a *SEEL-kee - that's what they called it."

Illustration and commentary from Oliver N. Wells, Myths and Legends of the Stawloh Indians *(1970).*

thing. I was shooting ducks, you know, and I passed by. About two hours after, I came back in the same way, and the thing was going about as far as where you are. I could see it went so fast. I seen it. I seen it with my own eyes. It didn't bother me. I didn't get crazy from it. I wasn't looking for the thing, you know. I guess he knows I wasn't.

The tape as we have it ends at this point, but the tape log indicates that further interesting material was gathered. The facsimile of Oliver's own notes shows how the tape continued. There are twelve more such pages of notes on this missing tape.

Albert Louie at Yakweakwioose, 28 July 1965[1]

WELLS: I forgot to get your age last time. I wanted to get your age. How old are you now?

LOUIE: Well, 1884, I was baptised one year after I was born, you see.

WELLS: Last time, Albert, you gave me the name of the Pilalt tribe. How do you say "Pilalt"?

[1]This is the date given in Oliver's tape log. The context indicates, however, that it must have been an occasion some space of time after the first interview, which is also dated 28 July 1965.

3.

it you know I guess he knew it
Skwiy-HAH-lah + Qoh-QIY-ah - are the same place

125 that SEEL-kee - that snake - one was made for a big smoke-house when I was a boy - they made it this size - 3 ft. wide post - the one head was pointed down & the other up - the middle was round like a tub - they had it painted - lots of red Indian paint - on the eyes - they just let the post rot down - that used to be the smoke house of the Indians - two men who dreamed about it were practising to be Indian doctors - ~~from~~ down at Quoh-KWAL-pull - they come down to where that fair-ground is - where Kipp used to live - to that big pond you have seen there - thats where that SEEL-kwee lived - Gr. father told me not to go there when shooting ducks - you keep away - Indian ways you know - when you see it - you pull your hair out of your head like that - you blow it at him - and when you do that you are hurting him - but when you see him - don't turn round or if you do you are going to twist all up.

Thats what my grand father tolds me.

Another SEEL-kee

My Gr. father - Chief Joe - he saw another one - in a big pond near Prest Rd. - there used to be a big lake then - he was hunting there - trying to get them geese - there were no settlers there then - and this thing was flying - he heard it - it come right down into that lake - just like a duck - when he got to that lake he found out it wasn't a duck, - he said it was just like a big tub - floating - and while he was watching its head come up & started talking - talked like a duck - like a mallard - quack - quack - quack - - not long before another head came up - he had two heads - & how that thing could fly - I don't know - but Indian said that thing could fly from lake to lake. - I don't understand but thats a great thing you know - but if you tell a white-man he wouldn't believe

A facsimile page of Oliver Wells's notes of a tape recording (now missing) by Albert Louie.

LOUIE: Pelólhtxw. They mostly say Pelólhtxw.

WELLS: Good. And the village where the smoke-house was that had the painted house-post?

LOUIE: Sx̲elá:wtxw. That's Rosedale. Yeah, x̲elá:ltxw, that means when you scratch like this, scratched around. You know, it's kind of a picture on a wall; like if you draw a pencil right around, that's what they call a sx̲elált.

WELLS: And do you know the name of the chief that was there in the early days, the first one you remember?

LOUIE: I don't think they had any chief. They scattered, that tribe, after they had a fight. The real chief was at Chilliwack Landing. Teméxwtel. That was the old chief down there. He was a warrior. Teméxwtel, yeah, meaning "the dirt." He used to be a fighter, and he had his power from the dirt. And his power was the thunder. When he got mad, you see, like this'd be lightning, lightning.

WELLS: Oh, I see, yeah. Very good.

LOUIE: He had a brother. He used to call that Skéweqs. You know that big raven? That was his power. The raven would jump from canoe to canoe. He used to do that when he was warrioring with my grandfather. Two brothers, they never joined religion; they died, you know, and they just keep their masks there. But my grandad he retired; he give up everything; he burned everything he had here, bow, arrows, and clubs, you know. And he had masks, that sx̲wó:yx̲wey mask; he burned that.

WELLS: But that other chief at Skwah reserve, he wouldn't change, eh?

LOUIE: Oh, no, no. He never got religion, or Catholic, or anything, you know.

WELLS: When you said the raven was his power, when he was out in this canoe business, he believed...

LOUIE: He jumped from canoe to canoe. The other fellow was thunder. My dad says they made him tell stories Easter Sunday. He just had a blanket on; he wouldn't have clothes on. And he was sitting down on his knees, he'd almost go over his head, that old, I guess. Teméxw, that means "the dirt." The other fellow was named T'á:ts', that fellow that jumps from canoe to canoe. T'á:ts' means when you barbecue a fish like that, you put three sticks this way, and you put it on the fire, they call that t'á:ts'. Well, that was his name.

WELLS: He was the man that had the power from the raven?

LOUIE: Yeah, the raven, right.

WELLS: Well, that's good. That's the old Indian history. You don't get it from anybody except somebody that heard it from the older people, like you, see.

LOUIE: Oh, yes. It's a long story if we only know. But we're telling you what *we* know, you see. But if they were living, like my grandfather and my father, they would have tell you the whole thing right through, how it would start, you see. But we just—I was pretty young at that time when I was just—you know, you take a little bit.

WELLS: I was asking you about Squiala, and you told me about the insects on the pond.

LOUIE: Oh, yeah, the fly. X̲wix̲wiyá:ye. I've seen them in not deep water when I was shooting ducks. Oh, they're as big as that, big hands on them, black, just like a crab. I asked my grandfather why it's black, and he says if it's a different colour that's no good. Them things has kind of a poison. Get that black in you, if it bites you, it'll kill you, just like a rattlesnake. Don't go in there.

WELLS: You told me about the seelkee that looked like a big snake. Well, then, the word slalakum, that's another form of—that's like a spirit in the lake?

LOUIE: Yeah, a spirit in the lake, a kind of different kind of animal, or fish, or whatever it is.

WELLS: Well, what's the difference between this and the seelkee?

LOUIE: Well, it's the same thing, you know. Same thing, yeah.

WELLS: Same thing. But do you ever see these slalakum?

LOUIE: Not really; but my father, early days, used to see a lot of them in the Lake. That's why they give it the name Ts'ewálí [Soowahlie]. And when the White folk come they give it Cultus Lake, means "a bad lake." My dad said he's see them big—even like you have big black fish in the salt water. That Lake must have had a bottom somewhere. That Lake is deep, Cultus Lake. They say 200 feet of rope, 300 feet of rope, couldn't reach there. That's what they say.

WELLS: The old Indian legends about the slalakum, they believed it come from the ocean a long time ago, like?

LOUIE: Oh, yeah. Maybe that lake got a bottom somewhere, that's what I think. Disappeared now, you see.

WELLS: I tell you I talked to the government man, and I got him to send me a book on the time, thousands of years ago, the glaciers were here, like. And he told me that when the glaciers went back, about 5000 years ago, the ice was in this part of the valley up to Vedder Crossing, but the ice cleared out of the Chilliwack River, and the Chilliwack River went through Cultus Lake, and it went out into the United States, out to the Birch Bay country, you see. And this would give the water channel out to the ocean, about 5000 years ago.

[LEGEND OF CULTUS LAKE]

LOUIE: The earliest story of the history of the water of Cultus Lake—there was a little lake on top of the mountain on this side, going into the States, right down to—what do you call that place across the Lake?

WELLS: Nooksack?

LOUIE: Yeah. And the fellow was practicing to be a doctor, you know. He was from Cultus Lake. He was the great-grandfolks of this Doctor George here, and Captain John, I guess. Swimming up there—so he dreamed about a lot of things. He got his thunder power there, and then he seen a fish, like them in a—a small fish. And he came down that lake. He dugged a hole there in that little lake, and that sloshed him right into Cultus Lake where it is, and run right into the Vedder. That was the history of it. That had a name for that old man, but I just forgot. He was an Indian doctor, practicing to be a witchdoctor or something. He was the great-grandfolks of the Doctor George and that Chief, Captain John, used to be there. That's what my dad used to tell me.

WELLS: That little lake in there—where Smith Falls come down?

LOUIE: Yeah, that side, right on top of the hill. There was a little lake there, where this fellow tear the bank down, and it came down to where Cultus Lake is.

WELLS: This is how Cultus Lake was formed?

LOUIE: Yeah, in the beginning. That's why they give it that name of Swílhcha. I guess that was on account of finding that little lake on top there, you see.

WELLS: That's a little bit like John Wallace. I asked John Wallace what Sweltzer means, and he says it has something to do that there wasn't any water there, and then pretty soon there was lots of water. This is the same idea.

LOUIE: Yeah. It came from a mountain, that little lake, when he took it right down there. All the same the Fraser River, this was a dead river right up by Yale, when one day they call X̲á:ls, that one that was changing the man and different spirit, like. Well, he made a sign there, you know, that'd be a river, and he told people that that's where the salmon's going to come in. That's why there's a lot of fish up to Yale and Hope, after the water running. Just the same as the fellow that done on the lake, he run the water, you know, like he opened it up. It was a day long ago there wasn't no Fraser River; just through that man, like he opened that little lake up there, now he opened the Fraser River the same way.

WELLS: Yeah, they call him Qwehqwahls, eh?

LOUIE: X̲á:ls. Changing things around, into rock or something, anything, animal or rock.

WELLS: What did the Indians have before the White people come, did the Indians have their idea of the beginning of the world? I think old Sepass makes it one of his poems, he has the story of the beginning of the world and what the Indians thought.

LOUIE: My dad said years ago that they know the flood before any White people come to them. Flood the whole earth, you know; they know about that flood. Afterwards they got that disease, what they call small pox. It killed, oh, half the Indians, all around the Fraser River there. But a few left, and that fellow that's left, he went down that bank there, I think, toward Bob Stevenson's. He put up the house there. He was at Kilgard when everybody died, and he come. He know that he lived here, and he took a woman along that wasn't his wife, but they lived together, and they made a family. That's how they growed up again like that, you see. He was the only one that was saved out of the hundred, two or three hundred that died. And he raised a family, and they lived on that bank between your barn and down to Stevenson, right up to Army Camp, both sides. That's where the Indians lived. They had a little smoke-house what they'd dry fish in, things like that.

WELLS: Very good. You gave me the word of Atchelitz.

LOUIE: Áthelech. That means it's round like a point like that.

WELLS: You told me about the word Ch.ihlkwayuhk.

LOUIE: Ts'elxwí:qw, yeah. As far as you can go with a canoe—you can't go no further. Ch'eláxw, Indians called it. You come there, and you can't go any further, and you're right in ch'eláxw, you see. It's what they call "far as your canoe can go": and they call that Ts'elxwí:qw. Then the White people have Chilliwack. (*Laughs.*)

WELLS: Yeah, I see, yeah. Coqualeetza, how is the old way of saying it?

LOUIE: Kw'ōqwálíth'a. Kw'ōqwál is when you beat your drum, like those women beat their drum, went after their husband, you know, and throw that feather, and spread that grey paint and that white paint. Kw'óqw, it means you hit something like that. Kw'óqw means you hit somebody. And when they were going after their men with sticks and that drum, that's how they made these fellows crazy. And they were talking their language, making them crazy. That's how their men scattered around. One of them was dropped right into that lake you were talking about, that's Qél x̲ótsa, you know, way up Katz, that big lake there.

WELLS: Kawkawa.

LOUIE: A couple were dropped in there; and this girl was fishing, oh, years later, fished them out. And they claim that the same fellow was around when the women had drove them away, and he flew up there, you see. And when that came back, these tribes here got that sx̲wó:yx̲wey was made here first, and scattered round right into Cowichan, now all over. Started from here, you see. My grandfather had three of them wooden masks, and all of his clothes that he'd burnt up. I wish that it was around; I'd create great changes.

WELLS: When they talk about Coqualeetza now, some people say it means the place where they beat the blankets to wash the blankets. Is this partly the same idea or is it—did the Indians go there to wash blankets especially?

LOUIE: Well, I never heard of that, but there's just that kw'ōqwál, where they beat the drum, you know, and makes them men crazy, like a witch-doctor talking to you, and you go off your head. It's a strong, different kind of power. My Chief Joe grandfather down there, he was one of them, talking to a person, you know, anything, even if it was a horse. When they used to run racehorses here, Joe Corey and them, you know, grandfather he used his power. The horse was shaking right here like he was going to drop; he'd put that rock in his horse's foot, you see, and make the horse kinda quiet down then. He took a prize, by God, he won lots of races, and he never lost a race in Chilliwack. White fellows got to know him around town that hold horses. "Joe," he says. "I want you. Come help me. I'm going to run tomorrow. I'll give you $100," he says. "Do you think my horse will win?" My grandfather says, "He'll win." He took her to town, run a mile, and his horse come ahead, and the fellow gives him $100 tip. Al Evans used to give him $100. Al Evans was a horseman, you know. He had eight or ten racehorses. "You got to get him." He'd come down and get him. If it was a man's footrace, he knew that one because, see, his mouth, strong.

WELLS: Will-power, like.

LOUIE: Yeah. He was going to show me how to go before he died, and give me that power. But he died a little too quick, and I didn't get it. He's just talking to you, you know, you get crazy like. He'd move his hand, and he'll put you to sleep, too, almost, you'll get sleepy and everything.

WELLS: Yeah, well, this today they call it clairvoyance. It's the same idea. I can hypnotise a chicken, but that's as far as I can get. (*Laughs.*)

•

LOUIE: The steamboat used to land there, early days, my dad says, right on the point of the Sx̲wóyehàlè [Squiala]. Oh, there used to be take-out grub. I used to take it up to Chilliwack Lake. The Mexican or the Spanish pack-train, fifteen or forty horses, taking grub up in there. They found some kind of a mine there in the early days. And they were working that mine, and they camped down there.

WELLS: I got some of this information from Washington, and some from Ottawa. I wrote to get it, you know, and they talk about this camp right where you say, right at Squiala. That was the head station, like. For the Boundary Line people it was a supply depot. And then maybe later the Spaniards worked the mine, maybe they found silver up there.

LOUIE: Oh, yeah.

WELLS: When the White people started to take out property, there was Reece and Kipp, and then on the outside of Wellington another Kipp took up a piece there, and he says, when he made the application for the land, this note from the Land Office, it said there was a Spanish corral on this land. Do you know where that was?

LOUIE: I guess it's down there towards Sx̲wóyehàlè. That's the only place they could pack up.

WELLS: Yeah, I've been reading about this in books, but, Albert, it's the first time that anyone ever told me about it. And you get it from your grandfather?

LOUIE: Both grandfathers. They always tell me about that pack-train and the mine that they camped there, these Spanish or Mexicans.

WELLS: I want to ask you where these big Indian houses were. This one, Quhqalahlel, up at the Crossing, how do you say that?

LOUIE: Qoqó:láx̲el. It was right there just where that Simpson's store is.

WELLS: But there was more land there then.

LOUIE: It was called a village there. It was some Indians right across the road that goes just where the Coopers, way up on the hill there, that's where they go hide when they're having a battle, these people go hides up there in them houses, high, you know. That's where they're having a war all the time. Frank Roberts told me he'd found a lot of flints in there, them arrow flints, right in them hills.

WELLS: Do you know where Bowman's farm was up on top there, up on top of the Promontory? Ed Blow lives there now.[2] He's found two or three of these big holes up there, lots of things, hammers and things. I photographed that stuff; about 25 pieces, good stuff.

LOUIE: Yeah. I worked for Bowman when he had a house on top there. He had a mill there too. And he moved down

The finished model of the "big-house" made by Bob Joe, now in the Chilliwack Museum.

[2]Dr and Mrs Weeden now own this property. At least one keekwilee hole can be discerned adjacent to their residence.

to pretty well where Dunc Wealick's. And from there he moved down to Sumas where he is now. I worked for him for four or five years. I've followed that trail right down to the Vedder River. And you go up the same way. That's quite a flat on top of there. It's a nice settlement there, you know, a lot of good farms up in there.

WELLS: Bob Joe's building a model of this big house that had the big eaves where the water come in.

LOUIE: Who, Bob? On that Qoqóláx̱el?

WELLS: Yeah. He's got it nearly finished.

LOUIE: It had a crow nose that way, and a crow nose this way. A big wood, and when you let it out, they got it plugged here, just like you cork in your thermos bottle. Pull the cork out, and the water runs that way.

WELLS: I'll have to get you to make the crow, then. Maybe he doesn't know how to make the crow.

LOUIE: Oh, I guess so. Bob is a good carpenter. I'm not a carpenter.

WELLS: Where Mrs Cooper lives now, do you know the name of that place? Kayluhs?

LOUIE: X̱éylés. It's a sidehill.

WELLS: It means slide?

LOUIE: Sidehill.

WELLS: Does it mean "slide" or "sidehill"?

LOUIE: Oh, just a sidehill.

WELLS: Sidehill. Maybe I got this wrong. I'm making this map and I mark places. When I get this finished, everybody'll be surprised. There was a big house at Skway too, was there?

LOUIE: Yeah, it was right by the Fraser River. There's a road that goes from the dump into what they call Macken's Mill. You cross that slough what you call Macken; there's a river goes down about a mile into the Fraser River; it was on this side where the big house was. I've seen it. It's a long house, about a hundred feet long, I guess, maybe more. Forty-fifty feet wide. It had no floor. And this big fire, you know, it's why the Indians call it a smoke-house.

WELLS: And the Pilalts, they had one at Kwawkwawapilt?

LOUIE: Oh, they had one, and them snake totems was on it. Oh, they had two there; one of them was a bear. It was like a big statue of a real bear. That fellow that owns it, that was his own power, that's why he built that. It's not supposed to be a real bear, but what bear he sees in a lake; not the bear you see around, different bear. If they only cut and saved them.

WELLS: I'm going to talk Frank [Malloway] and see if I can't get him to try to make these. I'll show him the description you gave me, and then if I can get him to do it, then you can tell him "just a little more here, just a little less here," eh? I mean, you'd give him an idea how it should be?

LOUIE: Yeah. Well, the one I seen, that sílhqey, you know, had a head on it just like that. It was something like a feather came this way round. And its teeth go from here round; but it's awful small. It was like a feather come from here, and way up high. I don't know what it is. I didn't see the real thing. I guess that fellow see'd it knows it, you know.

Albert Louie at Yakweakwioose, 5 August 1965

WELLS: One of the first things I wanted to ask about was some of the older people of the Chilliwack tribe, and these people were here maybe when the White people came. And you would know them; you would be a boy maybe, but you would know them. If we start down at the Fraser River end of it, we start at Squiala. Who was there?

LOUIE: Skoyhále? Well, there was Chief Pete, Chief Peter they called him.

WELLS: Did he have an Indian name do you know?

LOUIE: Well, I don't know. I never heard of his Indian name. I was pretty young them days, you know. I've seen him though.

WELLS: My grandfather had a friend; his name was Sweewuhluhs.

LOUIE: Yeah, Swíweles. They've got a lot of the Jimmy Swíweles children there. Yeah, Sam Jimmie, and he's got seven boys, all boys, and they're all living there. They're all growed; they're all married now.

WELLS: Well, then, if we come up this way into Atchelitz, who was at Atchelitz, the old-timer?

LOUIE: Oh, that's Chief William Dick's father, Old Dick. I never heard of his Indian name, but I know they just called him Chief Dick. His son was William Dick. He married Charlie Jim's daughter, down here at Scowkale.

WELLS: One of the old men that I remember was Jack, wasn't it? There was Jack; he lived opposite Albert Knight there.

Julius Malloway's mother and father, and their daughter, Susan Reid (Ritchie Malloway's aunt).

LOUIE: Oh, yeah, Jack from Scowkale. He was my uncle, he was my grandmother's son, you know. And his dad was from Katz.

WELLS: The Malloways—I can't remember that first Malloway. It'd be Ritchie's father, eh?

LOUIE: Julius?

WELLS: Julius, yes. Did Julius have any brothers?

LOUIE: No, I think no. He had a sister older than himself. She was married in North Vancouver to a fellow they call Charlie Reid. But after her husband died in Capilano, she came home here. Well, she died here.

WELLS: Mr Pearson told me that Julius never wanted to give up the language. He always kept his own language.

LOUIE: I guess, well, yes. But he'd speak English all right. He used to read that book Father LeJeune from Kamloops made, that *Kamloops Wawa*, you know. Father LeJeune used to come round here, and he'd give these fellows a lesson in Chinook probably on one or two nights. When he'd get done, he'd go down Qweqwe'ópelhp there for a couple of days with my grandfather. From there to Chilliwack Landing. He travelled around, you know. I had his Bible, that thick. It was burnt with my dad's house. It was a history of the Bible, the beginning of the world, you know, pictures; and then there's English, Chinook, and here's Halkomelem, old language. I couldn't read that Halkomelem. By golly, I could read the Chinook, I could read the English; I couldn't read the Halkomelem. Right along the history of the story, and the prayers, "Our Father," and "Hail Mary," and the Creed, and what you say in praying, it's all in there, you see.

WELLS: It would make a big book.

LOUIE: Oh, yes, it was about 300 pages. I paid three, four or five dollars for that.

WELLS: We never got the old Indian word for the Malloway family. Nobody can remember it, eh? Julius Malloway, did he have an Indian name?

LOUIE: Oh, yeah, Siyémches, that's Julius Malloway. But I don't know the name of the old Malloway. This Siyémches was a big shot, you know. He'd give big time; throw guns away and blankets, and money. What they call cultus potlatch; that's what people called it, cultus potlatch. Siyémches means you're kind of a big shot and a high man, you know, like a king or something. So Ritchie's dad got that name, you know, Siyémches.

WELLS: Bob Joe says he got a lot of his history from Michell.

LOUIE: Yeah, James Michell. That's the fellow who used to live at the old hall where they have their dance.

WELLS: Where did he come from? Would he be Chilliwack?

LOUIE: He belonged to this tribe, but he moved up there. My grandfather moved him.

WELLS: Nobody knows old Michell's name. Bob doesn't know it.

LOUIE: I don't know it.

WELLS: No.

LOUIE: Oh, yeah, I know it now: Siyámátel. That's my uncle, Michell, you know. Siyámátel, that's another kind of high name. All these name I've given you, they are for high people that throws things away in early days. That's the ones had a lot of money. They'd give someone a gun and blankets, and everything.

WELLS: The Saul Wealicks—the Wealick family—were they old Chilliwack or did they marry in from Sumas?

LOUIE: Oh, this Wilíléq's from here, but he married a woman from Nooksack. She was part Kilgard; and the biggest time of his life he lived at Kilgard. And so this trouble, you know, this Mesatchee Sam, when they go to hung him by the Line, and he got scared because they were after all them Indians there, so he beat it away with his son, James Wealick, and that Fred Wealick, and another woman that Jack Uslick married, Harry Uslick's mother. Her name's Qw'óselwet. James was the older, and she next, and then Fred was the younger. And they came here, lived down here by that cedar tree there, you know, where the ducks are, 't other side of the river. They made a smoke house; they had their own place. They lived there for one year, pretty near two years, till my grandfather moved them when he spoke for that Tzeachten, when they got it from Commissioners. Commissioner Sproat was travelling with a manager, and they were giving these lands. He give that Tzeachten; he give that Landing up here the all-grass reserve, the 160 acres. And he give that Sx̲elá:wtxw [Schelowat], you know, way up toward Rosedale. He give that in the early days. And that across Deroche, my grandfather Chief Joe he got that. That belongs to the five bands of Indians that lived down there. They call that in Indian Q'emlólhp [Skumalasph, Queen's Island], that's right round next to Deroche, that island that ran right down to Deroche, where that bridge is. They got that land in the early days, at the same time together. Another thing: Cultus Lake never got any land of anything the Government owned.

WELLS: The Cultus Lake people? They didn't ask for more?

LOUIE: No. Well, they had pretty big land, you know, right up to the Lake, and right down where Cooper lives there, hits that mountain, right to the Crossing there. They got about 2000 acres, there's supposed to be anyway. Captain John, they're supposed to give him that piece where that lake is, where that trap is, right to Smith Falls. But Captain John, you know, he had had nothing in his mind whether it's going to be good or bad. He didn't want that; he wanted his line to be this way. So they just lost it. If he only said "Yes, I'll have my line go over to the water and that," he'd had that lake. But he never done that.

WELLS: That's too bad, yeah.

LOUIE: So he lost that, Captain John did. Now it's a big benefit for the people who are running it now today. Of course they got big land; they didn't get any more land from

Commissioner Sproat. After James Douglas, the first Governor, and Governor Seymour—Seymour's the one that give out the map. You know, I give Ritchie that map. Ritchie was here the other day with his map, but this was way different. And I just showed him my map, and I told

Albert Louie outside the Catholic Church at Yakweakwioose.

him, "You can keep this map." I told him he was chief now. It's a better map. That was a map after they spoke for that, Bishop Durieu, you know, Father Paquette, another French fellow, they spoke to the Governor as how they got this. I think it must be about 1887 I think it was when they got that. But they stopped marking the map what date it was. That fellow that first surveyed that, his name was on there. So we got a good chance on that. But that new map he got from the Government it's way different.

WELLS: Is it, eh?

LOUIE: Course, they'd been surveying; they were cutting a lot of that. But when the Royal Commissioner was here in 1913 they had us out in that little church what Sepass had there. Well, the Commissioner says—there's five men—"Wherever the mountain runs like that," he says, "that's your line; don't imagine it." But these fellows had been straightening out the line right along from the Army Camp down to Bowman's Sawmill or down to Bailey's Road, you know. And they're making that line—well, it's a lot of people that's living in that place, five or six acres there, Vedder Road. It's White people, you see. But the old map what the Commissioner gives—"Follow the mountain," he says. "That's your lines," he says, "except when you straighten it out, so straighten it out like that, you might have a big piece like that, you know." Of course, the mountains are kind of crooked from Vedder, this way, that way, and this way. Course, there's quite a few settled and living right along that mountain on account of they straightened it out. But the Indians talked about it and thought it was their map. The young fellows would never get anything, but the older chiefs like my dad, Sepass, and Billy Hall, they never said anything about that.

WELLS: Yeah, well, might be able to get compensation on it yet. Where does the Mussell family come from? Did they live down there?

LOUIE: That old fellow I told you come from Vancouver Island, she was one of them grandfolks of the Mussells, and she got a daughter that got married, a fellow they called Harry Mussell from Harrison Mill. They lived down there biggest part of their time. From there they moved down to Chilliwack Landing. I was in school there, the Mission, when Harry Mussell moved. And he had a big family. He had Ed Mussell, Jones Mussell, and oh, five or six girls, I guess.

WELLS: Do you know how he got the name Mussell?

LOUIE: Well, he's working the boat, my dad said, early days, when the boat used to run from Westminster to Yale, and he used to pack a lot of heavy stuff, the boys then called him "Muscle." That's why he got that name, and he was Mussell all the time. That's not his name. This Stan Mussell, his dad's got a different name, only he has the real name, you see. But this "Muscle" was just a nickname, but everybody called him Mussell.

WELLS: Because he was strong.

LOUIE: He used to pack four or five hundred pound on the boat. He was a big man, like his Stan is. But he got a different name. Jones come to find out, he told me. He was past 65, but he went down to see Andy Paull. He couldn't get his birth certificate in the Mission. Of course this Mussell had a different name when Jones was baptized in his real name. There was no Mussell. He couldn't get it. I couldn't get mine. Of course, I was baptized by a priest, Father Peytavin; but he made haste, you know. He's writing in Chinook and French, and these priests here they got nowadays they're Scotch and English. That priest we had here lately, Father Bernardo, he was Italian. I tried to get him, and he don't understand the French. And an old priest there that I know round same time as Bishop Durieu there—they used to call him Plamondon—he asked him if he could find it. He took one book; he looks all over. "Right there," he says, "in the French, in Chinook." He could read Chinook. "That's Chief Louie Tíxwelátsa's son," he says. "His name is Albert Louie, that's the fellow you're looking for." He took it down; he marked it, and he printed it, you know. He gave it to me. So it was in the Indian Office when I got my pension. It's in the Indian Office now. I was born November the 6th. It was marked.

WELLS: You told me a little bit about the legend of the family that were bear hunters, and I was going to try to get that another time. You remember, these two men that were—?

LOUIE: Yeah, two brothers.

WELLS: Can you tell me this story so I'll get it on tape?

LOUIE: Do you want it?

WELLS: Yeah.

[THE WEALICK FAMILY]

LOUIE: Well, they used to live right there where George Wealick's house. They were born, and their dad died, you see. And they used to swim all the time, go there to the river. Every night they would go to swim before they go home. Well, he hunted there for years, and he just couldn't kill anything; goes right down Bailey Road, right up this way, Ryder Lake, down this way; but couldn't kill anything. And one day he was out hunting, and he seen two womens sitting down; one of them had a red hair and one of them had a black hair, you see. And he got kinda ashamed to have his bow. He wasn't hunting for no woman; he was hunting for animals. That's before he killed a bear, you see. And he come along; he sees them sitting down. They went and asked him, "Who are you looking for?" "Oh," he says, "I'm hunting, and I want to kill a bear." He says, "I wasn't looking for a woman. I got kinda ashamed to see people." "No," one of them says, "you're looking for us." They were bears, you see, but they were turned into womans. "You know what's wrong with you?" she says. "When you walk," she says, "you scratch your head like this. You pull out something, a flea or a louse. You throw those down, and your stomach round here is full of that slime, full of that stuff you swallow. Come here." Comes up to him, and this bear slapped him like that. (*Slap.*) He fainted. When he woke up he started to puke what he'd taken down, puked everything, got cleaned out, you see. He went home. She says, "Tomorrow, if you come hunt again you'll get us. When you're walking on the mountain," she says, "where you see kind of a little smoke comes out there and there, we're there. You know where to find us." This is a bear, this is a brown bear, this is a black bear; but they were womans when they were sitting on a log, you see.

The next day he went hunting. He went there. He was walking along there. There was a little fire; you could see that smoke. Well now, that's a bear. So the bear's killed. He killed the bear, you know. He butchered it up, and he called some of his friends that lived right there. They went and got the bear and bring it down out of there for him. From there he started to kill the bear, and then he seen what that bear done with him. Then he was a good hunter, oh, for years. For years he was hunting. And he saved something, you know, what he killed off a bear. I don't know if it's gall or whatever it is. He butchers it, and shoves it on a stick like that, saves it and dries it. He told his mother and sister, "Don't touch it; do not touch it." When it gets dry, he puts it in a little seal bag he uses for hunting, and he puts it away. Every bear he killed. For years. And then I guess the girl started to play with that. He wasn't home. That's what made him crazy. After he was a good hunter for years, he got sort of crazy. He went to sleep, and he hadn't eaten no meal, and he got up in the morning, and told his mother, "You folks must be touching that what I got put away. You're not supposed to touch it. That's what's making me crazy. But I'm hunting, and you have my brother to come along." I guess he was beginning to turn different, you know. And he went hunting the same way, the places there. And when his brother tells the history of when his brother become a bear, he slapped the tree every time like that. (*Slaps.*) Every tree he goes like that. He must have followed his brother for miles and miles away. He told him, "Well, I'm going to leave you." He says, "I'm going to turn into a bear," and he slapped a tree. Slapped a tree like that, and he climbed and looked down, and he could still talk, and he told his brother to take the bow home and the arrow. "And tell your mother, and tell your sister that I have turned into bear. But," he said, "you're not going to kill bears until after two years. When you kill the first he-bear, this'll be your song that you'll sing. When that bear dies, you'll sing." When he got home, he told his mother, "He's turned into bear. He went and climbed up a tree. He's going to see me no more. He told me not to stay with him." So when they tell that story, the Chilliwack tribe they used to cry over that, you know. Well, I think that's all I could tell you on this part here. Course, it may be longer, but. . .

WELLS: This is the same story Dan told me, only you've got the beginning of it more.

LOUIE: The old fellows like my grandfather and my dad, they got the history, you know, like a book right along there.

WELLS: Well, the first time I went to a big do up at the Tzeachten Hall, it was about 1923 or '25, that's about forty years ago, and this time when I went in, I just went in the door and stand there, and there was just Indians, you know, and all the women along this side, and down this side were older women, and they were all weeping. And if anybody come out—maybe one would come out and dance around the fire. But I asked somebody afterwards, and they said that this was weeping because of the people that had died before.

LOUIE: Oh, yeah, that's right. Oh, the Indians used to had a different way than they do nowadays. They had their own ways. They had their own prayers in Indian, my dad says. They know how to make the sign of the cross. There's no White man then in them days. That's what my dad says. But they gather up what they got, grub and everything, and Sundays they meet together, just for a preacher. He's like a preacher, just like if he knows the Book, like. He tell them everything that it was a wrong thing. But they had no book. My dad says they used to know the prayers, the Indians. I don't know where they learned it. They learned it themselves, in their own language. They had a little service, like a church, you know. Some from Cultus Lake, but they always gathered up here, my dad says. He mentioned a man's name that used to do with that. He didn't belong to this reserve. Ts'elxwíqw.

WELLS: Did the Indians give thanks to the Cheechel Seeahm?

LOUIE: Oh, yeah. Yeah.

WELLS: He's like their father, eh?

LOUIE: Oh, yeah. They say some kind of a prayer, anyway.

WELLS: When the first salmon come up and when the first berries come in the spring, do they have a special ceremony, like?

LOUIE: Oh, yeah. Pretty near every place is a little different, you know.

WELLS: When the Chilliwacks talk about their Cheechel Seeahm, their great high spirit, does he have anybody else, like, to help him?

LOUIE: No, they just know there's one, one god, anyway, like they believe in the Bible.

WELLS: The Transformer, this man that transforms, like, changes people into rock, this is the one you call Qwehqwahls.

LOUIE: X̱á:ls, yeah. They didn't know what kind of a man he was. The only one that beat him's up here above Hope, a place they call Choate. That's before the Fraser River got small. And this fellow he was working, trying to get them Indians. And them Indians, they were witch doctors, they could make you crazy, do anything. They were drumming this side, and that X̱á:ls was over there. These fellows had too much power. This fellow was throwing into them, and he couldn't do nothing with them. He left.

•

WELLS: These slaves they mostly kept them separate no matter what their rank was.

LOUIE: Oh, yeah, yeah. Well, there was a few over here that was from Vancouver Island. But they looked after them just same as a friend. But they couldn't go home, just like they're fighting the War: German picks you up or anybody, you can't get out, like. That's the way they were doing here. My grandfather had two of them, you know, two womens from Vancouver Island. But they were treated right by the Chilliwack tribe there; they wasn't mean to any of them. They had everything they wanted. He give them money when they wanted a little money, you see. And when they died he made a coffin for them. They died here, and my grandfather was the one what put them away, hang them up from them trees, you know, between this side of the English Church and the old grave cemetery. And they looked after them. That's the way it happened. Course, my grandfather'd never tell anything what he used to do, you know. He wouldn't tell nobody. He was a warrior, and he wouldn't say anything, what he was doing, and what the other one was doing with him. Whatever he done on Vancouver Island, nobody knows. "I'm going to tell nobody—just each keep it a secret." Just my father knows, you see. But my father told me that he's been there and there and there, you know. He'd been one of the warriors.

15. Dominic Charlie—I

Dominic Charlie, according to baptismal records, was born in 1885. He received the same Indian name as his famous great-grandfather, Syexwáltn, described as the "prophet" of the Squamish. He was half-brother to August Jack Khahtsahlano, as shown in the following family tree:

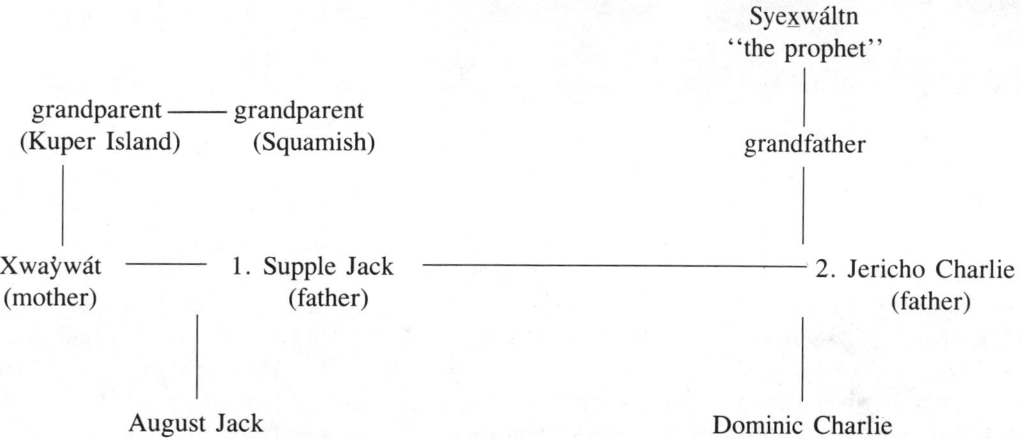

In his thumb-nail sketch of Dominic Charlie in *Squamish Legends*, Oliver Wells wrote:

> As a young man, Domanic worked for August Jack, who had a contract to boom logs down the Serpentine River in the days of hand logging. After ten years on the Serpentine River, Domanic worked as a boom man at the mouth of the Squamish River, working from his canoe. He later worked for nine years in a mill in North Vancouver.
>
> A congenial man, with high moral standards, he is much respected by native and non-native. He continues to preserve the songs and dances of his tribe, taking part in the Provincial Centennial Celebrations in B.C. Indian Festivals.
>
> He is a member of the SKWIY-kway dance Society and continues to practice "good medicine," as one of the few remaining Indian Doctors with a full knowledge of herbal plant medicine and its use.

Dominic Charlie at Capilano, North Vancouver, 4 August 1965.

WELLS: How old are you?
CHARLIE: I'm seventy-nine now.
WELLS: Seventy-nine. Were you ever chief here?
CHARLIE: Oh, no. Not chief.
WELLS: Is Khahtsahlano your brother?
CHARLIE: Yes, half-brother
WELLS: And how do you say his name?
CHARLIE: His Indian name X̱áts'lánexw.

Dominic Charlie and August Jack photographed by Oliver Wells in 1966 by the bridge over the Cheakamus River at the Paradise Valley Road turn-off.

WELLS: Very good. I like to get it on tape, then I got a record of it. When I talked to August Jack he told me about your family, or his family. He was born over at Jericho Beach.

CHARLIE: No, he was born across here at Stanley Park here. I was born at Jericho beach.

WELLS: What did they call the village then?

CHARLIE: Iy̓ál̓mexw. My father had a big house, you know, very big smoke-house, because he's a tayee man, he calls the people from all over B.C., have a potlatch.

WELLS: How far would the tribes come?

CHARLIE: Oh, they come from Skeena River, Nass River, up at Rivers Inlet, Kingcome Inlet.

WELLS: Did they come up from the Fraser River country?

CHARLIE: I think so. He keep them there about one week, or two weeks. I don't know. I wasn't born that time, see. One man from Kingcome Inlet he tell me he was there when he was a small boy. I don't know if he's alive yet; he's named Charlie Scow. He was brother to Johnny Scow, Chief Scow.

WELLS: I heard of that name. Chief Scow was one of the leading men when the White people come.

CHARLIE: My father give away everything, everything, deer skin, bear skin, goat skin, beaver skin, oh, everything, canoe; but I think he give away some money too, because my father had lots of money. He used to pack freight from Hastings Mill all over the inlet; he had a big canoe, packs, oh, about two tons, I guess. We used to pack everything, barley—some of them used the oxen, some of them, Jerry Rogers, he used the horses and he had about twenty mules; and my dad used to pack each logging camp, each day. One goes to Rogers, and one goes to, I think, Bob Preston, load with groceries, you know.

WELLS: How many men would paddle?

CHARLIE: Well, just my dad and my mother. Big canoe—oh, we used to have a hard time when the tide is coming in over here in the narrows. I had a little oar myself.

WELLS: Old Chief Sepass he made a big canoe to freight on Chilliwack Lake way up in the mountains. He made two oars for it at that time—it was about 1925. This would be White man's oars, like?

CHARLIE: Well, they make their own oars. They just used to use that cedar branch, you know, and put holes on the canoe and the oars go in there.

WELLS: When you had a chief in your Squamish tribe you call him "Tayee"?

CHARLIE: Siy̓ám̓. That's the big chief, siy̓ám̓.

WELLS: Seeahm, yeah. Now we'll talk about before the White man bring any religion, did the people have a chief spirit, like our God, you might say. . .?

CHARLIE: We'll come to that now? My great-grandfather had a great big house.[1] He make a big house because he found something in the mountain, see. And I don't know myself—I didn't see that, but I guess it's something written on, see. And he read that. He tell his people what's bad. He say, "Don't go fool around with another man's wife, and don't tell lies, and don't steal anything. If you want this thing, you ask for it, don't steal it." And he know when it's come to Sunday, see. Monday, Tuesday, Wednesday, Thursday, Friday, Saturday, Sunday. Sunday they get together all the Squamish people. They go to church, like. They cook what they going to eat on Sunday, and they put it in a basket. When they come in, well, they put it in the middle of the big house, each person. Each reserve they eat different way. When they finish praying they all sit down and eat, and you know your own food, see. They spread that they got on plates.

WELLS: I wonder what they make the plates of?

CHARLIE: Wooden plates. Just like a bowl, you know; they did 'em the ends high, oh, they make it pretty. And they put bones on, the bear teeth, you know, that is on the side, anything what you get, you just make it fancy, you know.

[1]This is the "church" previously referred to by August Jack, situated at Yekw'ts, across from the mouth of the Cheakamus River, now an unoccupied Indian Reserve (No. 12). The place in the mountain where the "Ten Commandments" were found is also mentioned by August Jack as Yelhíxw (Ashlu). In 1952 Wayne Suttles elicited this same information from Dominic Charlie—see "the Plateau Prophet Dance Among the Coast Salish" in his *Coast Salish Essays* (1987).

WELLS: Does each family have their own idea? Do some family have a beaver, another family have a bear?

CHARLIE: Oh yeah. But we never eat beaver.

WELLS: When they pray, what do they call the head that they pray to?

CHARLIE: Chilh siỷáṁ. My grandfather say "Na na7 kw chilh siỷáṁ."

WELLS: What's that mean?

CHARLIE: That means it's somebody up in the Heaven. That's the man he bring us down, see.

WELLS: And the Indians, their belief that this Cheechel Seeahm, that he created all the world?

CHARLIE: Yeah. Well, I tell you.

[ORIGIN LEGEND]

One man come on Gibsons Landing, and he made a house, not too big, but shake-house, see, and had everything fixed nice. After a while when he's ready there—he was alone, you know—somebody hit the roof, another guy come down, and nobody know where he come from. But he had a mask, and he had a rattle. Too bad I haven't got my—I could have shown you that thing that man had. He start to dance up there. This man down below, he went out to see what's going on, and he went in again. And this fellow on top, he told this man: "You're my brother, you down below me." And this fellow down below say, "No, I come here first myself. I'm the oldest, and you the youngest. You come after me." He say, "Come on in my house." This fellow come in; he had a mask on. Can't see his face. He start to dance when he come in, try to come in three times; he back up dancing, you know. And that's our history; that's sx̱wáyx̱wi.

WELLS: Oh, I see, yeah.

CHARLIE: And that's where we come from. I'm belong to that family. My great-grandmother belong to Gibsons Landing.

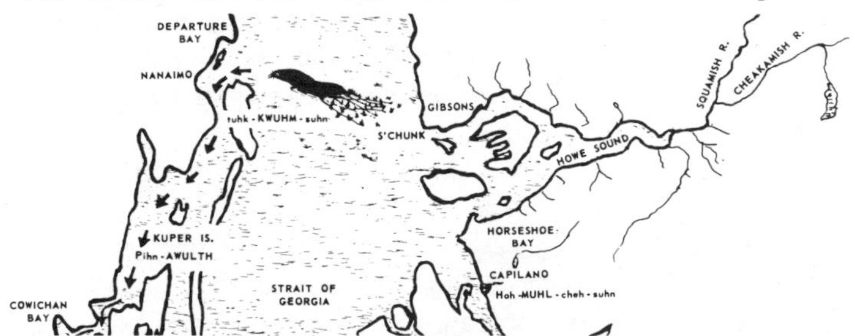

Map and drawing used in Oliver Well's Squamish Legends *to illustrate the legend of "Creation of the Squamish People" and the sea lion story.*

WELLS: Does your tribe have a name for this first man?

CHARLIE: I think his name's Sxwchaltn. That's the first man.

WELLS: And the second man to come?

CHARLIE: I think his name's Tíṁeỉtxw; and that's the name of my brother, X̱áts'lánexw, see. That's his other name. My oldest brother, his name Sxwchaltn; but my brother die, and that name's gone, see. He's got no children. But I thinking we come from them family, I should have named some of my grandchildren.

WELLS: Good to keep up the old names.

[SEA LION STORY]

CHARLIE: And this fellow dance all the time. This first man he get tired of his brother. See, he never give him a chance to do anything. All he does is dance and dance. And this first man, he's a powerful man, and he think, "I guess I better do something"; and he tell his brother, "You better move." You know that bay over Gibsons Landing, right where that ferry lands; there's a nice bay there, and he tell his brother, "You better move over there, build your own home over there." And this man tell his brother, "All right. I'll go." And he moved there, and he built a house. And I don't know how he get the woman, but I guess she just come just like them two, see. And they grow, the family grow.

And this first man, this man couldn't give him a chance; he's always greedy for everything. It's a reef out there on the point there where this nice beach, reef there, and that's where the sea lion comes on when he goes to sleep on the rock, and he goes there and they spear 'em. And this man never give his brother a chance to get any sea lion. And this man get sick and tired of him, and he thinks what to do, because he's a powerful man. And he carved that thing just like sea lion, see. And he carve a fir, fir log, he carved it just, oh, about as big as a sea lion. There's a lake there, I guess—I never seen that little lake—and he goes in there, and he get a kelp from the salt water; he rubbed that on to that, in the lake, see. And when he gets finished rubbing that kelp that thing gets alive. And that fir is too heavy, I guess; he just come up once, and he go down. And he change it, he made a cedar, red cedar; and that cedar come good. He come up just like sea lion. Sea lion come up, you know, sshoooo! goes like. He always come up; he don't go right down. He go around in that lake. This man he say it's alright: "You're alright." He keeps rubbing that kelp on to the wood. After a while he bring him down to the salt water, and he tell that sea lion: "You go around here," he says, "go around this bay. They'll have their spear; they'll spear you, see. When you got 'em all, well, you go straight across." He tell that to the sea lion: "Go straight across." And that they call that Gabriola Pass: "You go in through there,"he tell that sea lion. And when that people reach there, some of them cut loose on that side, see, and some of them cut loose on this side, both sides. He tell that sea lion: "You keep on going; go through Cowichan Pass, see." Some of them cut loose on that Kuper Island, a nice bay there, nice beach. And that thing keep on going till they come into Cowichan Bay, and they all cut loose there. We don't know what happened to that sea lion.

WELLS: That's a very good legend there.

CHARLIE: That's why we all friend to these people who live there. They're Squamish, see. They're all Squamish.

WELLS: You mean even the Cowichan?

CHARLIE: Penálx̱ets'. What they call Lhémelch'.[2] They're all Squamish. And we all friend to them.

WELLS: Oh, yes. I see.

CHARLIE: But my mother come from Penálx̱ets'—that's Kuper Island. I talk the language of my people. When my father go out, you know, work, my mother used to talk this language, and that's why we talk this language, my mother's language, from Kuper Island. Me and my brother August, we talk our language, see, Cowichan language; and I used to talk to them when we have a potlatch here, pow-wow, you know. I talk to my friends when I meet 'em.

WELLS: This is very near like the Chilliwack language.

CHARLIE: Little bit different. I understand them, you know, Chilliwack and the Musqueam, and the Tsawwassen same, and up to the Bellingham people. I can't understand them. Lummi talk different.

WELLS: When your people get together for this big Sunday gathering, this like religion before the White man came, when they pray, do they thank the big chief for the food?

CHARLIE: Yeah. They pray, and dance, and they got songs. My great-grandfather he know, he sing that. I'm sorry I didn't get that song. I had a cousin, but he never—I don't know why he never tell me.

WELLS: Is it like a song of thanks, like?

CHARLIE: I don't know how it is. It's something like if he goes like that, see. (*Beats.*) They all dance. I guess you never see Shaker people?

WELLS: No, I never seen them, no.

CHARLIE: They dance, you know, and they shake.

WELLS: If the Indian is hunting and he gets a deer, at that time did they think the deer is like one of my people? When you get up in the Upper Fraser they kind of believe the deer like one of my own people, like, you know.

CHARLIE: No, not that; different here.

WELLS: Do they say thank you for giving me this deer?

CHARLIE: Oh, yeah, yeah.

WELLS: And when they get a big catch of fish, when the first salmon come up, do they have any special—?

CHARLIE: Oh, yes, because they say it person if I die, see, I was the good hunter, see. I hunt everything, deer and goat, ducks, fish, anything, I get 'em easy. If I die, well, I turn to fish, me, I turn to blackfish.

WELLS: In the Indian religion, like, you don't go through anybody else, you don't go through any minister?

CHARLIE: Yes, my grandfather he was the only one, he was the only one at Squamish, see, because he's a great hunter.

[THUNDERBIRD LEGEND]

Every fall, every spring, he's up in the mountains. He's got place there for his home, up in the mountains, cave. And every fall and every spring he's there. And he was hunting and he was tired, and he made a fire, and he was laying down, his back towards the fire, and he heard something from up, up in the sky. He heard something coming, just like, you know, when the thunder goes he goes chchrrrrrr! My great-grandfather he never turn round, he never look. He knows somebody's coming down, see, that noise just like Thunderbird. He hit the other side of the fire; he know he hit the ground. He had a big fire here, and this man come down. He had—I don't know—a walking stick, like a talking-stick,

[2] The Lamalchi Bay people merged with the Penelakuts, the largest Kuper Island village, in the late 1800s. The sea lion story links the Squamish and the Island people mythologically. In speech they are quite different, Kuper Island (as Dominic indicates below) belonging to the group speaking what was commonly called "Cowichan" and is now called "Halkomelem."

and he poke my grandfather in the back. He asked my grandfather, "Are you asleeping or are you awake?" He talk our language, see. And my grandfather say, "Chen men wa es7úmsm, chen men wa es7úmsm." He means, "I'm awake." "Chen eslhk̲'í7s kwis i hem̓í." My grandfather say that: "I know you coming. I know you coming down from up the sky." And this man say, "Well, I see you here all the time, every spring, every fall. What are you doing?" My grandfather say, "Oh, my good man," he say, "I got lots of family home, and I come here to get their food, see, dry meat, and the wool. We use the wool for our clothing." And this man say, "Yes, I see you all the time." This man say that. "I see you all the time; you right here all the time. But that's why I come, I come to help you. I got something to give you." My grandfather never never turn round, never look. This man tell him, "I got something to give you." That's our story, like, see. And he told the top one: "You not tell lie." Second one: "Not steal anything." Third one: "Not go fool around with another man's wife." "And if you good good worker, and you have everything, you'll plant everything all around your home, everything your food," this man told him, see. "If these people believe you, they'll do what you tell them. They'll plant their food here and over here." I guess that's potatoes. "And you'll be planting berries so you won't go hunt berries up there." Used to go up, you know. The berries is ripe now, see, blue berries. Up Squamish there's lots yet, up in the hill, way up top.

WELLS: When these people give thanks, do they give thanks through your great-grandfather? Does he give thanks for all of them?

CHARLIE: Oh, yes, yes. These people come and they—because my grandfather he was just like the head man, and these people, that's just like if that's their father. They're all relation to him, you see, because we all come from one man, one woman, see.

WELLS: Oh, I see.

[TRANSFORMER LEGEND]

CHARLIE: This man he, nobody know where he came from. Same as these fellows over Gibsons; but this man he born up Squamish. And he didn't know his wife was going to get baby, see. And he know somebody coming. He know. There's a bird there, Raven; he go ahead of them three men, see. They tell the Raven, "You go tell everybody we coming." And this man he understand that bird. "Some man coming. Three men, three brothers coming." And this old man he get ready. There's a nice little mountain there, just fit his canoe. He tie his canoe here, and he got a pole, long pole. And this place wasn't very deep, you know, and he puts that pole down, and he ties moss on there. When the fish touch that moss, the slime caught on that. He was there and he knows them people coming. They reach Squamish already. And he had his pole like that, and the fish touch and he pulls it up; and he knows where the slime; he puts it in that wooden plate, see. He heard them coming coming coming. Them fellows know where he is and come across. He wouldn't look, just hold his pole like this. Them fellows coming, landed on the side of his canoe. They ask the old man what he's doing. The old man say, "Oh," he say, "you my grandchildren, I know you people coming, and this here I'm going to feed you people this. That's my food," he says. And he tell these people, "I got a house there, see, right there, just a little bay. You people bring your canoe there and come up." And he pull up his pole, and he had lots that thing, moss, you know, and he brings it. And he boil, the rocks hot, you know, and he gets the moss and puts it in there, and he makes soup, and he tell the man, "Sit down like this." He had a bench: "Sit down." And he had a big x̲wúk̲wem, plate; the man made that. He know the people coming; he made it real fancy. And he feed them. He had three spoons, three mountain goat horn, big one, I guess; he fix it and cuts it open, you know, just like spoon. And he feed them. He got mountain goat fat, inside the stomach there.

WELLS: Goat fat? You got a name for it?

CHARLIE: We call it x̲wastn because we—oh, my wife she loved that. Oh, I used to kill lots of goat. I cut 'em, don't cut that bag, you know, save that. I bring it home, and my wife dry it, put it on a rack. My wife used to come there and plate and just a little stick, you know, and warm it up, toast it.

Them three men eat that. The woman is laying down. Oh, she's going rolling, you know, and this man say, "I don't know what's wrong with my wife." But this man, head man, he know she's going to get baby, see. Tell his two brothers, "You fellows go across and get the medicine." He name that tree, x̱wáy7ay, that's the willow tree. "You fellows go across there and get that willow tree, the small one, green one. You scrape that bark, scrape it." And he told the old man if he's got any smaller x̱wúk̲wem. The old man say, "Yes, I got smaller one." That head man tell him put two rocks in there, and they put the bark that willow tree, just it in there; and he give that woman drink, he give her drink. Not long he call the old man, "You better go out." He tell his brother: "You fellows take your grandfather out and talk to him outside." He stay in there, the head man, he stay in there; and not long they hear a baby cry, you know. And this head man he fix him up. They had cedar bark all ready, all fixed up nice, you know, just like a little cradle, and they put that baby in this, fix him all up. This head man he show that woman how to do it, next baby, see. He tell him about the medicine, tell the old man when he come in and he got a baby, baby boy. First come born baby boy, and the next one a girl. Them two grow together, grow, come big, and they, this boy married his sister, see. Next baby come it's a girl, and the next one a boy again. There's four of them. Well, they do the same; they all married their sister. That's where we come from them; that's why we're all relation.

WELLS: I see, yeah. That's interesting.

CHARLIE: All relation. Same way Alert Bay. One man from Hardy Bay, nobody knows wherehe come from, but I guess the same as that one at Gibsons Landing, see, come down, you know, same as the one up Squamish.

WELLS: That's the beginning; that's the first.

CHARLIE: Yeah, yeah, that's the first, we call it X̱í7lánexw. Nobody know; he just come born.

WELLS: Well, it's been very good. I thank you very much, Dominic Charlie. I'm very pleased to have had this chance to talk with you, and you have given me a lot of information. This is August the 4th of 1965. Maybe twenty years from now this will be very important, when people hear this. When I get finished with it, I'll put it in the University or some place like this, you see.

16. August Jack Khahtsahlano—II

Wells interviewed August Jack on 13 September 1965, bringing with him the map, ''Sko-mish-oath: the Territory of the Squamish Indian People'' that August Jack had worked on with Major Matthews in 1937, later reproduced in *Conversations with Khahtsahlano* plate 8D. That interview is difficult to follow as Oliver asked August Jack to repeat all the names on the map. Oliver worked again with the same map when he returned on 2 November 1965; but after a few minutes with place-names, he went on to more general subjects.

August Jack Khahtsahlano at Squamish, 2 November 1965

WELLS: I'd like to start again asking you names around from Musqueam. Can you give me the name first of Musqueam?

JACK: Xwmétskwiỷem.

WELLS: And the next one up from that little place called Mahly, was it?

JACK: Máli.

WELLS: And you don't remember this fishing place, or a place called Cheahtun?

JACK: Ch'iyák̲.

WELLS: Before you get to the cedar trees was a place that looks like Homulsom. Do you remember this one?

JACK: Heméletsen.

WELLS: And there is a place just before you get out to the point where the University is? It looks like Kullakan.

JACK: K̲'élax̲en.

WELLS: And right out the point with the University is, Chitchulayuk?

JACK: Ts'ats'lhm.

WELLS: There is not one before that?

JACK: K̲wek̲w7úpaỷ is next, and then you come to—.

WELLS: And if come around now past the Spanish Banks, what do you call the Spanish Banks?

JACK: P'ékwcha.

WELLS: When you are coming down now from the Spanish Banks, it looks like Kokohpai, what's the next one there where Sasamat is?

JACK: Iỷál̓mexw.

WELLS: And then coming in towards Kitsilano?

JACK: Ts'mts'ámels.

WELLS: And then where the Kitsilano Beach is?

JACK: Sk̲w'áyus.

WELLS: Very good. And now we'll come in where the Burrard Bridge is.

JACK: Seṅák̲w.

WELLS: Snauq. Is that where you where born? Is that your home village?

JACK: No, no. I was born across there.

WELLS: O.K. We come in further where False Creek is, where Cambie Street is, Aunmaytsut?

JACK: Á7enmitsut.

WELLS: And then you go further into where the CNR yards are now.

JACK: It is called Sk̲wácháỷs.

WELLS: Coming back again, where Main Street goes across there: Kiwahusks? You don't get that one? I'll come around to the other side where Howe Street comes down. There used to be a trail through the forest there he's got marked here. Smamchuze. It's on a little bay there. Well, if we go out past where you get to English Bay, there is one Ayaulshun?

JACK: Smamk̲w'ch.

WELLS: Where English Bay is now, what do you call it?

A photocopy of this map was sent to Oliver by Major Matthews.

JACK: English Bay'd be Íyel̓shn.
WELLS: Where Second Beach is, Straitwouk?
JACK: St'ít'eweḵw'.
WELLS: And where Siwash Rock is?
JACK: Slhx̱í7elsh.
WELLS: Where the point is now, Prospect Point? Sahunz?
JACK: S7ens.
WELLS: How do you say this one here? Before you get to Beaver Lake there is a little place.
JACK: Áx̱achu7.
WELLS: That is Beaver Lake, eh? And then the district here, Whoi-whoi.
JACK: X̱wáy̓x̱way.
WELLS: Then Brockton Point is? Pahpeeak?
JACK: Pápiy̓eḵ.
WELLS: Yeah, and then where the Deadman's Island is?
JACK: Skwtsa7s.
WELLS: And in where the Lost Lagoon is?
JACK: Ch'elxwá7elch.
WELLS: Yeah, very good. And then we go right up to the end and come around by Seymour Creek.
JACK: Ch'ích'elxwi7ḵw.

•

WELLS: This name looks like Mulks.
JACK: Mel̓kw's.
WELLS: Was this an old historian?
JACK: Old man, yeah. I knew the man.
WELLS: You knew him, did you?
JACK: Yeah, I knew him.
WELLS: This man Professor Hill-Tout he told about when he went to get the history, why, they got this old man out of the back. Nobody knew he was there in the village, like, I mean, nobody except the people themselves. They brought him out and I guess they sat around a table, and the first thing they did they made six sticks for him, six tally sticks, like. And he was blind, but he was their historian. And this man Hill-Tout he asked him to tell about the beginning of the people. And then he told this story. He'd go so far, and then put one stick down, and pick another one. And then, why, he got so far, he'd put this one down and pick up another one.[1]
JACK: That's the way you tell history.
WELLS: That's the way you tell history?
JACK: Yeah, from way back, you got to have sticks. When you're through with one history, another person, you move that stick over, put another one here; and then keep on till you get the other one again. That's the way they do it before. That's only what you call it, like marking, you know, mark a piece of board or something.
WELLS: Yeah, like checking 'em off.
JACK: Yeah, checking 'em off.
WELLS: It makes like a chapter in a book. Do the old people do it now?
JACK: No, nobody. All gone.
WELLS: Well, this story that he told it was about the coming of the first man; and he gave the name of the first man, and when I write it down I think it's Kalana. You ever hear of this name in the stories, in the legends? Kalana, this is what he called the first man. Is there anything like this in your early stories?
JACK: No. You know, all that story is way back, and I don't know.
WELLS: Well, Mr Hill-Tout asked him about how the people began. And he started with the flood, and then the Great Spirit brought the mountains above the water, and then he created this first man. And then he gave the man a wife, and a chisel, and a salmon-trap. After this the people increased. Do you know this story?
JACK: No.
WELLS: When the people got so that they were no longer good, why, then he brought back another flood, and the Great Spirit he punished them all again. He left one man and his wife. And then the people built up again. The next time he sent a snowstorm, and the snowstorm covered everything so there was no food. You don't get this story?
JACK: Well, just part of it, just the big snow.
WELLS: You have this part of the story?
JACK: Yeah, that's as far as I know it. After that winter, the summer came too hot, and burned the whole Squamish, burned it from the mouth of Squamish up to the top. It was too hot.
WELLS: Well, the last time I talked to you, we were talking about the sun and the stars, and you told me at that time that the people at one time prayed that they take the sun further from the earth, so that it wouldn't be too hot. Has this got something to do with the same story?
JACK: Yeah, it's the same thing. Yeah.
WELLS: These old stories, they are the first history of the tribe. When this snowstorm was over, if I remember right, he had a bird bring the first food, like. This man killed an eagle or a fish-hawk with a salmon, and this was their first food. Does this have anything to do with the legend of the people about the Thunderbird?
JACK: They call them Cheakamus Indians. They're Squamish, you know, but they call it Cheakamus people.

---

[1]See Charles Hill-Tout's 1897 article "Notes on the Cosmogony and History of the Squamish Indians of British Columbia," in Ralph Maud ed. *The Salish People: The Local Contribution of Charles Hill-Tout* (Vancouver: Talon Books 1978) Volume II, pp. 19-25. Oliver asks Dominic Charlie about Mulks in the later interview, 15 November 1965; but he had already obtained from him the name of "the first man": X̱i7lan̓exw—see 4 August 1965 tape at the end. Hill-Tout's "Kalana" is his representation of the same name.

[THUNDERBIRD STORY]

After that flood there was only one man left. But nobody knows where he was when the flood was on. When the water went down, he was walking around there where the village was, and he says, "What's the use of me being alive and the rest of my people gone?" And he wanted to drown himself. This Thunderbird he come down and tapped him on his back, and he says, "It's no use you going to die same as the others. You come up. I'll give you a woman after." So he go in the curtain, grab the salmon, and give it to him. "Now this is a food for you, the salmon." And that Thunderbird's gone. Next day she was coming down with a big basket, everything all that what Indians can use, all packed up in that basket. And when she come to this fellow, he told her where to stay. So she come to this man; he looked and he said, "Well, sister, what you got? You got anything good to eat?" So she opened up the basket and give him everything he wanted, and he's got a food. That was the Cheakamus River people.

WELLS: I see. Very good.
JACK: And this, another one, down here at Howe Sound, that's the first people that was coming down.

[ORIGIN STORY—SEA LION]

This man he made his house, he made a little house. Of course it's a flat roof, so somebody dropped down on the top of the roof, and he started to dance, and you could hear the rattle rattle. And he says, "Well, I'm the oldest, older than you," he told the man that's inside. But the man inside says, "No, you can't be. You've just come now. I'm the oldest." The other says, "All right." He got a stick and he moved one of the boards, what do you call it—it's not a board, it's a cedar bark. He moved it up. He give him the step-ladder, and tell him, "All right, you can come down, and you sit over there." And this man, early in the morning he started dancing, with his costume, and evenings do the same. That's where we got this sx̲wáyx̲wi. (Any of those people that think they own the sx̲wáyx̲wi, but we, we own it, we're the owners.) After a while he says, "Well, brother," he says, "you better move. You go on that side of the bay, just the other side of the bay. And make your house there. I'll stay here in this place." This is Scheňk̲, Scheňk̲ people[2]. It's pretty good to know a long story.

There is five peoples, the old man and four of his children. These other peoples they don't give him a chance to get some sea lion. The sea lion comes there, and these other peoples goes out and get the sea lion first. They don't get nothing. So these other will make the sea lion. He's got cedar, cedar; he makes the cedar, made it just look like the sea lion, and he took him way up in the lake. He got the cedar all fixed, and he tell him, "You go down." He try to go down; the cedar's too light; he comes up. "Well," he says. He tell his family, "Well, we get another stuff. We go look for fir." He made the fir, so they try it, and he go down. Tell him come up way on the other side of lake, swim down, come down. Was all the power they got, you know, keeps that thing alive. And night time he took him down from the lake, took him down, and tell him, "Yeah. You go to that little island"—course, it's not big island, it's just a little island where the sea lion goes. He stays there. Now he get the wood in, and he start "bah-ahhh, bah-ahhh," trying to get those peoples to come out. The peoples come out, and they all go, everybody go there, and these peoples, these five peoples say, "You go and tell your aunt, you go and tell your uncle, 'Don't go. Stay.'" Some other peoples go. Everybody get that spear in her. Spear. Oh, lots of line, and towed over to Comox. That's where they cut the line off, and they stay there. They never come back.

WELLS: I see. That's the way part of the tribe got over there.

JACK: Yeah. They say, "All right. We can get our meat now." And the meat comes in. They can hear them starts talking, you know; the sea lion where he gets up he starts "bah-ahhh-bah," and they go out. They get that sea lion. That's the way.

[2]The name of the Squamish village on the western side of Howe Sound at what is now called Gibsons Landing—see also Dominic Charlie's telling of the same origin myth in the previous interview of 4 August 1965.

WELLS: That's a way of moving the people without killing them, like?

JACK: Yeah. Not kill them, just move it away. Now some of them stay over at Comox. I was with a fellow named Frank Joe, and he's got that sx̱wáyx̱wi. And he says, "You know this," he says. "That don't belong to me. It belongs to you fellows." "I know," I tell him, "I know who it belong to."

WELLS: Is this swhiykway, is this different than the Whoi-whoi in Stanley Park?

JACK: There's lots of them, you know. Lots of them stories.

WELLS: It is the same mask, like, is it?

JACK: Same mask, yeah.

WELLS: But different ways the people got the mask, different stories.

JACK: Yeah. Up on the Indian River, fellow was jigging. He got one. He pick it up; when it come up it was a mask. So he put him in a canoe. Well, them fellows forgot it. They never thought about this, this mask. I guess they don't use it anyway. But this one here, on this little island, Áx̱achu7, the fellow was cutting, going to make a canoe. He was cutting, and the tree fell, and this mask dropped out. That's why they call it X̱wáy̓x̱way.[3] I still got that same mask.

WELLS: Well, this belongs to the family, like?

JACK: Yeah. No other people can use it, just in our family.

WELLS: Does anybody else carve this mask?

JACK: No. My granny stay in Musqueam. Well, she was there for a while, and one person says, "You lend me that mask. I'll make some, copy it, you know." So they got seven masks, same kind, seven people. "You, you take this mask.You take this one, that one." So those are ones that are used by them there in Musqueam. But it don't belong to them. The mask belongs to me, and I still got the mask. Yeah, same as the Scheňḵ [Gibsons Landing]. We're same family, belong to that. The old man, the oldest man I know, oh, he must have been over a hundred, and he used to tell us, "You fellows belong to that sx̱wáyx̱wi." So I know we belong to that, same as the ones that was in the X̱wáy̓x̱way. [Lumberman's Arch, Stanley Park]But not very long, my uncle died in Musqueam, Johnny, Chief Johnny. Before he died, he says, "August," he says, "August, you take that mask. You take it home. It belongs to you. It don't belong to us. So you take that home."

WELLS: Is that right?

JACK: So I had a little money, and I gathered the peoples and tell 'em, "Yeah, I'm going to take that mask. I'm taking him home." Now this new generation they thought we don't own it. I said, "You fellows can keep on, 'cause you belongs to the old timers. You can keep on going."

WELLS: In your family, how many can dance?

JACK: My son. That keeps on moving down. It goes down. it never goes off.

•

WELLS: This is a song by Mrs August Jack.

[*Song*]

WELLS: I wanted to ask you your Indian name.

MRS AUGUST JACK: Indian name is Swenámya.

WELLS: This is how you got your song.

Mrs August Jack.

MRS AUGUST JACK: Yeah. I was picking blackberries, and I come to end of the log, and I look, oh, bear is coming, same logs where I go. And I was saying, "Oh, what I go do?" Bear he coming and I go this same log. I was scared.

[3]As Dominic Charlie explains more clearly in the next interview, 15 November 1965, the mask and paraphernalia were found inside the felled tree near Beaver Lake in Stanley Park, which accounts for the name X̱wáy̓x̱way "sx̱áyx̱wi mask place" for the nearby Indian village at what is now Lumberman's Arch.

And I think about for do this, my hand.
WELLS: Clapping your hands?
MRS AUGUST JACK: Yeah. Old man he tell me before, long time, "If you scared and you do this your hand [*Claps*]." I do this, and bear he turn around and go back, and I'm staying.
WELLS: I see. Very good.
MRS AUGUST JACK: I was scared, and I was looking for berries. That's why I go that log. Pick berries.
WELLS: In your song, does the word for bear come out in your song? What is your word for bear?
MRS AUGUST JACK: Míx̱alh, the Indian name, yeah, bear.
WELLS: Chief August Jack is going to give us another of his songs.

[*Song*][4]

WELLS: That's one of your old folk songs?
JACK: That's my own song.
MRS AUGUST JACK: Is for real Indian dance.
WELLS: Real Indian dance. Yes, well, that's very good. Thank you very much.

[4]Just as his wife's bear song above was her own syéwen or spirit-power song, so this song is August Jack's syéwen. It is a mountain song, and Louis Miranda used to sing it for him when August Jack got "too old."

17. Dominic Charlie—II

Dominic Charlie in North Vancouver, 15 November 1965

WELLS: There was one question I wanted to ask you first, Dominic: when I talked to August Jack last time I asked him about an old, old man that used to tell the history of the people. Now this man he's mentioned in the works of Hill-Tout, and he called him Mulks. Did you know Mulks?

CHARLIE: Yeah, I knew him.

WELLS: Where did he live?

CHARLIE: He live in North Vancouver reserve.

WELLS: What's the name of that?

CHARLIE: Slha7án̓ [Mission Indian Reserve No. 1]. Right beside that church, you know. It's like it "come close to the edge of the bay."

WELLS: That's what the word means, eh?

CHARLIE: Yeah, Slha7án̓.

WELLS: When Hill-Tout wrote about him he said when he asked about the history of the people they brought this man out. He was blind and very old. And the old men of the tribe they supplied him with six sticks and they sat around a table, and when he started to tell the story about the tribe he'd pick up one stick. And when he'd told so much, he'd put that down, and he'd pick up another stick. Do you know anything about this?

CHARLIE: No, no.

WELLS: He was an old man when you where a boy?

CHARLIE: He was very old. He used to paddle from here across there when it's low tide, to come down only when they are touching the ground with the paddle, they know it, you see. They follow the shore all along, to come to English Bay there. They were both blind, his wife and he old man.

WELLS: They would make the trip alone, even though they were blind, eh?

CHARLIE: Yeah, they were great people. They were staying at my aunt's; they were close relation. And when they left they go in, they go up towards False Creek. My mother told me, "You better go follow your great-grandfather. Go follow him." And they can't hear; they're deaf, they're all deaf. And I tried to catch up to them. Oh, they went way up right where that Burrard Bridge before I caught them. And I told them, "You'd better go across the other way." I told them, "Go that way." And I lead them, lead them right in the shore, and they got in the shore, and they say, "Húy̓malh-halh ch'ám̓ek̲w"—they call me "ch'ám̓ek̲w" because it's my great-grandfather. I say, Húy̓malh-halh ch'ám̓ek̲w huy̓." And they paddle touching the beach, and they say, "We're all right now." And they come, come around. I don't know how they get across here, and when they cross here. Well. they know. They know where they go.

WELLS: Can they tell how strong the current is through the narrows?

CHARLIE: They know. They're great old people.

WELLS: They live alone?

CHARLIE: The two of them, in one little shack at Slha7án̓, at this side of the church, over there, you know. The old people they like to live close to the salt water. That the way.

WELLS: Now there was an Indian name given by Hill-Tout, Kalana.

CHARLIE: I don't recall that name.

WELLS: Mulks told Hill-Tout that Kalana was the first man.

CHARLIE: I didn't know that.

•

WELLS: Can you tell me about the characters on your talking stick?

CHARLIE: Oh, you want the story?

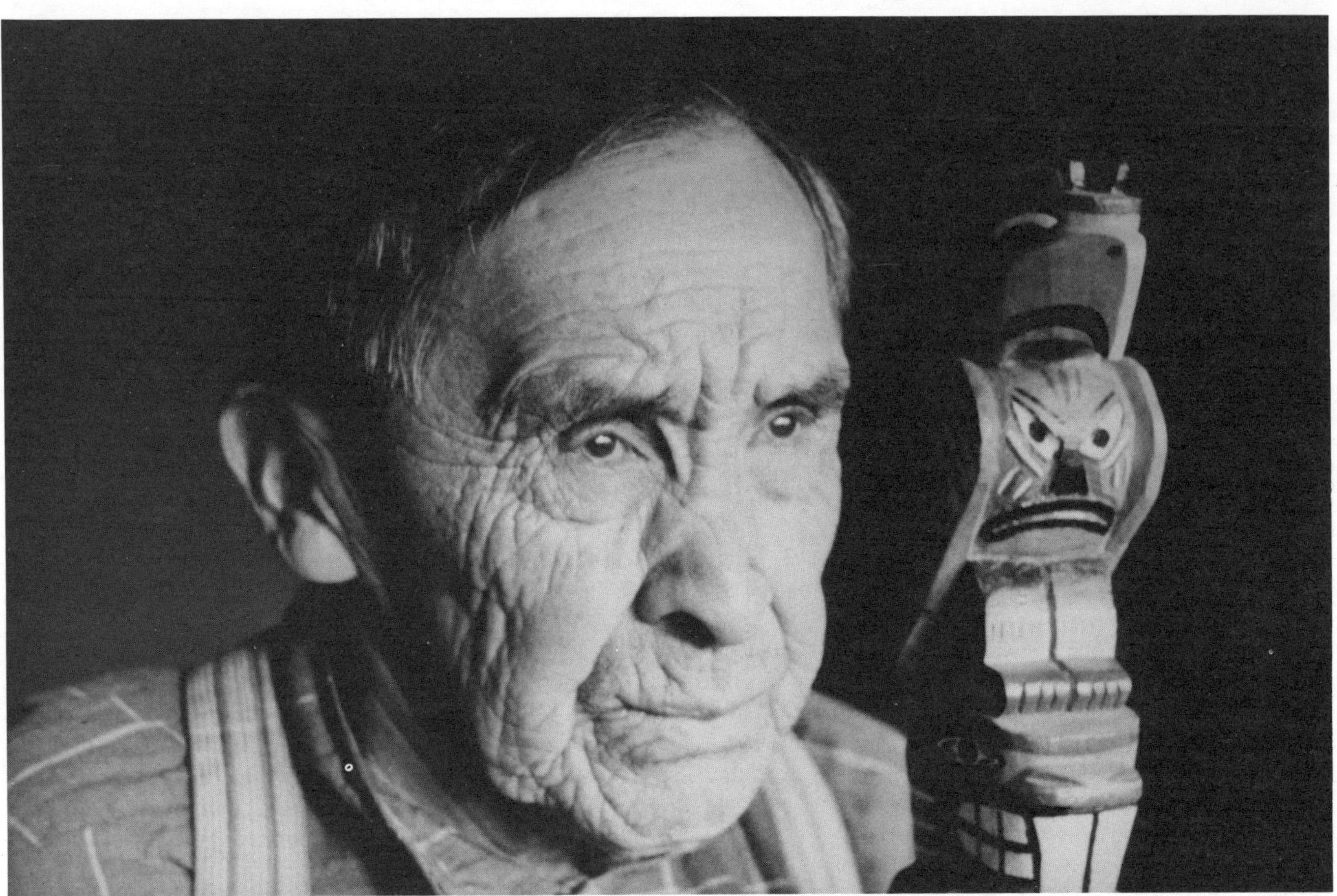

This photograph of Dominic Charlie taken by Oliver Wells on 15 November 1965 shows the "talking stick" with the images of the Thunderbird and the Beaver, as discussed in the interview.

[THUNDERBIRD AND BEAVER]

Well, this, it's the Thunderbird. He's the one that helped the people; he helped everything. He help one man when that big flood over the whole world, you know. The whole world had a big flood, and this man he was going to go away; he didn't like to live there because all his people all gone. He was the only one left because he went up to Garibaldi, see. When he come back, his home was as clean like that road, nothing, nothing there, and he was going to go away, see, and he started to go, and something hit him, come on his back, and that was the Thunderbird, see, and told this man not to do that. "You'd better stay here," the bird told him. He didn't know it was a bird, but he talk behind him, told him not to go. This bird told him, "I'll help you. Every morning you spread a hemlock brush down the beach." And every morning I guess that bird come down. He bring everything, fish, meat, deer meat, goat meat, everything on to that. And that bird told him, "I'll help you." This bird brought him a woman, and this bird told him to stay there, stay there, and build a home right where they used to live.

And when them people come, you know, two men, you know, changing the people, and they seen that beaver, and he told the beaver, "Why don't you work?" The beaver say, "I can't do nothing. I got no tools. I got nothing." Well, this people—we call them X̱eX̱e7ének̲ [Transformers]—they told him, "You got teeth. You can fall anything with your teeth," they told that beaver.

WELLS: That's why he's on your stick?
CHARLIE: That's why I put him on there. That's the story. I didn't want to put too many. I just wanted two of them.
WELLS: This represents?
CHARLIE: That's his fur.
WELLS: Thank you. When I get the picture, well, then I got the story to go with the picture.

•

CHARLIE: Will I talk in Indian or—?
WELLS: First of all, in English, tell me what it means?
CHARLIE: In English?

[RAVEN ROCK STORY]

The Raven tried to sling that up to Squamish, see, and some of his friend push his arm, and that thing slipped this way. He was supposed to sling it to Squamish, and he come to that Fisherman's Cove [West Vancouver], and he come to the ravine like this, and that rock's still there, yes, still there yet.

WELLS: It's a big rock in the—?
CHARLIE: Oh, a big one, big rock.

Drawing used in Oliver Wells's Squamish Legends *to illustrate the Siwash Rock story, and showing the rock "seen only at low tide."*

WELLS: Well, can you just tell me in the Squamish language the same story a little bit?

[*Story Told in Squamish*]

CHARLIE: They say "sch'elk̲'s"—that's the name because he sling that.
WELLS: O.K. very good. That gets a little bit of the Squamish language on the tape. You told me one time the story of Siwash Rock. Maybe there's more than one, but I think the story you told me about the two men coming along—.
CHARLIE: Three. You want me to talk Squamish again?
WELLS: O.K. Tell it in Squamish, and then tell it in English after.

[*Story Told in Squamish*]

WELLS: That's very good. It's nice to hear it in your own language. You make lots of expression with your hands; that's good too. I can't get that on the tape, but it's. . . Now, if you tell me the same story in English?

[THE STORY OF SIWASH ROCK]

CHARLIE: Well, them three men come by. They were coming, and the Siwash Rock was getting ready, getting ready to do something to them three men. And they didn't know he was in the water bathing, and he had that brush in his hand, that's the one he use for, like, soap; and the woman was on the other side of him, just other side a little ways, and she was sitting in the water. When them people come, they got the water, and they splash the water onto that woman, and they bring her right back in that hillside, you know, and that woman is there. And they come to this man and they ask him what he is doing, and he said, "I'm getting ready for them three men. I didn't want them to come my—that's my fishing ground here," he says. "Oh," them fellows told him, "that's us. We the people you heard coming." And they tell him, "You be standing there forever." And they get the water, and they splash him, and he went and turned to be a rock, and they got that brush—he dropped that brush, and they got it, them men, and they put it on his head, and that's why that tree, that little tree, used to be standing on the front his head, and one on the back. I could show you. The Siwash Rock. That was all.

They come by, and I don't know how—this, it's another one, this they call it Prospect Point, I guess, and we call it S7ens, S7ens. Well, they call it "Little Siwash Rock," but the Indian name is S7ens.

But there's another one this side of Siwash Rock; it's a woman. You can't see it only when it's real low tide you see it, sitting down, just like that. She was bathing too when them people come, and they ask her what she's doing. "Well, I just getting ready for them people coming, see." "Oh," them X̱ex̱e7éneḵ says, "that's us that's coming. We come to you people now." They splash the water, and they told her, "You be stay there for ever." That thing's still there.

WELLS: These three people, are they like the people the Stalo people called Qwahls?
CHARLIE: Yes. They call it different different language. They change the people, them three men.
WELLS: When Pauline Johnson come out, why, she made the Rock famous because she writes the poetry about the Rock. But it's good to have the Native stories. Where they put this Lumberman's Arch now in Stanley Park, August Jack he was telling me this is the place where the skwiykway mask comes from. How do you say skwiykway?
CHARLIE: Sx̱wáyx̱wi. Man named—You getting it down?
WELLS: I would like to get this story if you give me the story.

[STORY OF THE MASK]

CHARLIE: The man Syetx̱ím̓el̓txw he was falling tree in the lake in that little lake. When the tree hit the ground, and it split from the bottom, the butt, right up the top, and soon as that tree split, and that thing, that rattle we've got is in there with the mask, inside of the cedar. And this man named Syetx̱ím̓el̓txw he get funny, you know, get nervous, and he didn't know what to do, and he run home to Lumberman's Arch. He run down and he come to X̱wáy̓x̱way, and come and told his wife, "It's funny happen to me," he tell his wife. "As soon as the tree hit the ground it split right in half, right up the top," he said, "and there's something in there," he said, "a rattle and a mask," he said. We call that sch'etxw ["a mask"], see; this here is sch'etxw. And the woman told her husband, "You'd better go back. Take something good, your blankets, and go up and get that thing. Get 'em, go get 'em. That thing help you," that woman say that. This man say, "Well, all right." And he got something blanket, and he run back; got back there, and that thing still still going that, yes, that rattle, that shell, you know. And he brought it home, brought it home, and carry a blanket and it covered with the blanket; the woman seem to know. She said somebody help her husband to get everything easy, easy, see. And when he make that canoe, oh, I don't know how long he make a canoe and few days he's finished; make another one just a few days; he get big lined up with canoe in Lumberman's Arch. That's his business because that sx̱wáyx̱wi help him. He don't know where that come from, but it's in the tree.

WELLS: This became his power, like?
CHARLIE: Yeah, and that's the way it goes. And this man's name's Syetx̱ím̓el̓txw.
WELLS: Did his wife have a name?
CHARLIE: I don't know the name of the woman. I don't know.
WELLS: What's the name of the Beaver Lake, that little lake?
CHARLIE: We call it Áx̱achu7. X̱áchu7—that means "lake," see. But we call it Áx̱achu7, that lake.
WELLS: The other day in the *Sun* paper, and, like, the mist coming through the trees, the fog and the light coming through, and you can see the water in the background. I wrote to the man that took the picture, and I told him I'd like to buy it and I'd like to be able to reproduce it; and so he sold it to me, and I paid him $10 for it. It's a nice picture, and I would like to write about the Squamish legends, and I'll use this picture because its got the feeling of the legends, the light coming through the trees, and you kind of wonder what's on the other side, like.
CHARLIE: Yeah, it'd be all right if you could put my sx̱wáyx̱wi picture and put it on there. You know, I got one myself. And August got one.
WELLS: Yeah. Do you have the rattle? Could I take a picture of the rattle?
CHARLIE: All right. How about this?
WELLS: Well, maybe I'll take it afterwards, maybe when we get finished. I've got a little bit of time yet. I don't know if there is any more of these places that have got stories that you can tell me. Your home was at English Bay, was it?
CHARLIE: Kitsilano. That's August Jack's great-grandfather's name, X̱áts'lánexw. The White man just pronounce it Kitsilano.
WELLS: That's not right. O.K. I got it on there, now I'll know it. And what was the name of the village? The village was Khahtsahlano, was it?
CHARLIE: Sen̓áḵw.
WELLS: Yes, I remember he told me know. Up at Jericho?
CHARLIE: Iy̓ál̓mexw.
WELLS: And what does this word mean?
CHARLIE: It means, Iy̓ál̓mexw, use to be a nice beach, sand beach.
WELLS: And the word for the Spanish Banks is—?
CHARLIE: P'ékwcha—because it's flat, see.

WELLS: Yeah. That little island, they call it the Deadman's Island now. The name Squtsahs?
CHARLIE: I don't know.

Photograph of a scene in Stanley Park, obtained by Oliver Wells from the Vancouver Sun.

WELLS: August Jack he didn't know that one either. Maybe I don't say it right maybe.
CHARLIE: I don't know. I forgot the name.
WELLS: Seymour Creek?
CHARLIE: Ch'ích'elxwi7k̲w.
WELLS: What does that mean?
CHARLIE: Oh, I guess it ends kind of drop into this harbour.
WELLS: Yes, I see.
CHARLIE: There used to be sea serpent up, way up above there.
WELLS: Up Seymour too?
CHARLIE: Right across the Deep Cove there's a little island there, and they could see a rock, like that hole, that's where the sea serpent's head used to be, in there.
WELLS: Oh, I see.
CHARLIE: And the other end the sea serpent used to be across the inlet from up there, right up across that where that power house.
WELLS: At the end of Burrard Inlet?
CHARLIE: Yes. And them Indians can't come by. They used to live in that right across Deep Cove, it's a bay there, I don't know the name of it.
WELLS: Taytumsen?
CHARLIE: That's up at the Port Moody's different—Títem̓tsn, that's Títem̓tsn. But that bay I think the White people call it Graveyard Bay. It's a bay facing this way, see, and nobody could come through here with a canoe. And the Indians they made a skid, just like a skid road, up to the head of that, and when they want to come out they pull the canoe right over.
WELLS: They would do this rather than go where the serpent was? What did they call the place where they had the skid?
CHARLIE: Temtemíwtn, that's the name of that bay there, Temtemíxwtn [Belcarra Bay].

[THE STORY OF THE SEA SERPENT]

And used to be Indians live there, and people all died. They got sick, small pox, I guess, everybody died, just a few left, this one girl and a baby, I guess. And this girl she raise her brother, a boy, and she raise it, come little big, and I guess she get sick of the boy, she get tired of it, see, and she want to drown him. She throw it overboard, early in the morning she throw it overboard. And the baby crawl, he was crawling, he crawl, and he come ashore again. And he go in his house, and this woman, this young lady think, "I guess I better do that every morning, throw him overboard." This young lady do that, every morning throw him overboard, her brother. And that boy grow quick, grow fast. After a while he get big. And his uncle live, I guess, and he told his uncle make him a bow arrow. And this boy go hunt. He got a rabbit. After a while he get bigger, and a bigger boy, and he come big boy. He get grouse. After a while he told his uncle make him a bigger bow. And he get a deer and keep that girl train him all the time, every morning throw him overboard, every morning. And I guess this young lady dream that, to do that, see, to throw her brother overboard, because this serpent, they can't come by, see. And after a while this boy get bigger and bigger, and he tell his uncle to make him a canoe. They made him a canoe and spear, and he goes up and spear them seal. When the seal on the rock he spear him. And after a while he get bigger boy, and he always go swim every morning in the salt water. After a while, well, I guess the time comes the seal come after him when he was in the water, and they grab this boy, and they take him out. Everybody try to catch him, but the seal hold him up like that, you know, in the water. They come around, and they come around; they come around behind that little island, and he goes through, and he come right out, they come right out. People try to catch him; they never go down, they just hold the boy up; them seals come here, and they go, come to Siwash Rock. There's a big rock there out in the water, only when it's low tide you could see it. They came there, and then they went down. The seal went down, and that boy, and they say it's a hole from there right to Point Roberts, to come up there. Nobody know where they go. I guess they take that boy away somewhere, just like the seal kidnap the boy; they take him away; they go. That young lady keep his house just clean like this, keep him clean, and they burn a medicine round the fire, you know. I guess she dream that, to do that. And ten years, ten years, that boy come back, come back; and I guess when he come them dogs—somebody coming from the water, then the dogs run down and bark; and he go down again underwater. And this young lady told these people lived there to tie their dogs and put 'em away some place. "Maybe that's my brother come back," she say that. And he came back, fourth day he come in, come in the house, this bed all ready, his bed all fixed nice, fire on, and medicine, all medicine, just like for keep the fire going.

And that time there's one lady, young lady, when that boy disappeared, one young lady she trained, she trained, she wants to get married with that boy when he come back. This young lady trained; I guess she goes up to that lake, you know, where nobody see her, nobody know. In the day time they hide her, you know; Indians used to have just like a bunk, way up, when people come in they can't see it, it's all blind. And as soon as that boy came back they had a place just like this, they had everything; his uncle, that young lady, got everything, fur, goat skin, bear skin, they put it there for rug, you know. And that young lady come down, and she come together with that man; he got married right there. And that time that young fellow he told his sister, "I'm going to kill this animal, that sea serpent. I'm going to kill him." He dream that. Well, just like if he trained when he went away, see, for ten years, and he could kill that. And he, the serpent, told him what to do, what to do if he is going to kill. The serpent told him, "If you going to kill me, you get four, four stick of pitch, pitchwood, real black pitchwood, and sharpen it, sharp like a pencil, you know." And he jab him on his head, both ends, and that's finished it, like.

WELLS: Well, that's a very good legend. I'm very pleased to get it.

CHARLIE: Next time I give. . . .

[*Tape Runs Out*]

WELLS: You were going to give me the story about this legend about the upper Squamish. But I wanted to ask you first, if you could tell me, Dominic, about the idea that the hunters had that they should give a gift to the Master, like, when they come past Siwash Rock.

CHARLIE: Yeah. Now?

WELLS: Yeah.

CHARLIE: Well, he's supposed to be, he's a powerful Indian, you know, that Siwash Rock. And they turn him to a rock right there. And it's the story, if we give him an arrow, and when we hunting everything come easy, because we help, we give him that arrow. And its just like if he's hid. And that's the way that story from there.

WELLS: Very good. I just wanted to have a note on that on the tape. And then I wanted to ask you about the name of Garibaldi, the Indian name for Garibaldi.

CHARLIE: Oh, Nch'k̲ay̓, Nch'k̲ay̓.

WELLS: Very good. Now you were going to give me the story about the Transformers and the story on the face of a mountain.

CHARLIE: At Ch'iyák̲mesh.

WELLS: At Cheakamus.

[TRANSFORMER STORY]

CHARLIE: Yeah, well, the Ch'iyák̲mesh is a river, you know, when you see lots of fish, when you think you're going to get lots, maybe you only get one, and that fish all gone. They go in that little brush, but if you go look for them, you can't find them, because that man up in the mountain, his face—that's a face. That three men come and change everything. If he say it wrong, like with Siwash Rock, see, he says, "You're wrong, see." Says he was getting ready for them three people coming, and he wanted to do something to them, and they turn him to a rock.

And this man up Ch'iyák̲mesh, that's one of these three men, just like if his picture on the mountain there, to watch the river, if anybody go there. Lots of fish goes there, you know, and spawn, all kinds, steelhead, spring salmon, coho, dog salmon, trout, oh, there used to be lots of trout, but now no more. And in that little lake across that Paradise Valley—there is a little lake there [Tenderfoot Lake]—and when the coho go in there, they stay there, stay in the middle of the lake, stay there till February, about February. But now they go in this time, and they stay there, and February they start to spawn, late. But if you go there, you can't get any, them fish; they all go in out. Soon as they see somebody coming, they go out in the middle the lake; you can't get any because that man he watch that.

And further up, up Ch'iyáḵmesh, they put another, his older brother there, in the water. It's just like Siwash Rock, but small, oh, about ten feet high, I guess. It's in the water. And there used to be lots of trout there, right around the outside where that brother. And his head just like slant like that, and the grass it's, I guess, that's just like licorice ferns, you know, grow.

WELLS: You got a name for this?

CHARLIE: Tl'esíp. It grow just like if a hair on that rock. I don't know, I never been up there—it's a long time we been up there. We went up, me and my brother August, and old Ned and Jimmy Jimmy, four of us went up in a canoe. We speared this steelhead. Me and my cousin go together, and my cousin told me, "You spear the one on this side, I'll spear the one on the other side." We spear them same time, you know, so the fish won't get away. And sometimes when the fish close together, my cousin told me, "I'll get the both; you just stay away," he says. And he spear the fish, steelhead, you know, and he catch the two of them.

Dominic Charlie is showing Oliver the face of the transformer, Wáwnti, on the rocky face of the slope on the east side of the Cheakamus River, just downriver from the Paradise Valley turn-off.

WELLS: A three-pronged spear?

CHARLIE: Yeah, a two-pronged spear, like that, see. It's a goat horn, and we call that "miyách." When he spear the fish, that thing come off, see, and he can't get away. My friend was telling me to make one, but I never get time.

WELLS: Well, these men that become stone, are they one of the three, or do the three men make these others?

CHARLIE: Just like to watch the river, see, because when they turn to stone, when he's finished turning to stone, well, he go back with his brother again, and they keep on going. They keep on going and they come to one lake further up. I don't know what lake is that. It's four loon, I guess, always in the lake. When there is something going to happen to you, see, if you are not going to live long, well, the whole four of them holler. You know how the loon. . .?

WELLS: Yeah. Yeah.

CHARLIE: But if you going to live long: just one holler. The other three, and they go in the rock, in the rock, I guess, and they go down, and never see them no more. But they holler, you know.

WELLS: Do they do this because of the power of the three Transformers?

CHARLIE: Yeah. And I didn't know much this. It's way back our place, you know.

WELLS: Well, this river, is this the Squamish River?

CHARLIE: No, different. Ch'iyáḵmesh different. Squamish goes the other way. I think Ch'iyáḵmesh come from Green Lake. I don't know farther up. I don't know, I never been, I never go far. I went far as Green Lake; as far as I go. I work in the camp, you know.

WELLS: Yeah. Well, that's pretty good.

18. J. W. Kelleher

We do not know how Oliver got in touch with J.W. Kelleher and his family, but they were just the informants he needed to complete his picture of the Chilliwack's neighbors, the Matsqui, and their connection with the Nooksack.

Mrs and Mr J. W. Kelleher.

J.W. Kelleher, Mrs Kelleher, and daughter Irene at Abbotsford, 11 September 1966 & 6 October 1966

WELLS: Mr Kelleher, I should like to ask you first when your parents came? Would it be your parents or your grandparents?

KELLEHER: My father jumped ship in San Francisco, to go to the gold field in California. Then the gold fields broke down there, you know, and they conscripted him to fight the Yakima Indians.

WELLS: Is that right?

KELLEHER: Yeah. That's how he begin to come this way, you see. And he come with the rest of them, back there when the gold fields were struck in the '50s up here in the Cariboo.

WELLS: What nationality is your family?

KELLEHER: They're Irishmen. County Cork, Ireland.

WELLS: Good. And he married an Indian?

KELLEHER: Indian woman, yes.

WELLS: Indian woman. And what was her name?

KELLEHER: A Nooksack; she was a Madeline Job. He must have married her here, because they lived here in Sumas first, and then they went to where Mission City is now. And there's where I was supposed to be born.

IRENE KELLEHER: Their marriage is registered at the Mission Church.

KELLEHER: Oh, yes. They were registered there at the Mission. My father died in 1879, and they took me into the Mission.

WELLS: How old are you now, Mr Kelleher?

KELLEHER: Oh, up in the nineties, ninty-four.

WELLS: Is that right? Well, you're keeping your age well. And Mrs Kelleher, I should ask of your family. Where did your family come from?

MRS KELLEHER: My mother was from Port Douglas. You see, I don't understand his language, and he don't understand mine. But I know when they're talking Douglas.[1]

WELLS: Did you attend any of the schools, the Catholic schools?

[1]Port Douglas, once a thriving gold rush depot on the northeast shore of Harrison Lake, marked the boundary between Interior Salish and the Coast Salish. Below that point Halkomelem was spoken; above, the Lillooet language.

MRS KELLEHER: Oh, yes, the St Mary's convent. I was there for a while. I stayed with my sister most of the time. Then I stayed with Wades. Remember Wade's Landing down here?

WELLS: Yeah.

MRS KELLEHER: Well, I stayed with them for quite a bit, you see.

WELLS: Port Douglas in the time of your parents, it was a big town—it was booming. . .

MRS KELLEHER: Before they went to Yale, you see, they had to go through Port Douglas when they went to Cariboo. And my brother was just three weeks old, so I'll always remember it was in 1870 when they come to Wells's Landing.

Irene Kelleher with her mother, showing a photograph of Mrs Kelleher's mother, Julia, of Pt Douglas.

WELLS: And your father was John Joseph Wells?

MRS KELLEHER: Willard Wells. And they come from. . .

KELLEHER: Jackson County, Michigan.

WELLS: We have a Wells history, and I'll look it up and see if I can find it in the branch of the Michigan family. It's quite likely the same family I belong to; originally came from the States. They come up into Canada at the time of the United Empire Loyalists. They'd come earlier from the Old Country into the States.

MRS KELLEHER: Yes, that's the way with my father. There was a bunch of them come to New York from Wales. They scattered from there. My father was born in Michigan. That's all I remember.

WELLS: And your mother would be of the Port Douglas?

MRS KELLEHER: Oh yes, she was Port Douglas. At the time of the gold rush, you see, that's how Father met her. My mother's picture's up there.

WELLS: What was her name?

MRS KELLEHER: Father called her Julia. But her Indian name—can't you remember it?

IRENE: No.

MRS KELLEHER: I can't remember her Indian name, that's the worst of it. It'll come to me maybe before. . .

IRENE: Her father homesteaded at Hatzic.

MRS KELLEHER: He come right from Port Douglas right to Hatzic, and they called it Wells's Landing in the steamboat days. It was just the last few years it changed to Hatzic.

KELLEHER: They changed it from Wells's Landing to Hatzic when the CPR come through. They used to put a catch post there where they get the mail; the mail bag would drop on the ground; and the mail that goes out, it'd be to catch on this post, and put it in the car.

WELLS: Did you know the Indian that was the mail carrier on the Sumas River?

MRS KELLEHER: I don't know about the Indian, but there's a fellow that carried the mail over the mountain.

KELLEHER: Bill Bristol was the fellow that carried; he lived at Hope. He used to carry the mail from New Westminster up along there during the winter time, along Yale Road; then he'd come across from the Mission there. They'd be always watching for him.

WELLS: How old are you now, Mrs Kelleher, if you don't mind telling me?

MRS KELLEHER: Oh, I don't know. I was born in '76.

IRENE: She'll be ninety in October.

WELLS: Ninety in October! You're not like Mrs Amy Cooper; she won't tell me her age. Well, you've kept good health. And Irene, your daughter here, has been looking after you these past years.

IRENE: Just since December 19th, 1964. He made up his mind he had to leave the homestead.

WELLS: It's nice that you're able to look after them. And you, Irene, were instrumental, weren't you, in helping build up the history of the Sumas, the little booklet they put out on the Sumas.

IRENE: Oh, yes.

WELLS: Did you work with Christie Harris on that?

IRENE: Christie Harris, and Mr Meadows was the editor.[2]

WELLS: I've looked at it at different times, and this was the only place I could find the meaning of the word "Sumas."

KELLEHER: Semáth? It means a level place.

WELLS: Somewhere I read about Sumas referring to a big opening.

KELLEHER: Well, that's what it was: a big open flat ground.

WELLS: Oh, yeah, I get the idea then. One of these words down here referred to an easy portage from the Matsqui country through to the Sumas country. Did the Indians portage from one stream to the other?

KELLEHER: Not that I know of. See, they used to have a trail come from that way along the bank, then along the mountain to Semáth there.

IRENE: They call that the Riverside Road, but I don't know why.

WELLS: When the first explorers came in, I have a record of their diary, and they came up the Matsqui, and they portaged through here somewhere and went down the Sumas, and then they come up the Chilliwack. This was the Hudson Bay people.

KELLEHER: Well, they could have. You know, they come up to right down here where McClure's is, and then portaged over here to the Sumas River there, right through Sumas City now.

WELLS: Mr Hill-Tout, he made a study of the Indian archaeology, and he wrote quite an article on the burial mounds that are on Sumas Mountain. But these may be 2000 years old. They're beyond the time of the present day Indians.[3]

KELLEHER: The Indians as far as I remember as a boy, they buried them all up on the trees, on the cottonwood trees and cedar trees.

WELLS: Can you remember them on the Sumas River?

KELLEHER: I can remember them on the Sumas River, right at the outlet there. There used to be big cottonwoods there, great big fellows, yeah. And they'd carry them, and put them way up there in their canoe, and they would stay there.

WELLS: Mrs Bertie Nesbitt told me about that.

KELLEHER: The last one I seen was down here on Matsqui Prairie, you know Beharrell's place down there, down by the river. And there was a big cedar tree there, and this Indian from Douglas put his wife up on the tree there, before he took her back—she was all gone then, but just the bones I guess, when he took her back to Douglas. That's the last one I ever seen.

Picnic at Sumas Lake before it was drained. Photo: Vancouver City Archives.

WELLS: The draining of Sumas Lake made a difference in the country, didn't it?

MRS KELLEHER: Oh, my, yeah. My, we used to have a good time up on that lake, when we had the gas boat, and we'd get a crowd and go way up there to get out of the mosquitoes.

WELLS: Do you have any remembrance of the Indian village on Sumas Lake on top of the water? The Boundary Line Survey people, they described this village; and the people would take their canoes, and go out to the village; and they would get rid of all the mosquitoes before they left the land.[4]

KELLEHER: No, we never seen one of them. It's a funny

---

[2]The pamphlet, *Where Trails Meet* (no date), can be consulted at the Abbotsford Museum. It was compiled by a Historical Committee whose membership included Irene Kelleher and Christie Harris, the well-known writer on Indian subjects. The coordinator was S.D. Meadows.

[3]Oliver is referring to the Archaeological section of Hill-Tout's study of the Halkomelem tribes; see Ralph Maud ed. *The Salish People: The Local Contribution of Charles Hill-Tout* (1978), Vol. III p. 92: "Indians who live in the vicinity of these tumuli know nothing about them or their builders."

[4]Oliver is referring to the following passage from J.K. Lord's *The Naturalist in British Columbia* (1866), included in his worknotes:

> We knew these most unwelcome visitors were to be expected, from Indian information. I must confess I had a vague suspicion that the pests were to be dreaded—; for the crafty redskins had stages erected, or rather fashioned to stout poles driven like piles into the mud at the bottom of the lake. To these platforms over the water they will retire, on the first appearance of mosquitos.
>
> Mosquitos never venture far out over the water after once quitting their skin-canoe (egg sack), this fact the wily savage has taken advantage of. During their "reign of terror" the Indian never come on shore if they can help it, and if they do, they take good care to flog every intruder out of the canoes before reaching the stage.
>
> These stages each with a family of Indians living on them, have a most picturesque appearance. The little fleet of Canoes are moored to the poles and the platforms reached by a ladder made of twisted cedar bark. Often have I slept on these stages among the savages, to avoid being devoured. If you are restless and roll about in your sleep, you stand a very good chance of finding yourself soused in the lake.

On the subject of the round-fish, see footnote 1 to interview #10 above.

thing—we used to come from Matsqui here and go up there and have a good time in them sandbars there. No mosquitoes; and they'd be thick down here.

WELLS: Did you ever harvest what was known as round fish in Sumas stream? This book of J.K. Lord, the naturalist with the Boundary Line people—he described the Indians harvesting the "round fish." Now, I don't know what fish this is.

KELLEHER: Round fish? I don't know. I know them darn fellas over in Sumas brought them damn catfish. Shoemaker over there in Sumas, he brought them from somewhere in the East, and turned them loose in the slough right there, and, boy, they're everywhere now.

WELLS: How about the Indian settlement at the outlet of the Sumas River or near Miller's Landing there? Old Catholic Tommy was the last one on the end of the mountain there, wasn't he?

KELLEHER: Yeah, he was the last one, and he never had any family. That's all washed in the river now, ain't it?

WELLS: Yes, I think so, a lot of it.

KELLEHER: Everything practically. It's a funny thing to me that old Miller built that stone house there.

WELLS: Yeah, he built it on rock though. Do you remember Miller's Landing when it was way out in the river?

KELLEHER: Yes, I remember it. Oh, there was quite a bit of old dirt outside, you know, out on the Fraser River side.

WELLS: I took Jack Stevenson—do you remember Jack Stevenson?

KELLEHER: No, I don't remember him.

WELLS: I took him down there one time. He was born in 1885, I think it was. He said the Landing used to be, oh, half a mile out, you know. There were fields way out to the River. And the old maps show it all right. Well, now, the word Hatzic, this is an Indian name is it? Do you know what it means?

KELLEHER: Lake. It's the name of the lake there.

WELLS: Yeah, but what does the word—?

KELLEHER: Well, it means the name of that lake is just Hatzic, X̲áth'ex̲.

WELLS: The word Nicomen, do you know what the word Nicomen means?

KELLEHER: Neq'ámel, yes. That's the name of the big creek there, big slough. Neq'ámel means behind there.

WELLS: How do you say it again?

KELLEHER: Neq'ámel.

WELLS: Nekehmel, yeah.

MRS KELLEHER: He'll learn you to talk Indian pretty soon. (*Laughs.*)

WELLS: Well, the Indians along the Fraser so far, they use the "n"; and then on the other end they use the "l." And so Lekehmel or Nicomen, it's the same word, "n's" or "l's."

•

WELLS: Do you have any knowledge of the fact that Indians from up the canyon, Spuzzum and that area, came down and hunted deer, and took game back up the river again?

KELLEHER: Well, I have a story about them, the Thompson Indians coming over by Mt Baker there to live near the Nooksacks, trying to steal some of their women, or boys and girls, to make slaves of them. And they caught 'em.

WELLS: Well.

KELLEHER: At least, the women that they took with them up into the mountains, and when these Thompson Indians camped for the night (that's what Jack Jimmy was telling me) the women had to fix these Thompson Indians' buckskin moccasins, stretch 'em, you know, they're wet, and dry them. So when the Thompson Indians went to sleep, the Indian women took all them buckskin moccasins, and put them in the fire and burned them.

WELLS: And then they took off.

KELLEHER: The girls' people was following them up, and they went back with them home. And then, of course, these Thompson Indians didn't have any buckskin moccasins to put on the next morning in the snow, and so they never come back after that, he says.

WELLS: Yeah, that's pretty good. I made a map of all this country, and I call it *Indian Territory 1858*, and it shows all the trails, and I think I'm going to get this published now within two or three months. I'll make sure you get one, and you'll see these trails they used.

KELLEHER: These trails used to go over the hills, oh, I don't know where, somewhere up there and over Mt Baker.

WELLS: Yeah, I noticed in Jeffcott's, he refers to the hunting grounds way up the river.

IRENE: Course, the Nooksacks weren't a treaty Indian; they didn't sign a treaty with the Government.

KELLEHER: I had a job, you know, taking all of these Indian claims, you know, that they took up years ago.

WELLS: Yeah, I see.

KELLEHER: And I had to go in through all them places up there, and all across there; so I got quite a little, but I forget them now.

WELLS: That was quite a while ago, was it?

KELLEHER: Oh, when was that?

IRENE: In the 1930s somewhere.

•

WELLS: This is continuing recording at the home of Mr Kelleher on October the 6th. Mr Kelleher, I would like very much if you could give me any of the old legends of the Nooksack people, and I believe you have one which is connected with the story of the Flood.

KELLEHER: All right. Well, when I first come to the old mission up there in 1879, we was all out in the yard one evening, and the moon was out, and the sun had just gone down nicely, and you could see Mt Baker so clear and nice, like it's a big smoke, like out of a chimney, you know. And we were telling one of those there, an Irishman, by the name of Ryan, we says to him, "Look at the smoke over there. I bet it's going to bust out again." "No," he says, "it busted out here when we first come here," he says—oh, about five or six years before I got there. He says, "You could read a book over here, " he says, "plainly."

WELLS: Is that right?

KELLEHER: With the light that was shining over from that Mt Baker. That's a good many years ago. We all stayed up till quite late that night, thinking that it probably would bust up. And we could see the flames there; it was a real fire. But it didn't bust. It just had smoke all the time. So we went to bed.

WELLS: One of the geologists told me recently that Mt Baker is still almost a live volcano.

KELLEHER: It might be.

[VOLCANO STORY]

Well, then, the Indian story of this, you know, it says they were up there near Mt Baker. As you're coming down towards Shuksan, you know, there's a nice flat there, where the creek spreads all out, after it come down way up high in the mountains. Well, the dog salmon used to get up as far as there, and the steelhead, and the coho, but the other salmon wouldn't get up there. They weren't strong enough. But the Indians used to go up there and camp there and dry their salmon away up in the hills, you know. So they were all having a big time there, catching salmon and drying them. And first thing, the mountain started to rumble. He says it growled and growled, and "Gosh," he said, "we got scared. Oh," he says, "the first thing, it was boof! and come a big, big smoke, and," he says, "fire and stone was flying around you," he says, "and dropping all around red hot." He says, "We all run; we didn't take nothing, just run down the hill, farthest and fastest we could go."

"Oh," he says, "we got way down, oh," he says, "down, I guess, way down close to Everson," he says, "down that way until we stopped and wondered what we were going to do. We got all our blankets and stuff and all our stuff to eat up there." Well, this fellow says, "We can catch salmon here too." So they did. And then the chief—I can't think of his name—I've seen his name in that paper there some time—he volunteered to go up with four or five men to get some fire. So they went up and, of course, everything was burning, and the trees and forest was all on fire. They got up there and she rumbled again, and away they go again down the hill as fast as they could go. Well, four or five, the next day, they tried again, Well, that time they got some fire. The fire got a little further out, you know, then. And it'd keep burning the brush and stuff. So they got some fire. "And from that day to this," he says, "the women had to pack the fire."

WELLS: I see, yeah. This is the beginning of, when they moved from place to place, they used to carry their fire with them, eh?

KELLEHER: Whenever they had to stop, they'd have to get it out there, and she'd blow on it. He says he'd get this cedar bark, dry cedar bark, and fuzz it all on up, and put it alongside the coals and blow it and blow it, and start the fire.

IRENE: Then you were told about the Flood too.

WELLS: Was it Chief Jimmy that told the story about the flood?

KELLEHER: Yeah, Jack Jimmy.

[FLOOD STORY]

Jack Jimmy was telling about the flood. He says, "The flood started to come up." He says, "First thing," he says, "they come from down Lummi way and down that way, and running, fellows running, telling the people to get their canoes ready—there's big water a coming, big water. Oh, nobody ever believed 'em, you know, and they said that all that's all nonsense. Well, some of them got it, and the first thing, you know, they were saying that a big tidal wave coming in. Then they started to run around, hunt up their canoes and rafts and everything, put stuff on them." And Jimmy says, "All the little animals and things was all on the roof or in the canoe and every place else." And he says, "The worst of it is them darn snakes used to come in and stick their head over the canoe," he says. "We'd hit 'em with a paddle, you know, bang 'em," he says. "Oh, it was awful, you know, all the snakes," he says. "Big ones." And he says, "We kept coming up. They don't know what they were going to do. "Oh," he says, "nothing to eat. So one fellow says, 'Look over there; look at the deer over there swimming, way over there against the rocks.' Well, they went over and got what they wanted, you see, and let the rest go.'' And old Jack Jimmy says that the fellows down there in Chehalis in British Columbia, they had these cedar house, you know, slabs. Well, they made a raft of that, and put their stuff on it, and that floated and floated, and they are still up in one of them mountains there in Harrison Lake, away up on the top of the flat there, the cedar slabs are still there. You can see it if you go up there and see it. That's what he says. So I don't know. Jimmy says they had a hard time after that. When the water went down, there was nothing, you see. Everything was dead, you see. No green grass or anything. But it come quick, brush come quick, you see. But where the deer and other small animals come from, I don't know. He says, ''They come. We never see 'em. Maybe you get them on the big mountain there, I don't know,'' he says. But he says, ''They were there at pretty near the same time as we were down, down at the foot of the hill,'' he said.

Now let me tell you something my grandfather told me when I was half asleep sometimes. He says, ''Years and years—'' that is, his grandfather tell my grandfather and his great-grandfather tell my great-grandfather—''waa-aay back,'' you know how you do it, ''waa-aaaay back, that this earth was hit one time, like that.'' (*Slaps hands.*) I says, ''How did it do it?'' He says, ''Our god, my god and not the White man's god,''he says, ''he don't look after it. Our god, the Indian god,'' he says, ''has an armful of worlds like our, you see, balls. Yeah, he's packin' them, and he's going to hang them up there, and one slips out,'' he says, ''slipped, hit our house and rolled and rolled,'' he says, ''and, oh, we got drowned, see. Lots of our people drowned. Ohhh,'' he says, ''there was lots of people drowned, lots of big animals,'' he says, ''drowned. All kinds of big ones,'' he says. ''Biiiiiig ones—'' the way he'd get it way up in the air—''yeah, all died,'' he says. ''Small ones, not too bad; they get on top of the brush. White man says it rain, rain, rained. No water can stand around, eh? eh? Can it? No,'' he said, ''nobody knows everything. Indian says he come and shove 'em and he roll 'em, you see. Not catch 'em all,'' he says, ''catch 'em some. They roll 'em way up in there, I don't know where,'' he says. ''Killed 'em all, killed pretty near all anyway,'' he says. ''Lots get alive, lots come back, lots of them are not scared and run. Nothing can run away so fast. Got in canoe and put some grub in, and it was all right. They got man and woman, you see, put in canoe, and keep rising up with the water. But them that got scared and run, run and got drowned.''

Of course, the water, once it started to recede, my grandfather said, it went fast. ''It came fast and it went fast,'' he says. ''Then,'' he says, ''lots of the animals that was stuck on top of big rafts of logs and brush got saved, you see. But them that got under, that's why you find animals way deep in the ground, he says. You find the coal in the mountain.

WELLS: Oh, I see, yeah.

KELLEHER: Well, there's an article there about some professor coming into that too, up in the north, in the arctic.

WELLS: This is the Indian's explanation of it, then?

KELLEHER: It's mentioned in the old man's story, only in a different way, you see. Most likely this fellow is making a big guess at it too, like.

19. Mrs Lena Hope

Oliver sought out Mrs Lena Hope of Seabird Island for information about the Chilliwack's neighbors higher up the Fraser River. She was born at Spuzzum, which is usually considered on the borderline between the Stalo tribes and the Thompson.

Mrs Lena Hope at Seabird Island, 28 September 1967

WELLS: Mrs Hope, it's nice to be able to come and have a talk with you, and I had hoped to come at different times formerly, but. . . I talked to Edmund Joe Peters several times before he died, and from him I got a list of the villages which are in the Canyon, and a little bit about Seabird Island, and one thing and another; but I believe your family lived in the Fraser Canyon, did they?

MRS HOPE: Yes, they lived up Spuzzum.

WELLS: Were you born at Spuzzum?

MRS HOPE: Yes, I was born there.

WELLS: At that time, how many families would there be living in the area there, eight or ten or a dozen families?

MRS HOPE: Oh, more than that.

WELLS: And would these families obtain their living both from fishing and hunting?

MRS HOPE: They wash gold in them rockers, that was only the way that we got something to spend in the stores. I remember it very well because I stayed with my grandparents till I was about ten or twelve, I guess, and then they passed away. I used to be out with my grandparents out in the Fraser washing gold. I had my own little. . .

WELLS: Is that right?

MRS HOPE: Yes, they made me one, you know, just to keep me quiet.

WELLS: Wilson Duff, he did quite a bit of work on naming these villages—there was a little place called Suhseh.[1]

Mrs Lena Hope.

[1]Wilson Duff *The Upper Stalo Indians* (1952) p. 32.

MRS HOPE: Sése. Sése. The village right in Yale. There used to be a village there across the creek as you get into Yale town, and you cross the creek and there was a little stream that runs along there, and that's where they had their cemetery. Long ago they used to have it in big boxes, and they used to be on stilts. I just saw a little of it when I was a little girl.

WELLS: It was still visible?

MRS HOPE: It was still laying there, just crumbled up on one side, but my father told me that was the last one that was there, and the White people made them take it down and bury it. It had like a stilt, just the great big cedar poles.

WELLS: Was this on the same side of the river as Yale?

MRS HOPE: Yes. Above Yale. That little creek is not running any more, because of the highway. You can see the four mounds there now. They took these great big boxes. Each family has their own big box; I forget how thick it was. The people hewed this cedar, and when one dies they just wrap it up; and put it in. They had it so deep, my father says, it was almost half a tree that goes on top of that box, and it is hard to pick off, and I guess it just stays right on. He often told me that the mounds that was there, these are wooden boxes of people from long ago, way back.

WELLS: You can still see the mounds?

MRS HOPE: Yes. We always go up there and clean the cemetery. But I didn't know who they were because they were from long ago.

WELLS: When Simon Fraser came down through, I think they made a sketch of some of these burial places, and it showed these burial places above Yale there on the highway, these above-ground burials. But I don't know whether it gave the exact location, but this might possibly have been the location. Your own people would be buried up at Spuzzum, would they?

MRS HOPE: Spuzzum, yes. They had one like that too, I guess. There was one man that used to carve out, if it's a child, it'd be a little one, and if it's a little girl, it's sort of like had a dress on, and I don't know what color it was, because when I was a little girl I've seen a few, but I used to be so scared. There was one big one there; they didn't take it off after they moved the graveyard. Mother told me about it, and she says when she was a little girl she used to be so scared to go down there because there was all shapes of these like it was people standing all over.

WELLS: Would these represent members of the family that had gone?

MRS HOPE: Yes, each one has different. Each family has, but they all go in the same big box, yes.

WELLS: Do you know where they are making this excavation now above the CNR tracks, where Dr Borden is working? He's gone down—he's proven that the Indians were in that area 9000 years ago.[2]

MRS HOPE: No, I don't.

WELLS: I'm not just sure where it is, but they go in by the CNR; and the university students, they work there for two or three summers, like. I think they've come down through fifty feet of sand, and in this fifty feet they found different inhabitations of different periods of time; and at one time the Fraser River was up there fifty feet higher, and it left this sand and back eddies. The Native people, it was an area where they were fishing and cleaning fish, because they had these scrapers, and they've come down through three different periods of time. And they estimate that it was 9000 years ago. Isn't that amazing!

Old Indian grave on the Fraser River, photographed c. 1868. Courtesy of the British Columbia Provincial Museum, Victoria, B.C.

MRS HOPE: For goodness sakes! I remember my grandfather used to say—I don't know how he knew—that the river, oh, I don't know how many feet it was, it's gone down lower. It used to be way up. But one story that he told me is that he went up with—I forget who the other Indian man was—they were hunting grizzly bears, and they went up in that—you can see it from the tunnels—you can see it from the village too—that rock way up; it's kind of a little peak on it; they call that "Pointing," something—I don't know what it is now.[3] But up and below that peak there's a cave, and his friend that was with him went in there; they said they were going to camp in there. They wandered around there, and they picked up these sticks you use for the dry

[2]Oliver kept several clippings about the Fraser Canyon excavations conducted by Dr Charles E. Borden and students of the UBC Department of Anthropology. The one referred to here is probably "B.C. shovels uncover 9000-year-old clues" by Art MacKenzie; but the name of the newspaper and its date are not preserved on the clipping.

[3]Mómet'es, "Pointing"—see C.P. Lyons *Milestones on the Mighty Fraser* (3rd ed. 1958) pp. 43-44.

salmon, sticks that holds them spread, you know. It was in there, and they touched it, and it just turned to powder, like. But you can see it laying on the inside of the cave. It looked so like it was just put there recently, and they touched it and it just broke up. But how that got there they don't know. They wondered, I guess.

WELLS: This would be several hundred feet up from the river?

MRS HOPE: Oh, it was a way up in that mountain, yes. You can see that peak from the highway. And he said there were some—I don't know what they saw—some rocks, anyway, the Indians used to use to cook with or something. But later on my father went up there. He said there wasn't anything there. Some White people must have went there and took everything.

WELLS: Do you remember hearing of an old chief at Yale, Mahlihtluhk?

MRS HOPE: Yes, that's my husband's grandfather. He was the chief then when we first got married.

WELLS: Do I say that right?

MRS HOPE: Yes, you said that right, Maló:ylheq.

WELLS: Good. It's those combinations of letters that a White person can't get right.

MRS HOPE: I guess what Edmund was referring to as their prophet or something, well, there was one in Spuzzum. My grandmother's sister, and I think it was her cousins, there was three young women, and this old person was saying that "there was some strange people coming and their eyes are just like the sky there, bright as that, and they're blue." He said that "he doesn't know where they come from, and this one man there, his wife's got the same name as you have," he told my grandmother's sister. I can't think of it now. I used to remember it all the time, this name, Indian name. And he told her mother, "You'll have to watch your daughter. As soon as that boat lands in the mouth of the Spuzzum Creek, your daughter is going to run to this man because she has the same name as this man's wife in where they come from, wherever they come from."

WELLS: Well!

MRS HOPE: He told this mother not to say anything to her. When it did happen, I don't know how long, but one day—there will always be a boy or man always be way out somewhere watching when enemies or something come—they seen this boat, a strange boat, coming down the river, and it landed. Of course he had this story already there was some strange people coming, gonna land there, and they're not enemies or anything. But he thinks that they weren't enemies anyway. So of course I guess they watched these people coming in, and sure enough, this girl, a young woman—I don't know how old she was—she ran and she put her arms around this man. And they couldn't talk White people's language, and this man didn't know what to make out of it, getting loved up. Grandmother said his hair was long and just white. She said to the man her daughter's got the same name. So she got pushed away and they got on their boat and left.

WELLS: Well, that brought out quite a bit of history, that one word.

MRS HOPE: I have Maló:ylheq's picture enlarged somewhere, but I just don't know where it is now.

WELLS: Have you?

MRS HOPE: Yes, I'll look for it. I don't think I gave it away after my husband died. His cousin had somebody to paint it, and before she died she gave it to my husband. It must be somewhere in the house. I have a picture of my great-grandfather too. Well, I haven't got it now. I think Mrs Crane at Yale has it. But he was chief in Boothroyd.

Mrs Lena Hope with basket work in 1965, photographed by Oliver Wells. The basket on the ground was made by Mrs Hope's grandmother, Mrs James Paul.

WELLS: Can you remember the name—?

MRS HOPE: I can't remember the name of him. I must have been around eight or nine years when he died; and he was a hundred and one, I think. I remember certain little things. I know I used to go and give him a drink of water. He just had long hair, and it was just as white as anything. I remember I used to hold his pipe. He had one long pipe, you know, that it was stone. I used to fill it for him with that stuff they used for tobacco long ago, when he couldn't hold his pipe up when he was real sick. My grandmother took her father from Boothroyd, and he died in Spuzzum.

WELLS: In those days did people stay right within their own area most of their life—unless they married into another area, eh?

MRS HOPE: She goes to where her husband comes from. When the parents picks out their sons' wives, sometimes when they're just a little child, they say, "That's going to be your wife, son." When they get to age to get married, they come with their buckskins and food and everything. They sit her down; then they pile this stuff. It's like buying her gifts and all sorts of things. Then if the parents of this girl still agrees that they get married, well, they take her. Some of them, they change their minds, and they have to take back things they give.

WELLS: And were there different classes, like? A chief's daughter or a chief's son, would they necessarily marry into a different class than the average person?

MRS HOPE: I think there is classes, but I don't know about the chief. I don't think that they allow that what they call the lower third, lower class people. . . Depends on if they're lazy, they wouldn't let their daughter marry. Same with the slave-girls that they've taken from different places, the village, they wouldn't allow this man to marry a girl that had been a slave.

WELLS: Did the Thompson people occasionally make raids on the Lower Fraser people, or did they go to the Coast?

MRS HOPE: I don't know about the Coast, but mostly my grandfather talks about—oh, I guess they did, down this way, because he often tells me about a girl—they took a girl from the West Coast somewhere, and she was a slave there for a long time right in Yale. And the chief's son wanted to marry this girl, and the parents wouldn't have it, so they ran away, and they lived up in Siwash Creek, way up, half way up the mountain. Yes, I seen kind of a hole there I guess they'd kind of dug out. And my father says, "This is where the couple lived all their lives pretty near, till I don't know which way they went," he said.

WELLS: Is that right? Well.

MRS HOPE: They had children. They were outcasts I guess you would say they were called. He says his father never told him where they went after that. Maybe with the things changed, when people left, you know, they might have come down.

WELLS: From what Bob Joe said, the Thompson people came down sometimes to hunt above the Chilliwack River country, and would bring down dried meat down the Chilliwack River to the Fraser, and then come back up the Fraser.

MRS HOPE: My grandfather was one of the last ones, I guess. He used to tell me that when he was young he used to go up there, to Mt Baker. I don't know what month they'd go down, but I remember my grandmother said her first cousin got drownded going up. They came down too late, and then the Fraser was froze, and most of the places they had to haul their canoe past the frozen parts of the Fraser, and they got to one place, and she fell in with her child on her back. Most of them had long sticks, they said, so that they wouldn't go in if it breaks. But she didn't have any. She fell in with her child. I think it was the last time, they said, that the people went hunting.

WELLS: You've lived most of your married life on Seabird, have you?

MRS HOPE: Yes, I came here after I was married. My husband's parents got this place here, I guess. And they worked on it a little bit. My father-in-law went to work on the CN, a section hand. So they left. After we were married, they gave us this place.

WELLS: For a period of time I imagine it was the same as it was over at Chilliwack. They were quite good little farms, and people made their living from farming almost, and then the fishing was supplementary. Among the Chilliwack tribe I've been able to gather quite a bit of information about the people that were here when the White people came, and when I finally get to producing something in the way of a publication I want to refer to these people as a nation, you might say, or as a people, not just a reference to them being an Indian, or something like this. Because I think the whole subject of this early history, when it comes out, the people should be recognized as a civilization which was an important civilization rather than one that had to be brushed aside, you know, which it unfortunately was.

20. John Wallace

Oliver Wells's manuscript notes on John Wallace include the following items:

> John Wallace Born Sept. 25, 1905 at Hulbert's hop yard. "Born a hop picker," said John—Sept. 26/68.
> When 15 yrs old J.W. had hunting camp on Cultus Lake Mt. near boundary line. Old David's father had camp on the mt. Sampson and Old David intended to go up and stay with John but never got there—tried to go up after heavy snow. John spent winter alone—made snowshoes, trapped, had $1400 worth of furs in spring. Snow 15' deep.
> J.W. once tangled with a big Swede when he was a young man of terrific strength. The Swede was jibing at him about being an Indian. Finally John said to him, "If you want something of me, step outside." They plowed into fighting. They were both given 10 days on bread and milk in the "skookum" house. At their first meeting afterwards, they fought again, and John beat his adversary really badly. When they next got out after their 10 days confinement, it was Sunday, and they all had to file into church. John found the Swede sitting in front of him and tapping him on the shoulder said, "You want a fight." "No, no, no," said the Swede, and there was no more trouble. It was said John could lick seven good men.
> Once John had a new rifle, and he was up in the Liumchen country with Ed Wells, for whom he often acted as guide. A man suddenly came out of the woods saying, "You are under arrest." Edwin said, "For what?" The officer said, " For being in U.S. without any customs clearance. I'll have to take you to Bellingham." To John he said, "Give me your gun." John held his new gun calmly and said, "Come and get it." The man backed up, and took off into the woods. Nothing more came of the incident.[1]

In all John Wallace made seven canoes with Oliver Wells. There exists a photographic record of the canoe-making process at every stage. The following notes by Oliver show the progress of one canoe-making, with personal notes interspersed.

NOVEMBER 28—6½ hours

John smiled more broadly and talked more today than he has ever done since I've known him. He has now completed 70 hrs. of energetic work in carving a canoe out of a 15 ft. log of 22″ diameter. Today he spent 6 hrs planing down the bottom to a smooth almost hydroplane appearing surface which has a slight rise towards the bow and lesser taper toward the stern. Tonight as he finished he said "tomorrow I'll take a little more out of the ends on the inside and smooth it out inside—then we'll cook it a little and spread it—then we'll go for a canoe ride."

As he ate dinner with us today I asked him "what do you call this canoe in your own language, John?" "'tel-AY," he replied. I showed him a model canoe made by Joe Lorenzetto of Ohamil. "What do you call this one, John?" "WHAL-kwah-LIH-chum,"

---

[1]Oliver indicates the source of the last two paragraphs as "Notes from Fred Oakes." Oakes had worked with John Wallace in a logging camp, and was related by marriage to Oliver Wells.

he said. "That is used on the Fraser but it is no good for the fast water streams like the upper Chilliwack. You can't hold it when the fast water catches that sharp bow—the 'tel-AY is different—it slips over the rough waters."

"What do you call the bow of the canoe, John?" "'kuh-LAWLL," he said—then he volunteered the bow of the K'oh-wath is much higher—comes way out and up as high again as the canoe almost—"it spreads out for turning back the waves on the salt-water." "What do you call the stern, John?"; "s'ay-LAHK," he replied. "And do you have a name for the middle portion of the canoe?"; "s'UHL-wuh," he said.

After dinner I asked John in to see some of our original paintings which would be of interest to him—the Soowahlie Church and the Seabird Island Church by M. V. Thornton were of keen interest to him. He lives near the Soowahlie Church and had not known the Seabird Island Church had been taken down. The Brooks picture of the white-footed mice and the Raccoon were of interest to him; also of interst to him; also L. B. Hunt's big goose picture and Lodges Old Country Stag at Eve. Brook's G. Eagle and Wolf Howling and Lodge's Gyrfalcon. When he saw the "Eagle of Yen" totem picture by Rugh Harvey he showed more enthusiasm than is usual for him. "I saw that one on the Queen Charlottes," he said, "and there was a taller one which was about 16 ft. high."

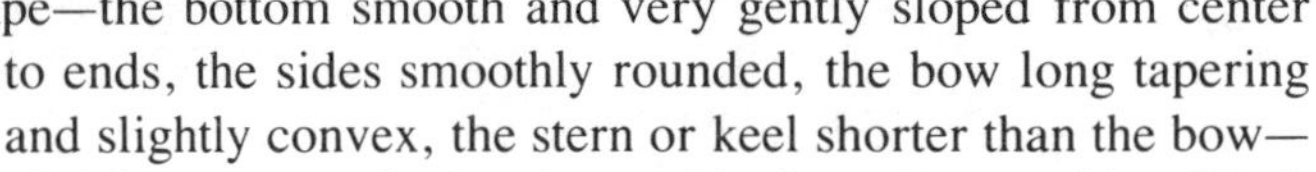

When we got back to the barn and started to work on the canoe John stopped to clean the shavings out of his plane. 'When I was a boy living with my grandmother—I was 7 years old then—that was at 'SKWAH-tehts (on the Fraser below Hope). There was an old canoemaker there—he was blind. I used to go for a walk with him, he liked that. He was blind—but he could make a canoe or paddle just as good as a man with eyes. Just someone gave him a start and he would finish it." And John went to work with the plane and his eye and the feel of his hand and the canoe took shape—the bottom smooth and very gently sloped from center to ends, the sides smoothly rounded, the bow long tapering and slightly convex, the stern or keel shorter than the bow—slightly convex at keel and smoothly fanned out to sides. The bow to slip over the water; the stern so it would not pull water behind it.

"What did the Chilliwack Indians use to smooth their canoes when finishing them before the White men came?" I asked when opportunity arose. "Rocks" he said—"rough, rough granite rocks. They would drop a rock and break it so it had a flat side—rough like a rasp or file and they rubbed the canoes smooth with that." An assistant with a sure form plane with convex and straight blades put in 6 hrs. smoothing down sides.

Biographical notes: John worked at several farms—Al Evans, Charlie Evans, Jackson, Woodruff.

NOVEMBER 29—6 hours

Today John turned the canoe over to clean out the throat of the bow of the canoe and also to reduce the amount of wood in the base of the stern. He used the long handled adze again and then smoothed out the new finished lines with a curved drawknife followed by rasp plane and sandpaper. This required 5 hours work. The canoe's lines were then brought into near perfect form with the use of the plane which required an hour's work.

The inside of the canoe is now ready for spreading. Inside measurements now being

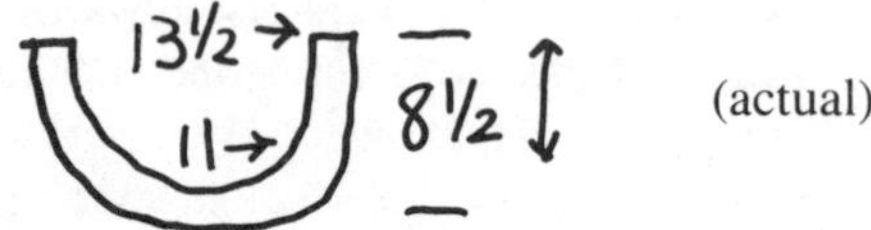

(actual)

Thickness and walls and floor of the canoe approximately 1¼″. John never uses a ruler to check any thickness; everything is judged by eye or hand.

Biographical notes: Over tea-time. John observed squared timbers of the old horse barn—broad axe work—which he used to do. He squared the timbers for two barns—one of which was Harry Capit (Kah-piht)—Chinook word meaning "you're too quick." August Sam was carpenter of the job. John also spent some months working with a Swede by the name of Olson cutting and squaring railroad ties for 2 cents apiece—also getting out telephone poles. John also worked for 2 years on bridge construction—wooden bridges—with contractor by the name of John Jackson—last two bridges built were over the Squamish River. Last winter when snow was on the ground John kept his brother Sam and his nephew Harvey and Stan Mitchell—3 meals a day. Only Stan helped pay for the grub.

NOVEMBER 30—5½ hours

John turns canoe over and uses plane to straighten and make uniform the outside walls of the canoe. This required 3 hours. Two threaded rods inserted to reinforce canoe—filler and glue used on cracks etc. 2½ hours. Canoe's finished lines close to axe line. Canoe ready for spreading.

Autobiography—Notes while working and at noon: John went North to Alaska as a crew member on a seiner. After the season he went onto a construction job and logging in Alaska. He and another then headed for Washington, D.C.—other man 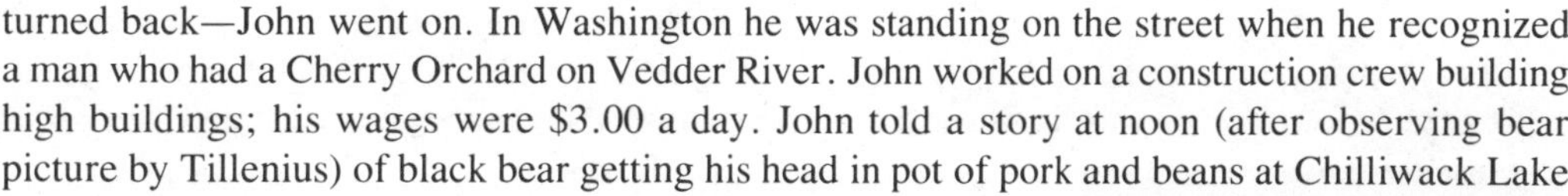 turned back—John went on. In Washington he was standing on the street when he recognized a man who had a Cherry Orchard on Vedder River. John worked on a construction crew building high buildings; his wages were $3.00 a day. John told a story at noon (after observing bear picture by Tillenius) of black bear getting his head in pot of pork and beans at Chilliwack Lake when camp cook put pot out on a stump. John proved to be in same camp as Ed Joe Peters and was in picture in 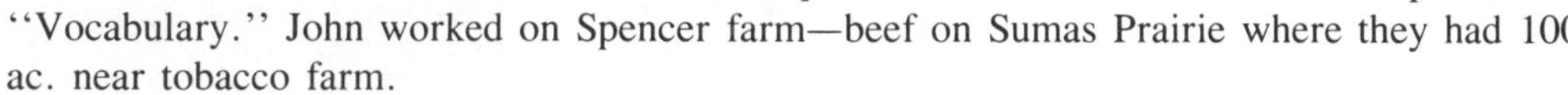 "Vocabulary." John worked on Spencer farm—beef on Sumas Prairie where they had 100 ac. near tobacco farm.

DECEMBER 1—3½ hours

John brought vine maple (green) stems about 1″ thick which he cut into short lengths and then split them in half. They were then ready to be used to spread the canoe. He then made 2 seats out of old dry cedar and 3 cross pieces which will all be inserted in the canoe after "cooking" and spreading.

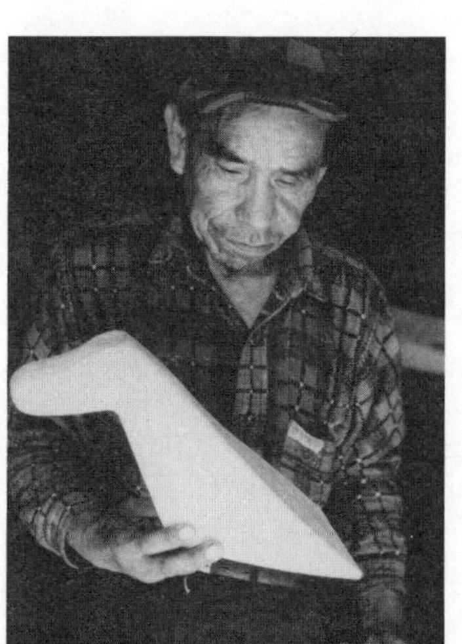

John helped dig a well for Stan Mussell at 27′ came to 4′ log. John helped dig a well for a White Rock man @ $1.00 went down 130′.

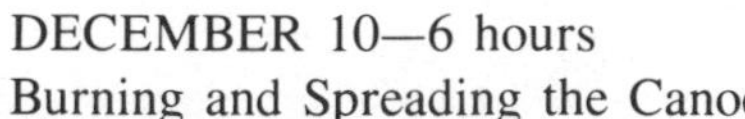

DECEMBER 10—6 hours

Burning and Spreading the Canoe

Canoe was moved outside and set up off the ground on blocks—Cedar Chips and shavings were used for fuel. Chips were scattered generously along full length of center section of canoe and then lighted. Fire was allowed to heat sides of canoe until they caught fire. A little burning was allowed—then burning chips were pushed back from side of canoe and fire was rubbed out with a green stick. If it would not rub out—wet mud was applied. Fire was thus kept under control until sides of canoe were charred black. When fire died down, green maple sticks which were about ½ inch thick cut to a length slightly wider than the canoe, were then pressed down into a half moon position. When the sticks got what John called "tired" with the heat (lost their tension) he threw them out and set others in their place. Frequently John took a sight down the length of the canoe to determine the amount the canoe had spread. He never measured with a ruler—only his eye. When a section was sufficiently spread he refrained from putting on more pressure in that area. When pressure was needed to make the lines uniform he set in more or stronger sticks. If the spread was sufficient on one side and not on the other the stick was set low on one side and high on the side which needed spreading. When the center section had spread sufficiently the fire was allowed to die out after it had charred the bottom to a depth of ¼″. Attention was then turned to spreading the end sections to a lesser amount. Kindling new fires was occasionally necessary to burn certain sections which had been missed. The measurement of how much fire to use, was the amount of charring done by the fire—when the wood was hot enough to burn then the desired heat for spreading was assured and the amount and uniformity of the spreading was thus governed.

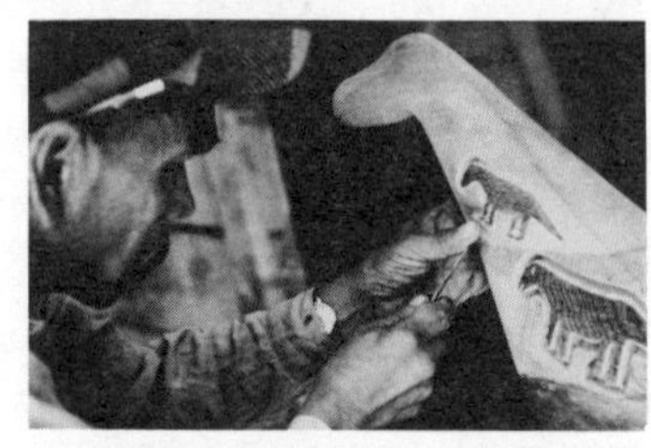

When the desired width and contour lines of the canoe had been established it was then allowed to cool in a cold rain with the vine maple sticks acting as thwarts to preserve the established shape of the canoe. Width between gun walls had been increased by 3″. The canoe was then moved inside and the thwarts of split cedar were cut to fit and set into place. The two seats which had been cut and ready to set on cedar cleats pinned to the canoe. The canoe was now cleaned of all loose charcoal and lightly sanded inside in preparation for the nature "paint" treatment.

Painting the canoe was traditional with the Native. To preserve the canoe, oil was used which had been heated and applied hot. Many sources of animal oil were used—the most desirable so far as the Chilliwack tribe were concerned was bear oil—rendered down from bear fat. For decorative purposes Native paint in the form of iron pigment was used to make a brick red which was traditionally the color for the inside of the canoe. tihm-MIHTH (the Native word for the red-rust deposits along the Chilliwack streams) was secured from the streams or soil and burned over the fire until it became a brick-red powder—cleaned of all foreign elements by fire. This powder was then mixed with oil and again the mixture boiled together and applied hot to the wood. In this case both outside and inside of the canoe were "painted" in order to preserve the wood and this permanently preserved the natural color of the wood. After the first oiling has dried into the wood a second oiling is applied and allowed several days to dry. The canoe is now ready for launching.

100 hours labour.

Biographical notes: John helped Harry Capit burning and spreading canoes. Canoe makers all went to SKWIY-ee to make canoes. Here logs drifted up on beach and were easily available for canoe making. Back water of Fraser—big whirlpool where Chilliwack met Fraser.

Oliver Wells and his grandchildren in John Wallace's finished canoe, in Sardis Park.

John Wallace at Soowahlie, 3 October 1967

WELLS: You lived here most of your life, eh, John?
WALLACE: Yeah.
WELLS: And I already got the name of your father. He was known as Doctor George, was he?
WALLACE: Well, his name was Xe'ílhatel.
WELLS: Shee'eetlahtuhl? How do you say that again?
WALLACE: Xe'ílhatel. That's his Indian name.
WELLS: Was he what we call a medicine man? Was he a doctor?
WALLACE: Yeah, an Indian doctor. Xwelá:m, they called it.
WELLS: And did he use medicines, or did he take the spirit out of people, like?
WALLACE: He never used no medicine. If you had a sore anywheres, you just tell him where it is. He'd draw it out with his mouth.
WELLS: Yeah. And would he sing while he does this?
WALLACE: Yeah, he would sing. He would sing with one of his singers, so he just goes ahead and draw it out, just pulled it out with his hands, and that was it. My mother used to drum for him. I used to drum too with him. And now I forgot all his songs. It's been a long time ago.
WELLS: What tribe did your mother come from?
WALLACE: Squatits, up by the Peters Reserve, they call it now. Just across from where we was the other day.
WELLS: Oh, yeah, from Seabird Island. And when you were a young boy, did you live right here at Soowahlie?
WALLACE: Yeah.
WELLS: And you remember the old people? Can you give

me the names of the old people that were living here then?

WALLACE: No, I don't remember no Indian names—only David, I know his Indian name was Seláqw'iyitel.

Capt John with Soowahlie hop-pickers. "Born a hop-picker"—John Wallace.

WELLS: Can you remember any of the big old houses that used to be over there?

WALLACE: No.

WELLS: They were all gone then?

WALLACE: Yeah.

WELLS: When you were a boy did you spend most of your time at home? Did you go to school?

WALLACE: No, never went to school at all.

WELLS: What year were you born, John? How old are you now?

WALLACE: Me? Sixty-two. Last Tuesday.

WELLS: Good, you're two years older than I am. How young were you when you started to work, John?

WALLACE: Fourteen.

WELLS: And where did you go to work first?

WALLACE: Worked for Bowman first. It was behind—you know where the army is, where they shoot targets over there, what do you call it?

WELLS: Oh yeah, Promontory. Up where Bowman had his home, later; he made a farm up there later.

WALLACE: Yeah, he made a farm up on top of the hill there, and we work on the side of the mountain.

WELLS: What were you doing when you first went there?

WALLACE: Buckin'. Buckin', a man's job.

WELLS: Buckin', is that right? With a cross-cut, eh? I see a cross-cut by the road here, is that your old cross-cut?

WALLACE: Yeah.

WELLS: Would you use a saw as big as that then?

WALLACE: Yeah. Seven feet. That's a logger's saw.

WELLS: And you were just fourteen years old. How many hours a day did you work?

WALLACE: Ten. Yeah, for two bits an hour. Two dollars a day in ten hours.

WELLS: Is that right? And did you live at home?

WALLACE: Yeah. Oh, I moved down to the mill. After I worked for two weeks for him, I moved down there, in between two Japanese. They had Japanese there, you know.

John Wallace (centre) with the Bowman logging crew.

WELLS: Well, after you worked for Bowman, where did you go?

WALLACE: I worked for the farmers for a while.

WELLS: For the farmers? What farmers did you work for?

WALLACE: Well, the first farmer I worked for was William Walker, up near Rosedale.

WELLS: Did you learn to milk cows at Walker's?

WALLACE: Yeah. They had thirty cows, and there was no milking machines in them days; you just squeeze 'em. My dad had lots of cows, and a lot of sheep and pigs and chickens.

WELLS: And where was your farm?

WALLACE: Just across from here.

WELLS: Across the Sweltzer Creek.

WALLACE: There used to be a big river there though, in them days, between where Jim is and Ted Cooper's. A big river was there, and one was through here. And one way down there where the other river is now.

WELLS: These rivers were coming through between the good land, eh?

WALLACE: Yeah. Oh, they take lots of land, that old man river. That was before they got wild; 1918 when it started to go crazy. You can't stop 'em.

WELLS: I think you told me one time you went to Westminster and worked at—.

WALLACE: Yeah, at Fraser Mills. About three years. I did

everything there; worked on the planer and off on a table sawyer—I get more money there, $7.50 a day. Biggest wages those days. I had to file the saw too, you know.

WELLS: Did you have any time on the river, fishing?

WALLACE: Oh, yeah, I fished there, had nets set out. Set a net there for a couple of hours, you get all the fish you want for a week.

WELLS: And when you caught sturgeon, did you catch them with a net?

WALLACE: No, you catch 'em with a line, and put some feed on it. Oh, you don't have to wait for them, just throw the line in there and go away, and you come back here, it'd be hooked.

WELLS: What kind of a hook?

WALLACE: Oh, it was just an ordinary hook, smaller than what I got over there.

WELLS: Smaller than a gaff, eh? Did you ever catch sturgeon from a canoe, spearing? Long pole with a spear on the bottom?

WALLACE: No, I never tried that stuff.

WELLS: That was the old way, eh?

WALLACE: Yeah.

WELLS: Well, after you left the Westminster Mills, where did you go?

WALLACE: Came home.

WELLS: To Soowahlie here?

WALLACE: Yeah, in Soowahlie. I just cut cordwood or shingle bolt or something like that.

WELLS: Did you ever get out, up the coast or anywhere?

WALLACE: Oh, yeah, I've been out, Alert Bay. I was fishing down there, Alert Bay, all over there with a seine boat, a skiff man.

WELLS: You were hired as a skiff man?

WALLACE: Yeah, that's right. You had to hold the end of the net, you know, about a quarter of a mile long, and keep rowing it away, keep it from going back.

WELLS: How many fish did you get in one—?

WALLACE: Well, the biggest haul we made there, that's the sockeye, that was about 6,588. Couldn't put it all in the boat; had to wait for the scow to come in.

WELLS: How long did you work on the seiners?

WALLACE: I stayed out there for about four months. Get cold and rough, I quit.

WELLS: Did you ever fish in the rivers up there?

WALLACE: Oh yeah, for a long time, in 1926, or was it 1924 up to 1926? I was fishing with Sitdown Jim.

WELLS: Where did he belong? Where was his reserve?

WALLACE: He used to stay with Harry Uslick. He lives there when he's not fishing. He had a crippled leg. One leg was bent, it was way over like that; he couldn't straighten it out. He would walk on his hands. That's why they called him Sitdown Jim.

WELLS: That would be on the Fraser? What boat would he use?

WALLACE: Oh, just a canoe, that's all. He was a crippled man, but he had more money than anyone else. Fished all the time, and he'd sell it down Mission.

WELLS: How were you fishing when you fished with him?

WALLACE: Oh, just gill net. Not any more than thirty feet, I don't think. We just tie it into the bank or somewheres, and set it where it's eddying; fish comes in there.

WELLS: Did you ever go up the coast further than Alert Bay?

WALLACE: I was up as far as Bella Coola. I done a little bit of hand logging.

WELLS: When you're hand logging, what do you do?

WALLACE: Well, there was no donkey, no nothing. Just a horse, a team of horses. You haul it down to the bank, and roll it down there and put it in a boom.

WELLS: Did you go further north than that?

WALLACE: I was in Queen Charlotte Islands for a while. I was a head faller there. That was falling with a saw, not no power saw, you know. There was no drag saw either in them days. We just buck 'em by hand, and they fall over easy.

WELLS: When you're falling, would there be two of you falling a big tree?

WALLACE: Yeah, one on each end of the saw. Springboards when you have to have it.

WELLS: What kind of trees were you falling?

WALLACE: Oh, well, mostly when we went in there we always logged the spruce. They were shipping it to England.

WELLS: Oh, I see, airplane spruce then.

WALLACE: That's the toughest wood they can have. I don't know, they making planes or something out of it. It's light wood when it's dry, and tough. Couldn't crack 'em.

WELLS: How long were you on the Queen Charlottes?

WALLACE: Oh, about six months. I had to stay six months to get my fare back.

WELLS: Seems to me one time you told me you did some construction work up on that coast there.

WALLACE: That's in Prince Rupert. We was logging up to Hazelton. That's behind Prince Rupert there.

WELLS: You told me one time you went to live with your aunt in the Skagit, I think.

WALLACE: Yeah, that's where my father comes from, or my grandfather.

WELLS: Well, would this be the same—like, Captain John's father?

WALLACE: Yeah. Captain John was older than my father.

WELLS: But they all had the same father?

WALLACE: Yeah. Oh, they all came from the Skagit, I guess, as far as that goes. They all moved down here, except my great-grandfather. He's still over there.

WELLS: He stayed in the Skagit?

WALLACE: He's buried over there.

WELLS: You don't know his name though, eh?

WALLACE: Ts'ō͟xéylém. He was a fighting man. I don't

know my grandfather, his name.

WELLS: Well, that's pretty good. I'm glad to get that much anyway.

WALLACE: Oh, they all got a name, but I just never remember them. I often hear my great-grandfather's name because he was a rough man. You just get him mad, you're gone, that's all. It's just like killing pigs, he'll kill 'em all. When he gets mad, he'll kill you.

WELLS: Is that right? Well, would he be their war-chief?

WALLACE: No, he wasn't no chief.

WELLS: He was just like that, eh? Well, this name that he has, does this signify anything?

WALLACE: Ts'ō<u>x</u>éylém means a, well, it means "a fighting man," "a destroyer," like.

WELLS: You used to go into the mountains here a lot with my father. You took my father up Cultus Lake Mountain one time, didn't you?

WALLACE: Yeah, we went up the other end of the lake, past Watt's Creek and climb up. He's intend to make a trail up there.

WELLS: He was trying to find a horse-trail, I think, wasn't he?

WALLACE: He never got started though.

WELLS: John, I was talking to somebody about the division line. A lot of the old Indians say that Indians in Soowahlie were different than the Indians at the Lake. In the old days, long time ago, was there a division up here, up the creek here a ways?

WALLACE: Yeah, there used to be a big settlement there just where the hatchery is. The call 'em Lhéchelesem. They got a different lingo than what we have here.

WELLS: Did they live in other places too?

WALLACE: No, they had a place there, and I wouldn't say that they were foreigers, but they lived there, near what they call Stútelō Creek there.[2]

WELLS: And would these same people—you told me one time you found a stone dagger on something that looked like an old Indian place up on the mountain, Vedder Mountain, up above Cultus Lake there—do you think there'd be a village site there, the same people?

WALLACE: Oh, yeah, way up on top, big flat up there. There used to be a bunch of Indians lived there some time ago. We found a knife all made out of stone in that creek.

WELLS: The headwaters of that little creek that comes down to the lake, eh?

WALLACE: Well, it used to head down that way, and then people changed it, and it comes up. That's how they get the water in Cultus Lake.

WELLS: Yeah, my dad helped change that. Can you see any big holes, like, where the people lived?

WALLACE: Oh, yeah, good level ground there where they used to live, I guess. We was just buggerin' around in the creek, and we run into that knife. That White man, he took it, and I don't know what he did with it.

WELLS: Who?

WALLACE: He was from Vancouver.

WELLS: Do you think it went into the museum? You don't remember his name, eh?

WALLACE: Well, his name was Bill Williams. He lived in Vancouver, somewhere around Hastings someplace. Bill Williams was up in that creek there, camped there for a week, hunting deer. I think they got about twenty of them before they went home.

WELLS: How long ago would that be?

WALLACE: Oh, around '23.

WELLS: Did you go into the Chilliwack Lake country one time with a man by the name of Johnson. One time you told me you'd packed beans for him or something.

WALLACE: Well, yeah, that guy he used to own that nickel mine, the one Sepass got. He's the guy that went in shares with Billy Sepass.

WELLS: Yeah, well, did you take him on a prospecting trip?

WALLACE: Oh yeah, we done lots of that. Oh, I didn't hear nothing but gold. We was all over the mountains. They was looking for gold, only they don't know what it looked like. They know what it looked like when it's in a little money, about that big—$25 for that, same size as a 25¢, you know, that's $25.

Oliver's caption on back of this photograph reads: "The 'Silver Chief'. A silver mine at Chilliwack Lake, located by Chief Billy Sepass (seated in picture)."

WELLS: Well, did you ever get way back in the mountains and then have to go down through. . . ?

WALLACE: Yeah, it was the same bunch of guys; we went prospecting, and we end off way down Skagit River, you know. We went through around Tamihi. We hit Nooksack

---

[2]Lhéchelesem is the name of the Nooksack language. Stútelō is the Nooksack word for creek; the Halkomelem word is stótelō. John Wallace here confirms that this site on the north side of Cultus Lake was probably a Nooksack village.

River first, and we passed that; and we hit Skagit River. We almost run out of grub then. Ten days, nothing to eat. I didn't mind it at all, but these men started getting sick. Hungry and tired, throwed all their stuff away, guns and everything, you know, can't pack it no more.

WELLS: Too all in, eh? Were you ten days without grub?

WALLACE: Ten days without eating. We still walked. They wanted to come back. I says, "You go back, go ahead," I says, "I'm going down here." Well, we got down there, and I see a creek running, running down that way. I told them, I says, "That creek must end off in some river," I says. I says, "You guys wait here," I says, "I'm going to look." I climb up the hill, and I looked down. I see a guy across the river making a canoe. So I came back and told them. I says, "There's a fellow down here making a canoe," I says, "Maybe we can bum something off him." So I gather some wood, and told them, "You guys stay right there." I went down there, got down there, and I holler at that guy. He came over, and I told him, "I got some mens up here starving." Well, he took me to his cabin, and give me something to eat, and he give me some lunch. I took off back to them guys, and they was glad to get something to eat, I tell you that, eat anything, dry fish, they eat dry fish. Of course, I got a little bit potatoes from that man.

WELLS: You were in high country with no game in it, eh?

WALLACE: Yeah. Well, next morning we went down there, and that man took us across, and we said we was going to walk down to Skagit, you know; but that old man says, "I'm going down and I'll take you guys down in the boat—canoe." So we went down river, and it was fast, too.

WELLS: Did he have a good-sized canoe?

WALLACE: Yeah. They were shovel-nose canoes. That's what they was making in there. That's all these Indians can use to go up the river, you know. A boat wouldn't do no good.

WELLS: Would the four of you go down at once?

WALLACE: Yeah. We came down about to the Skagit Indian Reservation, and from there they took us to Seattle on a buggy. We was travelling all day and half of the night. In them days, had to do a lot of complaining, you know, to get there. It doesn't matter to me; I can go either side of the Line.

WELLS: Well, that was quite a trip, eh? I knew that Johnson; he's still alive. But when did you lose your leg, John? How many years ago?

WALLACE: 1948.

WELLS: And where were you working then?

WALLACE: I was working for Bowman then.

WELLS: Falling?

WALLACE: Yeah.

WELLS: How did you lose it? What happened?

WALLACE: I fell off—the tree pushed me off the springboard, and down, and hit a blind stump. It didn't broke right off; it cracked it.

WELLS: How far did you fall?

WALLACE: About thirty feet.

WELLS: Is that right, John? You were on the side of the mountain, eh? Cultus Lake Mountain?

WALLACE: Yeah.

WELLS: They put you in the hospital?

WALLACE: No, I just went there; the X-rays says it was cracked. I thought it was all right, so I get out of there. It never bothered me till 1937. I was in Coqualeetza for a while. They took me to Vancouver with it, but it was too late; couldn't do nothing with it. I was in there for two and a half years.

WELLS: Did you say it was '37 or '47?

WALLACE: Well, it was '47 when it happened, '48 when I went in. March the 2nd. I was in Coqualeetza for, I don't know, about three weeks, I guess. They cut it open, and they couldn't do nothing. So they took me into St Paul's Hospital. They had that leg in a cast for eighteen months. It never do no good, just go for worse, and they had to chop it off.

WELLS: But then the compensation people, they wouldn't pay, eh?

WALLACE: Well, if it had broke right off, see, and stayed that way, I could have got it sure. And our doctor—I had Dr Roberts—he took off somewhere, I don't know where he went. He's not in town no more.

WELLS: Yeah. But because you went back to work, why, then—.

WALLACE: They said I might have broke it somewhere else.

WELLS: Well, how have you made out since? You'd get relief money after that, would you?

WALLACE: Oh yeah, but not very much—$6 a month, that's what they gave me. That's from Indian Affairs.

WELLS: Well, did you start living on your own or—?

WALLACE: I was staying with Ted Cooper when I first come out. I'd stay with Sam or Jim.

WELLS: You get more relief now, eh?

WALLACE: Oh, I get enough, sure. It's hard too—I feed them other guys, there.

WELLS: Yeah, that makes it hard. Somebody told me you helped build several barns. Old Harry Capit, did you work for him?

WALLACE: Yeah, I helped him. Samson Jim was the head carpenter.

WELLS: Kelly told me that you built his house for him. Did you build Mike's house?

WALLACE: Yeah. They were trying to hew timber for it, but they don't know which end to start on. He asked Sam to go up there, and, why, Sam he don't know—he couldn't use no axe. So I went up there, showed him.

WELLS: Did you help build other barns, John, in the valley?

WALLACE: Yeah. Oh, I helped build what-do-you-call-him's, Frank Williams', down at Langley Prairie.

WELLS: Did you do some work on the bridge construction?

WALLACE: Yeah, I worked there for quite a while too. Started from Hope-Princeton, right down, oh, and end off down at Squamish River—I think that's the last place we worked. We built one down just above where the Squamish Hotel they called it. I don't know if it's still there or not. I never been over there since I left down there.

WELLS: I went over a couple of times last year with Dominic Charlie. Before you go into Squamish, there's a deep canyon and a narrow bridge there, high bridge over a narrow deep canyon, a road bridge. That's not the one, eh?

WALLACE: No.

•

WELLS: Have you hunted on Elk Mountain?

WALLACE: Oh, yeah. Lots of times hunt there.

WELLS: Bear?

WALLACE: Bear, deer. I like to get a deer more than I do a bear. The only time I killed a bear that's when them guys want some rug.

WELLS: Do you know anything about the old Indian idea of when you're going to kill a bear and maybe a deer too, a long time ago, before the White people came, why, they kind of tried to make it right with the rest of the bears, so there'd be good luck for next time.

WALLACE: They want a rug, they fix it somehow.

WELLS: I think the Thompson people, when they kill an animal, why, then they do certain things. They're careful how they clean the animal and stuff like that—old Indian ideas?

WALLACE: I butcher the same as anybody else, you know.

WELLS: But did your father and the older people, did they take special care and do things?

WALLACE: Oh, yeah, they have; but I don't know nothing about it.

WELLS: Sepass, one time Bridge Bailey saw Sepass, he watched Sepass go down into the valley to shoot a bear. Then after he shot the bear, when he went up to the bear, he said he went through just like a, oh, like we call it a trance or something, you know. He just—he likely had a certain prayer, like, you know.[3]

WALLACE: Yeah.

WELLS: But this apparently was old maybe Thompson River custom.

WALLACE: Yeah.

WELLS: If I ask you—you know these stories about the water babies—if I ask you to draw a water baby, could you draw what you think it looks like?

WALLACE: Oh, I don't know.

WELLS: Eh? You told me one time before that they used to be at the Lake.

One of Bridge Bailey's jobs was to check the Boundary Line markers on the mountain peaks. He did regular runs up to Red Mountain mine. He once packed in a generator, divided into two loads. When the horses needed a rest, he built a tripod to get the weight off.

WALLACE: Well, yeah. That's what my grandfather told me. There used to be some there. But there's still some up Chilliwack Lake. Sometimes they play now out in the bank that's on the other end. My father told me there was a White man fished one out, and it got out of the water and screamed. And comes down the fog and rain, and the water came right up, water right up to that man's waist, and they let go of the baby; he got scared. So the baby went down in the water again, and the water went down.

WELLS: Some time I'll have to bring you a pad and pencil. You draw that Seelkee alright. I think you should take a pencil and draw up what you think these water babies look like.[4]

WALLACE: Yeah, well, I'll try 'em some day.

---

[3]In a recorded interview with long-time resident Bridge Bailey on 3 December 1965, Bridge described the occasion of Sepass shooting the black bear:

BAILEY: Billy went down to shoot him, and it was wonderful to watch the old guy. He crawled down there, and sneaked up to him. And then he got right close to him before he shot him. But after he shot him, you know, he went through sort of a prance.

WELLS: Is that right?

BAILEY: Well, I've never hunted with Indians excepting old Billy, but he reverted right back to the old Indian.

WELLS: Yeah, well, this particularly interesting to me because I read about this in the early research workers, and they tell about the fact that the Indian basically, when he shot a bear, his next thought was that he wanted to behave correctly so that the bear—the rest of the bear would not be angry with him. The bear world doesn't mind him shooting this, as long as he looks after it and does it properly. And if does it correctly, and treats it according to custom, why, then it won't be hard for him to get another bear.

[4]Wallace probably drew his idea of the "seelkee" when Oliver visited him on 26 February 1965 and the following conversation on the subject took place:

WALLACE: Oh, it was big. It'd be about four or five feet high. From his head to his tail it would be about twelve feet, I guess.

WELLS: Old Dan Milo he talked about them too, you know. And he said they were in Slesse Creek, near where they camped there. And he talked about 'em coming out—if you put something in the water for them, in the morning it would be gone. They would come and get it, and go again.[5] But did your old people ever talk about little people that lived in the high mountains, in the Skagit country and maybe in the Nooksack?

WALLACE: No.

WELLS: You never heard about that from your grandfather, the Skagit people, eh?

WALLACE: No.

WELLS: Well, we got a good tape, John. I think we got lots of things on the tape.

WELLS: Could you carve one out, with your idea of how big it—?

WALLACE: Oh, yeah, I started one. But didn't finish it though. Well, it was pretty near finished and then one leg broke off.

WELLS: I see. Is he a four-legged animal?

WALLACE: Yeah. Has four legs and got a long tail.

WELLS: Dan Milo has one of these seelkee stories about down near, oh, behind the fair-grounds, in that swamp down there. But the one they saw down there, it's a different type of thing altogether. It's a round-bodied thing with two heads.

WALLACE: Well, I guess there used to be a lot of queer things around this country before.

WELLS: Yeah, well, you carve one out for me sometime.

WALLACE: Yes, I will.

WELLS: And we'll have a model of them then, because he's a good Chilliwacker.

[5] Oliver in his notes recorded further information about ''Water-Babies'' from Dan Milo in 1962:

While the men were after timber for making canoes, the old Indians always fed their water-babies, that came out from the rocks, by throwing food in the water for them.

White men thought they would fish them out. The first one caught one, but it just held the line in its hands and stopped right where it was. The Indians all left (knowing something unnatural would happen, because the water bavy had been caught.)

The Baby opened its mouth to squeal, and fog came out of its mouth, and it filled the valley with fog.

I don't know if those water-babies are still there or not.

Epilogues

To provide a sense of what Oliver Wells considered to be one of his most useful achievements, we reprint the section ''Return of the Salish Loom'' from his pamphlet *Salish Weaving: Primitive and Modern* (1969). Part I was published in *The Beaver* (Spring 1966) pp. 40-45. Part II consists of notes added in 1969 to bring information about weavers up to date.

Finally, we print a significant letter written in the year of Oliver's death. It was addressed to Mrs Helen Richardson of Okanagan Falls, who had written to Oliver on 18 January 1970 after reading his Introduction to the *Sepass Poems*. We are indebted to the B.C. Indian Language Project for calling the letter to our attention, and providing a copy from their files.

Return of the Salish Loom

I

Members of the Stalo tribes of the Coast Salish Indians have again taken up the ancient art of loom weaving. They are weaving blankets, a craft almost completely abandoned last century, and rugs, which have not been made for some forty years. Instrumental in this revival were Mrs Adeline Lorenzetto of the Ohamil Reserve and Mrs Mary Peters of the Seabird Island Reserve on the banks of the Fraser, the river known to their people for generations as Stalo (river). To them, the Fraser had no other name, and from the River the tribes from Yale to the Coast took their name; they like to be known as "the Stalo people."

Early writings about the Coast Salish by such authorities as anthropologists Franz Boas and Charles Hill-Tout, naturalist J.K. Lord, and naval officer and explorer R.C. Mayne give detailed accounts that indicate these tribes made great numbers of blankets. They used them not only for their own comfort, but also as gifts to establish friendly relations, and as potlatch items in a display of wealth, at what were known as "blanket feasts." One of these blanket feasts, held on the banks of the Chilliwack River near the Boundary Commission supply depot established in 1858, illustrates the extent to which the blanket, regarded as an emblem of wealth, was used. According to Captain C.W. Wilson's journal: "We had a grand festival among the Indians, several tribes coming to a feast here; these festivals are annual, held at different places, and the Chiefs give away between 300 and 400 blankets." One writer referred to the social use of blankets as the mainstay of a thriving industry which kept the women almost continuously employed. In ceremonies of marriage union many blankets were involved as gifts between the families, and in the case of a girl of high rank the path from her home to her husband's canoe might be covered with blankets for her to walk on. At other ceremonies also, including burials, blankets figured largely among the gifts distributed.

Oliver used this reproduction of a painting by the travelling artist Paul Kane (1810-1871) to illustrate his article, "Return of the Salish Loom." His caption reads: "In 1846 Paul Kane painted this Coast Salish woman weaving a blanket of dog hair and mountain-goat wool. A shorn wool-dog sits by the loom and a woman in the background spins wool."

The original Native blankets were woven in a twilled or twined weave using principally wool from the wild mountain goats of the Cascade Mountains, which bordered the tribal grounds, or the hair of native dogs, which were bred for the purpose. Spinning the yarn was accomplished by the use of the spindle and whorl. In the homes of the Upper Stalo Indians three of these original type blankets have been proudly retained by their owners. One owned by Mrs David Charles of Seabird Reserve is a large heavy blanket, plain white in colour, with a twilled weave. Another, belonging to Mrs Hope of Seabird Reserve, is a blanket about 60 by 72 inches; it is made of a finer spun yarn and is ornamented with five stripes of red and brown colour, woven into it lengthwise at regular intervals. It is principally of a twilled weave.

The third blanket, owned by Mrs August Jim, has been given by her to the Chilliwack Museum. It was woven in a twilled weave, all white, except for inter-woven half-inch strips of a red commercial blanket material, which were introduced for ornamentation. The ends of this blanket have been finished with a three-inch wide strip of plain checkerboard weave, with loop ends of the warp extending about two inches beyond this. These blankets were probably made close to 100 years ago. Their owners are among the older of the present generation and do not remember having seen such blankets made.

Mrs Mary Peters.

Mrs Lorenzetto, who had an elementary school education, had not seen goat-wool blankets made, so she studied the weaves of old Salish blankets and read the published accounts. One was ''Organized Salish Blanket Pattern'' in the *American Anthropologist* by Mary Lois Kissell, who spoke of the textile industry of the Salish tribes in the lower Fraser River Area as ''one of the most novel in North America.'' She wrote about the Salish ''nobility blanket'' (usually about 30 by 36 inches), and of at least four distinct types, one of which was made at Yale and one in the Fraser Delta. Another account in the same publication was by Charles C. Willoughby in which he described the technique of the Salish Blanket. There was also a leaflet ''Woven Blankets of the Salish'' put out by the Heye Foundation. It was on such descriptions that Mrs Lorenzetto based her experiment, and she was successful in weaving two small blankets, one using mountain goat wool, the other using sheep's wool.

Mrs Mary Peters, who does not speak English, has been affectionately referred to as ''one who knows everything, because she never went to school.'' She is one of the few who retained the art of making the fine coiled basketry of the Fraser Canyon and Thompson tribes (her mother's people were from the Thompson). In her mind are clearly imposed the beautiful designs, traditionally those of her family, which she has taken from basketry to rug-making, an art she herself undertook to recreate in the fall of 1963. In a matter of months she became proficient and completed three beautiful rugs.

Reference to the type of loom used and the manner of weaving was made by Professor Hill-Tout in *The Native Races of the British Empire, British North America*, 1907: ''. . .they are woven upon a very simple loom which consists of an upper and lower cross- or yarn-bar. These yarn-bars are variously held in place. Sometimes they are tied. . . Sometimes, as among the Vancouver Island Salish, they are set in vertical posts which have slits or holes at intervals in them to permit of extending or reducing the length of the web.'' Weaving is done with a shuttle or by fingers alone, working from the top down, and rolling the web over the bars or rollers as the web in front of the worker is completed.

The blankets which came under Hill-Tout's observation were made entirely of the twined weave in which the weft thread was tied ''to the outermost warp filament in such a way that it is doubled, each end being wound upon a separate shuttle. One of these is passed over the warp filament and the other under; the threads are then twisted round each other and passed in the same manner over and under each successive filament till the last one is reached, when they are brought back again in the same way.'' Hill-Tout then points out that ''sometimes among the Salish more than one of the warp filaments is woven in at a time.'' He adds that, ''The blankets of the notables of the tribes often had patterns worked in them in black and red, similar to those in the old basketry of this region.''

When the Hudson's Bay Company established trading posts at Fort Langley in 1827 and a few years later at Fort Yale and Fort Hope, the fur and salmon trade brought a new way of life to the Coast Salish. Salmon which they could take in unlimited numbers, could be exchanged for trade blankets. In 1851, sixty fresh salmon would buy a blanket. In the great potlatches and blanket feasts the trade blanket soon replaced the Native woven ones. The coming of the White man in the Gold Rush, and the missionaries' determination that the Native must discard his old customs and dress, were the final blows which stilled the fingers of the Native women. Their ancient craft of loom weaving was gradually forgotten by succeeding generations.

In an effort to re-establish the craft among the Stalo people, the writer prevailed upon Mrs Lorenzetto to make a goat-hair blanket. The loom she used is similar in construction to that described by Hill-Tout. It is four feet wide, with slots in the uprights to allow for rollers to be either two feet or four feet apart. Using the closer slots, Mrs Lorenzetto wound her warp strands around the two rollers in a continuous manner. This method required careful finishing of both ends of the blanket before the warp threads were cut. Mrs Lorenzetto practised the various Salish weaves on a small loom about 12 inches square. Each end of the blanket was finished with a 4-inch width of close-twined weaving, which was bordered by a decorative design woven into the web of the blanket with black wool. Between these weaves, the central portion of the blanket was in the old twilled weave, a somewhat looser weave. Both types of weaving were cleverly worked into a smooth web on the same warp threads. The overall size of the blanket is 36 by 40 inches. Work was started with five pounds of washed goat wool plus a little naturally black wool for decorative use. On each panel of twined weave an arrow-head design in black and purple was worked into the web as weft material, making it visible from both sides.

Mrs Adeline Lorenzetto.

Mrs Peters' loom is of a slightly more rigid construction, in that the lower roller is fixed in a solid position, and only the upper roller can be wedged to tighten the warp when necessary. This loom also has a fixed cross-bar between the roller. It was designed and made by Mrs Peters from memory of looms previously used by her family for rug-making. She undertook rug-making on her own initiative, and the writer obtained her first rug for exhibition in Montreal. Her weaving is done entirely with the fingers on the face of the web, working downward across the full width of the warp. The warp cords were placed on the loom with the use of an additional loom rod. The warp cord at its beginning and end was tied to this rod; then, as it was passed up and down, it alternately went over a roller, over the loom rod and back over the same roller. When the rug was finished, the loom rod was pulled out and the rug lay full length without having to cut the warp. Mrs Peters used a twined weave at each end of her rug. In between is a twined weave in which each diamond of the pattern is worked separately, with two weft elements. In her first rug, the weave was left somewhat open between each row of diamond patterns. A second rug was made with a more complex pattern, in which the various diamond blocks were bound uniformly together. The material used was commercial twine for the warp, and strips of cotton material for the weft. Rugs measure about 20 by 42 inches. Her third rug, made with commercially spun wool with the pattern in squares, is a uniform twined weave throughout.

Oliver was planning to use this photograph of B.C. Indian chiefs to illustrate the styles of wool blankets actually worn. Photo: Provincial Archives, Victoria, B.C.

The last rug made by the Chilwheyuk band of the Chilliwack River known to the writer was made by Mrs David, an old-time rug maker, about 1920. It was made on a one-bar loom, the warp cords being held taut by the weights tied to the lower ends. The warp of this rug had been made from threads of sacking material which had been unravelled and then spun, with the use of a spindle and whorl, into a cord as thick as a pencil. The weft was made from strips of cotton dress material. Considerable pattern in colour was worked in wide or narrow bars across the web. The weave was twined throughout, and bound at the ends to prevent unravelling, by a special weave.

The fine woven work completed by Mrs Lorenzetto and Mrs Peters was featured in an exhibition of Salish Arts and Crafts sponsored by the Chilliwack Community Arts Council. The two weavers were presented with engraved copper bracelets in recognition of their work in re-establishing this native art. Further recognition came to them when each received a first prize, for goat-wool blanket and cotton rug respectively, at a handicraft exhibition in Montreal, at which Mrs Peters was also awarded a prize for the finest basket.

II

Mary Peters and Adeline Lorenzetto continued to weave—with time out for berry-picking and fishing season on the Fraser River. No other Native women, with the exception of Mrs D. Thomas (who is mentioned later) showed any special interest in trying to do likewise until the fall of 1967.

Mrs Lorenzetto had in the beginning prepared and spun her own wool. However, with her full time being required for weaving, Mrs Wm. Kelly, of Soowahlie, became the master spinner and spun wool for the weavers. Mrs Peters and Mrs Lorenzetto dyed some wool, but in this they were assisted by the writer, who, by the use of native plants and bark nature-dyed the wool used.

During 1967, Adeline Lorenzetto produced ten blankets each measuring 3′x4½′, of beautiful colour and original design. She modified her loom to facilitate her work. With short ends she created beautiful chair covers, which found a ready market.

Early in 1967, Mary Peters received an order to weave tapestry for the newly constructed Hotel Bonaventure in Montreal, Canada. The order had come as a result of the article, ''Return of the Salish Loom,'' which was published in *The Beaver* magazine in Spring 1966 issue. It was a large order—225 square feet of tapestry, carrying Salish design in colours of Gold and Black, Brown, Buff, Orange, Blue and Red. The tapestries were completed in three months and hung for the opening of the new hotel. This project, with the prestige and publicity which accompanied it, was undoubtedly the spark which ignited special interest in Salish Weaving.

Mrs Mary Peters.

In 1965, Mrs D. Thomas of Seabird Island Reserve, one of the older generation of weavers and basket makers, again began the weaving of tump-lines, an art that she executed so capably in the twined weave with the used of the single bar loom. She was persuaded to try weaving on the two-bar loom and completed a fine wall hanging. She then turned to rug making, which craft she had followed in years past. Using a burlap sack as a base, she applied a beautifully laid out design with the use of a needle. This art she had learned from ''a Coast woman'' (Native) who was following the old Native custom of applying design onto the finely woven cedar-bark mats and dancing aprons of the Coast people. The craft, while not of the true weaving type of rug making, is much appreciated by those interested in Indian design and special Native craft work.

Late in 1967, Mrs Gordon James (Martha) and Mrs Stewart (Anabel), of Skwah Reserve began weaving in the twined weave. They were soon producing beautiful items, useful as rugs, saddle blankets and wall hangings. At the time of writing, Martha, (who has won Canada-wide Handicraft competitions in sweater making) had produced no less than fifteen items. Anabel, one of the capable young weavers, is a grand-daughter of Mrs David, who was mentioned earlier as the last weaver among the Chilliwack tribe. Anabel has completed twelve peices, some of which have been made on order.

Mrs Irene James, daughter-in-law of Mrs Gordon James, learned the art from Martha and has woven two rugs.

Mrs Mabel Peters, of Seabird Island Reserve, who could remember her grandmother weaving, decided to try her hand at weaving. Mabel Peters has been totally blind for some ten years, during which time she continued her sweater making, at which she was most capable. She has woven two rugs and is ambitious to continue.

The youngest of the weavers to set her hand to the task is Miss Monica Philips, a fourteen year old grand-daughter of the ''Mother of modern weaving,'' Mary Peters. Monica is already capable of basket making and is, at the time of writing, weaving her first wall hanging.

These weavers are already recognized as those who have rebuilt an industry that had vanished and thus re-established the ancient art of weaving of the Salish people.

In 1968, the Chilliwack Arts Council, who have taken a special interest in the Native crafts, purchased ten pieces woven by these Native weavers. The fine collection is assembled and has already been on display to publicize Salish Weaving.

Items have been purchased that have gone as far afield as Eastern Canada, California, New York and across the Atlantic to Europe. As this publication goes to press an order for several articles of Salish weaving has been received from ''The World Handicraft Foundation.'' This non-profit organization with headquarters in Toronto, and whose representative personally inspected the items, has as its objective, ''the promotion, distribution, exhibition and sale of artistic and ethnographic handicrafts.'' Through them and others of like mind, Salish weaving is obtaining World Recognition.

Mrs Josephine Kelly and Mrs Sara Wells at an exhibit of Salish Weaving at the Chilliwack Arts Council Centre, Chilliwack.

Authentic Native weaving produced by the Salish is now officially identified by the Department of Indian Affairs official label. Inscribed on the symbol, the likeness of a Beaver pelt, are the words ''Authentic Canadian Indian fine Craft.''

A Letter

22 January 1970

Dear Mrs Richardson,

It was a pleasure to receive and read your letter. I believe we should get together some time and have a talk on this subject of understanding the inner religious nature of our Indians. In speaking of religion in this sense I mean that strong inner self of the Indian, which for generations they passed on in what we too often called their simple or childlike beliefs. I recently read a book on the Blackfeet Indians of Alberta and south. It was written by a U.S. Survey man who lived among them for two years and was accepted by them. They allowed him to enter into their most intimate ceremonials in regard to the sundance. It is an amazing revelation of how great a people they were, and how deep and firm were their religious convictions. It is out on loan now but I'll send it to you when I can.

I believe our Salish Indians here were as deeply religious, and for the most part were men and women of character, who lived by their beliefs—some of which were based on fear and superstition, which characteristics were made so much of by our missionaries that they forgot to recognize the many fine elements of the primitive people's life. I wrote the introduction to the *Sepass Poems* for Eloise Street Harries at her request to let the readers know that Sepass was a reality and a highly respected man.

The great pity of it all is the fact that we have already lost that which could have been a great help to the younger Indians in lifting themselves out of a very difficult situation: Pride of race, pride in their ancient beliefs of being as one with all nature and the over-all Great Spirit. I believe these are being rebuilt, but because they were lost for a generation or two, they will have to build on a new foundation.

Several years ago I made a contact with old August Jack Khahtsahlano of Squamish, and was successful in having several very worthwhile interviews with him. I went mainly because Eloise Street told me that August Jack had the same religious training and background that Sepass had. I was unsuccessful in getting what I went after—simply because I could not know how to present the questions to him which might have led him to give me the answers I had hoped for, viz. the beginning of life and their religious ceremonies, the symbols on their masks and what they represented etc. I have learned lately of a younger man who is familiar to some degree with the "high" language used by the religious and historical leaders. I hope to get a chance to discuss it with him.

I am one of a very few White people who get into the "power dances" which our local Indians are reviving. This is the closest I have come to being intimately associated with the Native in a primitive cultural experience. You have to see and hear it to realize it is possible. The wonderful thing about these big dances is that the Indians set a high standard of behavior and etiquette, and do their own policing, very effectively. Three or four hundred Indians, from babes in arms to old people—all in harmony, with maybe thirty drums beating in a small hall, makes an impressive accompaniment for a lone dancer dramatizing his "power."

Some of the finest people I know are devout religious men and women of our local tribes who have accepted Christianity but, like Sepass, see no wrong in the good things of the old ways. I doubt if we will ever find an Indian who still carries the basic old religious and historical beliefs of our Salish people. Eloise Street Harries is a remarkable person, and never ceases to try to prove that Sepass and his background of knowledge were of the old foundation.

I have compiled a History of the Chilliwacks and Neighboring Tribes, an early history up to the establishment of Reserves. It is copyrighted, and the Indians are amazed that so much has been written. As yet I have been unable to get financial assistance to publish it.

In writing the history I learned of the Salish weaving, and thought that this is one fine cultural undertaking which would give the Native people a lift if they could be persuaded to revive this fine old art. This is now an accomplishment, which is most rewarding—not financially for me, but it is for them, and it's developing.

I'm sending you some things I have been able to publish, which are doing much to interest the Natives in themselves, and also awakening the interest of many who never really thought of an Indian except as an Indian. The booklet on Salish Weaving is just off the press—revised edition. It cost me $2000 this time. I'll sell it at 2.50 per single copy. The Vocabulary is complimentary. I have a second printing of it with 1200 words, but this first edition has more of local interest in it.

This is quite a manuscript, and it still doesn't have the answers.

Sincerely,
Oliver N. Wells

Information Supplementary to *Indian Territory 1858*

The following pages, which exist in typescript, provided the basis for the information printed inside the covers of the map Oliver Wells published in 1966 as *Indian Territory 1858*. The lists provide, in effect, a summary of much of the ethnographic material gleaned from the tapes.

Tribal Areas

Chilliwack	The area drained by the Chilliwack River system with a frontage on the Fraser River.
Sumas	The area drained by the Sumas River system, which included Sumas Lake.
Pilalt	Tribal area extended along both sides of the Fraser River north and east of the present city of Chilliwack.

Indian Trails

Trails shown were being used by the Natives during Hudson Bay Co. days, and prior to that date. Each trail is identified.

Mountain Names of Interest

Cheam Peak	THEETH-uhl-kay, meaning the "Mother" mountain. Her three sons stand behind her to the east, and her daughters in front of her in order to watch the river (Fraser).
Tamihi	(McGuire Mt) T'ehm-ee-HIY, meaning "deformed"—a barrier mountain to which the "misfits" were taken and left to fend for themselves.
Sumas Mt.	Tuhk-KAY-uhq, meaning "gap left when large chunk broke away."

Names of Rivers and their Meaning

Chilliwack	*Ch.ihl-Ꝁ̶WAY-uhk* means "going back up stream" to the head of the tribe, or stream. The Chilliwack tribe were originally a mountain tribe with their head villages in the Upper Chilliwack River Area.

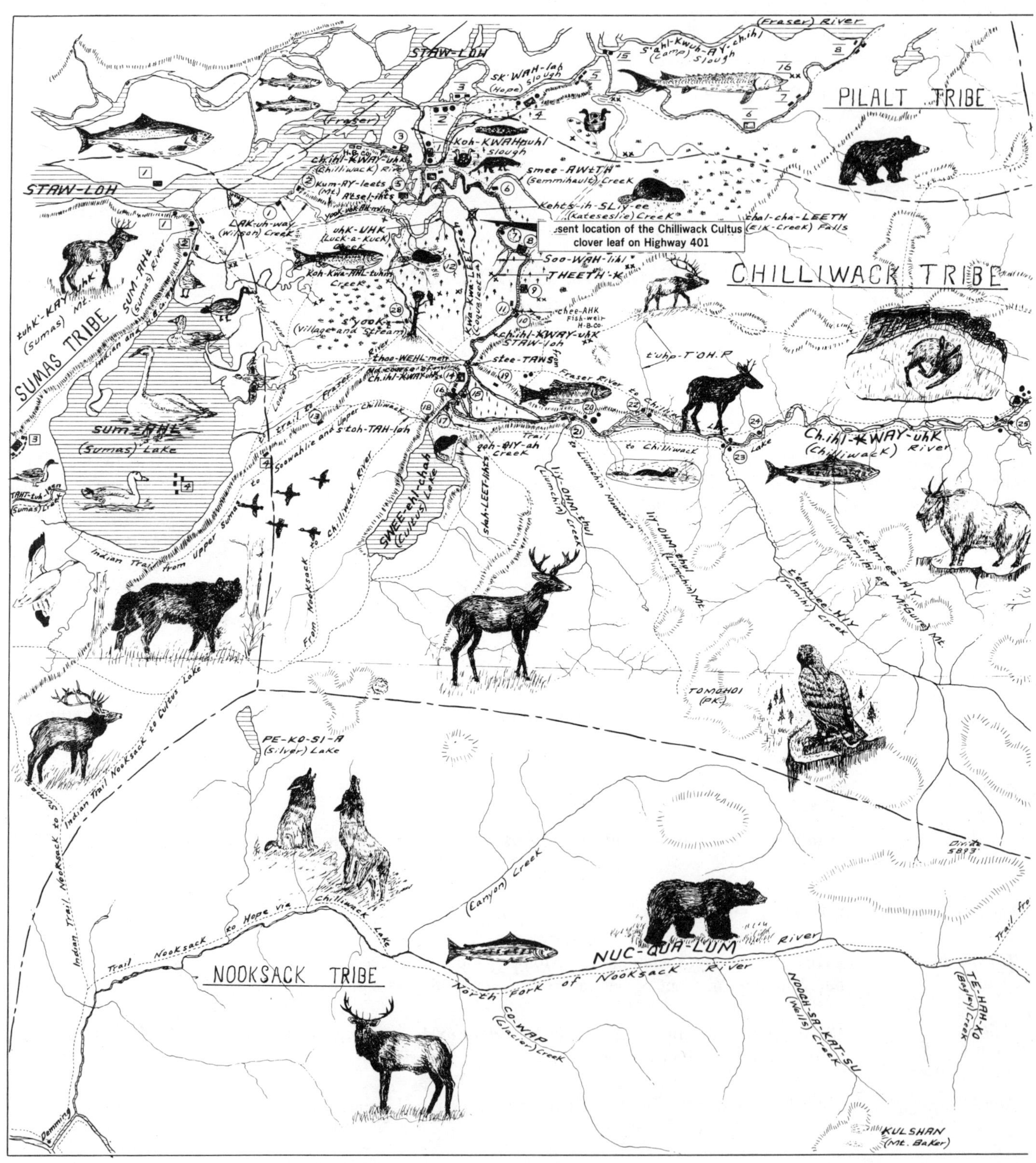

STAW-LOH
(Fraser) River
S'ahl-Kwuh-AY-chihl
(Camp) Slough
SK'WAH-lah
(Hope) Slough
PILALT TRIBE
(Fraser)
Koh-KWAHhuhl
Slough
Chihl-KWAY-uhK
(Chilliwack) River
Kum-AY-leets
(Mt)
Atsel-ihts
smee-AWtTH
(Semmihault) Creek
Kehts-ih-SLiy-ee
(kateseslie) Creek
chal-cha-LEETH
(Elk Creek) Falls
STAW-LOH
LAK-uh-way
(Wilson) Creek
uhK-UHK
(Luck-a-Kuck)
Creek
Present location of the Chilliwack Cultus
clover leaf on Highway 401
Soo-WAH-ihl
THEETH-K
CHILLIWACK TRIBE
Koh-Kwa-AHL-tuhm
Creek
chee-AHK
Fish-weir
H.B.Co.
s'yook
(Village and Stream)
chihl-KWAY-uhK
STAW-loh
SUMAS TRIBE
tuhK-KAY-uhk
(Sumas) Mt.
SUM-AHL
(Sumas) River
t'uhp-T'OH-P
thoo-WEHL-meh
stee-TAWS
Fraser River to Chilliwack
SUM-AHL
(Sumas) Lake
s'toh-TAH-lah
qeh-AIY-ah
Creek
Trail
to Chilliwack
Lake
Ch.ihl-KWAY-uhK
(Chilliwack) River
SWEE-ehl-chah
(Cultus) Lake
Indian Trail from Upper Sumas to Soowahlie and Upper Chilliwack
From Nooksack to Chilliwack River
TOMOHOI
(PK.)
PE-KO-SI-A
(Silver) Lake
Indian Trail Nooksack to Cultus Lake
Indian Trail Nooksack to
(Canyon) Creek
Divide
5893'
Trail Nooksack to Hope via Chilliwack Lake
NUC-QUA-LUM
River
NOOKSACK TRIBE
North Fork of Nooksack River
CO-WAP
(Glacier) Creek
NOOCH-SA-KAT-SU
(Wells) Creek
TE-HAH-KO
(Bagley) Creek
KULSHAN
(Mt. Baker)
Demming

INDIAN TERRITORY 1858.
1966 Compiled and copyrighted © by Oliver N. Wells, Sardis, B.C.
FOR PUBLICATION WITH OTHER SUPPLEMENTARY MATERIAL.
SHOWING
TRIBAL AREAS — 1 CHILLIWACK 2 PILALT
3 SUMAS 4 NOOKSACK.
TOPOGRAPHY —
Water Marsh Mountains Glacier.
VILLAGE SITES —
Pithouses Plank houses Ceremonial Un-named XX.
INDIAN TRAILS
HISTORIC SITES —
H.B.Co.
Cairns
WILDLIFE — OF SPECIAL INTEREST TO NATIVES,
Mammals Birds Fish
NATIVE NAMES — GIVEN IN P.P.S. PLUS COMMON NAME.
SCALE = 1 MILE TO 1 INCH
Technical Topography - Tunbridge and Tunbridge B.C.L.S.
8900 (Glacier) Peak
THEETH-uhl (Cheam) Peak
Skwuh-AWP (Cheam) Creek
uht-ZEET-zah (Fork) Creek
lah-see-SIHtP Lake
STAW-loh
Kleh-Kah-WA-lum (Lindeman) Lake
KOHK-oh-lum (Post) Creek
Trail Chilliwack Lake to Hope
PIHPS (Hicks) Creek
KLEH-KWUN-num (Silver Hope) Creek
Kleh-SIHL-Kwa (Klesilkwa) River
SKAGIT River
Trail from Chilliwack Lake to Fraser
Trail from Chilliwack Lake to Skagit
man-sel-PAHN-ikk (Mamselanik) River
Bypass trail to Hope
SHAW-ch-uhk-uhl (Chilliwack) Lake
stehee-AHK Creek
me-SA-Kwatch (Nesakwatch) Creek
sel-EE-see (Selesse) Mt.
CHU-CHUM Creek
sel-EE-see (Selesse) Creek
(Silver) or (Paleface) Creek
Chu-ch-CHEE-hum (Depot) Creek
(Dolly Varden) Creek
SK'EHL-OW (Beaver) Lake
KLAY-hoo (Valley)
7687
PUT-LUSH-GO-HAP
PUT-LUSH-GO-HAP (Tamihi) Lake
Trail to Head Waters of Nooksack River
Look-out C.W. Wilson Aug. 28 1859
Divide 6117
Lone Jack Mine
Darrah's Camp
Nooksack to Chilliwack
(Swamp) Creek
NU-QU-OI-CHUM (Ruth) Creek
Trail Nooksack to Chilliwack Lake
KLAHB-tah (Chilliwack) Creek
Trail Nooksack to Chilliwack Lake
Elev. 5451 (Hannegan) Pass
(Little Beaver) Creek
Indian Trail to Skagit
(Mt) SHUK-SAN

Coqualeetza	Kwa-kwa-LEET-sah—this was a spring water stream which flowed where the Luck-a-kuck is today, along Vedder Road. Its name means "the beating of blankets." This name originated in an old legend of the tribe.
Atchelitz	A'tsel-ihts—formerly an important waterway along which the tribe lived. The name implies it is "the place where the two rivers meet." The Atchelitz joins the lower Chilliwack.
Kateseslie	Kehts-ih-SLIY-ee—a tributary of the lower Chilliwack—navigable by canoe up as far as Sardis Village at the time of White settlement. Its course was past Cottonwoods Corner and under the Underpass of 401 Highway, at the Clover Leaf on Vedder Road.
Luck-a-kuck	Luhk-ah-KUHK, meaning "to straddle."
Thoo-WEHL-men	Now Vedder river—the Native name means "river that changed its course." At the time of White settlement, no water ran down the Vedder. However, several hundred years previous, it had been known as Thoo-WEHL-men when the Chilliwack river flowed west from Vedder Crossing.
Soo-WAH-lihl	A small springwater stream which now has its source in Sardis Park. Originally, it was a large stream which disappeared. The word "soo-WAH-lihl" meaning "stream that disappeared."
Sweltzer Creek	Originally known to the Native as Soo-WA-lay which means "to dissolve" or "to disappear."
Smith Falls Creek	(and Lake) was known as Slah-LEET-lihts—the place of bull-rushes.
Liumchen Creek	Liy-UHM-thul—which means "water swirling out in gushes."
Tamihi Creek	T'ehm-ee-HIY means "deformed."
Slesse	Sel-EE-see—meaning not definite, likely meaning "fangs" from Native word, "yel-IH.S" meaning tooth.
Ryder Lake	T'uhp-t'OHP.
Elk Creek Falls	Chal-chah-LEETH, meaning "rolling," or "falling water."
Hope River	Sk'WAH-lah—an important waterway for canoe travel moving up the Fraser. The name means "coming into the open."
Camp Slough	S'aht-kwuh-AY-ch.ihl—the name means "the centre stream." When the Fraser was difficult to ascend, the Native canoes used this slough.
Sumas River	Sum-AHL—meaning "the big opening." Likely referring to the fact disclosed by Simon Fraser's observation. When the Fraser was in flood, the whole Sumas prairie was "a big opening" to the Fraser.
Nooksack River	The North Fork—extending into the Mount Baker and Shuksan Country and providing a trail connection to the headwaters of the Chilliwack and Skagit Rivers. The Indian name, "nuc-Qus-lum" means "dog salmon," which salmon spawned there in great numbers.

Lakes

Chilliwack Lake	S'HAW-ch.uh-uhl—the name given the lake in the old language of the Chilliwack tribe.

Cultus Lake	SWEE-ehl-chah—the meaning is given as referring to the fact that there was in the beginning no lake there. Then the basin quickly filled with water to form a lake. This according to legend. The word Cultus is a Chinook word, meaning "bad." It is derived from the Salish word "kul," or "k̶ehl" meaning bad. This meaning developed from legends concerning the supernatural monsters, or SHLAL-lah-kuhm which were believed to live in the lake.
Sumas Lake	Sum-AHl meaning "a big opening." Formerly a lake of 10,000 acres in extent, which extended to 30,000 acres when the Fraser River was in freshet each spring. At this time, the Sumas River draining the lake ran in reverse, taking the Fraser River water into Sumas Lake until it extended over much of the valley and the water area had a "big opening" to the Fraser. In years past, the Nooksack river flowed out through Sumas Lake to the Fraser River.

Wild-Life Illustrated

Animals	
Grizzly Bear	kwayt-sh.ihl
Black Bear	SPAWTS
Cougar	SHWOH-wah
Mountain Goat	shee-LAHK
Deer (coastal)	'tl-puhlk'-TIHL-ah
Elk	k'AY-eh.ch
Coyote	snik-ee-YAP
Wolf	stuh-KIY-yah
Beaver	s'kel-OW̶
Birds	
Swan	SHWOH-kel
Canada Goose	hoh-MIHL-kum
White Fronted Snow Goose	k'woh-MEL-ak-ehl.aqa
Brandt	KLACK-wah-hahl
Duck	mow.q

Animals	
Grizzly Bears	in the high mountains in Cheam Peak, Chilliwack Lake and Upper Slesse Creek.
Black Bears	on Nooksack and lower Chilliwack Mts. and Valleys.
Cougar	illustrated in the Upper Chilliwack, but common in entire area.
Mountain Goat	native of the high mts, in Upper Chilliwack and Nooksack River.
Deer	common throughout entire area.
Elk	abundant in lower valleys of Chilliwack and Nooksack Rivers.
Coyote	the ancestor of the Native dog, bred and kept by Chilliwack tribe.
Wolf	friend of the Indian, was not hunted and looked upon as symbolic of tribal relationship with nature.
Beaver	trapped and used extensively for food and clothing and for sale.

Birds	
Swan	abundant on Sumas Lake and in the marsh lands of the lower Chilliwack Valley. Used extensively by the Indians for food and feathers.
Geese	Canada; White Fronted and Snow Geese and Brandt—used extensively for food and feathers.
Ducks	used extensively for food and feathers.
Fish Illustrated	
Along the Fraser River	
Spring Salmon	SKAW-kum, or PAWKW̶
Oolachin	SWAY-eh-wa, or SWEE-wah
Sturgeon	SKWA-wihch
In the Valley Streams	
Cutthroat Trout	s'PAWLT-sah
Along the Upper Chilliwack—proceeding up stream	
Cohoe Salmon	KOH-kwath
Chum, or Dog Salmon	KWA-lohq
Pink, or Humpback Salmon	HOH-lee-ah
Sockeye	SUHK:-ay
Kokanee	KIHK-eh-nee
Steelhead Trout	KAY-uq
Dolly Varden	k'oh-SAY'ch

Old Village Sites of the Ch.ihl-K̶WAY-uhk Tribe

(1) *LAK-uh-way*—meaning of name not known. Located at northwest corner of tribal territory.

(2) *Kuh-MEE-leets*—located on western end of Chilliwack Mt.

(3) *SKWIY-ee*—meaning of name—"a round vessel" located on large island at outlet of the Chilliwack River.

(4) *Skwiy-HAH-lah*—known as the "place where the SK̶WIY-kway mask was used.

(5) *A'tsel-ihts*—"the point where the two rivers meet."

(6) *SUHK-soo-koh-MIY*—meaning "the place where birch trees grow."

(7) *Skow-KAYL*—meaning, "going around a turn."

(8) *Yook-yohk-WHAY-oo.S*—meaning "burned out village."

(9) *SK̶WIY-k̶way-lah*—meaning "home of the SK̶WIY-k̶way mask."

(10) *Chee-AHK-tel*—meaning "the place of the fish weir."

(11) *SHAHL-kee*—meaning "place where dried salmon were soaked."

(12) *Kwa-kwa-LEET-sah*—meaning "the beating of blankets."

(13) *Kaw-kwiy-UHK*—located on the north side of Vedder Mt.

(14) *Quh-KA-lahk-el*—located just above Vedder Crossing on the west bank of the Chilliwack River on land long since eroded away. Site of the big house with the inverted gable—known as "watery eaves."

(15) *Skwee-KWIY-lehts*—meaning "coming in of the waters"—village site eroded away.

(16) *Soo-WA-lay*—meaning "to dissolve" or "disappear."

(17) *Qoh-ꝖIY-ah*—meaning "place of the maggot fly."

(18) *SWEE-ehl-ch.ah*—a Cultus Lake village on Sweltzer Creek.

(19) *THAH-them-ahls*—meaning "steep."

(20) *ꝀAY-luhs*—meaning "the slide."

(21) *Liy-UHM-thul*—meaning "water swirling out in gushes."

(22) *T'uhp''t'OH.P*—meaning "where vine-maples grow."

(23) *T'ehm-ee-HIY*—"the place of the deformed."

(24) *Ee-AY-thel*—the name signifies "from clear bank to clear bank" or "from rock wall to rock wall."

(25) *Sel-EE-see*—meaning the name has been given as "fangs" or "teeth" from the old language of the tribe.

(26) *Ch.ihl-ꝀWAY-uhk*—named by the author as information gathered would indicate this was one of the most important village sites over a long period of years.

(27) *S'HAW-ch.uhk-uhl*—meaning "the head" of the tribe in the old language which the tribe used before they spoke Halkomelem.

(28) *S'yook-ꝗ*—meaning "burned over place." This old village site was located on the upper part of the Atchelitz, that was known to the tribe as S'yook-ꝗ also.

(29) *Sen-EH-say*—a village site near Slesse Creek which was not previously named.

(30) *Ne-SA-kwatch*—a village site of importance, named after the creek which enters the Chilliwack River opposite the village site.

(31) *SWIY-ihl*—this name has been given to the location of a stone cairn located in the area in early days, later destroyed by vandals. The name, SWIY-ihl is the Hal-koh-MAY-lem word for "sky," also for "day."

Old Village Sites of the Sumas and Pilalt Tribes

Sumas

[1] *Sum-AHL*—a village on both sides of the Fraser River, just below the mouth of the Sumas River.

[2] *Tuꝁ-QAYL*—also known as T'uk-KAY-oh, a village on both sides of the Sumas River, near where the old highway crossed the Vedder Canal.

[3] *Qoo-ꝖWAY-ook*—formerly a large village protected by a stockade against coast raiders. Located where the Kilgard Reserve is today.

[4] *Nah-NEETS*—a village at the upper end of Sumas Lake, which moved out into houses built over the lake's surface during the summer, to get away from mosquitoes.

Pilalt

1 *Koh-KWAH-puhl*—meaning "place where crab apples grow." An important village site on Koquapilt slough, near the outlet of the Chilliwack River. The first church in the valley was built here in 1865.

2 *SKWEH*—means the "outlet", or the act of going through the outlet of the slough into the river.

3 *SKWAH-lee*—a small village on an island north of Hope slough, opposite the village of SKWEH.

4 *Sk'WAH-lah*—meaning "coming out into the open." The village takes its name from the slough. It was located at the west end of Little Mountain.

5 *Qwah-LAY-wee-ah*—a village on Hope River at the east end of Little Mountain.

6 *Shuhl-AHL-'qw*—(Schelowat), an important village on Hope River on the north bank, where Annis Road meets the old Yale Rd. The name signifies "the painted house" referring to the old house—post which was the "totem" emblem of the house.

7 *Sahl-KAY-wuhl*—"cracked trees."

8 *Chee-AHM*—meaning "wild-strawberry place," always an important village of the Pilalt tribe, which originally lived on both sides of the Fraser River.

15 *Choal-TEEL*—where Gravelly Slough joins Hope Slough.

16 *S'ch.ah-choo-kihl*—means "a going down."

The WHIHL-muh QWEHLT or Smoke-Houses

The *WHIHL-muh QWEHLT* were great ceremonial houses, in the homes of the "big" or important men of the tribe. Generally, they had a house-post totem, but not always.

6	*Skuhl-AHL-qw*)	
4	*Sk'WAH-lah*)	of Pilalt tribe.
1	*Koh-KWAH-puhl*)	
(16)	*Soo-WA-lay*)	
(14)	*Quh-KA-lahk-el*)	
(9)	*SKWIY-kway-lah*)	
(4)	*Skwiy-HAH-lah*)	of Chilliwack tribe.
(8)	*Yook-yohk-WAY-oo.s*)	
(5)	*A'tsel-ihts*)	
(3)	*SKWIY-ee*)	
[3]	*Qoo-QWAY-ook*	Sumas tribe.

SEEL-kee—Supernatural Beings (Supplement to Map)

Four of these are illustrated near Koh-KWAH-puhl where they were known to have lived in the legendary past.

Index